Hélène Thibault obtained her PhD in political science from the University of Ottawa. She joined Nazarbayev University in 2016 as an assistant professor in the department of Political Science and International Relations. Prior to this, she was a postdoctoral researcher at the Chair for the Study of Religious Pluralism and the Center for International Studies at the Université de Montréal. Her current projects look at changing matrimonial arrangements in Central Asia, especially polygyny in Tajikistan and Kazakhstan. She also took part in multiple election observation missions with the Organization for Security and Cooperation in Europe (OSCE) in Ukraine and has travelled extensively in the former USSR.

'This is a very interesting book which combines insights from political science and ethnography in an analysis which focuses on how Soviet policies toward, and discourses on, religion continues to inform how religion – in particular Islam – and its place in society is understood in Tajikistan today. It is well written and testifies to the author's broad and profound knowledge of the history of the country as well as the everyday lives of people from various walks of life there.'

Maria E. Louw, Aarhus University

TRANSFORMING TAJIKISTAN

State-building and Islam in Post-Soviet Central Asia

HÉLÈNE THIBAULT

I.B.TAURIS

LONDON • NEW YORK • OXFORD • NEW DELHI • SYDNEY

I.B. TAURIS
Bloomsbury Publishing Plc
50 Bedford Square, London, WC1B 3DP, UK
1385 Broadway, New York, NY 10018, USA

BLOOMSBURY, I.B. TAURIS and the I.B. Tauris logo are
trademarks of Bloomsbury Publishing Plc

First published 2018
Paperback edition published 2019

A catalogue record for this book is available from the British Library.

A catalogue record for this book is available from the Library of Congress.

ISBN: HB: 978-1-7845-3921-4
PB: 978-1-7883-1986-7
ePDF: 978-1-7867-3312-2
eBook: 978-1-7867-2312-3

Series: International Library of Central Asian Studies 12

Typeset by OKS Prepress Services, Chennai, India

To find out more about our authors and books visit
www.bloomsbury.com and sign up for our newsletters.

To my family

CONTENTS

LIST OF ILLUSTRATIONS

Figures

Tables

GLOSSARY

CARC	Council for the Affairs of Religious Cults 1944–65
Council of Ulemas	The official clergy of Tajikistan
CRA	Committee for Religious Affairs In Soviet times: 1965–91 Independent Tajiksitan: 1991–today
GBAO	A province of south-eastern Tajikistan where Pamiris live, an ethno-linguistic minority. Mostly referred to by its Russian acronym 'Gorno-Badakhshan Avtonomnaya Oblast'. Tajik: *Viloyati Mukhtori Kuhistoni Badakhshan*
Hanafism	The oldest of the four schools of Islamic jurisprudence, mainly found, though not exclusively, in Turkey and Central Asia
Hujum	Literally, the 'assault.' Soviet campaign for the unveiling of women that started in 1927
Imam	Prayer-leader in the mosque. In Tajikistan, it is often used interchangeably with the designation 'mullah'
Imam-khatib	Prayer-leader who delivers Friday sermons
IMU	Islamic Movement of Uzbekistan
IRPT	Islamic Revival Party of Tajikistan
Ishan	Comes from Persian 'they' as a form of respect Arabic: *shayk* or *pir*
Jamoat	District. Russian: *Raion*

Kishlok	A rural settlement, a village
Maktab	Arabo-Persian word that designates a school, mostly used for elementary schools
Maschidi Jomhe	Friday mosque, mosque. Russian: *Sobornaya*
Maschidi Panjvakhta	Literally, 'five-fold mosque.' Russian: *Pyatikratnaya*
Mazars	Any place with mystical properties, often burial places, which believers visit to honour a deceased holy person, pray, or make wishes
Mazhab	A school of jurisprudence in Islam
Medresse	An advanced religious school
Muezzin	The person who recites the call to prayer, generally from the minaret
Mufti	A Muslim scholar who interprets Sharia In Soviet Central Asia, it designated the Head of the SADUM. In today's Tajikistan, the Head of the Islamic Center and the Council of Ulemas is also called a mufti. Often used interchangeably with Qazi
Muhtasibs	A person who is charged to oversee religious behaviour. In Tsarist Russia, it was an official function
Mullah	Muslim religious figure, or scholar of Islamic law. In Tajikistan, it is often used interchangeably with the designation 'imam'
Nikoh	Exchange of vows before God, between a groom and a bride
Paranja	A burqa-like robe that covers the whole body, including the face, worn by women in some Central Asian societies prior to the Revolution
PDPT	Popular Democratic Party of Tajikistan (the ruling party)
Qazi	Originally, a judge in an Islamic court In Soviet Central Asia, it designated Republican representatives of the SADUM In today's Tajikistan, the Qazi is the Head of the Council of Ulemas. Often used interchangeably with mufti

Qaziat	In Soviet times, the Tajik Republican Branch of the SADUM
Ramadan or Ramazon (Tajik)	The annual fast to which all Muslims must comply. One of the five pillars of Islam
SADUM	Sredne Aziatskoe Dukhovnoe Upravlenie Musulman/Spiritual Muslim Board of Central Asia; Soviet Institution for the regulation of religion
Sharia	Islamic religious law that governs religious rituals and aspects of day-to-day life in Islam
Sovnarkom (SNK)	Council of People's Commissars. Russian: *narodnyx kommissarov*
Ulema	Muslim theologian
United Tajik Opposition (UTO)	Alliance of democratic, nationalist and Islamist forces during the civil war
Viloyat	Region or province in Tajik. Russian: *Oblast'*
Wahhabi	Soviets used this term to designate all islamist activists in the Ferghana valley and Tajikistan who opposed the official clergy. Today, most people use this term interchangeably with others to designate religious fanatics

A NOTE ON TRANSLITERATION

Generally, the US Library of Congress (LOC) system has been used with a few exceptions to avoid the use of unusual characters, such as ĭ used by the LOC for the Russian letter й; I prefer to use 'ii' instead, such as in tadzhikskii/Таджикский. Also, it seems more appropriate to use the most common 'ya' and 'yu' instead of LOC's 'ia' and 'iu' – for instance, Leninabadskaya/Ленинабадская and Kurgan-Tyube/Курган-Тюбе. 'Kh' is used to transliterate the Russian and both Tajik 'X' and 'Х'. The Tajik 'Қ' is transliterated simply as K. Finally, a single apostrophe ' is used for both the soft 'ь' and hard 'ъ' signs. I will use the 'J' for the Tajik 'Ч', such as in Panj (Панч) River. Unless specified, all translations are mine.

ACKNOWLEDGEMENTS

This book is based on research carried out in the course of a doctoral programme at the University of Ottawa and a postdoctoral programme at the Centre for International Studies at the Université de Montréal and was made possible with the financial support of the Social Science and Humanities Research Council of Canada, the Ethnicity and Democratic Governance Project and the Fonds de Recherche du Québec – Société et Culture. I am thankful to my professors at the University of Ottawa who offered comments and advice that helped me pursue my intellectual reasoning: my supervisor André Laliberté, Jessica Allina-Pisano, Dominique Arel, Cédric Jourde, and John Heathershaw from the University of Exeter. I want to acknowledge the support of Valérie Amiraux and Frédéric Mérand for welcoming me in their team at the Centre for International Studies at the Université de Montréal, which allowed me to turn my dissertation into this book. I also wish to thank the anonymous reviewers of this manuscript for their great input and recommendations. I am indebted to many of my colleagues for their friendship and valuable input: Laurence Couture-Gagnon, Jean-François Ratelle, David Rangdrol, Noah Tucker, and Ariane Zevaco. Other friends also contributed to this thesis by proofreading parts of it: Glen Perry, Jonathan Powers, Gabriel Shapiro, William Shapiro, and Jaime Yard; a thousand times thank you! Frank Johansen and Payam Foroughi, formerly at the Organisation for Security and Cooperation in Europe's office in Tajikistan, deserve a special acknowledgement for giving me the opportunity to work on an interesting project. A special thank you goes to my friend and 'boss' in Khujand, Lilijana Todorovic. I want to thank my mother Françoise for her affectionate support and editing skills, my father Jean for being an intellectual inspiration, my brother Sylvain, my sister Martine, and many other friends for believing in me. My most sincere thanks goes to the people I encountered in Tajikistan who welcomed me warmly and opened up with great generosity. I am greatly indebted to a number of people who I was fortunate to encounter during the fieldwork in Tajikistan; they facilitated my integration in Tajik society and offered help, shelter, and friendly advice. I owe special thanks to Ilhom Yakubov, who has generously opened so many doors for me in Khujand and helped me pursue my research. Finally, my most sincere gratitude goes to Mohiniso, my *moallima*, for her friendship, her support for my research, and her inspiring sense of justice.

INTRODUCTION

RELIGIOUS REVIVAL IN TAJIKISTAN

The Soviet socio-political engineering project was meant to rapidly and radically transform the societies of the USSR. It led to the implementation of brutal measures that in many instances had catastrophic consequences, particularly the terrible famines provoked by collectivization campaigns in Central Asia. Socially, damage was equally adverse: blind repression campaigns against 'petits-bourgeois,' clergy, and 'saboteurs' of the like are responsible for countless deaths and unfair imprisonments. Behind terrible stories, however, are also found tremendous achievements: near-universal literacy, millions of individuals who came out of poverty, promotion of women's rights, improved health and sanitary conditions, and so on, and all this within only a few decades. The rapid processes of secularization and modernization provoked phenomenal changes, and the peoples of the Soviet Union came to form a powerful ensemble driven by contradictory forces. This process was inspired by a formidable emancipating message yet imposed through highly repressive methods.

In Tajikistan, the extent of socio-economic transformation is especially striking when compared to its southern neighbour, Afghanistan. The two countries were part of an ethnic, cultural, religious, and linguistic ensemble until the consolidation of the USSR in the early 1920s and then were set on exceedingly different paths following the Bolshevik revolution. Tajiks in Afghanistan make 23 per cent of the total population,[1] approximately 8 million people, more than the entire population of Tajikistan. Tajiks in Afghanistan live mainly in the northern and western provinces of the country, in regions bordering Tajikistan. A quote from a middle-aged woman I met in the city of Qurghonteppa[2] in the Kathlon viloyat (province) captures this idea: 'I probably know more about Americans than I do about Afghans!' she said in an amused tone. 'I know we speak the same language, but we were completely cut off during the Soviet period so they are strangers to us. In fact, I'm afraid of them, they are radicals.' Adding to the irony of this statement is the fact that Qurghonteppa lies only about 50 kilometres from the Afghan border. In the northern Gonchi jamoat, an old imam told me that although most Afghans were also followers of Hanafi Islam, the Taliban promoted different ideas. The idea of women being forced to wear the *paranja* repulsed him and he would be 'ashamed to be compared to them, because what they are doing is not right.' The extent to which these societies were transformed is as fascinating as it is puzzling, and forms the starting point for my reflexion on post-Soviet religious dynamics in Tajikistan. Seventy years of Soviet rule have left a profound impression on socio-political orders, and the legacy of the Soviet Union has not entirely faded even 25 years after its dissolution.

The book reveals the traces of this legacy on formal institutions and the popular understanding of the place of religion in society in contemporary Tajikistan. I analyse the phenomenon with an institutional approach that considers institutions as constraints. More concretely it asks: how do Soviet atheistic policies and discourses continue to influence policy-making and social behaviour? By combining the theoretical tradition of neo-institutionalism to an ethnographic method, I revisit the concept of path-dependency to include not only policy-making but popular understandings of the place of religion in society. This ethnography of the particular helps to make sense of the post-independence religious revival from a local perspective while not neglecting the socio-cultural referents in which socio-political relations unfold. The book shows how Tajik state institutions continue to enforce a model of strict religious regulation and that the separation of state and religion remains an important political referent for the majority of the society, despite growing religious practice. It also explores the idea that some believers draw their religious identity from the proximity of Soviet moral and social codes and that it should be seen as a strategy to cope with changing socio-economic realities.

Islam is by far the dominant religion in Tajikistan. According to an official 2013 estimate, 99.4 per cent of Tajiks identify themselves as Muslims.[3] Yet, there are Christian communities all over Tajikistan, such as the Orthodox, Baptist, and Evangelical Churches, but the number of followers is small. The issue of increasing religiosity is a topic widely debated in the media, as well as discussed among ordinary people, and represents an issue of concern for the authorities. The phenomenon of religious revival since the late Soviet Union, albeit hard to quantify,[4] is significant. Hoji Ibodullo Kalonzoda, the respected imam-khatib of the Nuri Islam mosque in Khujand, mentioned that during Soviet times there were only 16 mosques in the whole territory of Tajikistan, whereas there are currently nearly 4,000 registered mosques as of February 2016.[5] Although there were no concrete numbers regarding the number of women wearing the hijab, this practice has increased dramatically in the last few years and has become an issue of concern for authorities. A 1996 IFES survey found that only one per cent of Tajiks prayed five times daily, whereas in 2010,[6] this proportion had jumped to 63 per cent.[7] Attendance at Friday prayers has also increased dramatically, from 13 per cent in 1996 to 52 per cent in 2010. In a 2010 OSCE-led survey conducted in Tajikistan, 73 per cent of respondents identified themselves as practising Muslims, while 17 per cent declared that they were not practising at all. Those who declared they were non-practising were mainly from urban areas.[8] In 2012, the Tajik newspaper *Asia-Plus* stated that according to a nation-wide survey conducted during the month of Ramadan, 88 per cent of Tajik respondents were fasting.[9] Interestingly, this article received many comments, a great majority of which pointed out that the numbers were certainly inaccurate. My own fieldwork experience indeed shows that a majority of Tajiks declare fasting but don't necessarily last through the whole month.

Suspicious of this religious revival and of the (former) popularity of the Islam Revival Party of Tajikistan (IRPT), the Tajik leadership exercises power to curb the development of religious groups by playing an assertive role in the regulation of religious practices. The Council of Ulemas and the Committee for Religious Affairs are responsible for shaping and implementing the rules concerning religious organizations, proselytism, religious education, and the education of clerics. Heir to the SADUM,[10] the Council is concerned with the spiritual aspects of religious life and training, whereas the Committee is a governmental body that enforces laws regulating religious practices and education. The 27 members of the Council are responsible for regulating all Islamic institutions and certifying imams. The Council is theoretically independent, but in practice it is greatly influenced by the government through the Committee for Religious Affairs. Advocacy organizations argue that in reality, the Committee stands as an executive body, and that real policy is formulated in the president's office.[11] Interviews with various stakeholders on the ground also confirmed the perception that this institution is not independent and that, as a result, it enjoys little legitimacy. Among numerous laws, decrees, and ukases, the most significant developments regarding the regulation of religious practice were the amendments made in March 2009 to the Law on the Freedom of Conscience and Religious Associations (modelled on a similar Soviet law), and the adoption in 2011 of the Law on Parental Responsibility in the Education and Upbringing of Children. Among other things, this law forbids minors from attending religious ceremonies, with the exception of funerals.

Contributions and Limitations

Most scholars portray the post-Soviet Central Asian states as secular and would describe the current politico-religious state of affairs as a continuation of Soviet practices, in terms of both institutional and ideological orientations. On the other hand, scholars acknowledge that Islam in Central Asia has become instrumental in national politics due to the fact that it is used for the purposes of legitimacy. Despite numerous publications addressing the issue of Islam in Central Asia, many facets of the puzzle still need to be addressed. As I will argue, the principal gap in the existing literature is that most scholars deal with Central Asia as a whole and tend to make broad generalizations on the state of affairs. More problematic is the fact many studies that deal with Islam focus on formal institutions and neglect the social and individualistic reasons that illustrate the religious revival. I acknowledge the usefulness of approaches that take into account the region's history and intertwining geostrategic interests, but not to the detriment of a deeper analysis of internal factors involving local discourses framing the issue of religious revival. As Adeeb Khalid rightfully stressed, 'Before we can speak of the political role of "Islam" in contemporary Uzbekistan, we have to comprehend what "Islam" means to the people of Uzbekistan.'[12]

This book addresses the issue of the place of religion in the society in terms of the legacy of the Soviet secularization process. It explores traces of this legacy in state policies and orientations as well as among ordinary citizens' attitudes and narratives. It investigates political circles, authorities, and opposition figures alike with a double objective: to show the extent to which these positions were influenced by Soviet practices but also to reveal the interactions of various actors' interests within state structures and expose the multiple facets of authority. It then considers perceptions and understandings of those labelled as 'secular' who support secularity and secular values and are concerned by religious revival. Perhaps more original is the consideration of those I designate throughout the manuscript as 'strict believers,' that is, citizens who embrace a rigorous Islamic lifestyle and live according to Sharia. The book paints a picture of everyday Islam in Northern Tajikistan, which in turn can improve understanding of the dynamics of the religious revival in the post-Soviet context.

The empirical contribution of the present work consists in offering innovative knowledge collected through ethnographic fieldwork on the issue of religious dynamics in Tajikistan, providing accounts of local discourses on religion expressed by a variety of actors. The idea was to move away from alarmist discourses on religious radicalism and present an argument that puts religious beliefs in context and downplays the threatening character of Islamic piety often found in a certain literature.[13] On that matter, Heathershaw and Megoran[14] warn that Western discourses of danger risk becoming self-fulfilling prophecies that could influence policy-making, which could actually endanger Central Asia. Instead, this book provides a valuable insight of a process of islamization without radicalization. The empirical contribution is especially valuable since political space is closing in Tajikistan and future fieldwork might be arduous, if not even perilous for scholars. My own research was conducted in 2010 and 2011 at a time when local and foreign researchers could still freely conduct fieldwork. I disposed of an incredible liberty and have never been seriously bothered by the authorities, even if I spent much time at the Islamic Revival Party of Tajikistan's (IRPT) office in Khujand, which represented the main opposition party at the time. However, authoritarianism tightened over the years and so did academic freedom. The detention of Toronto-based Tajik researcher Alexander Sodiqov in 2014 is a blatant example. Sodiqov was arrested on suspicion of espionage in June while working as a researcher for a project of the University of Exeter, funded by the British Economic and Social Research Council. He was detained during a meeting with opposition figure Alim Sherzamonov in Khorog, in the Gorno-Badakhshan viloyat. Sodiqov was imprisoned throughout June and released in July but not allowed to go back to Canada until the eve of the Shanghai Cooperation Organization Summit on September 12, 2014.[15] Finally, in the summer 2015, the IRPT, Central Asia's sole Islamic Party, was banned. This is an event which marked the end of the inter-Tajik dialogue and the tightening of authoritarian rule in Tajikistan.

The main theoretical contribution is to bring a new perspective on post-Soviet studies by moving away from the all-regional and state-centred perspective that permeates a certain literature on post-Soviet Islam and tends to reify both state and society as solid opposing entities. Instead, I propose an ethnographic perspective that gives importance to local narratives on religious politics. As Edward Schatz phrases it, political ethnography compels scholars 'to glean the meanings that the people under study attribute to their social and political reality.'[16] The research also gives a new meaning to the concept of post-Sovietism by looking for traces of the Soviet legacy not only in institutional design and governmental discourses but also in the most unexpected place, that is, in the narratives of those who most strongly rejected Soviet influence by adopting a rigorous religious lifestyle.

It should be clear that this book is not about Islam taken as a religious dogma. Rather, it is about a socio-political phenomenon in which religion plays a substantial role. Even though I learned a lot about Islam, Islamic laws and canons in the course of my fieldwork, I could not under any circumstances claim to be a specialist in Islam, and I leave to others the task of investigating Islamic theology and jurisprudence in the Central Asian context. Without making excuses for my lack of erudition, my focus is to some extent a 'symptom' of the object of study. Most people in Tajikistan have a limited knowledge of religious scriptures. Correspondingly, very few people know Arabic and a good number of people learn prayers by heart, with a greater or lesser knowledge of the prayers' meaning.[17] Akbarzadeh cites a 1993 survey that found that 'a third of Uzbek believers and two-thirds of Kazakh believers could not correctly translate from Arabic the sentence 'There is no God but Allah and Muhammed is his prophet,' which is the first and most important of the five pillars in Islam and marks one's belonging to the Islamic faith.[18] An 2010 OSCE survey revealed that only 3 per cent of respondents rated their personal knowledge of Islam as very good, 19 per cent considered their level to be good, 56 per cent average, 16 per cent listed poor and only 4 per cent admitted to having a very poor knowledge of Islam.[19] That being said, poor knowledge of religious scripts is not limited to the former USSR. Soviet author Tokarev points out that in America as well, believers have a relatively limited knowledge of the Christian doctrine. The author cites a 1954 Gallup poll in which 96 per cent of respondents identified themselves as Christians but 60 per cent of them could not give the names of the Divine Trinity and 53 per cent could not name the four Evangelists.[20] A 2010 survey conducted in the United States also testifies to a significant 'religious illiteracy.'[21] What is unique to Central Asia in this respect is that people in this region tend to regret their poor knowledge of religion. In particular, people blame the Soviet authorities for that lost wisdom[22] even though there were some prominent Islamic scholars in Tajikistan during Soviet times. Despite that, Islamic erudition was mostly limited to secret study circles.[23] I am in no position to judge Tajiks' religious erudition or lack thereof, and in fact, it is of little significance in the story because, as one person I interviewed put it: 'What matters is not the way you pray, how you place your hands, stand up and bow. What matters is to feel the presence of God in your heart.'

Organization of the Book

The book consists of seven chapters, including the introduction and the conclusion. **Chapter 1** introduces the theoretical framework, neo-institutional ethnography and lays out the main interrogations that the book tries to answer. It also presents the fieldwork and includes a reflection on the researcher's subjectivity and positionality and their impact on data collection.

Chapter 2 consists of an account of the Soviet secularization experience. Emphasis is placed on the ideological bases of Marxism-Leninism, its stance on atheism, the holistic character of the ideology and its ideological exclusivity. This chapter details the measures taken

by authorities to implement their social engineering project, meant
to eradicate religious beliefs. It also offers a reflection on people's
accommodation to the imposition of secularity.

Chapter 3 aims at situating the study in a description of Tajikistan,
and more particularly the Sughd viloyat, where most of the fieldwork has
been conducted. In particular it provides a thorough description of
postwar political actors and dynamics. It also offers a discussion on the
failure of political Islam in Tajikistan and the country's descent into
authoritarianism.

Chapter 4 illustrates the relevance of the path-dependency argument
by reviewing the functions and responsibilities of current regulatory
institutions as well as laws and official discourses framing religious
practices. The chapter evokes how citizens' virtue, especially of women,
has become associated with the perpetuation of national culture and values
as state discourses are used to define and impose a proper behaviour in line
with an idealized conception of a secular society.

Chapter 5 integrates the ethnographic analysis into the theoretical
framework and consists of a representation of the religious revival
through data collected during the fieldwork. It does so by describing the
conversion experience and everyday life of the main interviewees. This
chapter highlights the similarities of religious and Soviet codes and
portrays the extent to which religion is used as a source of morality but
also how it has become a source of tension within the communities in a
context marked by poverty and injustice.

The Conclusion recapitulates the main arguments presented in the
book and widens the discussion to recommend that religious disputes
be taken as signs of tensions between freedom and equality within a
polity. It concludes with a discussion on the prospect of radicalization in
Central Asia.

CHAPTER 1

A NEO-INSTITUTIONALIST ETHNOGRAPHY OF RELIGIOUS REVIVAL

Long kept in the shadow of the Soviet Union, the Central Asian region[1] did not attract much attention outside the USSR until 1991, with some exceptions, such as the works of Carrère d'Encausse,[2] Bennigsen and Lemercier-Quelquejay,[3] and Critchtlow.[4] The breakup of the USSR has boosted scholarly interest in Central Asia, but the study of this region remains marginal within the body of literature in comparative politics. The difficulty of access for foreign researchers, its isolation from leading publication and research centres, language issues, as well as difficult economic and living conditions make the Central Asian region less attractive to researchers. The politicization of Islam in Central Asia has nourished the field of post-Soviet studies after the emergence of armed insurgencies such as the Islamic Movement of Uzbekistan (IMU) and after the break-out of a protracted civil war in Tajikistan in 1991. Central Asia, and the Ferghana valley in particular, have often been labelled as a hotbed of radical Islam.[5] Other studies focused on geostrategic issues, especially after the Western military intervention in Afghanistan in 2001. Since independence in the early 1990s, observers have been expecting and predicting some sort of destabilization that has never occurred. References to 'The Great Game,' in allusion to the British–Russian competition for the control of the region in the nineteenth century were also common and granted the region a geostrategic importance in world politics.[6] In spite of the pessimistic prognosis, and with the exception of the Tajik civil war, the region has remained remarkably stable and both state institutions and political elites proved very resilient.

Among the Central Asian Republics, Tajikistan and Turkmenistan have received the least attention from the academic community. In the case of Turkmenistan, the dearth of scholarship can be explained by its exceptionally closed political system, limited freedom of movement within the country, and lack of access to people and documentation. In Tajikistan, the dangerous situation that prevailed in the country from 1991 to 1997 hampered the willingness of many scholars to conduct research there, but the country still receives far less scholarly attention than Uzbekistan, Kyrgyzstan, and Kazakhstan, for example. In fact, there are few scholarly articles, less so monographs, dedicated solely to Tajikistan. A recent monograph written by Nourzhanov and Bleuer, and published in 2012, offers a comprehensive and nuanced historical analysis, from antiquity to the civil war period. Among other influential research, many addressed the security situation in postwar Tajikistan. In particular, Driscoll,[7] Markovitz,[8] Nourzhanov,[9] and Heathershaw[10] have adroitly debunked the oversimplified common idea that the civil war opposed Islamists and secular forces. Instead, their work has shown that regional interests, which were defined and redefined throughout the conflict to suit the bidding of actors, superseded ideologies. Hence, the making of peace and the postwar equilibrium rested on the capacity of the winning elites to maintain patronage networks[11] as well as the manipulation of the peace narrative by elites.[12]

In the field of religion, many studies have provided useful and insightful accounts on the history and current status of the religious field in Tajikistan. Dudoignon, Epkenhans, Mullojonov, and Olimov and Olimova.[13] They shed a new light on the debate on parallel and official Islam in Soviet times and in today's Tajikistan by highliting the connections between representatives of official institutions and unregistered clerics in patronage networks as well as discussing religious debates. Although this scholarly production testifies of a profound knowledge of the religious field in Tajikistan, they tend to neglect the social and individual dimension of the religious playing field. This book should be seen as the ethnographic complement of the above-mentioned studies on religion. It concurs with a recent wave of ethnographic research on everyday Islam in Central Asia that focuses on lived religious experiences such as Louw, McBrien, Zigon, Pelkmans, and Rasanayagam.[14] However, this scholarship is coming to us from the field of anthropology and few studies have explored the political dimension of religious revival. Tajikistan is certainly worthy of greater consideration and, as I will argue throughout this book, scholars need to engage more actively in fieldwork to produce knowledge that is locally grounded. Yet, as I will discuss in Chapter 3, the current political conditions make the conduct of social science research very difficult, if not all together dangerous.

Perhaps because of the influence of 'Sovietology,'[15] in general, the literature on Central Asian Islam has not been a field for great theoretical debates. However, historical institutionalism and its concept of path dependency have dominated most research done by both historians and political scientists on the development of post-Soviet Islam.[16] Historical institutionalism is interested in discovering how past practices condition subsequent ones by encouraging societal forces to organize along some lines rather than others, to adopt particular identities, or to develop interests in policies that are costly to shift.[17] Jones Luong writes that: 'historical institutionalism depicts political identities as "investments" that individuals consciously make in response to their institutional surroundings and yet unconsciously maintain.' For her, this theory has the particularity to draw our attention 'to the structural incentives that make some identities more desirable and enduring than others.'[18] In particular, scholars have discerned the continuation of Soviet practices in Central Asia in:

(1) the nationalization of religious administrative structures;
(2) the adoption of regular and Constitutional laws defining the parameters of religious life;
(3) the repression of religious opposition;
(4) the assimilation of Islamic forces.[19]

Besides historical institutionalism, scholars have used innovative approaches to assess the great changes taking place in the region, especially the religious economy school[20] and ethnographic perspectives.[21] Both these approaches take into account agency in the redefinition of religious identities even though the latter looks at the way religious markets shape individual behaviour while the former focuses on personal interpretations and narratives to make sense of social and political dynamics. The religious economy school has the merit to move away from a state-centred perspective and consider a multiplicity of actors embedded in religious markets, and involved in the process of social change. If these studies incorporate the interests of political actors into the study of religious markets, they fail to contextualize the choices made and the attitudes adopted by actors. Two books by American scholars Paul Froese and Christopher Marsh illustrate how this is used for the study of post-Soviet religious revival. Both works demonstrate the failure of the forced secularization in the USSR as well as in China in the case of Marsh's comparative analysis of Russia and China. To explain the fact that the absence of religious market did not completely eradicate religious beliefs, Froese and Marsh rely on a common postulate: that the demand for religion or spirituality, as formulated by Stark and Finke, 'is an essential aspect of human condition.'[22] Yet, Marsh and Froese don't go very far in the exploration of personal motivations apart from the assumption that people are religious because they can. Ironically, tenants of the religious economy school who are the most interested in personal manifestations of faith and beliefs are those who neglect the personal dimension of research and investigation.

Overall, not much importance has been given to micro socio-political dynamics within the larger phenomenon of post-Soviet transformation. However, a new generation of ethnographic research proposes to dig deeper into local narratives and practices by using ethnography. Ethnographers attempt to provide accounts of local perceptions of politics 'to analyze the gap between the idealized representation and actual apprehension of events, people and political orders'[23] and try to uncover the power relations that lie behind the making, dissemination, and understanding of certain narratives in a given society. As Jourde wrote: 'when investigating Islam and politics, ethnography provides a sensibility that allows political scientists to "see" the large variation of meanings such a word [Islamism] can have across Muslim societies, as well as the complex struggles that are fought over this word.'[24] Also, as opposed to a certain literature, which claims that objectivity should be a guiding principle behind investigative social research,[25] ethnographers are usually conscious of their own subjectivity and the impact one's background (life experiences, values, and assumptions) has on the conduct of research. Reflexivity is seen as inevitable and useful.[26] Equally important is the subjects' reactions and interactions to and with the researcher. In their research on the former Soviet Union, anthropologists used ethnography to explore the overlapping of Soviet and post-Soviet periods and, most specifically, the connection between religious revival and Soviet legacies. Notably, Mathijs Pelkmans insists that scholars need 'to acknowledge that Soviet rule did more than simply repress religions. It also influenced understandings of religion and modes of religiosity.'[27] The interpretivist stance offers two possibilities: (1) to explore social narratives that have not been significantly considered in previous research on Central Asia, (2) to revisit common dichotomies of state and society, religious and secular, and Soviet and post-Soviet by showing the blurred boundaries between them. Ethnography is especially well suited due to its 'consideration of transtemporal and translocal effects.'[28]

The challenge that unfolds thoughout the book is to demonstrate the relevance of using an approach that insists on path dependency and the persistence of old patterns, while also focusing 'on the ways in which Islam is lived and experienced in practice.'[29] I combine a neo-institutionalist approach with ethnographic research to make sense of the religious revival in independent Tajikistan. The use of such a hybrid approach to study a phenomenon that departs from Soviet realities can appear to be incongruous. Per contra, I make use of historical institutionalism's central concept – path dependency – and a broad definition of institutions that includes ideas and norms to argue that the phenomenon of religious revival is subsidiary of Soviet legacies of understanding the social and political order. I demonstrate that Tajik state institutions and laws responsible for regulating religion have been greatly modelled upon Soviet institutions. On the other hand, I argue that the path dependency argument is also useful in decoding the behaviour of ordinary citizens as well as strict believers in their understanding of the place of religion in the society. I orient my interpretation along two critical axes: ontological and epistemological.

Ontologically speaking, I will seek equilibrium between the impact of the structure (Soviet legacy) on the individual (life and moral choices). I address religious revival, an ontological object subjected to diverse interpretations and debates. Indeed, many scholars refuse to frame post-Soviet Islam in Central Asia as a 'revival' given that religion did not disappear in Soviet times but was merely lived and practised differently and more or less secretly. My intention is to nuance the notion of revival in order to support the idea that there is continuity between Soviet and post-Soviet orders such that, against all odds, religious sentiments may even have their origin in Soviet values. By using the path-dependency argument, I aim to reconcile Soviet and post-Soviet orders by interpreting them not as antagonistic, but as overlapping.

Epistemologically speaking, it seems important to find a balance between what is a finding, a universalizable truth, and an observation. Seeking to grasp the significance of religious revival rather than to look for a sociological explanation reflects an epistemological supposition that reality is not made of causal relations waiting to be discovered by scholars. In this, I follow Davie, who renounces universalizable truths and refers instead to socio-political patterns which reflect the 'non-randomness of human living.'[30] Ethnography's emphasis on subjects' narratives makes available competing discourses on religion and illuminates 'the large variation of meanings and complex struggles'[31] that the interaction of religion and society typically entails. The theoretical perspective that I adopt supplements interpretivist and positivist epistemologies with concepts borrowed from historical institutionalism and political ethnography.

Both journalists and scholars often invoked the ideological vacuum to explain the resurgence of religion in the former Soviet space. Used and overused, this concept is both controversial and challenging. As Louw suggested, referring to the ideological vacuum argument is risky because it is used as a tactic by incumbent governments to legitimate authoritarianism.[32] Beyond such instrumental narratives, material from my own interviews iterates the experience of ideological vacuum after the dissolution of the USSR. Yet, I don't limit the definition of the concept of ideological vacuum to the disappearance of the Soviet ideological framework. Instead, the meaning I give to it encompasses both the ideological and material deliquescence that followed the break-up, which was particularly painful in war-torn Tajikistan. The dynamics I explore take place in a political context within which the post-Soviet ideological vacuum is coupled with failed attempts to construct new national histories.[33] The concept of ideological vacuum is also contentious because there is no clear boundary between Soviet and post-Soviet periods. The USSR collapse surely created a destabilizing and uncertain environment, but Soviet values were not suddenly discarded and forgotten. In accordance with the overall objective of the book, the concept of ideological vacuum has to be nuanced in order to avoid marking a definite line between Soviet and post-Soviet orders. The absence of delimitation between these two historical periods can be explained by the affinities of religious and Soviet moral codes.[34] Luehrmann's fascinating piece on religious education in rural Russia proposes to see the secular (Soviet) and post-secular periods not as opposed to each other but as 'sites of engagement that alternate and overlap in the lives of both societies and individuals.'[35]

In sum, the combination of neo-institutionalism and political ethnography produces a hybrid theoretical position that acknowledges structure, agency, and reflexivity. On the one hand, the concept of path dependency, more specifically the resilience of Soviet values, will be used to assess both state and individual orientations. For this, I abide by Smith and Grahame's evocation that 'the social organization which makes possible the daily scenes of life in contemporary societies isn't wholly contained within the local setting or its associated sensemaking practices. Rather, this organization is generated by social relations which originate outside of the local setting and which can only be partially glimpsed within it.'[36] This is precisely what this book is about: glimpses of local narratives about religion understood in the context of the Soviet legacy.

Conducting Research in Tajikistan and in the Sughd Viloyat

Tajikistan is a small country of 143,100 square kilometres landlocked between Uzbekistan to the west, Kyrgyzstan to the north, China to the east, and Afghanistan to the south. A majority of Tajiks today speak a Persian language close to the one spoken in Iran, but written with a modified version of the Cyrillic alphabet. Tajikistan is an ethnically diverse country: as of 2010, it was composed of 84.3 per cent Tajiks, 12.2 per cent Uzbeks, and 0.5 per cent Russians.[37] The country gained independence on September 9, 1991. Already the poorest of the republics during the Soviet period, the economic decline of Tajikistan was accelerated during the civil war: industrial production dropped 50 per cent between 1990 and 1998.[38] The economic situation during the war was catastrophic; the average monthly salary was less than five dollars, and the average monthly pension around two dollars.[39] The economy has never completely recovered from the initial shock and is still not very dynamic. Unlike some its neighbours, Tajikistan is not

Figure 1.1   Map of Tajikistan. Credit: United Nations.

blessed with fossil fuel reserves. Its soil is rich in minerals but its exploitation is limited due to the geography of the country. In fact, 93 per cent of the country is covered by high mountains, and 50 per cent of its territory is above 3,000 metres. Rashid suggests that this not only impedes trade connections, it also hinders the creation of national unity.[40] A critical lack of economic resources, bureaucratic weaknesses, internal instability, as well as regional isolation have led observers to question the viability of the country.

My fieldwork was conducted in northern Tajikistan, in the Sughd viloyat (province), formerly called Leninabadskaya oblast' up until November 10, 2000. Ancient texts refer to the region as Sogdiana and Transoxiana. Sogdiana comprised territories around Samarkand, Bukhara, and Kesh (Shahrisabz) in modern-day Uzbekistan as well as Khujand in Tajikistan. Transoxiana corresponds to present-day Uzbekistan, Tajikistan, and southwest Kazakhstan. Its name refers to the land across the river Oxus, that is, today's Amu Darya.[41] The region holds some of the oldest continuously inhabited settlements in the world. Around 329 BC, Alexander the Great led his armies to Asia and conquered the region, which had been under Persian influence since the rise of the Achaemenid dynasty around the sixth century BC. The region, located at the very heart of the Silk Road, flourished despite constant struggles for control of the area, variously ruled by Han, Kashgar, Persian, Scythian, and Turkic dynasties. After the conversion of Arabs to Islam in the seventh century, they launched a series of conquests to the east. They stumbled upon semi-independent principalities competing one against another, which eased their expansion in the region.[42] Historical writings demonstrate that although Zoroastrianism was dominant, it cohabited with Buddhism, Christianity, Manichaeism, Judaism, and local beliefs (Animism). New Arab leaders tried to limit the influence of those beliefs by destroying religious literature, imposing taxes on non-believers and by encouraging conversions mainly through inciting financial measures.[43] In the centuries that followed, the urban intellectual centres of Bukhara and Samarkand contributed to the dissemination of culture and science in the Islamic world and beyond. Poet and doctor Ibn Sina (Avicenna) and Islamic scholar and poet Rumi represent the most well-known figures of that Islamic Golden Age.

Despite the rapid conversion of the people of Central Asia, many animist tribes, particularly nomadic ones, kept performing their ancestral rituals for centuries.[44] In the thirteenth century, Mongol tribes were on their way to conquer the world and imposed their rule over Central Asia until their decline in 1346. Two decades later, the birth of Timur's empire in 1369 definitively marked the beginning of the Turkic domination in the region. Yet, Persian speakers continued to hold influential administrative and cultural positions. In the course of the eighteenth century, the empire was divided into three Khanates: Bukhara, Khiva, and Kokand, which later became Russian protectorates. The Russian military campaign in Central Asia started with the subjugation of the Kazakh territory in 1837 and came to an end when the Russians defeated the Turkmens in 1881.[45] After the settlement of the frontier, Russians were finally able to fully deploy their colonial strategy in the Russian Turkestan, formally established in 1867. The political structures of the Emirate of Bukhara and the Khanate of Kokand were maintained and used by Russians to rule indirectly. As for the Khanate of Kokand, which included the northern part of today's Tajikistan and the city of Khujand, it was abolished in 1876. The Khanate had a population of 80,000 people, 600 mosques, and 15 medresse in which about 15,000 students were taught.[46]

Russia's colonial strategy was one of non-intervention. For instance, military service was not mandatory for Central Asian subjects until 1916, and Islamic courts were maintained. Revolts broke out in Tashkent in 1892, but more important was the uprising in Andijan in 1898, led by a Sufi preceptor, Muhammad Ali, and 2,000 of his followers. The revolt was ended in two days but greatly affected Russian settlers. At the turn of the century, a new opposition movement emerged. Jadidists, whose name derived from the Arabic word *jadid* (new), were driven by the idea that Muslims should emancipate themselves through education, find a way to open up to the world, and participate in modern life while reinforcing their Islamic identity. The Jadidist movement was critical in the transformation of Central Asian cultural in the first decade of the twentieth century. Yet, they did not carry out significant political actions as they were later sidelined in the aftermath of the Soviet victory in Central Asia.[47]

The 1916 revolt, which started in Samarkand and spread over Turkestan, can be seen as the starting point of the Basmachi revolt that would last for two decades. The uprising occurred after an imperial decree that non-Russians were to serve in the Russian Army during World War I. Also central to the understanding of the revolt is the fact that the order implied fighting against Turkish Muslim 'brothers' who were allied with the Germans.[48] Despite its failure, the revolt revealed the possibility of Muslims fighting and resisting the colonizers. The outbreak of the civil war following the October Revolution in Russia threw Central Asia into a great turmoil, even though the fighting between the Red and White armies took place only in the northern part of the Kazakh steppe. In fact, very few native Marxists took part in the battle and most of the troops came from European Russia.[49] Victorious Bolsheviks established the Tashkent Soviet in March as a new revolutionary power structure and, on April 30, 1918, Turkestan officially became the Soviet Republic of Turkestan. Diverse political movements, centring on Muslim identity and advocating principles of national liberation as promoted by the Bolsheviks, were founded in Russia and Central Asia, but none of these achieved self-determination for the Central Asian nations.[50]

In 1918, the chaotic ambience and harsh economic conditions set the stage for the development of widespread thievery in the new Republic. For this reason, the Basmachi movement (in local Turkic languages, a *basmak* or *basmach* is a thief) was rapidly associated with marauders in order to discredit its actions. Yet Buttino suggests that many combatants were indeed involved in some kind of larceny.[51] The movement, inspired by pan-Turkism, an ideology calling for the unification of all Turkic people, was composed of various groups who at various times had more or less conflicting interests, which undermined the movement's scope of action. The movement attracted different political actors, such as supporters of the Emir of Bukhara, conservative local leaders, and Muslim reformists.[52] Fighting mainly took place on the actual territory of Tajikistan and later moved to Afghanistan. The clashes mutated into a guerrilla war, during which the rebel combatants never managed to dominate large portions of the territory. The Basmachis opposed the Bolsheviks until the death of one of its most prominent leaders, Ibrahim Bek, in Tajikistan in 1931. Even without being able to clearly define the goals of the Basmachis' endeavour, this episode makes it clear that the Muslim identity served as a catalyst for the struggle for the self-determination of the Muslim nations.

In Soviet times, the province of Leninabad (now Sughd) provided the country with most of its intellectual and governing elite, until the civil war forced a regional power shift favouring southerners. Indeed, from 1943 until independence, all republican Communist Party First Secretaries were from the North. This political arrangement favoured the Sughd region, which was and still is Tajikistan's most industrialized region. Yet, in 1987, Tajiks constituted only 48 per cent of industrial workers in Tajikistan.[53] Leninabad was also perceived as a very Sovietized region, with cities like Chkalovsk and Taboshar having large Russian populations. Taboshar was renamed Istiklol in 2012 while Chlalovsk was renamed Shohkant in June 2015.[54] Taboshar, a small town 40 kilometres north of Khujand and Chkalovsk, is located only 15 kilometres away from Khujand. Taboshar remains a restricted area due to the exploitation of uranium and the production of missile parts in Soviet times. Chkalovsk was also a closed town in Soviet times because of its uranium producing activities, but it is now accessible and even hosts the Khujand international airport. These cities' particular status also gave them special access to some resources and privileges unavailable to others.[55] However, some districts of Leninabad remained very conservative throughout the Soviet period – for example, Kuhistoni Mastchox, Isfara, and Asht. Today's Sughd viloyat extends to the Ferghana valley, at the crossroads of Uzbekistan and Kyrgyzstan.

During the civil war (1992–7), Leninabad oblast' was spared mostly because of its isolated geographical position and the relative neutrality of the northern elite. Most of the fighting took place in the southern province of Khatlon and around the capital and involved regional factions from the south and the Pamirs. During the civil war, the province was mostly cut off from the rest of the country, and goods came in and out of the region through Uzbekistan and Kyrgyzstan. However, a brief armed rebellion took place in January 1996, when local politicians and their supporters protested against the 'Kulyabization' of politics.[56] The mutiny, led by General Mumin Mamadzhanov, Head of the Leninabad oblast' military registration and enlistment office, was eventually suppressed and Mamadzhanov arrested.[57]

As of 2011, there were 2,251,700 inhabitants in the whole territory of Sughd. The region is densely populated, with 89.3 inhabitants per square kilometre. Urban and rural dwellers account for 25 and 75 per cent of the population, respectively.[58] As with many other regions of Central Asia, the Sughd viloyat is ethnically mixed and has a large Uzbek population. The ethnic composition of Sughd is 83.3 per cent Tajik, 14.6 per cent Uzbek, 0.4 per cent Russian, and 0.6 per cent Kyrgyz.[59] The Uzbek and Russian populations significantly dropped after independence: the region included 7.6 per cent Russians and 23.5 per cent Uzbeks in 1989.[60] Interestingly, there are no statistics on unemployment rates. However, the 2010 census documented 398,700 persons officially employed in Sughd, which represents 17 per cent of the region's adult population.[61]

Subjectivity and Positionality in Research

In total, I spent 11 months in Tajikistan, from May through to October 2010 and from April through to December 2011. If ethnography is defined as an approach that intends to make sense of a particular group's system of meanings, long stays become essential, though long-duration stays are also not a guarantee of genuine ethnographic work. For Cefaï, the ethnographic survey 'explores "perspectives" which unfold in social situations, as perceived, done and said by the persons concerned, *in situ*.'[62] Instead of starting from an overlooking viewpoint, the narrative starts from the perspectives of those who are surveyed. The idea is to uncover, rather than presuppose, individual's motivations and behaviours.[63] In the Tajik context, addressing a matter as touchy as religion required the establishment of trustworthy connections with interviewees. My research combined media reviews, review of the literature, as well as multi-level exchanges; formal and semi-directed interviews with state officials and clerics, attendance to workshops, participant observation and ethnographic in-depth exchanges with ordinary citizens, believers and non-believers. In most cases, exchanges were conducted in an informal manner, either at a tea house, the bazaar, my apartment or my interlocutor's place. I lived both on my own and with Tajik and Russian families for certain periods of time. I became entangled in banal events of everyday life as well as exceptional moments.

My fieldwork was for the most part conducted in Northern Tajikistan, in the Sughd viloyat and I spent most of my time in the capital of the viloyat, Khujand. I developed research sites in other towns of the viloyat such as Isfara and Buston as well as rural areas in the Bobojon-Gafurov and Gonchi Jamoats, where I made several field trips. I spent little time in Dushanbe, the country's capital, and mainly conducted formal interviews with state and party representatives while I was there. In 2010–11, the Islamic Revival Party of Tajikistan was still legal and active and I spent much time in their regional headquarters in Khujand. I was also invited to attend the 9th Congress of the Islamic Revival Party of Tajikistan in Dushanbe in September 2011. Institutions that were scrutinized are those of the Islamic Center, and its corollary Council of Ulemas, and the Committee for Religious Affairs. I conducted interviews with six representatives of the Committee for Religious Affairs (CRA), one in Dushanbe, two in Khujand, one in Isfara, one in Kistakuz, and one in Buston. I conducted one interview with the Head of the Council of Ulemas for the Sughd region in Khujand after repeated requests and use of connections but I was denied a proper interview with the Mufti in Dushanbe even though I was received in his office at the Islamic Center. This failed attempt to interview Mufti Said Mukarami Abduxodirzoda in Dushanbe is worth detailing since it is emblematic of other refusals that were not explicitly uttered. When I first went to the Mufti's office, his assistant told me that the Mufti's door was always opened to foreigners and that he would be happy to meet me the next day. I arrived the next day at the convened time and waited in the lobby for about 20–25 minutes. A different assistant wrote down my name and the purpose of my visit on a piece of paper and handed it to the Mufti, who was sitting in the adjacent office. I was then allowed in the office of the Mufti, who quickly told me (with a smile and in very good English) that he was very busy and had no time to talk to me. Instead, he pointed at another man in the room and said he was going to answer my questions. I followed the man, a jurist and Head of Department for International Relations of the Islamic Center, to his office. There I sat next to him at his desk and was told to write down my questions while he watched a foreign film about the life of the Prophet that was pending approval for mass distribution in Tajikistan. After I finished writing my questions with flimsy enthusiasm, I was told that answers would be available the following day. I called a couple of times in the next days but in the end, answers were never handed to me and they ultimately stopped answering my calls. I don't think it is exaggerated to affirm that a general lack of transparency pervades the culture in Tajikistan. Scholars who have conducted fieldwork in Central Asia are familiar with this type of avoidance behaviour. Straight refusals are hardly ever expressed, even sometimes for very banal demands, and it is difficult for outsiders to make out the meanings of unspoken words. For instance, when people meet acquaintances on the streets, they systematically invite each other home to drink tea, invariably accept but never go and it is considered proper behaviour. In fact, the opposite behaviour would be considered impolite and someone who would accept every invitation would be judged as a profiteer. I will never really know why I was denied an interview but it is easy to imagine that the Islamic Center was not very keen to talk to a foreigner who might be critical of its work.

In addition to formal interviews, I attended a dozen meetings where representatives of the Council of Ulemas and the CRA were present, such as focus-groups and round-tables in the framework of the Organisation for Security and Cooperation in Europe survey-project I was working on, Summer Camps on religion in 2010 and 2011. I also attended two international conferences where I could observe the interactions between the Council, CRA representatives, and other audiences. I also conducted interviews with Evangelical and Orthodox Christians in Khujand and Dushanbe. The minority position of these churches induces a particular relation with the authorities as well as with the rest of the community, since both ordinary citizens and the authorities sometimes perceive them as a threat against the Muslim faith and national values. Also, it seemed important to conduct research among Christian communities because, according to my research proposal, Christians would be facing the same issues. Religious revival is not only about the power of Islam to attract new adherents but about people turning to religion to make sense of the world they live in.

'Vostok – delo tonkoe,'[64] 'The East is a delicate matter,' many Tajiks told me all along. Although this idiom from a famous Soviet film bears a somewhat orientalist tone, I use it here in order to illustrate the challenges one can encounter when conducting research in a foreign land. Ethnography is about developing an insider's perspective, which can be difficult when the researcher is a Western agnostic female studying religious revival in Tajikistan. For instance, Iskandar, one of my main interviewees, once told me that if I really wanted to understand Islam, I needed to convert because 'Islam is like a house, and you, you just walk around it looking through the windows. But you have to go inside to fully understand it.' That is not to say that local researchers have it easy in comparison. Foreign and 'domestic' scholars encounter different challenges but both positions of outsider and insider and everything that comes in between can bear both advantages and disadvantages. As Bolak suggests: 'While a foreign researcher runs the risk of being culture blind, an indigenous researcher runs the risk of being blinded by the familiar.'[65] That being said, scholars should not think of outsider and insider as antagonistic positions. Instead, as Bolak proposes, it is rather a continuum in which the researcher's position is 'informed by the definition used by the participants.'[66] DeVault suggests that it forces the ethnographer to use his or her social competence as a guide toward interpretive analysis and that this position while, not that determinant, should be seen as a resource rather than a problem.[67]

As opposed to a certain literature[68] that claims objectivity should be a guiding principle behind investigative social research here, subjectivity is fully assumed. This is not only because, as many scholars would acknowledge, inevitable, but because it is also useful.[69] Yet, positionality and subjectivity do not only refer to the researchers' baggage and the way it affects his/her thinking, methodology, interactions, and reactions during fieldwork. It also refers to the fact that my personality and image influence the way people on the field interact with me. This has an equally important impact on the way research is conducted and data collected.

We have to keep in mind that the researcher is not all-powerful and, as Wolf so rightfully stated: 'We run the risk of patronizing our interviewees if we do not recognize their agency in the research relationship and how their reactions to us fundamentally affect the knowledge we are able to glean.'[70] Baker provocatively suggests that scholars have a tendency to study those with lower status than themselves: 'Indigent and poorly educated people do not have the resources or knowledge, the lawyers, or the "I'm too busy excuse" to fend off social researchers.'[71] This affirmation is shocking and makes the scholarly community feel uncomfortable because there is certainly some truth in it. I was often refused interviews, forgotten or ignored by people 'in power' whereas 'ordinary people' were most of the time willing and enthusiastic about talking to me.

Another less cynical explanation would be that people in subordinated positions are more likely to have grievances and see an opportunity to advance their cause in talking to a foreign researcher. It was clearly the case with the IRPT, which doors were always opened for me. The party had a favourable image and reputation abroad and knew that international support and sympathy was crucial for its viability in a context of increasing political pressure. The researcher can also be perceived as a threat to local culture or interests. Palmer talks about the sociologist as the 'chaperone,' the 'soft deprogrammer' who is susceptible to corrupt the interviewees' morals among other instrumental positions.[72] People in power might also be suspicious for fear of saying something that would do them harm. I was confronted to such a situation only once when I attempted to meet the city representative of the leading party, the Popular Democratic Party of Tajikistan. After politely welcoming me into his office, he asked me to leave when he heard that my questions were concerning religion and declared he could not answer without an authorization from his superior in the party hierarchy. I never heard from him again. Researchers can be instrumentalized in all sorts of ways. Adams refers to the 'mascot researcher' who can be used for instance to boost someone's prestige and/or legitimize certain cultural or socio-political practices.[73] I was never confronted to such behaviour towards me though at some occasions was reminded to 'write nice things about Tajikistan.' Conversely, performances for the foreigner can be set up and generic social narratives repeated.[74] It is the role of the researcher to distinguish common narratives from erroneous knowledge and interviewees' genuine thoughts or experiences.

I reckon that my religious and cultural background facilitated my research. Being non-religious or agnostic, yet interested in religious matters, meant that I was seen as a potential convert. Also, my non-judgemental attitude towards strict believers only fuelled their efforts to convert me since many of their acquaintances and relatives expressed disagreement with their religious lifestyle. More or less the same dynamics were at play in Christian settings. Though I did not develop close relationships with my Christian interlocutors, I was also subjected to proselytism and asked to reflect on my own faith and spiritual life path. Overall, my own religious beliefs, or lack thereof, did not impede my research on the contrary. I will further elaborate on that in Chapter 5.

Despite what one might expect, being a female scholar in a relatively patriarchal society proved not to be handicapping. Quite the opposite, it turned out to be an advantage because it granted me an almost equal access to both female and male circles. As Douglas suggested: 'women do not threaten either the women or the men. They are liked by and commonly share intimacies with both sexes. Men are simply more threatening to both sexes, even when they are the most sociable.'[75] Clichés aside, Tajiks are very amicable and it was easy to get in touch with women who were interested in showing me around, telling me about their life and their family. I had an easy access to their intimate life. Female friends and acquaintances invited me for sleepovers[76] and they shared memories and problems with me to the extent that a male researcher could have never experienced. I also had almost equally intimate discussions with some men who perceived me as a confidante who would not gossip about their problems. This is what scholars refer to as the 'third gender' that rendered social conventions inapplicable towards female scholars.[77] On one occasion, an imam whom I had previously met a couple of times, shook my hand when I entered his office together with a friend of mine who was an acquaintance of the imam. Jokingly, she told him that, for all those years, she had been waiting for him to shake her hand. Visibly amused, the imam replied: 'But it's different, she is a foreigner!' Indeed, men were very familiar with me, much more than they would have been with a local woman.

The other reason as to why gender matters is linked to laws of attraction. Whether female scholars like it or not, women are also judged based on their looks and 'sexual availability.' Rasmussen and Warren suggest that gender matters since 'respondents perceive us as women or men, as sex objects or not.'[78] I was myself more than once confronted with 'romantic' invitations. I received a number of marriage proposals from married men to become a second or third wife or from divorced men to become the first wife or simply asked on dates. I was what can be called a good party since I was tall,[79] looked young, educated, and potentially rich. Though I dressed conservatively wherever I went, men regularly flirted with me and I found it highly annoying at times even if men were overall polite. But this could also turn into an advantage: I had men's attention. Though I never flirted with any of my interviewees, my marital status certainly helped me to establish contact with some men. Yet, there is a downside to the laws of attraction. While non-threatening to most men, women can perceive the female researcher as a threat. That situation ultimately came up with Iskandar and Mera, a very religious couple who were my main interviewees. When Iskandar asked me to teach him the basics of the internet, we were sitting at the pierogi stall where Mera was working. I was not sure of what to do but he became very insistent so I accepted and we left abruptly. Understandably, Mera was very upset. I was quite embarrassed since I knew I did not act appropriately even though it was genuinely unintentional. I later had the chance to have a one on one conversation with Mera and she did not blame me for that incident. Afterwards, I explained to both of them that I did not want my presence to disturb their relationship and Iskandar tried to reassure me by saying: 'There is nothing to worry about, Mera will not be jealous any more. You have to excuse her, she did not know it was *haram* (forbidden) to be jealous.' This was an unfortunate incident that nevertheless taught me something about ethics, gender, and faith.

In a majority of cases, the observations recounted in this book are based upon informal interactions. Observant participation can create its share of ethical problems, even though people I talked to were always aware that I was a researcher. At the time I conducted my research, the political situation in Tajikistan was not as tense as it is today. Yet, I chose to conceal the names of my interviewees. That being said, I estimate that people who took part in my research faced no particular danger. The names of all respondents were changed at the exception of people who represent figures of authority with whom I conducted formal interviews. For instance, I report the names of representatives of the regional government, of the

Council of Ulemas, and of political parties unless they specifically required talking under the cover of anonymity, which happened only once.

I have outlined how I think my particular researcher's position affected the conduct of my research. But even if I am conscious of my own subjectivity, it is hard to fully grasp their impact on the ground. Scholars should be attentive, sensitive and responsive to the interviewees' reactions and try to act accordingly in order to maintain good relations with interviewees as well as to efficiently pursue research but it remains difficult to judge the effects of interviewees' perceptions on data collection. How differently would people have reacted to me and my questions if my identity would have been radically different? It seems impossible to speculate on that. However, what matters is to be conscious that the researcher is biased, interviewees are partial and that our position can represent an advantage or a disadvantage depending on circumstances.

The issue of religious revival concerns both national and local contexts, but since my fieldwork was concentrated in one relatively small area, its comparative value might appear limited. The discourses on religion that I study involve multiple voices, including those formulated at the national level by politicians and various institutions that deal with the regulation of religion. Even if, according to Gledhill, the study of micro-political processes can reveal that 'local level processes not merely reflect larger political processes and national-level conflicts,'[80] the analysis should not be hermetic. Local narratives should be understood within the broader national and historical contexts that shaped them.

CHAPTER 2

THE SOVIET SECULARIZATION PROJECT

Fifty years is ample time to change a world and its people almost
beyond recognition. All that is required for the task are a sound
knowledge of social engineering, a clear sight of the intended
goal – and power.

ARTHUR C. CLARKE, *CHILDHOOD'S END*

In Clarke's novel, benevolent aliens have been given the task of peacefully
leading earthlings toward a spiritual awakening, an endeavour which is
part of an even greater cosmic plan. Nor did Marx ever advocate using
force to lead people away from their God,[1] although the Soviet regime
ultimately resorted to this very thing. The eradication of religion was part
of a vast and ambitious socio-political engineering project, which aimed
at nothing less than the destruction of traditional institutions and the
establishment of a new socio-economic and political order on the territory
of the Soviet Union. This is what revolutions are about after all.

This chapter broadly introduces the social and political context of
Soviet Islam based on the idea that 70 years of Soviet 'management of
religion' continue to influence the understanding of religion and
its position in society in contemporary Tajikistan. While I strongly
emphasize the importance of history on the formation of social structures
and religious traditions, I don't pretend to offer any new groundbreaking
knowledge about the history of the region and the development of
religion in Central Asia. Numerous excellent works have covered the

history of the region and undertaking a long historical essay here seems only redundant. Moreover, in keeping with the overarching idea of the book, the objective is to focus on current practices and narratives with particular regard to identifying traces of the Soviet legacy.

This chapter focuses on the Soviet secularization experience as an aspect of the radical transformation the region's peoples underwent within a relatively few years. The first part of the discussion considers Soviet materialistic atheism and the resultant conception of secularity as the underlying philosophical and political principles that have impelled the Soviet state to undertake the eradication of religion. The second part examines the various stages of the secularization process itself and the measures taken not only to impose the separation of Church from State but also to persuade citizens of the backwardness of religious beliefs and of the importance of abandoning them. The third part details the spiritual role and administrative responsibilities of the institutions established to regulate religion. It is not my intent to offer a comprehensive analysis of Marxist-Leninist philosophy. That being said, I will present an overview of the philosophical and ideological orientation of the secularization project, with emphasis on the holistic character of materialistic atheism. The following sections are based on primary and secondary sources, both Western and Soviet, available in North American libraries, in Tajik bookstores, libraries, and personal collections. The works cited were selected for the purpose of highlighting the contrast between the very negative Western and very optimistic Soviet views of the secularization project. For instance, American scholar Christopher Marsh describes the USSR's forced secularization in such terms: 'Much like the Holocaust, this experience of inhumanity must be properly understood as a part of the larger phenomenon of religion's struggle with modernity itself.'[2] In contrast, Soviet scholar Okulov states that 'The October Revolution has shown that man's life having been liberated from every kind of social oppression, is naturally freed in all aspects from religious ideas, customs and rituals.'[3]

Soviet Scientific-Materialism

[Understanding Marxist philosophy] is the only efficient way to gain an insight into the process that have been taking place in Soviet society for the last seven decades.[4]

Dialectical and historical materialism are the founding doctrines of scientific atheism, which Pospielovsky defines as follows: 'The ontological model of materialism posits the existence of an objective, self-sufficient world in which laws regulate the order of things' while 'historical materialism aims at extending the materialist approach to the sphere of culture and society.'[5] Haldane, in his preface of Engels' *Dialectics of Nature* writes that dialectical materialism is 'a philosophy which illuminates all events whatever, from the falling of a stone to a poet's imaginings.'[6] More concretely,

> it is based on the foundation of all the philosophical, natural and social scientific, political, moral, and aesthetic views and convictions, which express the interests and ideals of the working class. The mastering of the scientific world outlook – the dominant element of the spiritual make-up of the Soviet people – helps in taking an active part in life and in solving pressing problems in the development of socialist society.[7]

As a corollary to dialectical materialism, atheism is an important aspect of Marxism. In the words of Marx's famous maxim: 'Religion is the opium of the masses.' In Marxist theory, religion or religious beliefs arose among primitive human societies as men, lacking scientific knowledge, tried to make sense of the natural phenomena that affected their everyday lives. In modern societies, religions have become entangled with political power. This relationship contributes to keep the masses in a state of servitude, passively accepting their fate, which they perceive as their destiny and therefore as inevitable. Servitude is driven by fear, which is itself brought upon people by the blind and brutal forces of capitalism.[8] In modern times, however, science provides the basis for understanding: gravity, illnesses, astronomy, mechanics, agronomy, and so on. Through science, men are able to understand the world they live in so they behave consciously and no longer need to rely on 'false beliefs' that place them in a state of ignorance. Hence, materialist knowledge and enlightenment are necessary to free the masses from the intellectual and material oppression imposed on them by the ruling class, whether aristocratic or bourgeois.

The theory of scientific atheism has two aspects: (1) the scientific critique of religion, (2) the study of the positive and creative role of atheism, including its role in the development of the cultural and spiritual life of society.[9] 'Materialistic atheism is revolutionary'[10] and, unlike atheism alone, materialistic atheism not only offers a critique of religion but anticipates and hopes for a revolution leading to the creation of a society in which the existence of religion becomes superfluous. According to another Soviet ideologue, materialistic atheism is distinguishable from the tragic atheism of the 'Nietzschean and existential type' and 'intends to revive man's confidence in man: to convince man that life has a meaning and is worth living.'[11] As in Western conceptions of secularization, the Soviet view emphasized the importance of social and economic development, and especially education, in the progressive decline of religion. But overall, Soviet ideologues were very critical of the secularization theory and processes, as defined and instrumentalized by Westerners. The *Soviet Atheist's Handbook*[12] summarizes the difference starkly: 'Western atheist ideas do not acknowledge that the antagonistic class structure is even more problematic than religion and that religion is used to reinforce the exploitation of the classes.'[13] Soviets also questioned the authenticity of the actual separation of Church and State in the Western world. For Rosenbaum, Western secularism was a fallacy because in some bourgeois States, Spain for example, the Catholic Church was recognized as the official Church, whereas in the USSR all religions were equal before the Law.[14]

Late Soviet thinkers, however, were far more critical of Soviet atheism. For example, in 1989, in the midst of Perestroika, Sadur explained that Soviet atheism held some anti-Muslim sentiments because it was greatly influenced by European atheism. Therefore, its rhetoric and terminology were filled with anti-Muslim stereotypes.[15] Without being benevolent-minded towards Islam, the *Soviet Atheist's Handbook* acknowledges that the reason why revolutionary movements in pre-Soviet Russia criticized certain religions and depicted Islam as idiotic was that they could not openly criticize Orthodoxy.[16] Nevertheless, Islam is pictured as a fatalistic religion since God is said to be Almighty and 'without God, not a single hair falls from a man's head' says the Atheist Handbook.[17] The book also quotes Karl Marx: 'Fatalism is the stem of Islam.' Islam is also depicted as a religion standing against scientific knowledge and encouraging backwardness. Finally, it is said to cultivate selfishness, because men are too busy thinking about their own salvation to care about other people and the world around them.[18] The *Atheist's Handbook* is certainly harsh towards Islam, but it is equally so toward other confessions reviewed in the book: Christianity, Judaism, Islam, Buddhism, Hinduism, as well as some mystical movements. In the case of the Soviet Union, it would be appropriate to say that the state had an equal aversion to all religions.

However, Lenin explicitly mentioned that if the state should remain neutral towards religions, the Communist Party could not because it does not consider religion as a private affair.[19] This became problematic since there was only one legal party in the Soviet Union[20] and it *was* de facto the state, commonly called a party-state. Hence, there could be no mistake about the involvement of the state in religious affairs. Later internal critiques were thorough and touched a fundamental aspect of state-religion relations; the actual absence of separation between Church and State in the Soviet Union. In the spirit of Perestroika, Furman wrote that: 'Church and State could not possibly be separated in the USSR because nothing was separated from the government.'[21] Indeed, Soviet Marxism-Leninism touched upon all aspects of life from religion to sexual health through housing and industrial manufacturing.

Soviet Materialism: A Religion?

Because Marxism-Leninism was a philosophy that had 'implications for just about every aspect of society, from the family to international relations,'[22] some authors conceptualize it as a religion in itself with its own ideology, worldview, moral codes, and rituals.[23] Codevilla suggests that: 'for its messianic and prophetic attitude, it [Marxist-Leninism] takes on a religious hue.' Like a Weltanschauung, the Soviet ideology, with its absolute values and objectives, aimed at the creation of a new society and a new man.[24] Soviet thinkers fully acknowledged the holistic character of the ideology promoted by the Communist Party. This was not perceived as something negative; quite the contrary. A noteworthy statement of this position is Lenin's famous quote: 'The Marxian doctrine is omnipotent because it is true. It is complete and harmonious, and provides men with an integral world conception which is irreconcilable with any form of superstition, reaction, or defence of bourgeois oppression.'[25] At the beginning of the Soviet Union, there were even deliberate attempts to create a new religion, although Lenin opposed any such undertaking. In particular, Lunacharsky, Gorky, and

Bogdanov were among top party members who proposed the creation of a Communist religion. For this, they were called *Bogostroitely*, that is, 'God-builders'[26] who aimed at building an atheistic religion that acknowledged 'a sense of connection with the past and future.'[27] Similarly, Lunacharsky thought to replace the traditional idea of God by building a new vision of humanity, positing, for instance, that socialism could become an object of love and adoration. Lenin strongly opposed this proposed direction, perceiving it as an attempt to 'dissolve Marxism into a mild liberal reformism.'[28]

Despite the fact that the Bogostroitely's project was never approved, Agadjanian underlines that in many respects, the Soviet ideology contained 'unmistakable religious connotations.' For instance, the *Moral Code of the Builders of Communism*, a 12-point party programme adopted in 1961 has biblical connotations even though it rejects religious meanings.[29] Froese's stance on the religious character of the Soviet ideology is somewhat ambiguous. On the one hand, he writes that Soviet communism was an alternative to religion rather than a competing religion.[30] On the other hand, he dedicates almost an entire chapter to a comparison between religious faith and cults and the Soviet ideology. First, he compares the League of Militant Atheists[31] to a Church because of its 'conversion' mission and its local cells, whom he finds reminiscent of religious parishes. When the League was abolished after World War II, it was replaced by a variety of organizations that actively promoted atheism, including the Knowledge society, Komsomol,[32] and the Institute of Scientific Atheism. Second, he associates atheistic science that proved the fallacy of religious beliefs to homily. Third, he sees as liturgy the new Soviet rituals and holidays (Women's Day, International Labour Day) and mimicry of religious practices at weddings and funerals.[33] Also, Froese suggests that perhaps the promises of Communism – the end of injustice and the advent of personal and social emancipation – might be considered analogous to the otherworldly rewards offered by religion.[34] Ultimately, he likens Marxist-Leninists to religious fanatics.[35] Gellner acknowledges the similarities between Marxism and other religions 'at the doctrinal and intellectual level the proud boast of Marxism was that it had exiled the supernatural from social life.'[36]

Despite the civic rituals, the cult and the myths Communists have built over time, I do not conceptualize Materialistic-Atheism as a religion. Instead, I regard Sovietism as a worldview, as the term is defined by Pospielovsky: '(1) A certain vision of the relationship between man and nature, (2) A concrete understanding of the relationship between man and society or groups of men and society, (3) A certain understanding of the meaning of life, of human nature and its destination.'[37] This definition I think captures the essence of what the authors cited above mean when they liken Sovietism to a religion, that is, a way to explain the world around us as well as the meaning of life, but without giving it a supernatural tone. Luehrmann suggests that this is why Soviet theorists of religion adopted a definition of religion that is not based 'on the contrast between the sacred and the profane, but always defined as faith in God or spiritual beings.' Therefore, they 'saw the creation of an exclusively human community as the ultimate goal of secularization.'[38] Whether or not we can consider Sovietism as a religion is crucial, because it determines the way we conceptualize its impact on Soviet peoples.

Secularization, Soviet-Style

There is a distinction to make between secularization and secularism. Secularization is seen as social phenomenon characterized by (1) the decline of religious beliefs and practices, (2) the privatization of religion, (3) the differentiation of the secular spheres.[39] Secularism – and its corollary the secular state – represents a political principle understood as 'a discourse and an institutional practice positing that religion should not be the final determinant of political outcomes and that religious institutions should not directly exercise secular power.'[40] Secularization processes are generally addressed from a Western perspective that depicts this process as stemming from an ineluctable evolutionary socio-economic movement.[41] As Marsh noticed, 'virtually none of the debate on secularization has considered the only part of the world where it actually became a state policy, and where tremendous amounts of resources were allowed to erasing religious faith and promoting atheism instead.'[42] In the following section, I will focus on the major features of the Soviet secularization project, from the physical destruction of religious institutions and the prohibition of religious performances and duties, the implementation of education and propaganda programmes, and the establishment of administrative structures to manage religion. All these elements contributed to the progressive decline of religion in

Central Asia and the making of a new socio-political order. As Schatz describes it: 'the destructive side of Soviet power accompanied the profoundly constructive transformations that Soviet rule brought.'[43]

Early promises and appeals

Husband argues that atheism was not a significant part of the Bolshevik's prerevolutionary messages nor did it influence their victory. Instead, the revolutionaries elaborated ad hoc the complex cultural strategies that would transform the face of the empire.[44] Keller insists that 'Soviet anti-Islamic action cannot be separated from Soviet policy toward the non-Russian peoples.'[45] At the beginning of the revolution, appeals from the Bolshevik party to 'toiling Muslims of Russia and the East' were full of promises. On December 7, 1917, the Council of People's Commissars published an appeal to Muslims 'whose mosques and shrines have been destroyed, whose beliefs have been trampled on by the Tsars and the Russian oppressors. Henceforth your beliefs and customs, your national and cultural institutions are declared free and inviolable.'[46] Later in 1919, while inviting the masses of the East to join the revolutionary movement, Lenin offered the following guidance: '[Unlike in Europe] You must be able to apply that theory [communism] and practice to conditions in which the bulk of the population are peasants, and in which the task is to wage a struggle against medieval survivals and not against capitalism.'[47] Because there was no proletariat as such, local traditions and religious habits were regarded as the social and ideological system to be overcome. Also, religion was inevitably associated with nationalism, yet another counter-revolutionary ideology.[48]

Overall, the Bolsheviks' appeal was not received favourably by local populations, even though the anti-Western discourse of the Soviets did prove attractive to some, especially the so-called 'Red mullahs,' as well as the Jadids, who represented a modernizing force in the region, albeit not a homogeneous one.[49] The modernist movement, with its roots in Tatarstan and Siberia, also attracted supporters in Central Asia.[50] Jadidists were driven by the idea that Muslims should emancipate through education, find a way to open up to the world and participate in modern life while reinforcing their Islamic identity.[51] Despite their support for the Bolsheviks, Jadids were later evicted from the political scene. The task of undermining religion in the Central Asian region was colossal, considering the dominance of Islamic Law and traditions in the Khanates, despite their having been under the Russian protectorate since the late nineteenth century. The three Khanates: Bukhara, Khiva, and Kokand,[52] were still administered in accordance with Sharia, which regulated courts, taxation, and education.[53] A report made by a Russian Communist party member indicates that in 1925, there were no less than 11,680 imams and mullahs in the Samarkand, Ferghana, and Syr Daria oblast's alone.[54] As we will see, in the early years of Soviet rule in Central Asia, the state maintained a prudent ambiguity towards the clergy.

The Soviets faced harsh resistance when trying to impose the Bolshevik government's authority in the early years of the revolution. The 1916 revolt,[55] which started in Samarkand and spread over Russian Turkestan, can be seen as the prelude to the turbulent years that followed. The October Revolution in Russia precipitated a great turmoil in Central Asia, even if the battles between the Red and White armies were confined mainly to the northern part of the Kazakh steppe. Also, the very small number of native Marxists meant that active participation in the military action was limited almost entirely to Europeans.[56] The victorious Bolsheviks established the Tashkent Soviet in March 1918, and on April 30, the former Turkestan became the Turkestan Autonomous Soviet Socialist Republic (TASSR, 1918–1924). However, the Soviet Army would meet resistance in the form of a loosely organized rebellion, the Basmachi.[57] This movement, more or less inspired by pan-Turkism,[58] was composed of various groups, with sometimes relatively conflicting interests,[59] which undermined its effectiveness. Most of the fighting took place in the territory of Tajikistan, later moving to Afghanistan. The struggle grew into a guerrilla war, but the rebels never managed to dominate large portions of the territory. Even after the Soviet Union had been established in its definitive form in 1922, the Basmachi continued to oppose the Red Army until the execution of one of its most prominent leaders, Ibrahim Bek, in Tajikistan in 1931. Poliakov suggests that there was still some Basmachi activity in Northern Tajikistan (Asht Jamoat) as late as in 1941.[60] Notwithstanding the absence of formal control over the region, the first actions against traditional institutions were taken in the early 1920s. These steps included the limitation and finally the abolition of the Islamic courts, the confiscation of waqfs,[61] and campaigns for the promotion of women's rights. These radical measures were coupled with the imposition of new social norms, which greatly affected the traditional organization of the society.

Victorious but unassertive

Much confusion marked the first years of Soviet rule in the newly created Turkestan Soviet Republic. Politics is often a process of trial and error, and so were the early Soviet policies by which leaders, in an uncertain administrative, political, and social environment, introduced rapid changes while trying to avoid creating too much unrest. In contrast, the Stalinist period that followed brought full-fledged repression of religious behaviour, institutions, and clergy.

The first legislation against established religions was adopted on December 18, 1917. A decree entitled 'On civil marriage, children and book-keeping of acts' recognized civil marriages and children born outside marriage, granted women the right to divorce and nullified the celebration of religious marriages.[62] Another significant legislative step was taken with Lenin's Decree of January 23, 1918, which separated Church and State by depriving the Church of its legal status and of its property rights, as well as prohibiting it from teaching minors religion in either state or private schools.[63] Article 3 of this decree provided the right for citizens to believe in any religion or in no religion at all, while Article 5 recognized the right to perform religious ceremonies as long as they did not disturb public order.[64] In Central Asia, the adoption of these decrees was followed by the confiscation of waqfs, which provoked so much outrage that Moscow later ordered Turkestan Communists to suspend the initiative.[65] Pianciola and Sartori argue that, contrary to popular belief, waqfs had never been requisitioned on a widespread basis and that the Turkestan Bolsheviks' attitude was very ambiguous, with state control over waqfs being more formal than actual.[66]

Lacking personnel and guidelines as well as facing opposition, Turkestan's revolutionary court system allowed litigants the right to refer to Sharia and adat[67] if the traditional norms did not contravene the interests of the working people.[68] Muslim courts were not abolished throughout Turkestan until 1927. Even after the new people's courts were set up, many individuals, especially women, were reluctant to use them because of social pressure.[69] In general, authorities took a relaxed stance on religious institutions until the late 1920s, except for what concerned education. From 1917 to 1920, the number of secular mixed primary schools in Turkestan increased from 576 to 2,022 until NEP measures slowed down these efforts.[70] In 1927, there were still 11 medresses in the Khujand district together with 99 secular schools.[71] A 1929 report on the state of the clergy in the newly created Tajik Soviet Socialist Republic relates that people continued to rely on clergy to settle disputes and to provide counsel on personal, family or health matters.[72]

The liberation of women from the patriarchal oppression imposed by feudal and capitalist societies was an important aspect of the socialist project, and the promotion of women's rights was an integral part of the political platform of the Bolsheviks from the very beginning. Indeed, laws promoting women's rights to education, to divorce, and to abortion were adopted in the early years of the Soviet Union. However, Stalin reverted the law on abortion in 1936[73] but the right to abortion was reinstated in 1955.[74] In Central Asia and in the Muslim regions of Russia, the promotion of women's rights had twin objectives: to ensure the equality of rights for men and women, but perhaps even more importantly, to undermine the Islamic clergy and religious traditions. In Marxist rhetoric, Central Asian women were identified as a 'surrogate proletariat'[75] because of their subordinate position within the patriarchal structure of both the society and the family. Therefore, women had to be liberated. This is how Soviet authorities started their propaganda campaign, which culminated with the *Hujum*[76] on the symbolic date of March 8, 1927 to mark Women's International Day. Agitation campaigns and public unveiling, as were organized from time to time by the Women's Committee (Zhenotdel)[77] of the Central Asian Bureau, proved not to be very effective and direct confrontations of women and men only triggered anger. In the 1930s, some communists were condemned as being too lenient in the fight against Islam, although at the same time, others were accused of being too zealous, especially in regard to *Hujum*, and therefore held responsible for discrediting the Soviet authorities by fostering discontent.[78] This kind of recrimination is typical of Soviet rhetoric and is found throughout the decades. In Tajikistan in 1948, there were cases of women wearing it while receiving awards for their 'communist labour' in the cotton harvest.[79] However, by the 1950s, the clergy had ceased to insist that women cover their heads, contending that it was not necessary and public opinion no longer censored women who would not wear the *paranja*.[80]

Before the 1930s, the pressure on religious communities was constant but diffuse compared to the more radical actions against religious figures and believers that would be taken by the Soviet authorities later during the period known as the 'Great Stalinist Purges,' between 1930 and 1939.

Full-fledged repression

Although he personally was a convinced atheist, Lenin was also a fine politician. He acknowledged that: 'war must never be openly declared against religion, for such a move would be an unnecessary "gamble of political war."'[81] Likewise, Sultan Galiev, a Tatar from Bashkiria and an influential member of the Communist Party in its early years,[82] also warned the Bolshevik Party to be careful in its attack against Islam or Muslimness (Musul'mantstvo) since Muslims perceived their own faith as a religion for an oppressed people who were victims of the economic and political oppression of Western imperialism.[83] That advice was followed in the early years, but soon enough there came a time when compromise was no longer necessary. The more the Communist authorities consolidated their power on the ground, in terms of both organizational and political capacities during the 1920s, the less it was felt necessary to ally with local reformist clergy. Spiritual administrations were closed in 1927 and religious schools, remaining Islamic courts and mosques began being closed or used for different purposes in the same year.[84] The collectivization campaign that started in 1928 created a momentum for the complete elimination of waqfs.[85]

By late 1927, local party cells were employing two complementary strategies towards the clergy, official propaganda and a secret campaign of terror.[86] Propaganda efforts to convince the population that mullahs and ishans (the oppressors) were profiteers living off the exploitation of poor masses.[87] This two-pronged strategy was based on reports from the field, which warned the authorities that brutal interventions could only lead to public outcry. For example, in Khujand in 1927, secular schools were vandalized with portraits of revolutionaries destroyed, and lands were withheld from state inventory following the arrest of five prominent mullahs, while five others left the area, fearing prosecution.[88] These are but a few examples of direct repression, among many other everyday tragedies that marked two decades. Repression was brutal and substantial and Keller affirms that between 1917 and 1939, 140,000 Muslim clergy were arrested, killed, or exiled.[89]

As a result, by around 1941, the number of mosques in the USSR had been reduced to five per cent of the pre-revolution total, from approximately 26,000 to 1,300.[90] As to Tajikistan, Keller's archival documents estimate the number of clergymen in Tajikistan in 1929 at 790.[91] That seems plausible until we look at the numbers provided by Ro'i. His research suggests that in the late 1940s, there were 150 mazars in the Leninabad Oblast' and 500 functioning ones throughout the Tajik republic in the middle of the following decade, served by some 700 mullahs.[92] Reports of the Council for the Affairs of Religious Cults (CARC) mention that, as of November 1958, most mazars had been officially closed.[93] Interestingly, a 1949 CARC report uncovered by Ro'i mentions that religiosity was not equally distributed in Tajikistan, with the Leninabad (Sughd) and Kulob (Kathlon) oblasts' showing higher rates of religious practice than elsewhere.[94] Notwithstanding discrepancies between statistics, the overall story is one of enormous efforts by the Central government and local authorities to curb religious beliefs and practice. Yet, physical restrictions against religion were indeed coupled with ideological programmes meant at turning Soviet citizens into 'enlightened godless subjects.'

Propaganda and education

Wheeler, writing about the establishment of a universal education system in the USSR, underlines the importance of the transmission of new Soviet values: 'In dealing with the Muslim masses of Central Asia, where it was not a question of re-education as it was in Western Russia, but of the introduction of education and political indoctrination where virtually none had existed before.'[95] This statement, while plausible on its face, is to some extent misleading because it tends to attribute a special character to Central Asians, as if propaganda and literacy campaigns were particularly effective since the lack of literacy made the people particularly vulnerable to propaganda. Even if literacy rates were low, there was a semblance of an education system, albeit limited, in Central Asia. In pre-revolutionary Bukhara alone, it is estimated that around 3,000 persons 'belonged' to mosques and Islamic courts, and there was one religious figure for every 30 citizens, or one for every 10 citizens over 20 years old.[96] In Kokand in the 1840s, around 1,000 students were enrolled at the medresse. Also, the memoirs of a Kokandi poetess, Dilshad, reveal that she taught literary arts to some 890 girls in the course of her long life[97] in Kokand.[98] Yet, Tajik historian Asimova's research shows that in 1897, the literacy rate among Tajiks in Eastern Bukhara was only 0.5 per cent.[99] In comparison, approximately 60 per cent of Russian men and 83 per cent of women could neither read nor write at the time of the revolution, and illiteracy rates were even higher in rural areas.[100] The differences in literacy rates that prevailed between peoples at the time do not matter much and, as Khalid remarked, Russians too had to be 'transformed and modernized.'[101]

As Gellner argues, modern education systems serve to inculcate shared understandings and values so that people understand, interact, and cooperate with each other in modern, production-oriented societies.[102] In August 1930, the adoption of a decree on General Compulsory Primary Education at the All-Union level was echoed in similar laws in each Republic, even though implementation proved difficult in the conservative environment of Central Asia.[103] Arabic script, then in use by Uzbeks and Tajiks, was replaced by the Latin alphabet in 1927 and entirely discarded in 1940 in favour of the Cyrillic alphabet.[104] As a consequence, people were cut off from the rich pre-Soviet literature and, most importantly, from religious scriptures. Also, Russian language courses became mandatory in 1938.[105] Education and literacy campaigns were conducted with newly printed Soviet books. 'The ultimate objective of the communist upbringing is to rid Soviet society of such "negative traits as individualism, bourgeois nationalism, chauvinism, indolence, and religious prejudices,"[106] Complete literacy in Tajikistan was allegedly attained in the 1950s.[107]

The word propaganda inevitably carries a negative connotation. Indeed, people usually understand propaganda as a Machiavellian attempt to disseminate false information in order to influence or fool people. However, Kenez suggests that, unlike the Nazis, the Soviets were not interested in the techniques or philosophy of mass persuasion, instead, they saw propaganda as part of education campaigns.[108] I was in fact quite surprised to hear people in Tajikistan use the word *propaganda* or *agitatsiya* to designate awareness and public information campaigns, understood as the action of 'propagating,' and not 'brainwashing.'

Soviet atheism specialists insisted on the educational aspect of atheist propaganda that would lead to the achievement of socialist goals. I distinguish four recurrent themes in atheist propaganda: (1) religious beliefs are fallacious and exist because men needed them to make sense of the world they lived in, (2) religions encourage submission and are therefore exploitative, (3) historical materialism provides a Weltanschauung that leads citizens to reject religion through education and material progress, (4) religious beliefs persist because of poor education and insufficient material advancement. Kurochkin, a Soviet ideologue, explains how the scientific and materialist atheistic Weltanschauung must be reproduced and expanded in every new generation of socialist society,[109] because according to him the danger of religious renewal was never far away. The following instruction of one Soviet ideologue evokes the need for, and the expected results of, atheist propaganda:

> It is necessary to conduct systematic extensive scientific atheist propaganda, to patiently explain the fallacy of religious beliefs that have arisen in the past due to the people's domination/pressure under elemental forces of nature and social oppression and their ignorance of the true causes behind natural and social phenomena. It should build on the achievements of modern science, which fully reveals the picture of the world, increases the power of man over nature, and leaves no room for the fantastic religion's fiction on super-natural forces.[110]

The first atheist lessons within the Communist party were drawn up in 1921. Soon, many atheist publications started being published: 'The League of the Militant Godless' was created at the beginning of the 1920s, but their actions started becoming visible in Central Asia only around 1925.[111] It was not until 1937 that a local branch appeared in Tajikistan. The League at first relied heavily on nonprint forms of propaganda (agitatsiya), since the number of literate people was quite limited.[112] Broad propaganda campaigns against Ramadan and Idi Qurbon[113] were designed in Moscow. These campaigns were intended to (1) unmask the counterrevolutionary essence of religion and national chauvinism, (2) increase the membership in the militant Godless, and (3) fulfil cotton-sowing plans and protect cattle from slaughter.[114]

After World War II, there was no organization in the Soviet Union solely devoted to atheist propaganda. The League of the Militant Godless was dissolved in 1947, replaced by the newly founded Society for the Dissemination of Political and Scientific Knowledge, which was renamed the Knowledge Society in 1963. The new denomination reflects a change in atheist strategies, from confrontation to dissemination of modern science as a more effective way to wean people away from religious beliefs.[115] The intensity of atheist propaganda was not constant over the years, but it never fell into complete disuse. To compare on only one measure, in 1954, 120,000 atheist lectures were carried out across the whole Soviet Union, while there were 650,000 in 1970.[116]

Beyond propaganda efforts, education and literacy campaigns truly became the capital agent of change. *Agitatsiya* can only give limited results and reach a limited number of individuals, whereas public education can sway a very large and impressionable young audience. Indeed, authorities thought that a high level of social and economic development combined with a materialistic atheistic education would inevitably lead to the transformation of the society, from god-fearing to godless.[117] Surprisingly, no particular antireligious propaganda was established in the school curriculum in the early years of the Soviet Union as the authorities were confident that 'Religion was irrelevant. So was any attack on it.'[118] However, reports about popular discontent started flooding into the office of the People's Commissariat for Education, or Narkompros,[119] confirming parents' anger at the removal of icons and religious education in schools. It seems that none of the players in the field of education were interested in introducing antireligious subjects into the curriculum because of fear of popular aversion, but most importantly, because of scarce educational and financial resources. There were no courses on atheism as such, with the exception of a general social science class in the last year of study. Instead, it was the teachers' prerogative to include atheist rubrics in the other subjects, complemented by extracurricular activities, mainly within youth organizations at the Pioneers and Komsomol Camps. Finally, in 1959, a course entitled 'Foundations of Scientific-atheism' was made mandatory in all fields of study in institutions of higher education.[120]

As much as they would have liked to get rid of competing religious ideologies forever, Soviet authorities had no choice but to acknowledge them as an inevitable and undesirable defect that must be dealt with. In fact, atheist literature is filled with conclusions and recommendations about the resilience of religion and suggestions for future adoption of methods to undermine it. Soviet figures from 1937 show that 66 per cent of rural and 33 per cent of urban dwellers were believers.[121]

Many of these were called: 'ordinary[122] religious believers.'[123] Okulov mentions that in some cases, 'pure reason' could not persuade believers of the 'absurdity of their traditional ideas.'[124] Such discourse survived Perestroika and could still be heard in the late 1980s.[125] The typical believers were found to be women, especially older ones living in rural areas. In spite of the socialist revolution which had supposedly liberated women, many of them remained housewives and could not access higher education. While acknowledging progresses made, Soviet social scientist themselves questioned the effective liberation of women and underlined the 'double burden' to which women were subjected due to their continuous involvement in household maintenance.[126] Low levels of education were also identified as a cause of religious resilience. However, personal and psychological factors were also held responsible for the persistence of religious beliefs. In this category were persons who had a weak understanding of social affairs, those of weak character, depressive or unhappy people, and those who had been traumatized, such as survivors of World War II.[127] Others who did not fit the description were considered 'unhappy' and under the influence of superstitious old women.[128] Clearly, the tone was very patronizing. There were regular calls for the conduct of special lectures for women. For instance, Dadabaeva, the director of the Scientific Atheism Department of the Philosophy Faculty of the Tajik SSR Academy of Sciences, writing in the newspaper *Kommunist Tadzhikistana* in 1980, called for a greater propaganda effort among women. Like others, she blamed poor education levels and household work for the superstitious character of women.

Many atheist discourses tended to avoid accusing or demonizing believers. In fact, many of the critical assessments conclude that propagandists failed because their message was insulting to believers. In an All-Union conference of the Council for the Affairs of Religious Cult in 1957, participants were told that they had to 'distinguish between clergy, who were "parasites" seeking to use religion for their own personal enrichment, and ordinary believers who, according to the party's injunctions, were not to be offended in the course of the struggle against religion.'[129] In what is perhaps a sign of softer times, another scholar, Abdulla, writes in 1989 that religion in the society cannot be separated from morality and that 'being a believer in a socialist environment shows that Islam does not take away the believer from the world but blesses him for serving the whole society.'[130] Despite the fact that in general this was a period of liberalization, the 1980s saw a revival of atheistic propaganda. In Tajikistan alone, 4,000 lectures on atheism were held in the first half of the 1908s for a population of 3.8 million people.[131]

Managing Religion: Constitutional Provisions and Laws

The first Constitution adopted by the Communist Party of the Russian Soviet Federative Socialist Republic (RSFSR) in 1918 confirmed the separation of Church and State and guaranteed citizens freedom of conscience (RSFSR 1918). The 1936 Constitution guaranteed the separation of Church from the State and the schools (Article 124), freedom of religious worship as well as the right to conduct *antireligious* propaganda.[132] In 1977, Article 52 stated that citizens were guaranteed the rights to follow a religion or no religion and to perform rites, as well as to disseminate *atheistic* propaganda. It also prohibited the incitement of hostility or hatred on the basis of religious beliefs.[133] By declaring that citizens had the right to propagate atheist 'beliefs' but not religious ones, the Constitution *de facto* prohibited religious proselytizing. Also, while the 1936 article mentioned the right to conduct *antireligious* propaganda, the 1977 provision refers to *atheist* propaganda. This change of wording epitomizes different political environments and political approaches, from Stalinist confrontation to an emphasis on at least limited tolerance, and to greater reliance on ideological persuasion. Finally an article added in 1977 officially brought a moral dimension to the upbringing of children. Article 66 stipulated that: 'Citizens of the USSR are to be concerned with the upbringing of children, to train them for socially useful work, and to raise them as worthy members of socialist society. Children are obliged to care for their parents and help them.' This article is tendentious because one cannot easily measure parents' success in making their children worthy members of the socialist society. Also, it stigmatizes a priori religious parents because their values are implicitly held to be contrary to those of socialism.

Various decrees and laws were adopted to further codify the practice of religion, especially the status of religious organizations rather than individuals, who were being addressed through other means, namely atheist propaganda and social pressure. As with Constitutional amendments, laws and decrees were frequently subject to change and reflected their respective socio-political times. I will mainly focus on the Law on Religious Associations because it significantly shaped religious life in the Soviet Union. Also, emphasis is justified by the fact that, in Central Asia, post-Soviet governments adopted very similar laws modelled after this very Soviet law. In 1921, the Presidium of the Russian Soviet Republic adopted decrees On the Exemption from Compulsory Military Service on Religious Convictions, Labour Service of Priests and On the Publication of Religious Literature and Religious Groups, Associations, and Congresses. It contained little reference to religious groups except for its confirmation that religious associations could not hold any legal status and needed approval before printing religious literature.[134] The 1929 Law on Religious Associations clarified the rules for registration but the criteria was vague, which gave the authorities broad latitude to reject applications. It regulated places of worship, listed forbidden activities, prominent among which was the organization of youth meetings or study groups. It outlawed religious charities and members of religious organizations could not be solicited for financial donations, thereby curtailing zakat,[135] except for the repair and maintenance of the prayer building. The law declared that all cult properties were nationalized, so that a religious group could not own a building but could be offered a place of worship by the district authorities. It granted religious associations the right to hold local, regional, republican, or All-Union religious conventions, but only with the permission by the appropriate level of government. After a period of relative religious tolerance during the postwar years, the period from 1958 until the end of the 1970s saw renewed persecution of religious elements.[136]

During the 22nd Communist Party Congress in 1961, Khrushchev called for the intensification of scientific-atheistic education and mobilized the Komsomol and the Academy of Sciences for this.[137] The criminal code was also modified to add violations of the principle of separation of Church and State. For instance, a provision entitled: 'The rights and duties of parents or guardians in the upbringing and education of children' was included in section 11 of the 1977 Law on Public Education.[138] This provision requires parents to raise children in the highest spirit of communist morality and respect for socialist property.[139] These laws seemed to have been firmly enforced, resulting in the closing of even more mosques, the interdiction of pilgrimages, and the closing of mazars as well as the prosecution of believers and members of clergy.[140] As we will see in Chapter 4, many elements of the Soviet laws just presented resonate with current Tajik laws that aim at restricting religion.

Institutions of Regulation

While a significant decrease in religious practice followed the implementation of these policies, repression and propaganda did not result in the complete eradication of religion. Authorities felt they had no choice but to try to channel religious behaviour by establishing religious standards, trying to make them as compatible as possible with Soviet norms. The creation of religious administrations in the postwar period provided authorities the means to influence religious practices. Four such administrations appeared throughout the Soviet Union during the war period: the Spiritual Administration for European Russia and Siberia in Ufa, the Northern Caucasus in Buinaksk (Dagestan), which moved to Baku in 1974, for Transcaucasia, and the Spiritual Muslim Board of Central Asia (SADUM).[141] Other faiths had their own religious administrations but, unlike for Muslims, their representation was not territorial. Russian Orthodox, Gregorian Armenian, Evangelist Christian Baptists, and Lutherans had representations, while Roman Catholics and Jews had no centre.[142]

The most common explanation for the creation of these bodies is they were a reward for Soviet Muslims who participated in the war effort[143] as well as an attempt to give a democratic image to the authorities.[144] Polat insists that the officialization of Islam was meant to purge Central Asian Islam of its external influences,[145] whereas Ro'i suggests that Moscow merely accepted the request of a group of Muslim leaders who hoped to bolster their position within the local clergy.[146] Dudoignon also suggests that within the context of repression, the creation of the SADUM contributed to the intensification of personal rivalries, particularly in Sufi circles.[147] Multiple factors doubtless came into play, but the bottom line may be that the decision to create religious administrations demonstrated that the regime perceived the clergy and religious communities 'as a defeated and controllable enemy.'[148] The end result was the creation of an official Islam in the USSR that was used to frame religious practices as well as an instrument of foreign policy when dealing with Muslim countries.[149] Perhaps the creation of these regional bodies also reflects the Soviet scheme of replacing religious identities with objective nationality categories.[150] As Pelkmans argues, Soviets eventually ethnicized religion by objectifying it and fostering a separate category that people refer to.[151] Indeed, as Schatz suggests, 'what distinguished an ethnic Kazakh from a Ukrainian was, among other things, the religious tradition associated with each reified ethnic culture.'[152]

Tasar has adroitely, and in very much details, analysed the tensions between the different organizations of regulation over the decades. He underlines the marginalization of both the SADUM and the CRA in their control of unregistered mosques at the profit of the district branches of government after the 1970s. Similarly, under Brezhnev, the conceptualization of Islam for official purposes was taken away from the SADUM and CRA and handed to the Soviet social science and propaganda communities.[153] Perhaps more importantly, Tasar's work serves to debunk the idea of the separation between parallel and official Islam and highlights the numerous official and non-official connections and collaborations between the two worlds.

Spiritual Muslim Board of Central Asia – SADUM

The SADUM was officially approved by the Supreme Soviet of the USSR on July 31, 1943 and held its first meeting on October 20 of that year in Tashkent. The Spiritual Directorate was headed by a Mufti, with a presidium or governing board and an auditing commission elected by a convention of clergy and believers. It had representatives in the territories under its jurisdiction.[154] The Mufti was elected at the general Kurultai, the assembly of all the Muslim clergy. The Kurultai also elected the presidium, later known as the Council of Ulama, which assisted the Mufti and acted as the editorial board for the journal,[155] *Muslims of the Soviet East*.[156] Soon after the establishment of the SADUM, Qaziyats were set up in each capital of the other Central Asian Republics. The Qazis represented the highest clerical authority within each of the republics, and were subordinate to the Tashkent Mufti.[157] Republican Qazis were in turn responsible for the appointment of religious clergy in each of their republics.[158] However, local committees of the Council for the Affairs of Religious Cults had to approve the nomination of each Qazi, based not on whether the candidate's religious training was deemed satisfactory but on whether he was judged suitable from a political standpoint.[159] Clergy members who were too popular or influential tended to be discarded.[160]

Babajanov identifies the following general functions of the SADUM: to regulate and control the religious situation, to strengthen the sense of unity, and to promote closer contacts between clergy and ordinary believers, especially in the absence of contacts with Muslims from abroad.[161] More specifically, Sadur lists the responsibilities of the SADUM as follows:

(1) To solve problems of religious dogma that concern faith and rituals, which decisions are given in the form of fatwas.

(2) To provide support to mosques, prayer houses, and religious organizations as well as to the Muslim clergy.

(3) To issue recommendations on the obligations of mullahs and muezzins of mosques accompanied with verifications.

(4) To dismiss mullahs and muezzins who have violated Islamic principles.

(5) To study attentively complaints and declarations of the clergy or believers that concern the competences of the Spiritual Administration.

(6) To publish the necessary literature, appoint muhtasibs,[162] representatives of local offices of the spiritual administration, and distribute the funds given to the local administration.[163]

In theory, religious education was under the close supervision of the authorities. From 1948 to 1991, there were only two functioning medresses in the whole of Central Asia, the Mir-i Arab, opened in Bukhara in 1946, and the Al-Bukhari in Tashkent, founded in 1956. In 1971, the Institute for Higher Islamic Studies was established in Tashkent.[164] There were no official medresses apart from the ones in Uzbekistan, so the opportunities to learn the basics of religion *legally* were nearly nonexistent, since private religious education was forbidden. Also, the pace of theological training in Bukhara and Tashkent was very slow.[165] In fact, these institutions trained a strikingly low number of students; between 1945 and 1970, only 85 students graduated from the Mir-i Arab medresse.[166] Partly as a result of this, the number of officially recognized mullahs was far too low to be able to serve the needs of the whole Muslim population and to perform the desired number of life-passage rituals such as weddings, circumcisions, and funerals.

The SADUM was subservient to the influence of Moscow, which perceived the spiritual administration as loyal to the regime. The SADUM and Qaziyats enjoyed little popular legitimacy, since the registration of mullahs meant that they were *ukaznie* (sanctioned) and therefore perceived as being too close to the authorities, on which they depended for their nomination.[167] Also, fatwas were regarded as bureaucratic edicts, devoid of any spirituality since all discourses, publications, and messages had to be submitted to state censorship before circulation.[168] In an interview with Hoji Ibodullo Kalonzoda, whose father Mirzo Ibodullo Kalonzoda held the title of Qazi Kalon between 1961 and 1988, he described the institution as a 'political farce' where only few people were working. It was also difficult for mullahs and clerics to retain their credibility among believers while straining to reconcile principles of scientific atheism with Islamic scriptures. To take but one example, a 1962 SADUM fatwa ordained that circumcision was not mandatory because it was said to be a pre-Islamic practice.[169]

Here we touch on one of the greatest paradoxes of Soviet and post-Soviet policy. Perhaps it is in fact mistaken to call it a paradox and maybe the good old carrot and stick approach best describes the strategies of Soviet authorities. On the one hand, atheist propaganda insisted on the fallacy of religious beliefs. Early portrayals of Islam as a backward, oppressive, and sexist religion were part of a long-term propaganda strategy to eradicate the influence of religion. This message was repeated over the years, such as in the *Atheist's Handbook* portrayal of Islam as a religion that encourages selfishness, passiveness, and gullibility. Other publications mention that Islam contradicts the principle of the friendship of all peoples by establishing a division between true believers and infidels.[170] On the other hand, some SADUM publications describe the ideology of Islam in the USSR as one of reason, humanism and progress, and say that Islam favours hard work, human rights, equality of men and women, and so on.[171] Dudoignon argues that SADUM's subordination to Moscow did not prevent it from pursuing some of its own interests. For instance, it promoted traditional (non-European) clothing and other non-verbal expressions of Islamic identity, and the restoration of the *adab*, the Islamic code of courtesy and good manners.[172] Ro'i also reports that if the clergy was not openly opposed to the new secular ceremonies, they nonetheless underlined their 'European' character.[173] Also, if the official clergy condemned the habit of holding expensive celebrations for weddings and circumcision parties, it did so because this was deemed contrary to Islamic teachings and not because it was an illusory ritual from the past as official propaganda suggested.[174]

Many religious figures engaged in the unregistered teaching of students. The existence of these secret religious study cells, or *hujra*, was an open secret, winked at by the KGB. Babajanov, who provides an excellent account of the internal factions within the SADUM, insists that many local mullahs were quite critical of the SADUM's decisions, opposing many of them and repeatedly defying the body's authority. In particular, he points to a group of mullahs from the Ferghana valley who opposed Hanafi rituals such as the reading the Qur'an at funerals and pilgrimages to tombs of local saints, and declared them 'unislamic.' The dispute opposed the group associated with famous Hanafi Tajik scholar Muhammadjon Rustamov, also known as Mawlawi Hindustani (1892–1989), to Rahmatullo Alloma and Abduvali qori Mirzoyev, who was himself a former disciple of Hindustani. Tasar describes Alloma and Mirzoyev as puritanists who condemned Hanafi's 'fanaticism' and the more liberal views of Hindustani and his followers. Hindusatani was even criticized for his 'immoderate taste for cigarettes' (CAS 2011, 61).[175] They called for a return to a more rigourous practice of Islam. In return, Hindustani labelled them as 'Wahhabi.'[176] In 1989, the attempt of the new Mufti Muhammad Yusuf Muhammad Sodiq, who had been a student of Hindustani, to rally the Presidium for the adoption of a joint fatwa condemning the Ferghana group revealed profound splits between members, opposing *grosso modo* Hanafis and the so-called Wahhabis. The split with the SADUM was perceived by the Tajik Qazi Turajonzoda, however, as a maneuver by external political actors seeking to divide Muslims.[177]

Dudoignon also tells us of socio-linguistic rivalries within the Qaziyat between Uzbek and Persian clergy, who opposed an Uzbekization of Islam within the Tajik SSR during most of Soviet period. He also highlights the roles of registered and unregistered mullahs in forming religious study cells, or *hujra*, which rightfully contributed to reducing the separation between official and unofficial

Islam.[178] Shortly after the creation of SADUM, initiatives to open
medresses in Tajikistan were turned down by the authorities, despite the
fact that these initiatives was supported by Tajikistan's Qazi, Salih
Babkalanov.[179] There also seem to have been a rivalry between official
and unsanctioned imams; Ro'i reports that in 1961 Tajik official mullahs
complained that unregistered clergy dubbed their official counterparts as
'Soviet,' a term deemed discrediting.[180] Yet, Tasar tells us that 'a broad
network of ulama in Central Asia served as a complement to the muftiate
rather than functioning as a source of competition'[181] since some of them
were employed by the SADUM at various points of their life, their
students found positions within registered mosques, and held religious
views close to the one of SADUM. For instance, Hindustani allegedly
served as imam at Dushanbe's Yaqubi Charkhi mosque in the late
1940s.[182]

There were 17 to 18 mosques officially registered in the Tajik SSR
between the beginning of the Khrushchev era and the end of the Soviet
Union and many more unregistered places of worship.[183] Official figures
from 1987 estimate at 230 the number of holy places in Tajikistan,
although that number was denied by the republican authorities, which
claimed that it was mostly women and children who visited such
places.[184] In addition, in the late Soviet period, the official clergy grew
more independent during the general liberalization attendant on
Gorbachev's Perestroika movement, as well as because of the flamboyant
personality of the Qazi, Hoji Akbar Turajonzoda. Among other things,
the Qazi attempted to gain more control over the nomination of imams
and asked the authorities to switch the day off from Sunday to Friday and
to forbid the selling of non-halal meat. 'For the first time in 70 years of
Soviet power, the Muslim clergy appeared in Tajikistan as a virtual
challenger to the political authorities.'[185]

Council for Religious Affairs

State-religion relations were under great political pressure from the early
years of the revolution. First being under the jurisdiction of the
Commissariat of Justice established in 1918, religious issues were later
managed by the National Commissariat for Internal Affairs (NKVD) in
1922. Religious matters were later transferred to the Ministry of Cults
created in 1924, returned to the NKVD in 1938, until the creation of
the Council for the Affairs of Religious Cults (CARC) in 1944.[186] The

CARC's main tasks were:

(1) To maintain a link between the government of the USSR and the leaders of religious associations on questions of faith that required the intervention of the central government.
(2) To draft laws regarding religious issues.
(3) To give instructions and supervise the implementation of such laws.
(4) To inform the government on the situation of religions in all regions
(5) To compile and transmit statistical reports on the number of prayer-houses provided by local soviet organs.[187]

Local representatives of the Council for the Affairs of Religious Cults were in turn responsible to:

(1) Maintain an institutional link between religious communities and the state.
(2) Register prayer-houses.
(3) Review and submit to the CARC the material concerning the closure, construction or refurbishing of prayer-houses.
(4) Receive clergy representatives and answer their questions, receive complaints from citizens, follow-up on complaints, and inspect prayer-houses.[188]

Luchterhandt emphasizes that the pre-1965 CARC sought cooperation between religious associations and the state, resolved local disputes, and presumably earnestly engaged in its role of ensuring freedom of religion. Although the 1965 reorganization under Khrushchev brought little change in CARC's mission and responsibilities, its actions were decidedly more repressive.[189] However, Ro'i suggests that the Council did not necessarily favour repressive measures, and he observes that the CRA in fact consistently urged its local representatives not to shut down illegal mosques but instead to assist in their registration, because this facilitated the control of Islamic activity.[190] Even though both SADUM and CRA were useful for the authorities, the two bodies were very distinct and pursued different objectives. While the former was an administrative body dedicated to the implementation of the law and the preservation of normalized relations with believers, the latter was a spiritual organization with its own political agenda, and subject to internal and external fights. Nonetheless, these regulatory institutions greatly contributed to the shaping of religious life and in particular, to the emergence of a specific understanding of state-religion relations.

In 1965, the Council for the Affairs of Religious Cults (CARC), the regulating body for state-religion relations, was renamed the Council of Religious Affairs (CRA). It consolidated the Council of Religious Affairs' grip on the development of religious associations, and confirmed the status of the CRA as the 'liaison body between the Church and the Soviet government.' The nature of the liaison was not purely administrative; the CRA was also reporting regularly to the KGB. Despite that, one amendment represented a small victory for religious organizations since it contributed to their eventual recovery of a legal status.[191]

The Soviet Modernization Project: Views on Success and Failure

Contrary to Gellner's opinion in 1991 that, in the USSR, 'faith has now totally disappeared,'[192] religion did not vanish. Despite the coercion of religious leaders, severe repression of believers and 70 years of persistent atheist propaganda, religious beliefs and rituals lived on, albeit altered. Many authors have underlined the failure of the Soviet's transformative attempt in terms of culture, language, and religion.[193] Rywkin has most strongly stated the failure of Soviet policies in Central Asia and 'USSR's Muslim problem.'[194] Myer's survey of the literature shows that a majority of scholars endorse the idea of a failed transformation. Roy[195] and Naumkin[196] see the adherence to Sufism, because it was widespread, as a cultural marker. In particular, they emphasize Central Asian peoples' distinctiveness, manifested through the persistence of local languages, the survival of cultural traditions (respect for elders, gender division, large families), and the resilience of religion. That last point is what authors see as the breaking point dividing Muslims from Russians and the main reason why assimilation did not work.[197] Yet, DeWeese refers to the discussion on the success or failure of secularization efforts as a 'fruitless debate' and argues that when comparing Central Asia to the rest of the Islamic world, it is easy to conclude that the Soviets definitely 'succeeded all too well.'[198] In this line of thought I compared present-day Afghanistan and Tajikistan in the Introduction. Therefore, the question should not ask if the Soviets managed to transform the societies of the former USSR, but how? On that matter, Adams, in her investigation of the cultural revival in post-Soviet Uzbekistan, mentions: 'The story that I find myself telling is one not of an Uzbek cultural renaissance blossoming in the wake of independence but, rather, of the successful institutionalization of a Soviet cultural schema that continue to define Uzbek culture and national identity.'[199] The focus here should not be on the extent to which atheistic ideas conquered the hearts and minds of individuals but rather on the way it affected people's understanding of the role of religion in society.

The following discussion revolves around the effects of the forced secularization and the social engineering project. I focus on socialization and education and argue that even though secularization was not entirely successful, in the sense that Soviets failed to eradicate religion completely, the attempt to secularize the society deeply informed the understanding of the world for generations of Soviet citizens. I will make a case to interpret Tajiks' current understanding of the place of religion in the society in terms of accommodation of values rather than passive resignation[200] or resistance.[201]

Among the few ontological debates that divide the community of researchers, the issue of 'parallel Islam' is one of the most salient. The term was borrowed from Soviet sociologists and first introduced by Bennigsen and Lemercier-Quelquejay in 1968.[202] It refers to the type of Islam practised during the Soviet period as opposed to the Islam labelled as 'official,' which was promoted and controlled by the SADUM. Parallel Islam was clandestine but supported by a network of underground organizations, mainly Sufi Brotherhoods.[203] Ro'i underlines the importance of parallel Islam by pointing out that the number of official mosques in the Soviet Union comprised only 1 per cent of the actual total.[204] By way of comparison, in the 1980s, there were officially 200 'central' mosques in Central Asia,[205] three of them in Northern Tajikistan (two in Khujand and one in Proletarsk). Poliakov's ethnographic expedition,[206] however, estimated the number at around 200, a number at least equal to that of pre-Soviet times. In 1982, in

Tajikistan, no less than 21 underground schools were discovered.[207] During my stays in Central Asia, many Central Asians told me of secret religious rituals, including Islamic weddings (*Nikoh*), circumcisions (*Hatna*) and funerals (*Dzhanoza*), as well as hidden mosques in caves or trees, or secret night bike rides to attend religious classes. Such activities placed people at great risk, for they could be prosecuted for performing or attending unsanctioned rituals.

The concept of parallel Islam is contentious mainly because many researchers acknowledge that some religious practices were not always hidden and often conducted with the complicity of local authorities. In particular, some rituals, such as circumcisions, remained the norm rather than the exception, even if they were officially condemned. At the local level, many of these manifestations of faith were tolerated, and even party officials often participated. Ro'i concludes that, in many places, the Muslim burial rite was tolerated because it 'was looked upon as a national custom rather than a religious rite.'[208] Poliakov, although to his great chagrin, also acknowledges how deeply embedded the rural religious authorities were in production networks and political life in the late 1980s. Rasanayagam, too, mentions that some local Uzbek political leaders worked with unregistered mullahs and other community leaders to mobilize workers.[209] Dudoignon[210] and Tasar[211] have also shown the deep connections between members of official and unregistered clergy. Such findings make it difficult to justify the use of the word 'parallel,' since the practice of Islam did not run alongside, but rather was intertwined with, local political and administrative realities. Thus some scholars favour the use of alternative terminology, such as 'popular,' 'political,' or 'non-official'[212] to describe the type of Islam practised in Central Asia. Olimova, for example, argues that the practice of popular Soviet Islam was a way to cope with atheist policies and withstand the effects of modernization.[213]

What comes out of the above discussion on parallel Islam is that there is no clear distinction between what should be considered 'Soviet' and what is more accurately seen as 'traditional.' This does not mean that this discussion is sterile, but rather that categories are blurry and distinctions are not easily made. In this spirit, Northrop argues that these two labels 'are historically produced, fluid, mutually constructing, and continually shifting categories.'[214] For that reason, it seems preferable to approach the Soviet secularization experience in terms of accommodation instead of using a binary perspective opposing passive resignation and resistance.

Accommodation in Context

The concept of accommodation supposes that imposed practices and discourses are not only contested or passively accepted but can be negotiated in the making and remaking of personal and socio-political identities. Thinking in terms of accommodation instead of resistance or resignation allows us to give agency to individuals in a broader sense than by referring to the concept of resistance. Indeed, resistance usually implies a concerted and motivated defiance of authorities. James Scott's examination of peasant resistance in Malaysia described 'everyday form of resistance' as actions that required little or no coordination and which were conducted with 'ordinary weapons of relatively powerless groups such as foot dragging, dissimulation, false compliance, sabotage, etc.'[215] As a result of these mostly non-violent actions, peasants engaged in low-intensity conflicts with the authorities. And yet, while Scott's study gave a new understanding to the concept of resistance, it did not allow for the consideration of different responses to authoritative change because people don't always resist; many comply, many defy, but many more accommodate. As suggested by Husband: 'In a larger context, far more citizens everywhere practice accommodation than ever take up activism.'[216]

Historians and anthropologists have made better use of the concept of accommodation. In the Soviet context, Husband looked at secularization campaigns in Russia between 1917 and 1932 and studied the way people tried to resist and to accommodate the imposition of a secular lifestyle. In trying to break the image of passive submission conferred to populations, Husband writes that it created 'circumstances in which individuals and groups not only had the opportunity to reevaluate their relationship to the sacred, but indeed could not escape doing so.'[217] Northrop goes in the same direction by focusing on strategies of Central Asians to cope with Soviet colonialist policies, in particular, the transformation of gender relations in the absence of a proletarian class. Northrop focuses on the discursive and physical battle over the definition of proper forms of everyday life Soviet Uzbekistan. He acknowledges that by the late 1960s in Uzbekistan, 'the Russians' self-styled European mission appeared, at long last, to have achieved hegemony among Central Asians themselves'[218] and that in contemporary Uzbekistan, the *Hujum*, the Soviet campaign for unveiling

Central Asian Muslim women, is almost universally seen as a positive mark of progress and a landmark of the Uzbek nation's development.[219] Yurchak has adroitly touched upon the issue of accommodation with his study of the appropriation and reinterpretation of Soviet values and discourses:

> The relationship of the last Soviet generation with official ideology did not simply involve a resistance to ideology, or its opportunistic use for self-advancement, or a dissimulated repetition of official ideological statements, but also entailed interesting and creative acts of rendering communist ideology meaningful within the broader framework of human values.[220]

Beyond literacy campaigns and the transmission of values via a standardized education, Suny argues that the Soviet authorities and the intelligentsia managed to foster emotional connections 'first to the Revolution and Civil War, the project of creating a new world, then to Lenin and Stalin as personifications of the Soviet project, later to the victory over fascism.' The end result was the creation of a powerful civic culture that connected persons from an extended space.[221] Likewise, Lane suggests that Soviet rituals were effective tools because they often blended with 'interpersonal values that bind the individual to his family and his local community' and 'rechannel them towards the large and more impersonal political collective.'[222] Indisputably, Central Asia ended up being profoundly transformed by the Soviet social engineering project. But given the resilience of traditional customs and religious habits, there is no doubt that Sovietization was not entirely successful. The Soviet transformative process cannot simply be described as the imposition of foreign atheist modernistic norms and values upon traditional societies. Opposing both the idea of the resignation of Soviet peoples and the exceptionalism of the Soviet experience, Suny argues that: 'supposed Russian exceptionalism is to see the ethnic or national as self-generated and the socialist and Soviet to be an artificial imposition.'[223] The social engineering project should rather be seen as a process of forced negotiation between foreign and local norms in which some local actors retained agency.

In the chapters that follow, I mean to illustrate the continuity between the Soviet and post-Soviet periods by identifying what exactly is path-dependent in the story – laws, attitudes, social norms. Wanner suggested that secularization did not lead to the eradication of religion but rather that secularization processes drew on 'particular views of how religion should relate to politics, governance, and public affairs and lead to religious change.'[224] This is to corroborate an idea widespread in the literature: that the 'Central Asian elite will long continue to be determined by the Soviet habitus.'[225] The idea is to look at how new institutions borrow from old ones, how customs become laws and the way in which the existing institutional world circumscribes the range of institutional creation. Informal practices also play an affirmative role in the definition of the state's orientations and are observable through the actions and dispositions of the current leadership, who are successors of the Soviet Nomenklatura. If we agree that informal institutions influence actors' political inclinations, it seems relevant to observe the reflection of values and norms that guided the actions of political figures and the public for decades.

CHAPTER 3

TAJIKISTAN'S POLITICAL LANDSCAPE IN THE AFTERMATH OF THE CIVIL WAR

This chapter provides a thorough overview of the recent political history of Tajikistan while giving the reader an impression of the context in which the fieldwork was conducted. It also highlights many of the continuities with the Soviet period when it comes to the issue of religion. Narratives about the civil war as well as the threat of Islamic radical organizations today coalesce to impute political Islam for instability in the country. Heathershaw tells us that the Tajik notion of *tinji* (peacefulness or wellness) as a 'practical ethos of post-conflict survival found in Tajik localities' has become pervasive in official and local discourses.[1] This emphasis on stability should be understood in the context of a slow but steady marginalization of Islamic actors and the affirmation of authoritarian rule in Tajikistan.

Civil War

Because of the identity of the belligerents, the Tajik civil war is often portrayed as a conflict between secular and religious forces. However, the political dynamics were much more complex. A majority of specialists agree that the regional factor was decisive. As Olivier Roy put it, 'regionalism is the key to the Tajik political game.'[2] Yet Roy also argues that it was the elite's intransigence and desire to stay in power that thwarted the political process.[3] Most authors recognize the Islamic character of some of the belligerents and yet highlight the amiguous non-religious actors' motives to engage in conflict. Mullahs, supporters of the Islamic Revival Party of Tajikistan (IRPT) and traditional strongmen loosely coalesced into the so-called 'Islamic opposition.'[4] Driscoll contends that in some of the areas where strict Islamic rules were enforced, such as in the Tavildara district by the United Tajik Opposition commander Mirzo Ziyoyev, the local population returned to its old ways once Ziyoyev became part of the government as part of the peace agreement.[5]

The outcome of the civil war was a regional power shift from the hands of northerners (Leninabadis), who had been dominating the political sphere in Soviet times, in favour of southerners (Kulobis). The Tajik civil war represents a thorny case, since the losers actually did not actively fight during the war. Most of the fighting took place around the capital city and the southern provinces of Khatlon and Gorno-Badakhshan (GBAO)[6] where Kulobis opposed the Gharmi (Rasht Valley) and Badakhshani units, while Leninabadis who first supported Kulobis remained on the sidelines for most of the conflict. Discussing the cases of Georgia and Tajikistan, Driscoll argues that 'they were essentially ruled by criminalized military juntas in the early 1990s. Presidents were installed to act as figureheads.'[7]

In the late 1990s, great economic and political instability gave opposition groups the opportunity to mobilize and seek a power shift in their favour. In 1990, the unemployment rate was around 22 per cent and 58.6 per cent of the population had incomes below the poverty line, which stood at 78 rubles a month in the USSR.[8] In the meantime, Moscow's transfers to the Republics slowed down, which resulted in a degradation of services. Budget transfers only stopped after independence, but the economic and financial disengagement of Moscow began in the 1970s, contributing to a worsening socioeconomic situation in a context of strong population growth.[9] In the context of Perestroika, opposition movements emerged and started formulating demands, such as the promotion of national values and Islamic religious heritage. Rastokhez, a popular movement of nationalist liberals, was born on September 14, 1989, at Dushanbe Tajik State University. Their programme focused on the promotion of national values and the promotion of independence from the USSR.[10] The Democratic Party of Tajikistan (DPT) started to function in 1991 and enjoyed a membership of around 10,000, mostly among urban intellectuals.[11] The Islamic Revival Party (IRP) was formed out of underground youth religious organizations active since the 1970s but officially started its activities in 1990. On June 9, 1990, the All-USSR Islamic Revival Party was founded in Astrakhan, Russia, and the meeting was attended by some Tajik representatives. Back in Tajikistan, IRP leaders tried to register the party, but their demand was rejected, as religious organizations were forbidden to get involved in political activities. Yet, on 6 October, 1990, the Tajik Branch of the IRP was established in secrecy. Their programme was oriented toward popular spiritual revival and the sovereignty of the Republic.[12]

The Islamic Revival Party of Tajikistan was not the only force promoting the role of Islam within Tajik society. Appointed in 1988, the *Qazi Kalon* Hoji Akbar Turajonzoda was the most influential figure in religious and political life in the country at the time. He enjoyed his position thanks to his prominent clerical family background as well as his useful connections to Tajik officials and religious leaders abroad. Acknowledging the lack of competent clerics and Islamic scholars in the country, he promoted a step-by-step religious revival insisting on the importance of training teachers and clerics. His plans concretized when he founded an Islamic institute in Dushanbe and a number of medresses.[13] Also, from 1990 to 1992, the publication of the Qaziat's newsletter, called the *Tribune of Islam* (*Minbari Islom*) facilitated connection with the population. Although it mainly discussed religious issues, political matters were also addressed. Alongside critics directed to Marxist ideology and the Communist Party, the Qaziat, foreseeing the aggravation of regional tensions, insisted on the importance of national unity for Muslims in Tajikistan. The Qaziat retained close links with the members of the IRPT. Bushkov and Mikulskii underline the complementarity of their activities during the period preceding the civil war: the Qaziat was dealing with religious and spiritual issues, whereas the IRPT was promoting a political agenda.[14] As a member of the Supreme Soviet, Turajonzoda tried to introduce reforms concerning the re-Islamization of the society. These included the adoption of Thursday and Friday as the weekly days off and of Islamic holy days as official holidays, the slaughtering of livestock according to Islamic law, and the exemption of mosques from land taxes; these were all rejected by the assembly.[15] Despite his prominent position, the authority of

Turajonzoda was challenged by the emergence of the IRPT, which he later joined. His alliance with the IRPT automatically led to his dismissal as the head of the Qaziat. Fatkhullo Sharifzoda was appointed as the new Qazi in December 1992 after President Emomali Rahmon came to power. A decision by President Rahmon transformed the Qaziat into a Muftiat in 1993. Sharifzoda and his family were murdered in January 1996.[16]

Despite efforts from the opposition to have the Islamic heritage of the nation recognized in the Constitution, the Constitution's adoption in November 1991 confirmed the secular character of the state, in which the direct influence of religion remained limited, constrained by strict institutional rules. Yet the authorities were rather tolerant of foreign religious groups, and a number of proselytizing groups from Iran, Turkey, Pakistan, and Saudi Arabia appeared in Tajikistan in the early 1990s. The authorities' tolerance can be explained by the fact that these groups' presence was supplemented by financial support, which allowed the construction of mosques.[17] However, as soon as the first demonstrators demanding a greater place for Islam in state affairs appeared on the streets of Dushanbe, a number of deputies virulently denounced the increasing religiosity and designated reactionary Islam as the number one public enemy.[18] Abdullaev writes that one has to be familiar with the rhetoric of Islamists to engage in a dialogue with them, which was obviously not the case for Soviet-born and educated elites.[19]

At the beginning of 1991, while Communists tried more or less successfully to update their political platform, opposition parties pressured the authorities to initiate reforms promoting national language and religion. In the spring, a series of protests were organized in the capital, demanding political openness. These events took place against a background of financial scandals, which uncovered the misdemeanours of some political figures.[20] Events took a new turn in August 1991 when President Makhamov supported the failed putsch against Mikhail Gorbachev. His support was denounced by the opposition, and, facing pressure from the street, opposition parties, and his own camp, Makhamov resigned on August 31. The president of the Tajik Supreme Soviet, Qadriddin Aslonov, became the President of the Republic *par interim*. Later removed from office by the Supreme Soviet after he banned the Communist Party of Tajikistan and allowed, under pressure from the street, the toppling of the statue of Lenin in Dushanbe's main square,

Aslonov was replaced by Rahmon Nabiyev on 23 September 1991,[21] who quickly restored the Communist Party.[22]

Beyond nationalistic issues and religion, economic considerations – such as land reform and distribution – became rallying issues for different political factions.[23] Rasthokez, the Democratic Party of Tajikistan, and the IRPT combined their efforts by forming the so-called islamo-democratic coalition to challenge the Communist Party in the presidential election of November 24, 1991. Nine parties in total participated in the presidential elections held after the proclamation of independence in September. Roy mentions that Central Asia's freest elections in the newly independent Central Asian states were held in Tajikistan and Uzbekistan. In Uzbekistan, Muhammad Solih for the Erk Party (Freedom) managed to win 12 per cent of the vote. In Tajikistan, Davlat Khudonazarov, a Pamiri filmmaker who was the candidate for the islamo-democratic coalition, took 30 per cent. Meanwhile, Rahmon Nabiyev, a native of Leninabad and chairman of the Supreme Council, secured 57 per cent of the vote.[24]

On December 2, 1991, Nabiyev refused to swear an oath on the Qur'an during his inauguration as President.[25] This gesture symbolized his opposition to any religious orientation and contrasted with the presidents of neighbouring Central Asian countries, who carefully associated themselves with Islam.[26] After his election, Nabiyev followed his predecessor's footsteps and proposed reintroducing the Persian alphabet and limiting the use of the Russian language in the writing of the Constitution, but the alphabet was not changed.[27]

In early 1992, the limitations on freedom of expression and the repression of opposition leaders after the presidential elections, as well as the financial scandals revealing misappropriation of economic goods by Khujandis, triggered the mobilization of opposition forces,[28] who rallied on Shahidan (Martyrs) square.[29] In April, counterdemonstrations were organized in Ozodi (Freedom) square by people who had come from Kulob. On May 5, 1992, the President established the National Guard, composed of units of Kulob supporters.[30] Dudoignon summarizes the political arrangement thus: 'Khujand Communists and the southern Kulobis on one side versus the Pamiri party Lali-Badakhshon, the Democratic Party of Tajikistan, and the Gharmi-dominated IRP on the other side.'[31] Facing a nearly uncontrollable political situation marked by rallies, raids, and clashes, Nabiyev formed a new coalition government composed of opposition members.

This compromise, however, was not accepted by any of the parties, and clashes broke out in Kulob, where pro-government factions purged the city of opposition supporters. In the meantime, Lali-Badakhshan, a Pamiri autonomous opposition group joined the islamo-democratic coalition in March 1992. Armed fighting in Dushanbe began on May 1, when the newly restructured Presidential Guard clashed with protesters. The Anzob pass, located on the road between Dushanbe and Khujand, was blocked, severing the Leninabad oblast' from the rest of the republic and thus protecting the region from the fighting.[32] On September 7, 1992, President Nabiyev was stopped at the airport while fleeing to his native Leninabad and was forced to resign at gun-point by a pro-opposition group.[33] Akbarsho Iskandarov, a Pamiri, took over as acting President. Fighting continued until December 1992, when the Popular Front of Tajikistan (PFT) reconquered the capital and defeated the opposition forces. The Popular Front was composed mainly of Kulobis, Uzbeks, and Khudjandis, and it benefited from the military support of Russia and Uzbekistan. Its military victory was coupled with a political one when Emomali Rahmon, a representative of the Kulobi faction, was designated as President of the Supreme Soviet in December 1992. The opposition retreated to northern Afghanistan in early 1993. Opposition leaders reorganized their political and military structures and created the Movement of Islamic Revival of Tajikistan (MIRT), headed by Said Abdulloh Nuri. At this moment, Hoji Akbar Turajonzoda was named First Deputy Chairman of the MIRT, and Muhammadsharif Himmatzoda, Deputy Chairman. At the end of the war, United Tajik Opposition (UTO) troops numbered around 8,000.[34]

Combat in the capital ended in January 1993. However, fighting continued in other regions, mainly Kathlon and Gorno-Badakhshan, until 1997. Reports estimate the number of casualties to be between 60,000 and 100,000 and displaced persons to number around 600,000. The majority of displaced persons were Russians who had the opportunity to emigrate to Russia. Nearly 400,000 Russians emigrated permanently between 1990 and 1997. Others were Tajiks who fled to Uzbekistan and Afghanistan.[35] Negotiations between opposing forces started as early as 1993, but it was not until 1997 that an agreement was reached.[36] The political dead end, economic chaos, and external pressures forced the parties to sign a peace agreement under the auspices of the United Nations on June 27, 1997.[37]

In this regard, the politicization of Islam in Tajikistan did not harm the eroding institutions as such but served as a catalyst for the expression of antagonisms between the regional factions that then led to the civil war. The ideologization of the conflict resulted from the necessity for the actors to stage the conflict in ideological terms rather than regional or economic ones. This dynamic also explains the internationalization of the conflict. Sharing an extended border with a country where Islamists and secular factions were engaged in an enduring civil war fostered the external perception of the Tajik conflict as a threat. For the same reason, however, the United Tajik Opposition (UTO) found allies in Afghanistan and among political forces in other Islamic countries with which the UTO had connections. Vinatier argues that the UTO, once it retreated to Afghanistan, started to strengthen its religious rhetoric. Cut off from the social realities of the country, the coalition needed to reinforce its ideological dimension, this being the only nonbelligerent strategy at their disposal.[38] Second, given the character of the conflict, the government in Dushanbe could use the spectre of political Islam to seek external support, as illustrated by the involvement of Russia and Uzbekistan.

As a consequence of the peace agreement, Tajikistan is the sole Central Asian country to have ever legalized a faith-based political party. The peace agreement devised the allocation of 30 per cent of ministerial positions to the opposition. In 1999, 5,377 veterans of the United Tajik Opposition, mainly men from the Gharm and Pamir regions, joined the Army ranks as well as frontier and regular police services.[39] Among the key positions granted to former UTO affiliates was Deputy Prime Minister, given to Turajonzoda upon his return to Tajikistan. He then served as a member of the National Assembly (Majlisi Milli), the upper house of parliament, from 2005 to 2010. Other positions included the Head of the State Customs Committee, the Deputy Chairman of the State Committee of Border Protection, and the Chairman of the State Oil and Gas.[40] Yet the peace agreement was slowly implemented and its goals remained largely unaccomplished. By 2003, of the 53 high-rank functionaries drawn from the opposition, only 12 were still in office.[41]

Postwar Tajikistan

Heathershaw talks about the peace enforcement in Tajikistan as a process that insured stability and reinforced authority but at the detriment of the citizen's capacity to influence the government.[42] Since the end of violence in the late 1990s, the situation in Tajikistan has remained stable but tense: 'the war-time political division between the state and the opposition thus remains,'[43] and warlordism continues to pose a threat to stability. In recent years, several violent events have contributed to political instability. Peace was not so easily implemented and several events threatened to destabilize the country after June 1997. In November 1998, Colonel Khudoberdyev, an ethnic Uzbek military commander and former pro-government warlord from the Qurghonteppa region who had been in exile in Uzbekistan after a failed insurrection in June 1997, invaded the Leninabad oblast' from Uzbekistan. Government forces put down the rebellion after a week of heavy fighting.[44] Some zones remained out of governmental control until 2001.

Some opposition leaders had rejected the Peace Agreement completely even though UTO fighters and commanders were given amnesty for crimes and actions committed before 1997. One of these leaders was Rahmon Sanginov, often nicknamed Hitler for his cruel ways. He and his followers continued to control areas east of Dushanbe and, according to the Interior Ministry, committed some 400 serious crimes from 1998 to 2001, including 270 murders. In June 2001, his group abducted 15 persons and demanded the release of four former UTO commanders detained by the authorities. Hostages were freed unharmed, but the government seized this opportunity to get rid of Sanginov and his supporters once and for all. They launched a military operation that led them from the outskirts of Dushanbe to the region of Tavildara, bordering the Rasht valley. The operation went on for two months until Sanginov was killed in a clash with security forces on August 10, 2001.[45]

Another former UTO commander, Mirzokhoja Ahmadov, who had been in charge of fighting organized crime in the Rasht district, fell into disgrace when the government attempted to arrest him in 2008. Government troops faced strong local resistance, and fighting led to the death of a senior commander. Ahmadov was forced to retire, though he seems to have remained influential. In the spring of 2009, the Tajik

Interior Ministry launched Operation Kuknor (poppy), an anti-narcotic operation in the Rasht Valley. This move coincided with the alleged return to Tajikistan of another opposition field commander, Abdullo Rahimov, mostly referred to as Mullo Abdullo, who had opposed the peace agreement and who had been in exile in Afghanistan since then. In the Rasht valley, he and his men were allegedly under the protection of Ahmadov. Mirzo Ziyoyev, another UTO former commander and ex-Minister of Emergencies, was sent to Rasht to convince Mullo Abdullo to give himself up to the authorities but was killed in the crossfire between government forces and local fighters in July 2009.[46]

Driscoll confirms the slow but steady reinforcement of the Kulobi elite over two decades at the detriment of other regional factions. Former Gissar (centre-west) commanders were purged in the early 1990s while other purges in the early 2000s removed former UTO combatants from Gharm and elsewhere. In the meantime, Pamiri commanders who 'reinvented themselves as police officers in rural Badakhshon,' remained in place.[47] Yet, as we will see, further marginalization of former commanders intensified after 2010 and confirmed the dominance of the Kulobi clan over all regions of Tajikistan.

The summer of 2010 was particularly dramatic and violent. On August 22, 2010, 25 political prisoners escaped during a mass prison break from a high-security prison in Dushanbe. Among them were the brothers of Nemat Azizov, a former UTO commander killed by security forces in 2009, the sons of slain ex-Minister of Emergencies Mirzo Ziyoyev, several members of the Islamic Movement of Uzbekistan, four citizens of Russia, two natives of Dagestan and two from Chechnya. The prison break created a commotion, throwing into question the reliability of high-security prisons as well as the trustworthiness of the prison staff.[48] On September 19, in the course of the chase for escapees, a military convoy passing through the Kamarob Gorge in the Rasht valley was attacked. The assault killed at least 25 police officers and soldiers. This was followed by several months of fighting against 'insurgents' in the Rasht valley. The government blamed former opposition commanders Alovaddin Davlatov and Mullo Abdullo for the ambush.[49] Davlatov and seven followers were killed by government forces in a controversial operation in the village of Runo in January 2011, while Mullo Abdullo was killed along with ten of his followers on April 14, 2011.[50] While authorities portrayed the conflict in Kamarob as an

Islamist insurgency involving foreign actors, evidence suggests that local commanders 'acted autonomously against the government as they felt threatened by the further incursion of the Dushanbe government into their region.'[51] The pursuit of the escapees lasted more than a year and in the course of the operation, eight people were killed and 13 detained, four of whom were Afghan citizens and served their sentences in their home country.[52]

On September 3, 2010, only two weeks after the mass prison break, a suicide bomber drove into a police station in Khujand that housed the Anti-Organized Crime Unit of the Police of the Sughd Province, a dreaded institution locally referred to as the Sixth Department. Two police officers died as the result of the explosion, and 25 were injured.[53] I myself was three kilometres away from the station when the bomb exploded and clearly felt the detonation. The event created a commotion in the city since it was the first suicide bombing attack ever in the territory of Tajikistan. To this day, the identity and motives of the perpetrator(s) remain unclear. The government initially blamed the Islamic Movement of Uzbekistan but offered no evidence to support its accusations. Responsibility was later claimed by an Islamic group that had been unknown until they released a video on a Chechen website, Kavkazcenter.com, but the authorities declared that there was no evidence of this group's involvement.[54] Fourteen alleged members of the Islamic Movement of Uzbekistan were later detained in connection with the bombings.[55] On the ground, people were speculating about the motives, suspecting possible revenge by previous detainees or the families of detainees who had been tortured in the infamous police station. Some also questioned the veracity of the story told by authorities, alleging that there was no one in the car, that it was not driven into the station but parked close to it when the bomb was set off, and that there were certainly more casualties than what had been reported. Other sources indicated that the attack was intended to interfere with the investigation of the murder of Homidjon Karimov, the owner of Isfara's Bazaar (*Bozorkom*) who was shot dead in his home village on August 30. Karimov was known to be involved in criminal circles and had previously been convicted for criminal activities.[56] In general, people were not surprised that this particular station was the target of an attack, since it has such an adverse reputation because of systemic torture allegations.

Two years later, violence touched Gorno-Badakhshan in the Pamir region bordering Afghanistan. The conflict was touched off by the murder of General Abdullo Nazarov, the chairman of the Directorate of Tajikistan's State Committee for National Security (SCNS) in the Badakhshan viloyat. Nazarov, a former KGB agent who fought alongside the UTO during the civil war, was linked by a Tajik Court to the August 2010 mass jail break. This was quickly followed by a crackdown in the province against so-called 'militants' and their alleged leader, Tolib Ayombekov, the general of the border guard directorate of the SCNS. Ayombekov also happened to be a former UTO commander.[57] Clashes resulted in the deaths of 70 persons, some 20 of them civilians.[58] Ayombekov claimed his innocence in the murder of Nazarov,[59] denied that the matter was connected to tobacco smuggling, and declared that the authorities had accused him because they wanted to get rid of former opposition field commanders. Adding further complexity to the matter, Sabzali Mamadrizoev, the Islamic Party's local representative, was killed on July 25, 2012,[60] while Imumnazar Imumnazarov, a respected informal community leader, was killed by gunmen in his home in Khorog on August 22.[61] Making the situation even more opaque, all telephone and internet connections were cut entirely for several days during the clashes. Authorities claimed that communication lines had been hit by bullets, an explanation that convinced no one.[62] Ayombekov surrendered to the authorities on August 14, 2012, and remained under house arrest for few months before being given amnesty in 2014.[63]

Khorog was again the theatre for deadly clashes in May 2014, when an alleged anti-drug operation left four people dead. The gunfight, which took place in a residential area, led to protests, and several buildings, including the provincial police headquarters, were set on fire. Protesters also allegedly denounced the appointment of people from other regions to high-level government posts in the province and demanded more autonomy.[64]

Because Badakhshan is a transit hub for goods coming in and out of Afghanistan, these matters may also have been connected to financial interests and black market activities. It is estimated that nearly 25 per cent of Afghan opium bound for Europe exits through the northern route via the poorly monitored 1,000 kilometre-long Tajik border. Given the economic importance of the opium trade, there are suspicions that high-level officials might be involved. De Danieli argues that in the mid-1990s drug networks went through a process of 'vertical integration' and that drug-control policies had the adverse effect of strengthening the 'political-criminal nexus.'[65] It is also believed that militant groups are involved in drug trafficking.[66] Based on the identity of the protagonists, mainly connected to the opposition, these violent events appear to be the result of political competition for the control of the region. Yet they are rooted in a complex web of events and socio-politico-economic interrelations and cannot be easily explained.

Finally, in September 2015, violence again threw Tajikistan into political turmoil. On August 30, 2015, a 23-year-old resident of Vakhdat, a town located just 20 kilometres east of Dushanbe, was beaten by the police and succumbed to his injuries several days later. He was allegedly apprehended by the police because of his long beard. The incident incited anger from his relatives and from the local population, and several days after the incident, nearly 100 people gathered in front the hospital where Bobojonov lay in a coma; they demanded that an investigation be opened. Bobojonov died on September 4, 2015.[67]

That same day, an attack was launched on the local police station in Vakhdat at dawn and resulted in the death of four servicemen. Quoting local policemen, Radio Ozodi first reported that the attack on the local police station had been conducted by Bobojonov's relatives after they had seized weapons from a nearby military outlet.[68] Almost simultaneously, another raid was conducted against an arsenal near the capital, Dushanbe. In the clash with security forces, nine attackers were killed and six others were detained.[69] Yet two days later, the Interior Ministry denied that any Bobojonov relatives were implicated and accused Deputy Defense Minister Abduhalim Nazarzoda, also known as Hoji Halim, of having led the operation. The search for Nazarzoda and his followers led security forces to the Romit Gorge, 55 kilometres east of Dushanbe. The special operation lasted 12 days and ended with the death of Nazarzoda on September 16, 2015. The official statement of the KGB indicated that 'negotiation attempts to induce them to surrender voluntarily did not give any results. Returning fire, the leader of the gang Halima Nazarzoda Hoxha, former Deputy Defense Minister of Tajikistan, Eshoni Dzhunaydullo Umarov, and ten of their accomplices were eliminated.'[70]

Before his death, a text claiming Nazarzoda's innocence surfaced on a website associated with Tajikistan's political opposition. An unidentified author claimed to have been mandated by Nazarzoda to publish a statement. In it, he declared Nazarzoda innocent and suggested that the attacks were an inside job organized by the government to frame and discredit IRPT associates and yet another former UTO commander.[71] Khovar, the National Information Agency of Tajikistan, quickly recalled Nazarzoda's involvement with the UTO during the war and established a connection between Muhiddin Kabiri, the IRPT's leader in exile, and Nazarzoda.[72] On September 16 and 17, a total of 13 IRPT members were arrested in connection with the Nazarzoda case. Kabiri described the accusation as absurd. Further accusations were announced on state television channel Safina, where it was said that plans to attack and seize government buildings were found in the IRPT's office in Dushanbe.[73]

The events recounted above are surrounded by confusing and contradictory reports. Some episodes seem to be escalations of local conflicts, yet they must be interpreted in the context of broader political, regional, or national dynamics. Interestingly, what may be perceived as political violence could actually be an act of violence in connection with local personal matters and dynamics. However, it is certainly more convenient for the authorities to blame events on extremist or insurgent groups. These incidents are yet another example of 'rhetorical battles for control over defining the event and [they] testify to the impossibility of truly making sense of social reality in light of divergent interpretations of events by different actors.'[74]

By relating these events, I have underlined the fragile nature of national politics in Tajikistan. Thorough research has yet to be conducted on the causes and consequences of these episodes of violence. Yet events in Badakhshan, the prison break, and the ensuing manhunt in Gharm point to the salience of regional identities and discontent with the concentration of power in the hands of the Kulobi faction. Subsequent military interventions by the government appear to have been a determined attempt to reaffirm its authority. The 2010 Khujand bombing and the 2015 Vakhdat raid appear to be the desperate attempts of ordinary citizens facing mistreatment to challenge the authorities through unlawful methods, given the absence of institutional channels for expressing discontent, let alone initiating political change. The recent episodes of violence and the physical elimination of former opposition figures, as well as the ongoing campaign against opposition parties, suggest that the political equilibrium reached by the signing of the peace agreement in 1997 is in jeopardy. As one Tajik observer put it, these events confirm the dismantling of Inter-Tajik peace agreement.[75]

Tightening Authoritarianism

Central Asian elites value stability more than anything else and political leadership almost seems immutable. In Tajikistan, Emomali Rahmon has occupied the positions of Head of State since 1992 and President since 1994, while Kazakh President Nursultan Nazarbayev has been in charge since 1990. In Turkmenistan and Uzbekistan, the deaths of Saparmurat Niyazov (nicknamed Turkmenbashi – the Father of Turkmens) in 2006 and of Islam Karimov in 2016 have led to a change of political leadership but did not result in significant political nor social changes. Kyrgyzstan is the sole country that had a political alternation via elections as well as 'revolutions' in 2005 and 2010. Clientelism, nepotism as well as authoritarian practices have insured political stability since the independence. Yet, political continuity is not limited to the stubbornness of political figures but should also address the resilience of Soviet-style policies and institutions.

In Tajikistan, genuine opposition forces formed and contested the hegemony of the Communist Party on the eve of the civil war. The situation dramatically degenerated and led to violent conflict, but the political parties formed in 1991 survived and remained active. In contrast with neighbouring Uzbekistan, dissident voices were not completely silenced, even though politics have been heavily and consistently dominated by President Rahmon's Popular Democratic Party of Tajikistan since 1994. Political repression has increased in recent years. Correspondingly, Tajikistan's democracy scores have decreased yearly since 2006, according to Freedom House ratings.

Apart from the defunct IRPT, opposition parties are either very weak or blindly supportive of government policies. The remaining parties after the 2015 parliamentary elections are the Agrarian Party, the Economic Reform Party, and the Socialist Party, which are overall supportive of the authorities. Each of them has two seats in Parliament. The Democratic Party and the Social Democratic Party, which are both critical of the government, fell short of the 5 per cent threshold. The Communist Party has been very compliant toward the authorities over the years, but in 2015, its leader, Shodi Shabdolov, vehemently criticized the elections, which he called 'a political farce.'[76] Indeed, the OSCE's electoral observation mission concluded that 'elections took place in a restricted political space and failed to provide a level playing field for candidates.'[77]

Regardless of the strength of political parties, parliamentary politics are not of primary importance: Tajikistan certainly qualifies as a super-presidential political system in which decision-making is made exclusively at the executive level. The Constitution was adopted in 1994 and amended in 1999 and 2003. A 1999 constitutional referendum extended the presidential term from five to seven years, while the 2003 amendments extended the number of terms that a Tajik president may hold office, from one to two seven-year periods. At the time, only one party, the Democratic Party, boycotted the 2003 referendum in protest against the concentration of power in Rahmon's hands.[78] Like his Kazakh counterpart Nursultan Nazarbayev, Emomali Rahmon has legally secured and consolidated his grip on power. A law entitled Law on the Founder of Peace and National Unity – Leader of the Nation, adopted in Parliament on December 9, 2015, grants Emomali Rahmon a special lifelong political status. The law gives him the right to oversee the activities of the government even after he retires. The law also grants Rahmon and his relatives lifelong immunity from judicial and criminal prosecutions. Finally, he will retain his properties as well as many financial benefits.[79] In January 2016, the Constitution was amended to lower the required age for presidents from 35 years to 30. The legal change has been interpreted as a measure that would allow Rahmon's 28-year-old son to run for president in the 2020 elections. On May 22, 2016, a referendum put those constitutional amendements to a popular vote; 94 per cent of the population approved the changes.[80]

As mentioned earlier, power shifted to the hands of Kulobis after the war, and opposition figures were progressively sidelined. There is a strong sense that patron-client relations as well as regionalism are preponderant in determining the structure of power in Tajikistan.[81] A quick survey of the executive as of September 2015 shows that top positions are mostly occupied by people who come from the south. Among the 21 top executives, four are originally from Sughd, four from Dushanbe, two from GBAO, and 11 from Khatlon. Among those 11, five are precisely from Dangara, the birthplace of the President.

Nepotism is also prevalent. Emomali Rahmon has seven daughters and two sons, and over the years, many of his relatives have been appointed to strategic positions within the state apparatus. For instance, his daughter Parvina, previously a senior tax inspector, was appointed Tajikistan's Consul General in Russia. Another daughter, Ozoda, was First Deputy Minister of Foreign Affairs from 2014 to 2016, after which she was appointed Chief of Staff on January 27, 2016. Her husband, Djamoliddin Nuraliev, is First Deputy Minister of Finance. The President's brother-in-law, Hasan Asadullozoda, runs the country's largest commercial bank, Oriyonbank.[82] The president's 28-year-old son, Rustam Emomali, was also the head of the Agency for State Financial Control and Combating Corruption from 2015 to 2017.[83] Finally, in January 2017, Rustam Emomali was appointed mayor of Dushanbe, succeeding Mahmadsaid Ubaidulloev, who was mayor for 19 years.[84]

Legal measures to consolidate power have been coupled with the elimination of political opponents, whether they represent a real threat or not. One of them is Said Zaidov, the former Industry Minister and a successful businessman. He was sentenced to 26 years in prison in December 2013, several months after announcing his intention to found a new political party. He was charged with financial misdemeanours, polygamy, and sexual aggression. A year later, in January 2015, the lawyer who defended Zaidov, Shuhrat Qudratov, was himself sentenced to nine years in a high-security prison on charges of fraud and attempted bribery.[85] This appears to have been a politically motivated accusation and was obviously meant to send a message to lawyers tempted to get involved in political cases. This is one of the reasons the IRPT had problems hiring lawyers for the 13 members of the Political Council who were arrested in September 2015.

The most dramatic episode of this political sidelining is undoubtedly the murder of Umarali Kuvvatov in Istanbul in March 2015, four days before the parliamentary elections. Kuvvatov was a successful business-man who used to be close to the Rahmon family. He fell into disgrace and left Tajikistan for Turkey in 2011. He then founded an opposition movement called Group 24. In 2014, using social media, he attempted to organize a demonstration in Dushanbe, but his plans failed and his organization was declared a terrorist group. Kuvvatov was shot on the street in front of his wife and kids after leaving a friend's house in Istanbul where they had eaten dinner.[86] His bodyguard was declared guilty of the murder by a Turkish court, although five other individuals were accused. Though the motives are unclear, it was reported that Kuvvatov had compromising information about the Rahmon family that he intended to reveal.[87] Two years before that, in 2012, there was an assassination attempt against Dodojon Atovulloev, founder of the Tajik opposition monthly *Charogi Ruz* (*Daily Light*). He had left Tajikistan in 2001. He was stabbed in Moscow but survived the attack and has continued his opposition activities in Russia.

Freedom of the press is limited and therefore hinders the actions of the opposition. Even so, Tajikistan has a better track record than most of its neighbours, with the exception of Kyrgyzstan and Afghanistan. The absence of dissident and critical voices in television programmes suggests that public and private TV stations are under strict control. Journalists still enjoy some freedom in the written press. The news agency *Asia Plus*, which publications I use extensively in this book, and which manages a very popular website as well as a printed newspaper, is a notable exception. Yet, journalists are nevertheless subjected to constant pressure and therefore report events in a fact-based manner, rather than analysing them within greater socio-political trends. Some topics seem too taboo to be addressed. For instance, no media ever directly criticizes the President or his family. When a video of an apparently intoxicated Rahmon seen dancing and singing at a wedding appeared on YouTube in May 2013, Tajik authorities cut access to both YouTube and the independent Central Asian TV channel K + between May 18 and May 27.[88] What could be a funny anecdote of yet another bizarre cult of personality surrounding a Central Asian President actually speaks to the considerable control the government holds over the media.

Table 3.1   Freedom of expression in Central Asia

Country	Freedom of press 2015, 0 = best 100 = worst
Afghanistan	67
Kazakhstan	85
Kyrgyzstan	67
Tajikistan	82
Turkmenistan	95
Uzbekistan	95

Source: Freedom House 2015.

On numerous occasions when a sensitive event has taken place, telephone communication systems (including text messaging) have been disabled and social media websites such as Facebook or Odnoklassniki blocked. This was the case during the clashes in Gorno-Badakhshan in 2012 and 2014, and in early September 2015 when IRPT members were arrested. One of the major media players in Tajikistan, the Information Agency Asia Plus, consists of a twice-weekly newspaper in Russian, a website in Russian, Tajik, and English updated daily, and a radio channel. Its website came under attack in April 2015 and it took three days to get it back up. Control of information as well as communication extends to the private sector. In August 2015, the IRPT had booked a room at the Sheraton Hotel in Dushanbe to hold a press conference and, at the last minute, the hotel administration cancelled the reservation, alleging an electrical problem. It was not clear if electricity was actually intentionally cut or if the hotel administration yielded to political pressure. The press conference later took place at Kabiri's house in Dushanbe.[89]

Civil society has not been immune to the closing of the political space. Several non-governmental organizations (NGOs) were forced to close down in the last several years. In Sughd, several important NGOs fell victim to political pressure. One of these, Amparo, a prominent association of young lawyers, was shut down in January 2013 for failure to re-register within the Ministry of Justice. The Association used to provide free consulting and legal support to students, conscripts, and other disadvantaged members of society. The NGO had also prepared a draft law 'On alternative military service,' which was supported by most human rights organizations in Tajikistan but which has never received the assent of Parliament. The closure of the organization attracted foreign attention and support from Amnesty International as well as from the EU High Representative for Foreign Affairs, Catherine Ashton, but their statements did not change the Tajik authorities' decision.[90]

During my time spent in Tajikistan, I collaborated with the director of a small NGO in Khujand. Her organization, *Tsentr Grazhdanskovo obshestvo* (Civil Society Centre), worked on various small-scale capacity building projects, such as media training for students of journalism and training for teachers, as well as organizing monthly meetings for political parties to get together and discuss various sociopolitical issues. In the summer of 2011, her NGO relocated into a newly built state office building, and its activities came under close scrutiny, especially her acquaintance with the IRPT and other opposition parties. When IRPT members, whose regional office was nearby, tried to pay her a visit at the office, they were denied entry in the building by the security guard who checked their ID. Initial intimidation attempts finally resulted in a January 2013 court decision that her organization must be shut down for using the wrong address in its registration documents and for failure to clearly define its leadership.[91]

In addition to judicial repression, Parliament passed amendments to the Law on Public Associations in August 2015, which have been denounced by international law associations as being too restrictive. The main contention concerns the requirement that NGOs register foreign funding with Tajikistan's justice ministry in order to be able to implement programmes supported by foreign grants. It is not clear whether the government would have the authority to approve or deny a grant's registration or what the consequences would be for failing to do so.[92] The detention of Toronto-based Tajik researcher Alexander Sodiqov in the summer of 2014 exemplifies this fear of foreign interference. Sodiqov was arrested on suspicion of espionage in June 2014 while working as a researcher for a project of the University of Exeter funded by the British Economic and Social Research Council.

While the Tajik government showed promising signs of political openness and compromise after the peace agreement was signed in the late 1990s, the Presidential clique's grip on power has significantly increased. The authorities have resorted to all the tools available to prolong their rule such as eliminate the possibility of rebellion as well as legalizing autocratic rule through Constitutional reforms.[93] The clampdown on civil society was supplemented by the complete marginalization of Tajikistan's first opposition party.

The Islamic Revival Party of Tajikistan: A Slow but Steady Marginalization

The following section details the history, philosophy, and activities of the Islamic Revival Party of Tajikistan, which used to be Central Asia's sole legal Islamic political party. While many commentators and scholars have been discussing 'political Islam' in the region for two decades, they have witnessed very little, if any, successful Islamic mobilization. Political Islam can be defined as a sociopolitical movement founded on Islam defined as much in terms of a political ideology as in terms of religion.[94] Islamists, according to Roy, are to be differentiated from fundamentalists in the sense that unlike the latter who are interested in the return to traditional values and idealize a distant past, Islamists make modern society the focus of their actions. Yet, political Islam failed in Tajikistan. Roy suggests that political Islam is doomed to fail because of its incapacity to reinvent the political structures in which political parties evolve and offer a true game-changing alternative to populations. In Tajikistan, the IRPT was coopted when it signed the peace agreement and its high-profile members were given specific enviable positions. The party adopted a critical yet not too confrontational approach towards the government of Emomali Rahmon. However, its compliant attitude towards the authorities did not suffice to protect it from the concentration of power in the hands of the presidential clique. Even though the party has been disbanded and outlawed, its active participation in national politics and mobilization throughout the country over both religious and secular issues legitimized and normalized the association of Islam and politics to a certain degree.

The Islamic Revival Party of Tajikistan actually emerged as a movement in rural Tajikistan in the 1960s and 1970s. Dudoignon and Qalandar argue that the party has distinguishable geographical roots among the populations from Qarategin (now referred to as the Rasht valley) who were resettled in the Qurghonteppa area, a claim denied by the party's leadership. Indeed, the party was aspiring to a certain universalism and rejected any regional or ethnic affiliation. Roy argues that Islamists are not clerics but political actors the IRPT emerged out of fundamentalist circles, from the Muslim Brotherhood model.[95] Eventually, the rapprochement with the Qaziat, headed by Turajonzoda, encouraged the de-radicalization of the party in the early 1990s.[96] Fundamentalist views of Islam were not very popular in a society as secular as Soviet Tajikistan, and the party was careful to not advertise its radical positions on the imposition of Sharia or the creation of an Islamic Republic. However, Vinatier argues that the United Tajik Opposition, when it retreated to Afghanistan, reinforced its ideological dimension, this being the only nonbelligerent strategy at their disposition.[97] Tajik political scientist Abdulloh Rahnamo also emphasized the ideological shift operated by the party's founder, Said Abdulloh Nuri, in the 1990s. It implied a normalization of relations with the traditional clergy, a rethinking of the party's undsertanding of democray accompanied by a discursive shift from the use of 'Islamic state' to 'Muslim society' to describe their political project.[98]

Even after the peace agreements were signed, it was not until August 12, 1999, that the Supreme Court lifted the ban on religious parties and the IRPT was allowed to resume its activities in Tajikistan. The IRPT redefined its programme, with a focus on secular issues such as national unity, ensuring national independence, and education; it barely referred to Islam. That confirmed the IRPT's moderate attitude and its nationalist tendencies. Naumkin outlines the following objectives for the IRPT at the end of the civil war:

(1) Ensuring the development of economic, social, and cultural life in the republic.
(2) Ensuring the development of democracy, rights, and social regulation.
(3) The development of Islamic values, as well as national and human values, among the people of Tajikistan.
(4) Raising the political and cultural level of the population, especially women and youth, through their participation in political activity and state government.
(5) Ensuring the political, economic, and cultural independence of Tajikistan.
(6) Realizing its aims through the public authorities and legislative bodies with the participation of members of parties in their activities.[99]

The party's position on secularism was unambiguous — at least at the official level. In 2009, commenting on the possibility of establishing an Islamic Republic if the IRPT were to win the elections, Party Chairman Muhiddin Kabiri stated: 'Our party complies with our country's Constitution, which backs the [secular] system in Tajikistan. Our Sunni Hanafi sect of Islam does not support the idea of theocratic governments.'[100] In November 2011, I attended a meeting organized by the IRPT in Sughd to discuss constitutional matters. Representatives of all political parties attended except for the ruling party, the Popular Democratic Party. At some point, the discussion moved to the topic of the compatibility of Islam and democracy, which led to a heated debate when IRPT members suggested that the Islamic Caliphate was an early example of democratic rule. In general, the idea that Islam reflected democratic values and promoted social justice was constantly put forward by IRPT members. However, secular members of society remained very suspicious and considered Islam to be an authoritarian religion whose strict behavioural prescriptions were incompatible with democracy.

Because I had been frequenting the IRPT's office in Khujand since 2010 and had acquaintances there, I was invited to attend the IRPT's quadrennial ninth Congress in Dushanbe on September 24–25, 2011. The event was well attended and many media were present. The crowd was composed mostly of party members, both men and women. The older men were given the best seats in the front, followed by younger men and women. There was indeed a great number of women, young and old, present at the Congress. The rooms and chairs were organized in a way that men and women were separated. Yet, there were also many representatives of different national and international organizations, national political parties, and embassies who also enjoyed good seats close to the main stage. In this section, the segregation between men and women was not respected. The presence of so many foreign guests was surprising and was meant I assume, to provide the party with international visibility as well as an aura of legitimacy in the eyes of the local public. Some of the guest speakers were representatives of Islamic parties from Pakistan, Indonesia, and Iran. The IRPT had also invited a representative of the ruling party, the People's Democratic Party of Tajikistan to offer a speech, which in today's context sounds truly astonishing. Hoji Akbar Turajonzoda was also among the guest speakers as well as Abdulloh Rahnamo, a scholar formerly close to the IRPT.

The ideas expressed at this event supported the secular viewpoint, and the most 'radical' ideas were not communicated by the IRPT's leadership but by foreign guests, mainly Geidar Jamal, the founder of the original Islamic Revival Party in Astrakhan, and Russian journalist Maxim Shevchenko. Jamal, a Shiite, is a well-known yet controversial figure in Russia due to his radical leftist, Marxist-inspired Islamic political views. His speech, which received the loudest applause, was crammed with references to Kafir – a derogatory Arabic term used to refer to unbelievers – and to powers oppressing Muslims, the Zionist threat, the

Figure 3.1 9th Congress of the Islamic Revival Party of Tajikistan, Dushanbe, November 2011. The banner says: Islamic Revival Party of Tajikistan condemns all kind of secular and religious extremism. Credit: Hélène Thibault.

lessons of the Caliphate, and the importance of unity between Sunni and Shia Muslims.

At the local level as well, popular discourses on those issues sometimes differed from the IRPT's party line. Iskandar, one of my main interviewees, had an IRPT membership card but was not an active member. He was confident that in the event of an electoral victory of the IRPT, the party would slowly implement Islamic law, and he believed in the possibility of one day living in an Islamic Republic. One of his friends, Tolib, was not supportive of the IRPT and did not even agree with the very concept of an Islamic party. This kind of position is often associated with either neo-fundamentalists or Salafis, who reject partisan Islam and are more concerned with individual expressions of faith and who see in the application of Sharia the solution to social and political problems.[101] For example, the Hizb ut-Tahrir does not recognize nation-states and refuses to engage in national politics, but calls Muslims to work for the establishment of a world Caliphate governed by Sharia. In general, the ordinary people I spoke with did not show great interest in or animosity toward the party but admitted to not being very familiar with it. When I asked people to give their opinions about the IRPT, a typical answer was: 'Said Abdulloh Nuri was a great man, he made peace with the President, but I don't know much about the new leader, Muhiddin Kabiri.' Others questioned the very necessity of an Islamic Party in Tajikistan. An imam in the Gonchi district considered religious parties useful in European countries where many religions co-existed but did not see the necessity of having a party that promotes Islam in a predominantly Muslim country. He added, 'Anyway, our President is there to promote and protect Islam.' On October 2, 2015, only a few days after the IRPT was banned and declared an extremist organization, the Center for Strategic Studies, a research unit affiliated with the office of the president, conducted a survey of public opinion on the IRPT. Not surprisingly, opinions were largely negative. One of the questions was, 'Do you think that the IRPT promotes religious hatred in the country?' to which 47.2 per cent of respondents answered in the affirmative, 21.5 per cent in the negative, while 31.3 per cent did not answer. In addition, 53.1 per cent of respondents considered the IRPT a terrorist organization.[102] If we question the neutrality of the survey questions and its results, there is little doubt that it constitutes a smear campaign against the IRPT, which will affect its image in the broader population.

In happier times, the IRPT managed to gather support within all regions of Tajikistan and it enjoyed a membership of about 40,000, half of whom were women. The party used to publish a weekly bulletin called Najot (Salvation), with a print run of 5,000 copies since 1999; it started to publish Naison (Spring), a magazine for women, in 1999. However, the publishing house was closed down in August 2015 under the pretext that employees had not been provided with proper uniforms and medical care.[103] The party's website, http://www.nahzat.tj/, whose content was available in both Tajik and Russian, was updated daily. Both the printed journals and the website were forbidden when the party was listed as a terrorist organization.[104]

When I conducted my research in 2010 and 2011, the party's regional branch in Sughd counted 13,000 members. Ilhom Yakubov was president of the Youth Committee of the IRPT's regional branch in Sughd when I first met him in 2010, before he became the chairman in 2013. When I asked Yakubov why he joined the IRPT in the first place, he replied: 'Democracy is part of Islam and I want to defend it.' Though he did not mention it, the fact that his father was the previous chairman of the party's regional branch certainly played an important role in his decision to become politically active with the party. 'Our party also focuses on raising awareness about respect of human rights, not only about Islam; we actually talk more about politics and other topics, liberty and rights, than religion,' said Yakubov. He explained the party's popularity in the region by the fact that northern people had been spared most of the fighting during the war, and unlike people in Dushanbe and Khatlon, they were not afraid to get involved politically. Alternatively, Schatz attributes the IRPT's popularity in the north to the regional power shift that occurred during the civil war, when northerners grew more alienated from the centre of power.[105] Indeed, the IRPT in Sughd was very dynamic, by and large because of the massive involvement of women in the party's activities. The party organized weekly mixed political and religious lectures, offered language classes to men and women, and provided a prayer room for women, which was the only legal one in the Sughd region. Once, after a religious lecture at the party's headquarters where the majority of attendees were women, one female representative asked me what I thought of 'their women.' Before I

Figure 3.2   IRPT's office in Khujand in 2011. The building was destroyed in 2014. Credit: Hélène Thibault.

had time to reply, she proudly said, 'We are the ones who are going to make the revolution!'

Finally, the party in Sughd also took an active part in the region's political affairs, organizing press conferences and seminars on a variety of topics such as education and suicide. The national suicide rate in Tajikistan among youth (15–19 years old) has seen a dramatic increase in the last few years, which concerns mostly young women from the Sughd viloyat.[106] During the seminar, discussions focused on how the Islamic faith could prevent suicide. Some outlined that one way to discourage people from taking their own life was to propagate the idea that suicide is considered a sin in Islam. Someone also suggested that the Council of Ulemas should prohibit imams from reciting prayers for those who committed suicide. This idea shocked others, who found it unfair to people struggling with psychological problems, and who suggested that imams should instead act as counselors and spiritual guides for distressed individuals. Overall, everyone, including the representative of the ruling party, agreed that Islam could play a positive role in preventing suicide. Yet people disagreed on the idea of who should be responsible for teaching religion: families, schools, or medresses.

The IRPT in Sughd was also very vocal in the scandal surrounding the opening of a toll road between Dushanbe and Khujand in 2010. Chinese companies built the road through a loan from Beijing, which the Tajik government is expected to repay with taxes collected by the private company operating the toll. Innovative Road Solutions (IRS), the company operating the expensive road, is registered in the British Virgin Islands and its ownership is a 'trade secret.'[107] Clearly, the concerns of the IRPT went beyond religious matters.

When they addressed the ban on the hijab in public and educational institutions in 2009, the IRPT even downplayed the Islamic character of the issue. In an interview with Radio Free Europe in 2009, Party Chariman Kabiri stated: 'For us, the hijab issue is about human rights. It's about freedom of choice, which is guaranteed by our Constitution. The Education Ministry or any other bodies have no right to ban the hijab anywhere.'[108] At the national level, the party offered financial assistance to Davlatmo Ismoilova, a Dushanbe University student who brought a lawsuit against the authorities regarding the hijab ban. Though she was ready to go up to the Supreme Court, her case did not go very far since her request was judged inadmissible by the local court. The IRPT branch in Sughd

received more than a hundred complaints from desperate parents. It was
reported that some girls threatened to commit suicide if they were not
allowed in school with their hijab.[109] Representatives of the IRPT
Women's Committee in Khujand commented that many girls came to the
party's headquarters looking for help in resolving the problem of the hijab
ban. Members of the IRPT's Women's Committee argued that the hijab
ban not only hindered freedom of faith and access to education, but also
violated the Constitution. The issue was indeed framed as a human rights
issue more than a religious one. Ultimately, the party could not be of much
support to those families without going against the law. In Khujand, the
party hired a very competent English teacher – who could not find work
because of her hijab – to teach bi-weekly English classes at the party's
headquarters. Though the party was not directly involved in any judicial
pursuit, they were very vocal about this issue, invoking it at every political
gathering in which they took part. However, the Islamic Revival Party has
remained silent on many issues regarding the restriction of religious
practices. Muhiddin Kabiri, who, together with Muhammadsharif
Himmatzodah, was one of only two IRPT members in Parliament, was
not present at the time the new Law on Freedom of Faith and Religious
Associations was passed in the Majlisi Namoyandagon (Lower Chamber) in
2009. Reacting to the adoption of the new law, Kabiri expressed concerns
over limitations on religious associations but agreed with the imposition of
Hanafi Islam in schools as well as with the non-compulsory character of
religious education.[110]

Because of its popularity, the IRPT has been subject to increasing
pressure in the last few years. This started with the eviction of IRPT
members from executive positions in 2006 and was followed by
insidious political pressure, such as repeated accusations of propagating
extremism, attacks on IRPT's property, suspected aggressions toward
party representatives, and continuous political pressure that culminated
in the ban on the party in September 2015, almost exactly 14 years after
the party was legalized at the end of the war.

As mentioned earlier, the integration of Tajik United Opposition
(UTO) leaders and commanders after the war remained incomplete, and
political cohabitation ephemeral. In 2000, the IRPT lost the Ministry of
Economy, headed by Davlat Usmon between 1998 and 2000.[111]
Immediately after the 2006 presidential election, which the IRPT had
boycotted, President Rahmon implemented a drastic reorganization of

the administration, following which the IRPT was even more marginalized.[112] In 2006, IRPT Chairman Muhiddin Kabiri did not enter the presidential race for reasons that remain unclear. In an interview with Radio Free Europe, he declared: 'We didn't want to place our country and our party at the front line of criticism that Islamic movements are very active here.' The same article reports that a lack of trust in the Central Election Commission and flaws in the country's election law are the two main reasons cited by party delegates to explain their decision. Some analysts claim that the IRPT was pressured by the presidential administration and then decided to quietly withdraw from the race, foreseeing likely defeat. Others argue that the party was too weak to mobilize a sufficient number of supporters for an election campaign only two months after Kabiri took over the party leadership following the death its founder, Said Abdulloh Nuri.[113]

From 2000 until 2015, the IRPT retained only two seats in the lower house of parliament, the Majlisi Namoyandagon. The party won 7.7 per cent of the vote during the parliamentary elections held on February 28, 2010. The IRPT leadership rejected these results and claimed to have won at least 30 per cent of the vote, citing their increasing membership and popularity. Muhiddin Kabiri suggested that these results could not possibly be accurate, as the number of party supporters had been increasing steadily since the last election, reaching around 34,000 in 2011.[114] In Kistakuz (Sughd viloyat), a local IRPT representative I talked to in 2010 was also suspicious of the results: 'Overall, they gave us 7 to 8 per cent but in reality, we obtained 30 to 40 per cent.' He also claimed, although he could not be certain, that in the Rasht valley region, the IRPT may have received up to 90 per cent of the vote.

The IRPT was again quite unsuccessful during the 2013 presidential elections. The IRPT's designated candidate, long-term female social activist Oinikhol Bobonazarova, could not enter the race because the party gathered only about 202,000 signatures out of the required 210,000. Bobonazarova claimed that her coalition was unable to collect the required number of signatures because of negative publicity against them.[115] Indeed, the period preceding the March 2015 parliamentary elections was characterized by political intimidation using alleged sex tapes of male and female representatives of the party.[116] The party garnered a mere 1.5 per cent, leaving it with no seats in Parliament for the first time in 15 years.[117] Soon after the elections, voices loyal to the authorities called for the interdiction of the party. In March 2015, several imams across Tajikistan called for a referendum to disband the party.[118] On April 2, Rahim Karimov, a professor at Dushanbe's Islamic University, called for the IRPT to be listed as a terrorist organization.[119] In June 2015, things escalated when the party's leader, Muhiddin Kabiri, announced that he was in a self-imposed exile in Turkey, fearing prosecution. In June 2015, the IRPT's leadership sent an official letter to the President, asking for his protection, but the request was left unanswered.[120] On July 1, the IRPT even addressed the guarantor countries of the 1997 peace agreement as well as various international organizations to help promote peace and stability in Tajikistan.[121] Various Tajik politicians and strategists disapproved of the IRPT's initiative and went so far as to question the IRPT's entitlement to speak as a stakeholder in the 1997 peace agreement.[122] In an interview with *Politrus*, a Russian magazine, in August 2015, Muhiddin Kabiri expressed fears that the government was planning to decrease the number of IRPT members in government to a minimum and then declare the party 'inoperative,' using the law that requires an active party to be represented in 50 per cent of administrative centres.[123] His predictions turned out to be right.

Besides political marginalization, the IRPT's representatives and assets also suffered physical attacks. In 2010, a suspicious fire destroyed the IRPT's women's mosque in Dushanbe. In several cases, party representatives were severely beaten, and one party representative in Khorog was murdered in 2012. In January 2014, an IRPT activist from Isfara, Umedjon Tojiev, died in prison. He was reportedly tortured during his detention and died after falling from the third floor of a prison building in Sughd.[124] In June 2014, the IRPT's regional headquarter office in Khujand was entirely demolished by city authorities on the pretext that it was part of a new urban configuration (see Figure 3.2).[125] Finally, the main IRPT office in Dushanbe was temporarily 'sealed' on August 19, 2015, since it allegedly did not respect proper fire safety regulations. Interestingly, the ruling Popular Democratic Party of Tajikistan was also closed down for the same reason, as well as the Social Democratic Party, another opposition party.[126] However, the IRPT's national headquarters never opened its doors again.

In June 2015, dozens of IRPT members publicly repudiated the party in what seemed to be an orchestrated campaign of political shaming. In June 2015, dozens of party members from different regions publicly announced their resignation, often by way of online videos in which they declared that the IRPT was irrelevant or even dangerous for Tajikistan.[127] Ilhom Yakubov, the former IRPT chairman in Sughd with whom I remained in contact, is one of those who were forced into exile in the summer of 2015. Yakubov had been under surveillance since 2013. He was harassed in person and online and repeatedly and unnecessarily stopped by traffic police; his business interests were hindered by administrative pressures, and he was forced to put an end to his car-selling business. Yakubov's situation worsened in June 2015. When several policemen arrived at his home with a warrant, Yakubov was forced to follow them to clarify the case. At the police station, he was shown photos of individuals whom he did not recognize. The police pretended to have the men in custody for their involvement in extremist activities. They had allegedly confessed that Yakubov was their accomplice. The police presented a case against him and threatened to prosecute him unless he agreed to make an official statement to disavow his party. His 'declaration' was videotaped and later put on Youtube, Facebook, and other media. Yakubov was released in the evening but the police called him in once more the following day and threatened him again. Fearing he would be prosecuted and jailed, he fled to Europe several days later, where he was later joined by his family. Since then, his property has been seized by the authorities.

The IRPT was finally suspended on July 8, 2015. The General Prosecutor's office announced that the party had lost its political party status, citing its poor electoral performance and the recent desertion of many party members, as well as criminal cases connected to party members, including charges of extremism.[128] Earlier in June, the party's leader, Muhiddin Kabiri, announced that he was in self-imposed exile in Turkey, fearing judicial prosecution. On August 28, the Ministry of Justice commanded the IRPT to stop all its activities because it contravened Section 3 of the Law on Political Parties, since it no longer had party cells in most cities and districts of the republic.[129] On September 29, Tajikistan's Supreme Court declared the IRPT a terrorist organization in connection with the rebellion fomented by Nazarzoda, and even accused the party of co-operation with terrorist organizations such as the Islamic Movement of Turkestan and the Islamic State.[130] More members of the IRPT's political council were detained, including a woman, Zarafo Rahmoni, who was the party's adviser on legal issues.[131]

The same day, Buzurgmehr Yorov, the chairman of the Bar Association of Dushanbe, who was an IRPT activist and designated lawyer for dealing with the latest wave of arrests, was himself charged with mass-scale fraud.[132] In an absurd chain of events, the authorities also arrested the lawyer who defended Yorov, who was himself defending other arrested IRPT members.[133] In total, 16 party members were standing trial in May 2016.[134] The May 22 referendum validated the prohibition of faith-based parties.[135] Tajikistan used to be the sole Central Asian country to allow religious political parties and the new Constitutional provision marks the end of lawful political Islam in Central Asia.

In the end, despite its mild critique and very moderate political stance, the IRPT could not survive the latest authoritarian thrust. The demise of the IRPT is no doubt the result of intensifying political repression. Yet the party also lost some of its political leverage over the years as it became integrated into the power structures. Its increasing dependence on the government for the attribution of positions hindered its legitimacy in the eyes of its constituents. It also had to be careful to not advocate ideas deemed too 'Islamic,' for fear that it would be shut down. Karagiannis even identifies a de-Islamization of the party reflected in its political platform; this alienated it from a significant part of their electorate and also contributed to the growing popularity of the Hizb ut-Tahrir.[136] Other radical Islamic groups, such as *Taqfir* (accusation of lack of faith/unbeliever) founded in Gharm, oppose the IRPT, accusing it of 'compromising with the government and selling out Islamic values.'[137]

When I first met Iskandar, one of my main interviewees, he was wearing an IRPT T-shirt, on the back of which was printed (in Russian) the following slogan: 'Instead of emptiness – Faith' (*Vmesto pustoty – Vera*). Confronting an ideological vacuum and the absence of a mobilizing national discourse, the IRPT saw itself as an ideology provider. In fact, the party perceived its role as that of a buffer that could offset radicalization processes. Ilhom Yakubov, of the IRPT in Sughd, said, 'Can you imagine the kind of situation we would have in Tajikistan without the IRPT? Our party is moderate and we are here to prevent the youth from joining radical underground groups.' Surprisingly, this kind of rhetoric was even echoed by the representative of the ruling party in a speech at the IRPT's Congress in September 2011. A prominent researcher at the Centre for Strategic Studies under the President of Tajikistan, Abdulloh Rahnamo also declared in 2011:

Today the IRPT plays the role of a legal channel for the socialization of the immense potential of political Islam in Tajikistan and, thus, contributes to the strengthening of national security. Many citizens who would like to participate in politics precisely as Islamic activists, today have the opportunity to realize this through the IRPT. When they join this legal party, they socialize, develop their political culture, and move away from radical positions, and so on. Without the IRPT, we would face a massive manifestation of radicalism.[138]

This kind of position could not be defended by anyone after the party was banned, at the risk of facing charges of extremism. But this narrative has always been very important for the party and certainly represented a way to justify its relevance, even more so after the party was banned, since it has theoretically resulted in the creation of a void in the field of Islamic politics. In a conversation I had in September 2015 with Yakubov, who had been in exile since June, he shared his apprehension about the future of Tajikistan. For him, the void created by the withdrawal of the IRPT will soon be filled by underground radical parties, which, in contrast to the IRPT, reject democracy.

The Other Islamic Opposition

Used by Soviet authorities to describe subversive Muslim activities, the term *Wahhabi* is still employed by Central Asian leaders to portray foreign and 'illegitimate' Islamic trends in the region. The term originally referred to a Saudi variation of the Hanbali law school in Sunni Islam that emerged in the eighteenth century. It was a reform movement that advocated purging Islam from idolatry and restoring its pure monotheistic worship. Today, the inaccurate use of the word *Wahhabi* to describe Central Asian groups is intended to frighten, alarming the national and international community and justifying the imposition of harsh control over religious groups.[139] In general, the fundamentalist threat is often exaggerated by Central Asian governments in order to curtail opposition. It is even exaggerated by some advocacy groups just because it is commonplace to assume that increasing piety in Central Asia leads to violent radicalization.[140] Yet, their existence is undeniable. The Islamic Movement of Uzbekistan

(IMU) and the Hizb ut-Tahrir (literally, the Party of Liberation), and more recently the Islamic State in Iraq and Syria (ISIS), are the main movements responsible for publicizing the phenomenon of radical Islam in Central Asia. Over the years, Tajik authorities have identified a considerable number of extremist organizations. As of May 2017, there were 14 groups on the list of banned organizations.

Some, like Al Qaeda and the Islamic State, are notorious, while others are less known, and perhaps even dormant or no longer active. Among them, Bayat burst on the scene in April 2004 when 20 people were arrested in the Isfara jamoat (Sughd viloyat) and charged with crimes ranging from arson to murder. Little is known about this group, but the authorities claimed it had ties with the IMU and the Taliban. Some groups are known for their violent actions, while others, such as the Muslim Brotherhood and Hizb ut-Tahrir, may hold fundamentalist views but are nonviolent political parties. Jamaat Tablighi[141] is considered to be a peaceful missionary organization,[142] while Salafiya, as it is referred to in Tajikistan, is not a group but a theological orientation. The term Salafism is derived from the Arabic word *salaf*, meaning 'ancestors,' and refers to a branch within Islam, in which the followers strive to practise a pure Islam as it was in the times of the Prophet

Table 3.2   List of banned organizations

List of extremist groups banned by the Supreme Court in Tajikistan as of May 2017
Al Qaeda
Call to Islam
Tojikistoni Ozod (Free Tajikistan)
Hizb ut-Tahrir
Group 24
Jamaat Tablighi
Lashkar e-Toiba
The Muslim Brotherhood
Islamic Revival Party of Tajikistan (IRPT)
Islamic State of Iraq and Syria (ISIS)
Islamic Movement of Uzbekistan (IMU)
Salafiya
The Taliban
Turkestan Islamic Movement

Muhammad. Naumkin[143] attributes an inherent violent character to Salafism, while others other like Adeeb Khalid recognize the multiple orientations of Salafism, from pietistic to jihadi.[144] In fact, Salafiya appears to be the post-Soviet incarnation of 'Wahhabism,' and the authorities use the term more and more frequently to portray expressions of conservative Islam. Finally, Free Tajikistan and Call to Islam are completely unknown to the public as well as to scholarly communities.

The Islamic Movement of Uzbekistan (IMU) is a militant organization originating in the Fergana valley of Uzbekistan before extending its activities to neighbouring countries. In the early 1990s in Namangan, Tahir Yuldeshev, and Jumma Namangani founded Adolat, a political movement that later morphed into the IMU. The leaders of the group made a turbulent public appearance in Namangan in January 1992 in the presence of Islam Karimov and challenged him to establish an Islamic state.[145] Shortly after this incident, the party was banned, and its leaders and followers went into exile; some got involved in the Tajik civil war along with the United Tajik Opposition. In 2000, they migrated to Afghanistan, where they enjoyed the support of the Taliban. Their aim was to overthrow the Uzbek government, to fight oppression, injustice, and corruption, and to establish an Islamic state.[146] The IMU is considered responsible for several armed incursions into the Fergana valley in the mid-1990s. The Uzbek government also accused the Islamic Movement of Uzbekistan of being behind the 1999 and 2004 bombings in Tashkent.[147] The international intervention in Afghanistan in 2001 is said to have greatly diminished the movement and resulted in the death of founding member Jumma Namangani. In August 2006, Tahir Yuldeshev claimed responsibility for an intrusion into Kyrgyz territory and warned Central Asian leaders to stop oppressing Muslims, threatening them with the prospect of terrorist attacks similar to the ones in Madrid and London.[148] According to Brill Olcott, IMU leaders provided little ideological innovation and were generally perceived as fighters rather than enlightened jihadists.[149] The relocation to the Afghan–Pakistani border implied a change in the group's objectives, which were supplanted by the 'need to survive in the tribal areas [such that] the group gradually became part of the military-political landscape of the rugged mountain area along the Afghan-Pakistani border.'[150] For that reason, the IMU 'has ceased to be a Central Asian group in anything other than name, not being active in the region.'[151] The extent of the group's presence in Tajikistan remains uncertain, but every year, dozens of Tajik citizens are convicted of membership in the Islamic Movement of Uzbekistan.

If the authorities are concerned with the Islamic Movement of Uzbekistan, they seem to apprehend even more the ascension of the Hizb ut-Tahrir (HT), which was officially banned in 2000. In the early 2000s, there were more HT than IMU members in Central Asia's prisons.[152] Although it is hard to assess of the importance of the party, many reports point out that their proselytizing activities were intensifying in Central Asia in the 1990s and the 2000s. Created in East Jerusalem in 1953 and exiled to Great Britain since the 1980s, Hizb ut-Tahrir aims at establishing a worldwide Caliphate. It proposes reaching this ultimate goal by peaceful means and rejects the use of violence. HT is careful to never use the word jihad in its publications. Yet its ideology is radical and very conservative on a number of topics, such as homosexuality and abortion. It has anti-Semitic tendencies and rejects any other form of governance than the Sharia.[153] The whole secrecy about the party comes from its particular structure. It is organized in secret, decentralized, five- to seven-person cells. The cells' main activities are directed at proselytizing, distributing leaflets as well as CDs and cassettes. The secrecy surrounding the activities of the organization makes it hard to determine who joins the party and why. The party appeared to have been extremely popular in the Sughd region in the late 1990s. One of the leaders claimed that there were 20,000 supporters in this province.[154] In 2005, scholar Emmanuel Karagiannis estimated the number of HT members in Tajikistan at 2,500 to 3,000.[155] These figures are already ten years old and very few scholars have dug into Hizb ut-Tahrir's presence in Central Asia, so numbers are very approximate. In 2010, one HT leader in Kyrgyzstan claimed that Kyrgyz prisons represented good recruiting grounds for the party since they were filled with an army of people who, after spending time in jail, were not afraid of anything any more.[156]

During my own fieldwork in northern Tajikistan, I came across very few instances of HT's presence. In general, people talked about it in a way that reproduced the government's discourse on Hizb ut-Tahrir. In spite of not knowing any HT members, people said that HT members had been misled by malevolent figures through either ignorance or cupidity. The idea that Tajiks received financial remuneration for their participation in Hizb ut-Tahrir activities was widespread, though this claim has not been substantiated. In Tajikistan, a judge from Khujand who sentenced HT members in 2003 later said: 'Many are from good families – there's no material interest there, just ideological.' The great majority of adherents still come from the unemployed class. The International Crisis Group (ICG) report recounts that of the 118 Hizb ut-Tahrir members who were detained in 2000 by security services in Sughd province, 64 per cent were between the ages of 21 and 30, 72 per cent were unemployed, 11 per cent were students, 2 per cent teachers, and 1 per cent Muslim clergy.[157] Since Karagiannis, no scholar studied the presence of HT in Central Asia. The only ones talking it recently have been HT members themselves.[158] Recent arrests in Tajikistan and Kyrgyzstan prove that the party is still active. The lack of reliable intelligence reports makes it difficult to get a good picture of their activities. It is not clear if the activity of Hizb ut-Tahrir' has actually decreased or if it just fell off the spotlight at the profit of what seems to be a more serious threat: ISIS.

Continuity with Soviet practices is also rhetorical in the sense that leaders carefully underline the threatening character of religion. Islamic movements are always problematic, they always represent a danger but its names change over time. In Soviet times, Sufim was repeatedly characterized as 'non-conformist Islam' that opposed Soviet outlooks.[159] It was later replaced by Wahhabism, which held even more radical and violent views.[160] Today, there seems to have been a rhetorical shift to Salafism, incarnated mostly by ISIS. All groups combined, thousands have been prosecuted and condemned for their involvement in one of the banned organizations over the years. In 2014 alone, Tajikistan opened 348 cases for charges of extremism and radicalism or for support or promotion of extremism and radicalism.[161] In comparison, the United States prosecutes on average 40 individuals every year for terrorism or related offenses.[162] Tajikistan has an exceptionally high conviction rate. In 2010, of 7491 defendants tried in criminal cases, only two were acquitted.[163] Prison sentences tend to be heavy in Tajikistan, and convicts receive sentences from 5 to 30 years.

In spite of accusations to the contrary, the Islamic Revival Party of Tajikistan (IRPT) has always denied having any connection with banned groups. Yet it is believed that many UTO fighters, unhappy that the IRPT came to an agreement with the secular government, chose to join the IMU to pursue their jihad.[164] The IRPT considered HT to be a competitor, capable of seducing people away from the IRPT. For instance, even though Hizb ut-Tahrir's content and message is grounded in local issues and contexts, it is part of a greater network aiming at the (re)creation of the Ummah. The IRPT vows to defend the integrity of the Tajik state and preserve its secular character, and it sees Islam as compatible with parliamentary politics; on the other hand, the Hizb ut-Tahrir, with its vision of recreating the Caliphate, strives against the global order and the nation-state. The IRPT also opposed Salafi circles as well as the Jamaat Tablighi movement, both of which have emerged and gained in popularity in the last few years. In an interview with news agency Radio Free Europe, Kabiri declared: 'We don't support the extremist view of the Salafi movement. We also oppose the Jamoati Tabligh group, which is promoting elements of foreign culture in the name of Islam, such as the so-called religious dress code and beard. It gives a completely wrong impression about Islam.'[165] Opposing the court ruling that declared the Jamaat Tablighi a terrorist organization, in 2009, Hoji Akbar Turajonzoda has urged the IRPT to make efforts to remove it from the list of terrorist organizations, arguing that it is peaceful and non-political.[166]

Most recently, recruitment by the Islamic State has been a matter of concern for Tajik authorities. Although ISIS has no presence in Central Asia, it appears to be actively recruiting Central Asian nationals. In April 2015, a shocking event raised other security concerns in Tajikistan. Gulmorod Halimov, the Tajik Commander of OMON (special paramilitary forces of the Interior Ministry), disappeared after telling his wife he was going on a business trip. A father of eight children, Halimov is a lawyer who joined the Tajik police in the early 1990s. He had received counterterrorism training in Russia and the United States and was appointed the head of OMON in 2012. Halimov resurfaced a month or so later in a video posted on YouTube in which he claimed to have joined the Islamic State, in protest of Tajikistan's anti-Islamic policies.[167] In the video, he threatened the Tajik and US governments. Apart from the shock and insult this betrayal brought upon the Tajik authorities, Halimov's expertise and knowledge of anti-terrorist and security operations have made his defection particularly worrisome for the government.

Research shows that social media propaganda and outreach represents an important recruiting method and almost half of Central Asians in Syria and Iraq were recruited among migrant worker communities in

Russia.[168] Tucker argues that migrants are seduced by the positive image associated with the Caliphate, the utopian vision of society accessible to everyone no matter their background.[169] He also suggests that Central Asian recruits 'embrace Islam as an identity that offers solidarity, a sense of belonging and an explanation for economic hardship and discrimination that they experience.'[170] Current figures estimate the number of Tajiks in Syria and Iraq to be between 300 and 400. In January 2016, Tajik authorities revised this number upward and announced that around 1,000 Tajiks have joined ISIS.[171] In 2015, ISIS even started operating *Furat*, a Russian-speaking service on social media websites. *Furat* is present on Twitter, Facebook, the Russian social network VKontakte, and the website Furat.info.

Both Russian and Tajik media and state actors have repeatedly warned against the threat posed by ISIS, claiming that it had built up a heavy presence of militants just across the Afghan border and was prepared to invade Tajikistan.[172] Consequently, in May 2015, 2,500 troops of the Collective Security Treaty Organization (CSTO) conducted operations in Tajikistan that simulated an ISIS attack. The exercise was repeated in September at the CSTO summit in Dushanbe. This time, 95,000 troops were involved in a containment scenario 'of an international armed conflict in the Central Asian strategic direction.'[173] Certainly, the threat of ISIS in Central Asia is exaggerated given the vast distance between the Middle East and Central Asia and the limited appeal of such extreme and brutal methods for Central Asians. Yet as religious repression continues in Tajikistan, ISIS jihadist rhetoric against the enemies of Islam might become attractive.

Tajikistan used to contrast with its neighbours in terms of political and religious pluralism, but repressive practices have now become too prevalent to ignore. In 2012, Markovitz described Tajikistan as a 'soft authoritarian country' in which presidential power and coercive capacity were limited by inadequate access to rents and resources. Even though access to resources has not been improved to a real extent, the ruling Kulobi elite managed to effectively sideline its opponents by invoking the spectre of Islamic violent radicalization.[174] The presence of the IRPT, the only faith-based political party in the whole of Central Asia, has been held up as a positive example of political pragmatism in the post-civil war nation, but the evolution of the situation in recent years tells a different story. It is difficult to foresee what the consequences will be, but this latest case of political repression is yet another manifestation of authoritarian consolidation in Tajikistan. The decision to ban the IRPT is puzzling. Although it is beyond the scope of this book, it seems very unlikely that the party was involved in the attacks allegedly perpetrated by Nazarzoda in September 2015. Banning the country's most substantial opposition party, a party that was mildly critical, yet which gave a voice to Tajik Muslims and which played by the rules, might actually backfire. Cutting all channels that allowed the legitimate expression of dissent – while increasing pressure on believers – may well be counterproductive, in that it may lead the development of an underground opposition that is not as 'loyal' as the IRPT used to be. Robert Dahl's striking citation, 'Opposition that would be loyal if it were tolerated becomes disloyal because it is not tolerated,'[175] accurately depicts the political dynamics that prevail in present-day Central Asia.

This chapter was meant at providing the reader with a thorough description of the political context in a postwar Tajikistan in which the fieldwork was conducted. A context marked by complex and unstable power relationships between the different regions, as exemplified with the conflicts between the authorities and opponents in Gharm or in Badakhshan. As a foreign researcher, I enjoyed relative freedom to conduct interviews and move around freely without any serious problems. Up until 2007, and even more so after 2011, the political situation hardened in Tajikistan and authoritarian practices became more prevalent. In regards to the purpose of this book, the present chapter has also emphasized the clampdown on religious movements and parties, an in particular, the IRPT. As we will see in the next chapter, these authoritarian practices and the overall negative perception of Islam and Islamic actors greatly resonate with Soviet practices.

CHAPTER 4

STATE POLICIES AND DISCOURSES IN INDEPENDENT TAJIKISTAN

As John Schoeberlein underlined, there is a curious contradiction in the fact that observers and scholars inescapably describe Central Asian governments as ineffective and weak but, at the same time, devote a great deal of attention to those same authorities and as a result neglect other relevant social elements.[1] The International Crisis Group has the gloomiest conclusion of all, going as far as describing the Tajik authorities as 'a virtual government in a hollow State.'[2] State policies do not unidirectionally influence the evolution of the religious field but they certainly contribute to shape religious life due to the numerous rules and laws that regulate religion and religious behaviour. As mentioned earlier, there are four aspects of policy that testify of the continuation of Soviet practices in terms of religious management.[3] Two (repression of religious opposition and the assimilation of Islamic forces) were already addressed in the previous chapter and the remaining two (religious administrative structures and regular and Constitutional laws defining the parameters of religious life) represent the focus of this chapter. In this sense, Tajikistan is no different from other post-colonial states that have 'adopted some permutation of religiously neutral and distanced state institutions,' which they see as 'being foundational attributes of their own independence.'[4] The chapter also explores the similarities between Soviet and post-Soviet institutions and discourses by illustrating the authorities' attempt to subordinate religious practices and define an Islam consistent with national ideals.

In terms of organization, the chapter will start with a review of relevant constitutional amendments, followed by the introduction of the two most important laws as well as regulatory institutions that deal with the practice of religion. A second part will survey official discourses and present the dominant orientations of the Tajik leadership. Apart from referring to legal documents, I will integrate elements from fieldwork interviews as an attempt to disaggregate state structures and to question the common conception of the state as a unitary actor. There are indeed multiple levels of authority and my intention is to demonstrate that actors' interests and local contexts matter in the implementation and enforcement of laws that regulate and promote a certain form of secular life. Ultimately, the chapter will also reveal the uncertain separation of state and religion in Tajikistan. Paradoxically, this type of assertive secularism enforced by the authorities combined to the reiterated threat that Islamic groups pose to Tajikistan 'endangers citizens more than it secures them.'[5]

Laws Regulating Religion and Religious Practice

Constitution

The Constitution was adopted in 1994 and amended in 1999 and 2003. The 1999 Constitutional Referendum extended the presidential term from five to seven years while the 2003 amendments extended the number of terms that a Tajik president may hold office, from one to two seven-year periods.[6] Rahmon, who was due to leave office in 2006 but was re-elected in the November 6 election. As mentioned in Chapter 2, a new referendum to approve Constitutional changes was held on May 22, 2016.

Five articles refer to the issue of religion in the Tajik Constitution.[7]

- Article 1. The Republic of Tajikistan shall be a sovereign, democratic, law-based, secular, and unitary state. Being a social-oriented state Tajikistan shall provide relevant living conditions for every person. The names 'Republic of Tajikistan' and 'Tajikistan' shall be equivalent.
- Article 8. In Tajikistan public life shall be developed on the basis of political and ideological diversity. Ideology of any party, social and

religious association, movement, and group shall not be recognized as a state ideology. Social associations and political parties shall be established and function within the framework of the Constitution and laws. Religious organizations shall be separate from the state and shall not interfere in state affairs. The establishment and activity of public associations and political parties which encourage racism, nationalism, social and religious enmity, and hatred, as well as advocate the forcible overthrow of the constitutional state structures and the formation of armed groups, shall be prohibited.

- Article 26. Everyone shall have the right freely to determine his position toward religion, to profess any religion individually or jointly with others, or not to profess any, and to take part in religious customs and ceremonies.

- Article 30. Everyone shall be guaranteed the freedom of speech, publishing, and the right to use means of information. Propaganda and agitation, kindling the social, race, national, religious, and language enmity and hostility shall be prohibited. State censorship and prosecution for criticism shall be prohibited. The law shall specify the list of information constituting a state secret.

Before the 2016 Constitutional referendum, Article 28 guaranteed citizens the right 'to participate in the creation of political parties, including parties of democratic, religious and atheistic character, trade unions, and other public associations, voluntarily affiliate with them and quit.' This was a unique feature in Central Asia's political landscape since neighbouring countries prohibit ethnic and religious parties. This article is the direct consequence of the UN-backed 1997 peace agreement, which terms imposed a power-sharing deal to opposing factions and allowed the integration of the IRPT into state structures. In May 1998, the Parliament, dominated by the President's Popular Democratic Party, proposed a Constitutional amendment that would have forbidden the creation and participation of religious-based political parties. The move infuriated the opposition and the proposed changes were not adopted.[8] Yet, it was implemented in 2016 after the IRPT was banned. In May 2016, Article 8 of the Constitution was amended and now outlaws 'the creation of parties of national and religious character, as well as financing of political parties by foreign states and organizations, foreign legal entities and citizens.'[9]

Overall, provisions of the Tajik Constitution are rather standard and do not reveal much about the current dynamics of state-religion relations. It certainly testifies of the Soviet heritage because in reality, a minority of countries explicitly mention the secular character of the state in their Constitution;[10] those include the five Central Asian countries, but also France and Turkey.[11] Ultimately, even if the state does not endorse an official religion, its neutrality vis-à-vis religious matters is dubious due to numerous laws and decrees that restrict religious practices and because of the trenchant positions espoused by politicians.

Law on Freedom of Conscience and Religious Associations
We find in Tajikistan, as well as in the other Central Asian Republics and Russia, a law called Law on Freedom of Conscience and Religious Associations. Like its earlier Soviet version, the law regulates freedom of religion, and relations between the state and religious communities. Over the years, the law became increasingly detailed and restrictive. Originally adopted in December 1994, the law was amended in 1997, 1999, and 2001. It was profoundly redrafted by the Committee for Religious Affairs in 2006 but adopted only on March 5, 2009. Before and after its adoption, the law was denounced by local and international advocacy organizations as one of the most restrictive laws on religion in the region.[12]

Among the most significant addition is the preamble that enunciates 'the special role of the Hanafi school of Islamic religion in the development of the national culture and spiritual life of the people of Tajikistan.'[13] The text also serves to establish the Hanafi Sunni branch of Islam as the official religious teaching in the country. On the day the law was voted, Mirzoshohrukh Asrori, Minister of Education, told the Parliament that since all religious institutions in the country were registered as belonging to the Hanafi school of jurisprudence, it should be declared the official religious teaching of Tajikistan.[14] This decision, combined with the requirement for religious schools to submit their curriculum to the Committee for Religious Affairs for approval, indicates how the authorities intend to reinforce their control over religious instruction. It is particularly interesting to draw a parallel with the establishment of the Imam al-Bukhari Islamic Institute by the Soviet government in Tashkent in 1971 since Brill Olcott tells us that it served as an instrument of enlightenment albeit on a highly restricted stage and that it restored the Hanafi tradition in the region.[15] Although nothing in the law specifically mentions that the other schools of Islamic jurisprudence are forbidden, in August 2015, Colonel Zikrullo Saidzoda of the Ministry of Internal Affairs, while addressing a crowd of believers in a Dushanbe mosque, warned that Tajiks must stay away from foreign Islamic trends and that those who do not pray according to the principles of the Hanafi branch of Islam could be interrogated.[16]

While Hanafism has been somehow officialized, Article 7 stipulates that in order to preserve state neutrality towards religious associations, state education is secular and religious teachings in public schools can only have an informative character and not be accompanied by religious performances. The law does not outlaw private religious education but Article 8(4) requires that 'teachers' receive a state authorization. Article 8(5) indicates that students from age seven until 18 can receive religious education with the authorization of parents. However, as we will see, the Law on Parental Responsibility contradicts this article and unequivocally forbids minors to take part in religious ceremonies.

In 2006, the first draft of the law generated lots of criticism because of the numerous restrictions to religious practice. The OSCE stated that the new law discriminated against religious minorities. It also noted that it restricted non-registered religious activity, free manifestations of religion or belief, religious activities of non-citizens of the Republic of Tajikistan and the religious rights of minors.[17] Numerous provisions on the regulation of religious practices appear rather intrusive. For instance, the law deals with the number of mosques that can be erected. The law distinguishes between two types of mosques: (1) Friday *Jomhe* mosque (*Sobornaya* in Russian), (2) *Panjvakhta* mosque (*Pyatikratnaya* in Russian) literally, 'five-fold mosque.' Article 11 stipulates that Friday mosques can be created in areas with populations of 10,000 to 20,000 people except for the capital where they may be set up in areas populated by a minimum of 30,000 up to 50,000 inhabitants. In every village with a population of between 100 and 1,000 people local mosques may be set up, while in the capital, they can be erected in areas with a population ranging from 1,000 to 5,000 inhabitants. Finally, the same article stipulates that the selection of imam-khatibs and imams must receive the approval of the responsible state organ, that is, the Committee for Religious Affairs (CRA). This last provision is a measure that unambiguously violates the neutrality of the state as well as undermines the independence of religious communities. By law, the CRA has no right to interfere with the selection of imams. Local communities are responsible for selecting their own imam through negotiation and deliberation. They then send the decision protocol to the local CRA, which will provide the license. However, it appears that the CRA has a say in the choice of imam-khatibs.[18] A representative of the IRPT in Kistakuz mentioned to me the case of an imam who failed to receive a registration because he studied abroad.

Among other controversial provisions, procedures for the registration of mosques and religious associations have been complicated. Also, clauses in Article 33 stipulated that existing religious associations were required to resubmit all necessary documents to seek a re-registration under the new terms of the law before January 1, 2010. Those seeking to register a new organization must provide local authorities with 200 signatures in support of their association. The 200 required signatures thus limits the possibilities for small communities, especially non-Muslim groups, to set up an organization; because of the small number of their adherents, they can hardly gather support from the greater community. This is a restriction that is reminiscent of Soviet practices as authorities considered small groups more suspicious than established religions, because they could not be easily monitored.[19] Proselytism per se is allowed since religious communities have the right to inform people about their faith and beliefs; however according to Article 23(4), they may not do so in state buildings, schools, and private homes, which greatly restrict the capacities of communities to reach out to the public. Finally, Article 9(3) states that public officials, public servants, leaders, and members of political parties cannot fund or be employed by religious groups, which created membership issues for the Islamic Revival Party of Tajikistan.

Minority groups are not the only ones being targeted by the law. There seems to be a bias against Muslim communities since an entire article (11) details the registration and creation of mosques while there is no mention of other places of worships in the text. Surely, it was perceived as such by members of minority religions. In an interview with leaders of the Baptist Church in Khujand in September 2011, religious leaders declared that they did not feel concerned by the law arguing that Christian communities were not the real target. Instead, they saw it as an attempt to temper rapid islamization. There was indeed a certain laissez-faire regarding their activities. There were a total of

15 functioning Baptist Churches in the country but only six of them were officially registered. For instance, the pastor in Khujand mentioned that the Church in Taboshar had no registration but held regular meetings in their office located right in front of the local KGB office. As mentioned earlier, Taboshar used to be a restricted town because of the presence of a factory producing missile parts in Soviet times. The town, which used to be populated mostly by Russians, now resembles a ghost town plagued with water supply problems, exceptionally high unemployment rates, and alcoholism problems. The Baptist pastor in Dushanbe explained this tolerance due to the particularity of the dire town: 'A lot of people have left, the town is in bad shape and they want people to stay there, not chase them away. It is also a human factor, they see how people live there and they know the Church helps the community.' Local conditions can also hinder registration efforts of small communities. The pastor mentioned that in some places, local authorities are hesitant to provide legal documents necessary for registration because they are under pressure from a neighbourhood which is hostile to non-Islamic groups. In 2004, a Baptist pastor was shot dead in Isfara. He was allegedly killed by Islamic extremists.[20] He reckons that most of the time, bureaucrats' incompetence represents the core of the problem. However, right after the adoption of the Law on Parental Responsibility in November, the church in Taboshar was closed down after an intrusive visit of the KGB because of the 'illegal' presence of children. Agents were reportedly filming people who were present at the Church but did not arrest anyone. Confusion in the implementation of the law also comes from the fact that religious communities as well as law enforcement bodies are not always up-to-date with legal and administrative changes.[21]

Interviews with members of religious associations revealed that registering a religious association can be arduous. In 2010, the Hukumat refused to register a Baptist church in Chkalovsk even though the Church had been operating without registration for years with the blessing of the previous mayor. Another imam from the region of Mastchox I talked to also said he previously was teaching children but had to stop his activities due to the law. He prepared all documents but was denied registration on administrative accounts. He reported that: 'They make problems all the time, they will deny registration for a comma at the wrong place.' The medresse in Buston suffered the same fate, although what really happened remains unclear. The case perfectly exemplifies the complexity of social science research since I collected many different accounts from a one-day visit to the town but lacked information to put all the pieces together. When I visited the medresse in June 2011, it was under renovation and was non-functional. An imam, who used to work there as a teacher, explained that the CRA denied the re-registration due to some administrative issues. He was therefore trying to improve the facilities to welcome more students in the future. However, during my visit, a man who identified himself as the 'caretaker' of the medresse came up to me in private and told me I should not trust the imam. He explained that the medresse was closed down because this imam was unqualified and no one wanted to study there. Afterwards, at the local Hukumat, the representative of the Ideology Department told me that: 'They closed the medresse because the conditions there were bad, they had nothing to offer to students. This imam wanted to open his own place, do something for himself and not for the benefit of students.' Notwithstanding the real reason behind the closure, the actors' narratives indicated that perhaps local power politics were being played out. However, because the case is not an isolated one, it is most probably part of a concerted action to limit access to religious education.

Religious education

In September 2009, a new course on Islam, called Knowledge of Islam (*Ma'rifati Islom*) became mandatory for schoolchildren. Hoji Akbar Turajonzoda strongly reacted to the release of new textbooks, saying in a open letter to the media that he was 'outraged and appalled' that revelations in the Qur'an were presented as some sort of political agreement reached between the prophet and tribe leaders in Mecca. 'Even Soviet-era textbooks, which were openly atheistic, didn't deny historical facts like our current authors do.' He accused old-fashioned Soviet-era atheist government officials of taking part in a wide government campaign to restrict the increasing influence of Islam in Tajik society.[22] Members of the Council of Ulemas also expressed their regret that the Ministry did not consult religious leaders for the elaboration of the new textbooks.[23] Ultimately, religious classes were cancelled only few months after they were introduced and replaced by a course called 'History of the Tajik people.'[24] In the course of my fieldwork, I asked school principals, teachers, and students a number of times as to why religious classes were removed from the curriculum but no one could tell for certain why they stopped.

On many occasions, the President has denounced religious education and its perverse effect on radicalization.[25] Lutfiya Roibova, a representative of the regional Department of Education accused imams of 'inculcating pupils with superstitions.'[26] Already in 2007, President Rahmon had blamed 'parents who bring their child to a half-educated mullah, and with a stick he tells them to learn the Qur'an by heart.'[27] The number of religious education institutions has greatly decreased over the years. In 2003, the Islamic Institute in Dushanbe as well as 21 medresses were responsible for providing religious teachings.[28] In July 2011, there were only five officially registered medresses whereas there were ten in 2010.[29] Also, in June 2011, a special police operation, called 'Operation medresse' in the Sughd viloyat, led to the inspection of eight local medresses, 93 Friday mosques and 955 other mosques and resulted in the closing of 11 illegal religious institutions.[30] A similar operation in the Kathlon viloyat resulted in the closing of 47 illegal schools in which almost 400 students studied.[31]

Finally, in the summer of 2013, the authorities suspended five of the country's six remaining medresses, which were all located in Sughd. The CRA invoked that they failed to provide proper documents for registration.[32] As such, the Medresse Abu Hanifa in Dushanbe, a joint project between the Tajik and Swiss governments, is now the country's only functioning medresse but its future operation is now jeopardized. In June 2015, a Dushanbe court ordered the transfer of responsibility of the medresse's building to the Pedagogical Univesity, which will turn it into student residences.[33]

The Ministry of Education is responsible for approving the medresses' curricula, which should include secular topics and languages in addition to Islamic courses. Medresses do not receive any state funding but tuitions fees are not very high in comparison to Universities. Tuition fees at the Khujand medresse were $100 per year whereas University fees can reach $1000 depending on the institution. Students can enter after completing the ninth grade.[34] After following a three-year course, male students receive a diploma, as teacher and imam-khatib. Female students receive an attestation that they finished a two-year course at the medresse. However, the Ministry of Education does not recognize the

Figure 4.1   2011 view from the Panjshanbe bazaar in Khujand of the Sheikh Maslikhatdin mosque, mausoleum and the medresse project that was never completed. Credit: Hélène Thibault.

diplomas issued by medresses. If most men have the possibility to be employed in a mosque, women cannot expect much from their degree. In fact, it seems that many girls who study in medresses do not do so to increase their employment opportunities but simply 'to study Islam more deeply' and many women suggest that they do so to become good mothers.[35] Women at the IRPT insisted that contrary to popular interpretation, the Qur'an actually encourages women to get educated since women should hold important positions in society and not only stay at home. Yet, they were very keen to mention to me that my studies were important because it meant that I would later be able to raise my kids the right way, also suggesting that I would convert to Islam eventually and raise them in faith. As a matter of fact, the Director of the medresse in Khujand admitted that many girls do not complete the whole training because they are not allowed by their in-laws to finish their studies once they get married. This situation is also common in secular institutions.

The Tajik Islamic State Institute is an institution of higher education that was established with the support of a special state fund in November 2007 following a decree of the Tajik President on October 30.[36] The decision was to broaden the curriculum of the Tajik Islamic University Imama at-Termizi, created in 1991, by including secular topics such as humanities and mathematics.[37] In March 2009, a Presidential decree renamed the Islamic Institute as the Imomi Azam Tajik Islamic Institute. The full name in Tajik is: Imomi Azam Abuxanify Numan ibn Sabit. This coincides with the announcement that the Year 2009 in Tajikistan was dedicated to the Great Imam, 'Imomi Azam' or 'Abu Hanifa,' a medieval Islamic thinker and founder of the Sunni Hanafi school of Islamic jurisprudence.[38] In 2010, it switched from being under the authority of the Ministry of Education of Tajikistan to the authority of the Committee for Religious Affairs. In 2010, it also received full recognition from the Ministry of Education and diplomas are now recognized by state authorities in the same way as diplomas delivered from secular universities.[39] Therefore, students, especially women, can expect to find jobs in schools or state agencies more easily. As of January 2013, there were 1,342 full-time students and 585 studying by correspondence. The Institute has 156 teachers, including five foreigners.[40]

Limited access to religious education certainly contributes to the popularity of foreign Islamic institutions. However, many religious figures as well as political figures complain that the level of theological knowledge is very poor and that this encourages students to pursue their studies abroad.[41] Even the Consultative Council of the Muftis of the CIS is of this opinion and suggested that the Council should take measures to raise the level of education of religious leaders.[42] Perhaps more importantly, mullahs are not necessarily equipped to answer the questions and provide guidance to young people who have 'modern' spiritual concerns.[43] During the numerous focus groups and round-tables on radicalism I attended in the course of my fieldwork, the poor knowledge of 'self-taught' imams and, consequently, the lack of respect they inspire, were identified as one of the main reasons as to why people fall for radical leaders. In comparison, 'foreign-taught' individuals appear more articulated and knowledgeable to the general public.

The shortage of qualified and respected clerics encourages a growing number of Tajiks to pursue their studies in different Islamic countries. In the summer of 2010, I asked the Director of the Sheikh Maslikhatdin medresse in Khujand, Orifjon Baiizoyev, whether or not he saw differences between the Islam taught in Tajikistan and in foreign countries. In his opinion, there was no need to go abroad because true Hanafi Islam was taught in Tajikistan. On the contrary, he said, 'when you go abroad, you are spoiling your own traditions and the Hanafi mazhab. Foreign sheiks teach their own mazhab, they provide food and money but their teachings are different and when our students come back, they have changed and conflicts arise.' He suggested that some of the pupils study abroad as 'partisans,' implying that they monitor other students' whereabouts. Baiizoyev mentioned that when they come back, the KGB asks them where they have been and why, and so on. 'It's the right of a government to ask where its citizens have been what they have been doing and what they plan to do next.'

The authorities' inclination to control religious education exceeds national borders and a year later, movements of Tajik students abroad have severely been curtailed. Concern over foreign education became especially salient after a Presidential speech in August 2010 in which Emomali Rahmon urged parents to 'bring their children home.' According to him: 'Most of them will become extremists and terrorists, because those schools don't only teach religion.'[44] Beyond fears of radicalization, the Law on Freedom of Conscience actually stipulates that Tajik citizens may pursue religious studies only after receiving religious education in the Republic of Tajikistan and with the written consent of authorized state bodies on matters of religion and education (Article 8(6)). Following the President's plea, Tajik authorities forced the return of hundreds of Tajiks who were studying in foreign medresses or Islamic Universities. Families of students were allegedly pressured by security enforcement agencies to urge their offspring to come back,[45] after which some of them also had to face prosecution.[46] Tightening measures rose to the point where the authorities prevented in extremis aspiring students from boarding a plane at the Dushanbe airport prior to its departure to Iran.[47]

Returnees and their families were promised help to find a job or a position in an educational institution but it seems that these promises were not kept. A year later, disillusion was palpable. In 2010, there were reportedly 2,413 Tajik citizens studying in Islamic countries, though not necessarily enrolled in religious programmes. As of September 2011, almost 2,000 students were back in Tajikistan. According to head of the Department of Education of the Committee for Religious Affairs Idibeka Zieaeva, of those returnee students, 129 were enrolled in the local educational institutions, 67 in public schools, 57 in various universities, and only eight in medresses.[48]

Law on Parental Responsibility in the Upbringing and Education of Children[49]

Years of rhetorical attacks and warnings against extremist elements finally led to the elaboration of this controversial law that deals with the education of children. The law drew lots of criticisms and the Communist Party of Tajikistan seems to have been the only opposition party in favour of the new legislation. The Communist leadership commented on the interdiction to let minors attend religious prayers at the mosque in such terms: 'We have students who leave aside their studies to hurry to the mosque, the state must necessarily respond to this.'[50] Such discourses are pervasive in Tajikistan and carry a negative tone that is reminiscent of Soviet anti-religious propaganda.

The Law was adopted on August 3, 2011 and came into force on August 6.[51] It coincided with the beginning of Ramadan and the timing was considered doubly offensive by many detractors. Yet, the government claimed to have received 4,000 comments of support for the law.[52] It is plausible that an important portion of the population supported the initiative given that popular discourses often refer to the loss of values among the youth and the need to educate younger generations. Mavjuda Mirchopoeva from the CRA in Sughd expressed this concern by saying that civility was really an issue and that people were not as respectful of authority, laws, and elders as much they were before. To others, this law is a sign that policy-making in Tajikistan has reached high levels of absurdity.[53] In an interview with members of the IRPT in Khujand, one man in his early 30s expressed this opinion in such terms: 'People in power are proud to say that we have 3,000 years old traditions, yet they think that we don't know how to properly raise our children. Did they really have to adopt such law? It's ridiculous.' Indeed, earlier that year, the leader of the Parliamentary Committee on Education, Marxabo Dzhabborova, declared in an interview that the law was necessary because: 'millions of parents do not pay attention to their children.'[54]

Article 8, entitled 'Parental education duties' is the one that sparked the strongest critique. Its most contentious provision forbids parents to let children participate in the affairs of religious associations at the exception of those who are officially enrolled in religious education institutions. Basically, this provision forbids minors to attend prayers at the mosque. In the opinion of many, this article not only contradicts other national laws but the Constitution as well as international legal texts.[55] Responding to critiques made by the US delegation at the 870th OSCE Permanent Council Meeting, Tajik authorities stressed that the unstable situation in neighbouring countries requires that the government address 'violent extremism and radicalization' and that 'the proposed law, by setting a minimum age for attending the mosque, can effectively protect children from the growing religious pressure to which they have been subjected during the past few years.'[56]

The Head of the Committee for Religious Affairs (CRA) in Khujand, Mavjuda Mirchopoeva, described the law as a truly 'national law.' Commenting on the prohibition for minors to attend religious services, she said that: 'instead of wasting their time at the mosque, children should do something more educative. Anyway, they can still read the Qur'an at home.' In contrast, a representative of the CRA in Isfara brought up the topic of the controversial law by showing me some passages of both laws on Freedom of Conscience and Parental Responsibility, which contradict each other. He expressed regrets that young people could not receive proper Islamic education, something that, in his opinion, could prevent radicalization. In any case, he thought that people would find other ways to be taught 'secretly, just like we did in Soviet times.' This state representative is the only one interviewed who openly criticized the law. Interestingly, he is one of the few apparatchiki to hold an Islamic degree.

Yet, even at the CRA's Central Office in Dushanbe, the Head of the Department of Education, Saiivali Khimmatov, agreed that the Law on Parental Responsibility contradicts the one on Freedom of Conscience and he did not know why the Parliament adopted such law. In any case, he underlined that children can nevertheless study the Qur'an at home. Finally, when I asked the Head of Shuroi Ulamo in Sughd about Article 8 that prohibits children from participating in religious ceremonies, he did not disagree nor approve but said that it was still possible to lobby even if the law had been adopted. Interviews reveal a lack of consensus among stakeholders who do not necessarily agree with directives but won't necessarily try to provoke changes.

Moreover, my observations indicate that the enforcement of the prohibition of children to attend religious ceremonies was not done systematically. In Khujand, it was carried out in very few places and seemed to have been limited to Khujand's Sheik Maslikhatdin main mosque. Whereas the Baptist Church in Taboshar was shut down due to lack of proper registration, the one in Khujand had not been visited by police forces even three months after the adoption of the law and many children were present at the Sunday mass when I attended the service in November 2011. However, stories on the monitoring of mosques circulated at this period and few cases were reported in the media.[57] Overall, it seems that authorities were not able to allocate sufficient resources to systematically control Sughd's thousand of places of worship and monitor children's whereabouts.

Other controversial articles include provisions about the transmission of 'national values.' In particular, Article 8 invites parents or tutors to give children names with 'national consonance.' Already in 1990, while the opposition demanded the promotion of national religious and language traditions, the Communist Party's First Secretary had set up a committee composed of historians and linguists to produce a list of non-religious patriotic names.[58] In January 2016, the authorities carried the idea further and the Parliament voted in favour of amendments to the country's Civil Registration law in order to forbid the registration of names considered too Arabic. From now on, registry offices will not register names that are alien to the local culture, names denoting objects, flora, and fauna, as well as names of Arabic origin. Interestingly, the changes apply to ethnic Tajiks only and not to other minorities such as Russians and Uzbeks, even though the latter are Muslims as well.[59] Also, in 2007, the president dropped the Russian suffix 'ov' from his last name and encouraged the population to do so in order to get rid of Russian/ Soviet influences.[60] Yet, the use of Russian endings in family names is still the norm in Tajikistan.

Most importantly, the Law on Parental Responsibility holds parents responsible for raising children 'in the spirit of the love and respect for the Motherland and national values.' This is again reminiscent of Soviet practices that meant to produce loyal subjects. For instance, Article 66 of the Soviet Constitution stipulated: 'Citizens of the USSR are to be concerned with the upbringing of children, to train them for socially useful work, and to raise them as worthy members of socialist society.' Other articles are greatly interfering with parenting. For instance, parents should forbid children to carry cell-phones to school, wear jewellery, and let children under 20 years old (even though the legal age is 18) go out at night in 'entertainment centres' such as internet cafes and bars. There is no doubt that these laws are patronizing but it is so intrusive and necessitates so many resources that authorities can hardly fully implement them. Though, as we will see next, the authorities did not hesitate to infringe on the rights of many believers they perceived were acting contrary to the religious behviour deemed acceptable and patriotic. To some extent, the Tajik paternalist state has replaced the Soviet totalitarian one. Not it in its brutal methods but in the sense that both dictate citizens the proper way to live their lives, in line with the convened nationalist secular ideology promoted by the state.

Institutions of Regulation

In Tajikistan, the presence of institutions such as the Islamic Center and the Council of Ulemas[61] and the Committee for Religious Affairs, heir to the Soviet Qaziat and the Soviet Committee for Religious, affairs also clearly illustrate the institutional continuity with the Soviet period.[62] The Council is more concerned with the spiritual aspects of religious life and training whereas the Committee is a governmental body enforcing the laws regulating religious practice. Just like in Soviet times, these institutions are not perceived as independent and often criticized for following the official party line. Another element of similarity is found in the marginalization of the Council of Ulemas in the administration of religious celebrations and ceremonies at the profit of state organs, such as the Committee of Religious Affairs (CRA). The CRA's responsibility have indeed been extended to include the registration of cult sites, the registration and renumeration of imams, as well as the preparation of the Friday sermons.

The Council of Ulemas and the Islamic Center

Appointed Qazi Kalon (Supreme judge of the Qaziat) after the dissolution of the SADUM in 1988, Hoji Akbar Turajonzoda was dismissed in 1992.[63] It led to the reorganization of the institution in a Muftiate in 1993, and the nomination of Hoji Fathulloh Khon Sharifzoda at its head. In January 1993, Rahmon transformed the Qaziat in a Muftiate and nominated a pro-government cleric at his head. This decision can be interpreted as a first step for the control of religious affairs in the republic.[64] After the brutal murder of Sharifzoda and his family in January 1996, the institution went through another transformation and the Muftiate was renamed into the Council of Ulemas in June 1996.[65] Hoji Amunullo Negmatzoda has occupied the function of President of the Council from 1996 until his death in 2010. In October 2010 the Council elected a new Mufti, Saidmukarram Abdukodirzoda, a 47-year-old graduate of the International Islamic University in Islamabad, who had previously worked as the Head of Religious examinations at the CRA.[66]

The 27 members of the Council have the responsibility to guide the population in accordance to the fundamentals of the Hanafi tradition, to regulate Islamic institutions, to train and attest imams, to oversee the import of religious literature in the country, to develop education curricula, and to nominate the Mufti who serves for seven years. The Council is also the only legitimate organ to emit fatwas. The Islamic Center (*Markazi Islomi*) is the administrative counterpart of the Council of Ulemas. It includes the General Assembly of the Founders, the Presidium of the Islamic Center, the Council of Ulemas, the President of the Islamic Center, the first deputy chairman, vice-chairman, secretary, and other administrative staff. It is responsible for monitoring the country's medresses and the Islamic University. The Head Office is in Dushanbe but there are regional offices in the three provinces as well.[67]

In the early 2000s, the government started to express its concern over the qualification of imams as well as over the issue of their political affiliation. In August 2002, together with the Council of Ulemas, the State Committee for Religious Affairs imposed religious tests on imams to assess their knowledge and prove their fitness for the job.[68] Yet, it appears that testing was not consistent over the years and tests administered only sporadically.[69] However, after years of discussion around the qualification of imams, a training centre for imams was established within the Islamic Institute in 2012.[70] There are surely lacunae in Tajik clerics' religious knowledge as it is estimated that almost 90 per cent of rural clergy do not have any formal religious education.[71] Even though the imposition of tests gives the authorities another opportunity to dismiss undesirable elements,[72] in Sughd, only 45 imams out of 991 failed the test after the first round of testing in 2011.[73]

The government is keeping a close eye on the activities of the mosques and imams are expected to convey messages of patriotism and unity instead of radical ideas.[74] The implementation of a measure concerning the salaries of imams confirmed the executive character of the CRA. In July 2013, at the occasion of a special meeting between the President and stakeholders involved in religious issues, the President asked the CRA to think of a way to remunerate imams in order to avoid their dependence on foreign revenues.[75] The Head of the CRA, Abdurahim Kholikov, supported the initiative. In his opinion, it does not contradict the laws of Tajikistan since according to the Constitution and the Law on Freedom of Conscience, the state has the right to help religious associations.[76] In the spring 2014, nearly 400 imams started receiving their salaries from the government, a sum of approximately $300 per month, which is higher than the average Tajik salary.[77]

In 2011, the Council of Ulemas announced that it would release a list of 52 topics, prepared in collaboration with the CRA. According to the Regional Head of the Council of Ulemas in Sughd, the initiative was allegedly motivated by the desire to support imams-khatibs with poor knowledge of Islamic scriptures to deliver their sermons. In May 2013, imam-khatibs were instructed to explain and retransmit a Presidential speech dedicated to issues of domestic and foreign policy.[78] In January 2014, the CRA announced the introduction of uniforms and dress codes for imams as well as the release of a 300-page manual containing 45 sermon topics for Friday mosques. The CRA and the Council of Ulemas approved the uniforms which consist 'of a grey satin shirt, trousers, a turban, and a long powder-blue robe highlighted by traditional white embroidery on the cuffs, lapels, and front trim' that will include 'national elements.'[79]

Disavowal of the Council of Ulemas and accusations of its connivance with state authorities are common in Tajikistan and facts could hardly rebuff these accusations. The Council did not oppose most restrictive measures infringing the free practice of religion such as the ban of hijabs in schools, of beards and Islamic dresses in the Islamic Institute, and the prohibition for people under 18 to attend Friday prayers. In some case, they received the Council's approval through fatwas. I will address these issues at greater length further in the book, in Chapter 5. The implication of the Council of Ulemas in political intrigues became more obvious with the eruption of a public dispute involving the Mufti and the Turajonzoda family. On December 9, 2011, the Mufti Saidmukarram Abdukodirzoda accused the Turajonzoda brothers of performing the Ashura, a Shiite religious celebration, in their popular Muhammadya mosque in Turkobod. As such, they were accused of violating the terms of their own Sunni religious association. Alerted by this accusation, the CRA then looked into the affairs of the mosque and as a consequence revoked the license of the imam-khatib Muhamadjon Turajonzoda and nominated one of his assistants to the position only one week after the incident allegedly took place.[80] The mosque was shut down for three months in December 2011[81] and its status was downgraded from a *Jomhe* mosque to *Panjvakhta* mosque after being reopened.[82] The Turajonzoda brothers denounced this as a politically motivated accusation due to the fact that the eldest brother Nuriddin is vocal about his opposition to the government.[83] Already in 2008, he had been warned to not make 'anti-democratic' speeches.[84]

As the Turajonzodas' case demonstrates, the affairs of the Council of Ulemas and the Committee for Religious Affairs are so intrinsically connected that it seriously questions the Council's independence. Khalid argues that the Islamic Centre is 'completely subordinate' to the government[85] and many critics have also denounced its subjection.[86] Responding to such critics, a member of the Council Ismail Muhamadzoda and imam of the main mosque in Gissar, stated: 'Luckily God has sent us a president like Emomali Rahmonov. Thanks to our president, Tajik Muslims enjoy full rights.'[87] Yet, Saiivali Khimmatov from the CRA claims that the Council of Ulemas is independent and works in collaboration with the CRA. For instance, in the preparation of prayer guidebooks for imams, the Council gives recommendations and the CRA approves. Still, the interconnection is undeniable and interestingly, authorities do not deny the control exerted over the Council. It is in fact presented as a necessary measure to protect Islam against deviances. On that matter, the words of the President of Tajikistan, Emomali Rahmon are unequivocal:

> The state in the framework of the acting legislation has authority to oversight activities of religious organizations in order to protect peace, stability, noble birth and cultural values of the people in the country. The direct obligation of the Islamic Centre and the Council of Ulemas of Tajikistan is to consider their sermons and moral admonitions. Therefore, it is the obligation of the concerned state government bodies to consider the cases when such sermons

and moral admonitions contradict to the Constitution and other
acting laws of Tajikistan.[88]

Cooptation of the clergy is reminiscent of past practices and shows
how the clergy can be mobilized to convey the ideology proposed by
leading political circles. It is through the control over their training,
assignment, and their speeches that the state can communicate preferred
religious beliefs and orientations. In an OSCE-led survey, only 8 per cent
of respondents declared that they would turn to representatives of the
Council of Ulemas if they faced a problem of religious nature, as opposed
to 42 per cent who would turn to local mullahs.[89] The Council does not
appear to be well connected to local clergy members as well as to
parishioners' realities. Epkenhans suggests that: 'The Islamic Centre
does not engage local and regional religious leaders in order to facilitate a
debate on doctrinal normativity, religious practice and eventually the
role of Islam in Tajikistan's society.'[90] The Consultative Council of the
Mufti of the Commonwealth of Independent States also acknowledged
that religious authorities should strengthen their relations with citizens,
especially youth, as well as intensify their dialogue with regional, local,
and state authorities.[91]

   In Sughd, most people I talked to knew who the regional Head of the
Council of Ulemas was. Yet, the Council's presence and involvement in
the community appeared to be negligible and limited to sporadic
television appearances on special occasions such as the Ramadan, Idi Fitr,
and Idi-Qurbon. When I asked an IRPT member from the Bobojon-
Gaffurov district what he thought of the role of the Council, he declared
that it was there 'to manipulate people' into adopting certain behaviours
that are not even Islamic, for instance, rejecting the hijab. He compared
the lack of legitimacy of the current religious leadership to the one of
SADUM. He recalls that Soviet-era mullahs were often 'set-up' by KGB
who were taking their pictures with people who were drinking alcohol
and which were then published in newspapers to discredit the Islamic
clergy. He said: 'And now this Musuzoda [Hoji Hussein Musuzoda,
Head of the Council of Ulemas in Sughd] sometimes finds himself
sitting among people who drink and does not even care!' He reported
another anecdote involving Musuzoda at a meeting in the regional
Hukumat, during which the death of a former colleague was announced.
According to tradition, the cleric should have said a few words about the

deceased but Musuzoda did not intervene, which apparently created a malaise in the audience. Like the SADUM in Soviet times, the Council of Ulemas does not enjoy much legitimacy and appear to be disconnected from local religious life. Presumed cooptation definitely impedes the confidence the population might have in the spiritual authority.

The Committee for Religious Affairs[92]

The Committee for Religious Affairs is a governmental body enforcing the laws regulating the registration of religious communities, religious education and private religious practices. This institution's very name and functions testify of its likeness to the Soviet institutions and similar structures are found in many of the former Soviet republics, including Russia and the Central Asian republics. Advocacy organizations report that the Committee for Religious Affairs stands as an executive body and that real policy is formulated in the President's office.[93] As part of a ministerial reshuffling following the November 2006 Presidential election, the government dissolved the State Committee for Religious Affairs (SCRA) and established the Department for Religious Affairs (DRA) under the Ministry of Culture. The SCRA's Chairman was appointed Deputy Minister of Culture.[94] In May 2010, it became an independent body as a result of two separate developments: the fusion of the Department for religious affairs with the one on culture and traditions and the nomination of Aburahim Kholikov as Chairman until February 2015, when Davlatzoda Solomon Pirkhon replaced him.

It is represented by the Central Office in Dushanbe as well as by departments in the three viloyats and in various towns and jamoats. There are three directions: (1) regulation of traditions, (2) religious expertise/audit of religious literature, and (3) religious institutions. The Committee for Religious Affairs operates according to two laws on Freedom of Conscience and Religious Associations and on Traditions, Celebrations and Ceremonies, to the extent that this law regulates traditionally religious ceremonies such as weddings, circumcisions, and burials. The latter law also raised a lot of criticism because of its strict regulation of social and traditional gatherings. For instance, it specifies the maximum number of guests for celebrations, rites that be performed, what gifts can be offered, and so on. Weddings can have up to 150 attendees, while burial ceremonies can be organized strictly on the fourth day and serve 80 guests one meal only. Celebrations for the return of pilgrims and birthdays can only be celebrated in private.[95] Before the adoption of the law, Rahmon criticized the fact that rites were often not conducted according to the provisions of Sharia but instead represented an arrogant display of wealth.[96] This is a position that recalls Soviet criticism of religious celebrations as mentioned in Chapter 3. In Central Asian societies, people are known to organize oversized costly ceremonies and families often feel pressured to conform to social norms. As a result, many get loans or send family members, mostly men, to labour migration in order to cover the expenses of such costly celebrations. Overall, many citizens welcomed the law since it relieves many families from an important financial burden.

The resolution on the creation of the CRA displays an extensive list of responsibilities for the Committee that is too long to be reproduced here in totality. In my interviews with representatives of the CRA, the main responsibilities that were mentioned were: the registration of mosques and medresses and the organization of the annual pilgrimage to Mecca. In Soviet times, less than a dozen individuals were allowed to perform the Hajj every year. Today, Saudi Arabia's annual quota for Tajikistan, which is of nearly 5,500 persons, is always reached. While, in most countries, the pilgrimage is arranged through private accredited travel agencies, in Tajikistan, the CRA organizes and plans the whole journey for a fixed amount of around US$3,500.[97] Depending on their place of living, pilgrims depart in charter flights from Dushanbe, Kurgan-Tyube, and Khujand. In 2011, the CRA started to impose a uniform to pilgrims: a light blue knee-long blouse and trousers with a Tajik flag sowed on it.[98] In April 2015, it announced that citizens younger than 35 could not undertake the Hajj. The CRA explained that it wanted to give older Tajiks the opportunity to do the pilgrimage, since Saudi Arabia limits the number of pilgrims for each country.[99] Overall, the Committee for Religious Affairs has increased its influence on religious life by approving the nomination of imams, the erection of mosques, by preparing a list of approved or suggested topics for Friday sermons and by delivering permits for citizens who wish to organize private religious classes.

Altogether, the laws and policies that deal with the regulation of religion appear to be restrictive and in many ways contradict the alleged neutrality of the state. The recognition of the Hanafi mazhab as the official teaching in religious institutions neglects to acknowledge the presence of minority religions such as Ismailism, practised by the majority of Pamir's inhabitants as well as Christianism and other religions. The Law on Freedom of Conscience and Religious Associations also gives the state plenty of possibilities to interfere in the affairs of religious associations, once again violating the principle of separation of religion and state. Regardless of the severity of the law, its application seems in some cases to be depending on local dynamics, either favouring or hindering religious associations. In some sense, Tajik secularism fits the *assertive secularism* ideal-type proposed by Kuru in which 'the state excludes religion from the public sphere and plays an "assertive" role as the agent of a social engineering project that confines religion to the private domain.'[100] Turkey and France are considered as good examples of assertive secularism. This type of 'regime' emerged as the result of ideological struggles between old and new forces and especially influenced by the presence or absence of an *ancien régime* based on monarchy and hegemonic religion, which was the case in both those countries. Though they were not driven by an atheist ideology, these states' colossal efforts to reduce the influence of the clergy and of religion in general is also part of a social engineering project meant at transforming the society. What is remarkable in Tajikistan is the fact that the legacy of the Soviet Union holds very strong. Even though atheism has been discarded, the Tajik state's institutions aim not only at controlling and limiting the importance of religion at the state level, but also at the society level by restricting the access to places of worship so much as to dictate the way citizens should practise their religion. In that sense, the Law on Parental Responsibility directly interferes with the private life of Tajik citizens by forbidding minors to participate in religious ceremonies and instruct parents on the right way to raise their children. Again, what we see here is a strong resemblance with Soviet politics that aimed at fostering a loyal communist community. The promotion of a specific type of believer and citizen, that is both pious and loyal to the state, will be detailed in the upcoming chapters.

Interestingly, the state interference in religious affairs does not seem to represent a particular problem for many clerics, including representatives of the IRPT. Muhiddin Kabiri, has described the issue of the continuation of Soviet practices in such terms: 'We are so used to debate according to different categories that it becomes a problem. We have built our religious institutions on the basis of different religions. And that is why inside our very Tajik state, we should start defining with our own categories and religions.'[101] In the above-statement, Kabiri deplores the remaining Soviet influence but does not question the state's involvement in defining religiousness. Similarly, at a conference on state-religious dialogue, held in Dushanbe in December 2011, clerics and representatives of the IRPT demonstrated their commitment to the state's engagement in regulating religious issues. This is also what emanated from the discussions I witnessed during numerous workshops and round-tables; the state is expected to get involved. It is seen as a solution to ease social tensions, especially in terms of religious education, which is perceived as a glaring problem in Tajikistan. There seems to be a unanimous position among clerics, IRPT and NGO representatives, and education professionals that improvement in religious teachings is a solution to a plethora of social problems. That management extends to the definitions of boundaries regarding the proper manifestation of religious behaviour.

The Patriotic Muslim

Following Panchenko's recommendation,[102] I investigate the cultural resources used for the elaboration of institutional and public discourses of morality, what it means to be Muslim while remaning a loyal citizen. Such recurrent patronizing state discourses are used to define and impose a proper behaviour in line with an idealized conception of a secular and moral society. Again, these narratives are seen in light of the continuities between Soviet and post-Soviet practices. I will first introduce the legal and discursive aspects of the hijab ban and contrast them with accounts from ordinary citizens as yet another way to represent the multiplicity of positions regarding the place of religion in the society. I will also consider to a lesser extent controversies over the interdiction of long beards for Muslim men. Finally, I will discuss how citizens' virtue, especially that of women, has not only become associated with the perpetuation of national culture and values, but reveals the difficulties of nation-building in Tajikistan.

The Hijab Issue

None of the issues connected with the practice of religion better illustrates the battle for the establishment of moral standards than the debate surrounding the hijab ban. In the early years of the Bolshevik revolution, the liberation of women from centuries-old patriarchal oppression was a priority for the Soviet authorities. The promotion of women's rights in Soviet Central Asia had two objectives: to ensure the equality of rights for men and women, and, perhaps even more importantly, to undermine the Islamic clergy and religious traditions. The *Hujum*, the brutal unveiling campaign of women that started in 1927, was an important step in the secularization project. Today, dressing up has become once more a patriotic affair in Tajikistan. As the hijab gains in popularity, female clothing and, more broadly, the female persona, have come to embody the secular and progressive character of the nation. Yet, if women are accused of propagating extremist ideas if they wear a hijab, they are also criticized for dressing up in 'sexy' European clothes that also betray national values. To a lesser extent, men's appearance, especially the beard, also falls under state scrutiny.

Up until the independence in 1991, few Central Asian women wore the hijab. It was tolerated by society at large for older women but rarely worn by younger ones. Today, it is difficult to assess the proportion of veiled women in Tajikistan but it represents a growing minority. Khujand-based imam-khatib Kalonzoda acknowledged a generational gap in terms of religiosity. The conversation reported here took place in the presence of a friend of mine who was a familiar of the imam. Both were in their mid-50s. He conceded: 'Me and her, we are half-Soviet. I've been telling her to wear a hijab[103] for the last ten years but she can't do it. Now ask a 20-year-old girl to take off her veil, she will never agree to it, even for money. The new generation is clearly different.' However, the narratives I will present later demonstrate that the generational gap is not that pronounced. Indeed, many of the strict believers had been socialized in Soviet times and had not been concerned with religion until very recently. Though the hijab is often portrayed in the media as backward and foreign, many women's decision to wear it is 'in line with new visions of modernity.'[104]

Hijabs have become common in conservative regions such as the Isfara or Matschox districts in Sughd, but are also in fashion in the capital city and less so in the city of Khujand, for instance. Highly conservative women wear hijabs that cover their head and neck with ample dark robes. However, most wear it over 'traditional' Tajik dresses, the long and loose colourful dresses worn over baggy pants. Others, inspired by Turkish Islamic fashion, wear it in a very stylish way by carefully matching colours and textures, meticulously wrapping the veil, and not refraining from wearing heavy makeup. Indeed, beyond religious considerations, hijabs also fall under a certain oriental fashion trend. Sights of women who wear niqabs, which cover the entire face except the eyes, are very rare; in fact, I have seen only three women in all of Tajikistan wearing it. When I asked Mera, who was always wore a hijab and conservative dark robes, about her views on the niqab, she argued that no one in Tajikistan could wear that because 'people would stare and gossip too much.' Interestingly, she promptly alluded to potential social intimidation and left aside the religious aspect of the niqab, whether it is desirable in Islam or not.

A negative campaign against the hijab started in the mid-2000s and became more aggressive over the years with cases of veiled women being harassed in public spaces. One of the most prominent forerunners of the anti-hijab campaign was Abdudjabbor Rahmonov, the Minister of Education from 2005 to 2012. Not long after his nomination, he stated that wearing the hijab and other religious symbols 'is unacceptable in secular schools and violates the constitution and a new law on education.'[105] Similarly, in April 2007, Emomali Rahmon condemned the behaviour of girls wearing the hijab as well as inappropriate clothes such as miniskirts and plunging necklines at school. A few days later, the Education Minister carried Rahmon's initiative further, officially prohibiting the Islamic hijab as well as inappropriate clothes in schools. The decree compelled young women to dress 'in accordance with their status and national traditions,' and avoid clothes that are 'provocative,' for instance tight jeans and miniskirts.[106]

In 2008, the Education Minister also ordered male students at the Islamic University of Tajikistan to wear suits, ties, shave their beards and announced the introduction of teacher uniforms and a ban on headscarves.[107] Attacks against the hijab reached a new height in the autumn of 2010, when Rakhmonov, who was addressing a crowd of students at the inauguration of a new school in Dushanbe, condemned parents who send their children to study with mullahs as well as women

who wear the hijab, going as far as to call these women 'monkeys.'[108]
When he became Rector of the Pedagogical University in Dushanbe in
2012, Rakhmonov continued to dictate the standards of womanhood.
He issued a decree instructing future female professors to wear high heels
(maximum height of 3 cm) so that they look more professional and feel
more confident.[109]

That case illustrates that there are not only proper ways to be
'religious' but also to be 'secular.' Similarly, when I was in Tajikistan,
I took the habit of wearing a light scarf, tied at the back of my head, with
my 'European clothes.' I did it mainly as a protection from the sun but
also as a sign of respect to my most conservative interviewees when I had
meetings with them. Most people complimented me and appreciated the
fact that I was respectful of 'their traditions.' Yet, one on occasion, I was
told by a friend of mine to not wear my scarf. It was the day celebrating
20 years of independence and we were going to the big parade organized
by the regional government. She argued that scarves were for old women
and that it was strange for young modern women to wear it. I found her
comment particularly puzzling since she had a sister who wore a hijab
and was very respectful of her sister's choice and yet considered my
headscarf inappropriate.

I can further illustrate the malaise surrounding the scarf with an
anecdote involving one Khujandi policeman during my second
fieldwork. In late October 2011, a policeman conducted a passport
check in my building. Because they were not many foreigners in
Khujand, he was curious about me and chatted a bit. He also asked me
for my phone number. Though I was uncomfortable with this,
I complied, not knowing if he had asked for personal reasons or for
monitoring purposes. He was sometimes texting me, which I thought
was outside the purview of his job. He came back for another passport
check three weeks later while I was having dinner with my main
interviewees Iskandar and Mera, who happened to look very
'religious.' I was dressed conservatively and wore a scarf, though not
a hijab. The policeman was shocked by the scene. When he checked
Iskandar's passport, an argument broke out because Iskandar had
written something in Arabic in it. The argument did not last long
and the policeman left but only to come back later around 11pm.
He asked me to go for a car ride with him. Unsure if his motives were
personal or job-related, I was hesitant to hop in. But because he was

very insistent, I accepted reluctantly. In the car, he quickly started to question me about my guests: Who were they? Why was I dressed like that? Had they tried to convert me? And so on. He was very suspicious of 'such fanatics' and he said:

> I was surprised to see you with them because we have terrorists here you know. We don't like these people. You did not wear a scarf before. Our girls dress in modern clothes you know.

His reasoning very much matched the state rhetoric on radical Islam. Yet, the policeman did not seem to follow orders he received and I had the impression that he did this because he was truly concerned about me, that 'these people' would lead me in the wrong path. Even though his motivations might have been personal, it did not change the fact that he was concerned about me and felt compelled to intervene. I was afraid my guests would later have problems but he did not follow-up on that. This example shows that formal and informal practices intertwine and that local dynamics and interests play an important role in the actions of law enforcement authorities and state structures. More importantly, it reveals how religious signs are associated with extremist beliefs.[110]

At the beginning of the school year in 2010, the hijab ban was widely discussed in the media, especially since a number of veiled girls were denied school attendance.[111] Yet my fieldwork revealed that the hijab ban in state facilities and schools had not been applied unilaterally but depended on a multiplicity of factors: the type of school, school directors' position on the issue, teachers' views on the matter, and relations within the neighbourhood and with the local Hukumat. In the city of Khujand, it was still possible to find private schools where some pupils and even teachers were wearing hijabs. In 2011, during a visit to Mastchox, a region known for its religious conservatism, I was told that many girls were going to school with their hijab, which they took off only when school board representatives were visiting. Yet, one school director I spoke to in Khujand in 2011 reported that the year before police officers raided his school with video cameras to document if schoolgirls were wearing hijabs. The measure was obviously only dissuasive because no further action was taken in the months that followed.

In 2011, Farangis, one of my interviewees, was working for a governmental service in Khujand and was still allowed to work with her hijab despite having to suffer the taunts of many of her colleagues. Indeed, she was sometimes mocked and criticized for not being 'part of the team' since she refused to join them at parties where alcohol was served, for instance. She was eventually dismissed at the beginning of 2012 for refusing to come to work without her veil. The anti-hijab campaign even expanded to public spaces, with women working at bazaars in Tajikistan's main cities complaining that authorities were pressuring women who wore hijabs.[112] On that matter, the deputy head of the Kulob main bazaar said that officials 'merely advised women to wear "national clothes".'[113] In the summer of 2010, Mera and Iskandar, who had a stall at the bazar, also indicated that 'Hukumat people' visited the main bazaar in Khujand and took the names of the women with hijabs and those selling religious literature. As those bazaar stories demonstrate, the hijab issue involves not only the national or local authorities, but engages a variety of civil actors, even bazaar directors.

Over the years, anti-hijab actions intensified. Several other public figures have publicly criticized women's clothing style, whether 'Islamic' or 'European.' Even the Council of Ulemas, Tajikistan's quasi-official clergy, recommended women to wear Islamic clothes that conform to the national culture, and not those of Iran, Turkey, or Arabic countries. Though it did not issue a fatwa on the subject, the Council did not disapprove of the government's campaign against the hijab[114] and even suggested that foreign-made hijabs reflected a tradition alien to Tajikistan. They also advised against wearing the hijab for practical reasons since it is 'too tight.' Instead, they recommended women to wear Tajik 'traditional clothes' that meet Islamic requirements.[115]

The standpoint adopted by Tajik Islamic clerics is ambiguous but understandable because of its subordination to governmental authorities. What is more surprising is the declaration of the leader of the Islamic Revival Party of Tajikistan Muhiddin Kabiri in an interview with Radio Free Europe. In 2009, Kabiri declared: 'We don't support the extremist view of the Salafi movement. We also oppose the Jamoati Tabligh group, which is promoting elements of foreign culture in the name of Islam, such as the so-called religious dress code and beard. It gives a completely wrong impression about Islam.'[116] Even though the party has supported the cause of hijabi women, the party was careful to not associate itself with what is perceived as foreign interpretations of Islam.

The hijab issue in Tajikistan not only challenges the definition of what it means to be Muslim but also what it means to be a Tajik. For instance, in a heated debate taking place between representatives of different political parties in Khujand in the summer 2011, a representative from the Democratic Party, who also happened to be a historian and school Principal, said he regretted that young people dressed in Arabic clothes because Islam was not the true religion of Tajiks. He argued that it had been imposed on them and instead considered Zoroastrianism to be the Tajiks' true religion. He also complained about the 'European' outfits worn by young females and wished they would dress in 'national clothes.'

In the midst of the escalating political repression against the IRPT in 2015, the anti-hijab campaign intensified in 2015. In March, it was reported that a number of prostitutes were wearing hijabs in order to avoid public or police harassment.[117] The story was picked up by the authorities, and used to delegitimize the veil as well as to question the morality of women who wear it. In May 2015, the mayor of Khujand in Northern Tajikistan announced the organization of a series of meetings with women to discuss ways to dress properly, in accordance to national traditions. He also underlined the need to conduct raids in clothing stores in order to prevent the selling of Afghan and Iranian clothes.[118] The President himself has associated the hijab to extremist ideas in a speech delivered at the occasion of Mother's Day in May 2015. Rahmon condemned women who wore foreign clothing, saying that they were propagating extremist ideas in the country. In August 2015, Mahmadsaid Ubaidulloev, Dushanbe's former Mayor, declared war against foreign clothing and even instructed relevant state bodies to put an end to the import and sale of foreign clothing in Dushanbe.[119] In August 2015, even Colonel Zikrullo Saidzoda of the Ministry of Internal Affairs felt compelled to criticize women for wearing 'European-style clothes,' and suggested that they wear 'traditional clothes.'[120] In January 2016, the Council of Religious Affairs saw fit to clarify what exactly is considered to be 'foreign clothing.' According to Shokirov Hussein, Head of Religious Associations of the Committee for Religious Affairs, the problem concerns the niqab, which is 'opposed by the entire civilized world.'

Though he conceded that black clothes that show the face do not pose any problems, he stated that: 'All the studies done in the world today show that basically all women who wear the niqab are members of extremist organizations.'[121] These public interventions tell of a concerted effort to delegitimize and securitize Islam by associating it with security issues.

In return, men's clothes are scarcely evoked even though some men who are more conservative wear clothes that stand out and are also considered 'foreign,' such as long loose shirts that go below the knees and trousers that stop above the ankles, a dressing style associated with Salafism. They represent a minority and authorities appear more concerned about beards than they are about short trousers. That being said, most Tajik men dress in regular 'Western-style' shirts and pants, suits and ties that do not seem don't seem to betray national traditions in the eyes of the authorities despite their 'European' origin. However, over the years, there have been many reports concerning police harassment toward bearded men, and even reports of some being forced to shave.[122] In 2009, the Council of Ulemas even established a norm for the length of beards, which should not exceed the length of a fist.[123] During the time I spent in Sughd, I've heard stories that were so extravagant that they seemed to me too bizarre to be true at first. I heard about a first case in 2010, which was presented as the 'authorities' fight against Islam.' An IRPT representative from the Bobojon-Gaffurov district mentioned an incident in Istaravshan in which an IRPT member was stopped at a checkpoint by Road Safety officers who made fun of him because of his beard and allegedly burned part of it with a lighter. Another case I was told about took place in the Gonchi district in the summer of 2011. In September 2011, one bank clerk in his late 30s reported to me that in his village in the Gonchi region, some police officers had recently caught young men in the streets, brought them to the hairdresser, and forced them to have their beards cut. Though it did not happen to him, the man who told me the story was very resentful. A month or so later I visited said village and asked the young local imam whether or not the story was true. He confirmed that the police came to visit him and a few other local informal leaders but said that they were not threatening them and that the Head of Police was a good and understanding man. The chief police officer told them to be careful of those who might be too zealous and to keep their beards short. Interestingly, the Gonchi imam did not see this as a problem and said: 'I think it's better to keep it short anyway. It's not very pleasant for others when one has a long beard, it's not very hygienic.' Reports of mass shaving became more and more frequent over the years.

In 2010, the police held nearly 30 Dushanbe residents over concern for their beards. The police declared that the problem with bearded men was that the pictures on their official identification documents did not match their current appearance, which is why the police could detain them for identification.[124] Another case that received much publicity in Tajikistan is that of Parviz Tursunov, a member of the football team Khair from a Dushanbe suburb. Tursunov was barred from taking part in a national championship because of his beard.[125] In 2010, the CRA Chairman denied that men with beards were being harassed by the authorities. Interestingly, he added that growing a beard represented an Islamic tradition and therefore they had no right to forbid it.[126] In early 2016, however, there was no more official denial and the police announced that it had shaved nearly 13,000 men in the last year in their efforts to counter radicalism.[127]

Positions over this issue are divided. While the imam in the Gonchi region was very compliant, the fellow villager who first told me about the forced-shaving story seemed very bitter. It is easily conceivable that the imam avoided criticizing the police in front of me. When I asked both the father and son (who both served as imams in the village) about local problems regarding the hijab ban in schools, they claimed there were not any problems because very few girls were wearing the hijab in their village. Despite being religious figures, their position on the hijab was very liberal. Interestingly, the young imam's wife was not wearing one but his sisters were. Later in the conversation, the father and son mentioned the fact that some local women complained to the police that some men were pressuring them to wear Islamic clothes. They were very critical of this kind of religious pressure and said that it was against Islamic principles to force religious behaviour upon someone.

Musin, who was a close friend of the Gonchi imams, had two daughters who were in the fourth and sixth grade, respectively, and a son who was four years old. In 2010, his daughters were still allowed to go to school with their hijab. When I mentioned the renewed warnings of the Education Minister regarding the hijab ban, Musin declared that he would have no problems complying with the law. He would allow his daughters to take off their hijab, but only to go to school. Although it was contrary to his faith, Musin said he would comply with the law because 'if they adopted this law, it means it was needed because they [the authorities] know better.' I first interpreted Musin's reaction as a sign of political conformity. Indeed, Musin's compliant attitude fits paternalist frames of authority in Central Asia, which Liu define as a 'tendency to believe that as ordinary people, they are not able to fully understand issues of government, much less voice consequential opinions or press for effective changes about them.'[128] Also, his way of using 'they' to refer to the authorities by avoiding attribution can be seen as a Soviet discursive tradition, but 'it is also characteristic of subordinated populations more generally.'[129] I also saw it as an interesting mixture of religious and secular behaviours. In my view, his position on the hijab ban symbolized the porous character of the two in the sense that he did not see a contradiction between his religious obligations and legal conformity. But in the autumn of 2011, I met Musin again at the Panjshanbe bazaar and we discussed the Law on Parental Responsibility that forbids children to attend religious services. In contrast with his reaction about the hijab ban the year before, he was very upset about the new law and said he was defying it by bringing his son to the mosque nevertheless. So what I interpreted as compliance to the law in 2010 was perhaps the sign of different levels of importance given to the religious practices of girls and boys.

In 2010 and 2011, I have met quite a few university students who were compliant with the law and were taking off their hijab at the gate and putting it back at the end of the day. Even though they were split between religious observance and their desire to pursue their studies, they did not have the impression that they were betraying their faith. Yet, this is a compromise that not everyone was willing to make. Hoji, another interviewee, was outraged when I mentioned those cases and suggested that these girls should drop out of school. When I asked him what he would do when his daughter would be of schooling age, he said they would move to another country because he would not betray his religion. During this conversation, Hoji also asked me if the classes at the university were mixed. I replied that they were and he seemed rather surprised and offended by the news. He reiterated that his daughter would not attend regular schools because of that.

An IRPT member from the Bobojon-Gaffurov district raised an interesting contradiction regarding the hijab ban: 'They say they want women to dress in traditional clothes but what really is traditional? It's the *paranja*!' Indeed, before the Bolshevik revolution, women living in the sedentary regions of Central Asia such as present-day Uzbekistan and Tajikistan used to wear burqa-like robes called *paranja* or *chavchan* that covered the whole body, including the face, until the Soviets launched the *Hujum* campaign in the late 1920s. Therefore, the definition of what represents 'tradition' is very problematic. In his speech on Mother's Day, the President assured that ethnographic studies prove that since ancient times, Tajik women wore colourful and beautiful clothes, not black ones. What the authorities and secular-minded people refer to as traditional clothes, that is, the colourful long two-piece ensemble and a light scarf, is in fact a Soviet creation that has been reified as traditionally Tajik.

Figure 4.2 Woman in *paranja*, Samarkand, 1910. Credit: Sergei M. Prokudin-Gorskii Collection at the Library of Congress.

Figure 4.3   Khujand, 2011. Girls and women in 'traditional' clothes. Credit: Hélène Thibault.

Indeed, the *paranja* shown in the picture below is light blue and not black, but it is in no way comparable to the clothes Tajik women wear today. The *paranja* was meant to hide the female body entirely whereas today's outfits are modest but reveal the head, neck, part of the chest, and arms. The use of pre-colonial legacies requires a distortion of history that authorities are willing to make so that it fits the nationalist secular programme they are promoting.

The Virtuous Tajik Woman

In addition to their choice of clothes, women's virtue is also targeted and associated with patriotic secular values. In his speech at the occasion of Mother's Day in March 2015, Rahmon labelled mothers as guardians of the mother tongue, and talked at length about the sanctity of women and how maternal authority fosters the future builders of the state and society. The President also insisted on the importance of the mother, described as a unique creature 'who swings the cradle with one hand and with the other, the planet.' Such paternalistic rhetoric conveys the message that women are responsible for the perpetuation of the nation through the appropriate upbringing of children as well as through the display of proper social behaviour, such as the celebration of national values and the rejection of foreign influence, whether Islamic or Western. In his annual televised address at the occasion of Mother's Day in 2016, Rahmon stated that as the world is becoming more complicated and plagued with terrorism, parents play an important role in the prevention of extremism. He highlights the special responsibility of 'dear mothers' who can prevent their children from falling under criminal influences through love, constant care, and education.[130] Citizens are encouraged to act in conformity with national values: according to the President, 'there is no greater sin than the betrayal of parents and of the Motherland.'[131] Constantine observed a similar phenomenon in neighbouring Uzbekistan where the newspapers and media emphasize the 'feminine' qualities of women and their role as wives and mothers, which, she argues, is part of a reconfiguration of Uzbek national identity.[132]

To be able to properly fulfil their maternal and national duties, women should stay away from Islam. In this sense, one of the most controversial fatwas adopted by the Council of Ulemas forbids women to pray in mosques. It was adopted in 2004 on the basis that mosques do not have the necessary facilities to allow men and women to pray separately.[133] It is true that women had not traditionally attended mosques in Tajikistan, but separate praying spaces for women can easily be organized as is the case in most Muslim countries. In Tajikistan, there is nearly no possibility for women to pray in religious facilities. The prayer rooms in the head and regional quarters of the IRPT, where women used to pray legally, are now closed. The only remaining places where women are allowed to pray are Ismaili prayer houses (*Jamoatkhona*), where women and men pray side by side and which are mostly found in Gorno-Badakhshan. Also, on very special occasions such as Idi Fitr and Idi Qurbon, some Friday mosques may welcome women in their facilities and organize a special separate space for women.

During a visit at the Islamic Centre in Dushanbe, the Head of the Department for International Relations explained to me the fatwa in the following terms: 'The prophet himself said that women should pray at home. They should take care of the house. If a woman goes to the mosque, who will look after the kids? Something can happen to them while she is away, it is better if they pray at home.' Leaving aside a certain willingness to marginalize faith, such paternalistic rhetoric resonates within the Tajik society, which remains quite conservative. Indeed, different piety standards appear to apply for men and women. The impossibility for women to pray in mosques is the most prominent example. Musin's willingness to leave his girls go to school without hijabs compared to his stark reaction against the law forbidding him to bring his son to the mosque is another. Also, during the meeting at Hoji's place, he left briefly to go perform the noon prayer in another room but his wife and my acquaintance Farangis skipped the prayer to stay with me and went praying only after he got back.

In a 2004 address to the nation, Rahmon called on women to obey this particular fatwa and also prevent their children from being distracted by religion. He mentioned how detrimental religious education could be for the country's future: 'We can't hide the fact that we are not allowing our children to learn a profession, to study technology.' Insisting on the importance of education and training for the well-being of the nation, he mentioned that: 'We can't build the Rogun hydro-energy plant because of this. For three years, we have been negotiating the purchase of three Boeing, but we can't buy them because we have no pilots.'[134] In this speech, religion and religious knowledge is understood as being anti-modern, as opposed to secular and progressive knowledge. This resonates with the Soviet discourse on the importance of education for scientific and technological progress. A passage from a book called *The Atheist Education of Students* is evocative: 'Soviet students represent the social force of our society, of distinguished high ideas and scientific levels and they can accomplish a lot for the future improvement of the effectiveness of workers' atheist education.'[135]

A case that took place at the beginning of 2016 perfectly epitomizes the amalgam of female virtue, submission, and political loyalty. A Tajik journalist who was a friend of Muhiddin Kabiri, IRPT's now exiled leader, said she was harassed by the authorities, who wanted to prove that she had an affair with Kabiri, a married man. She admitted that he had been in love with him but that their relationship was strictly platonic. She claimed that she suffered pressure from the authorities and that her bank accounts were frozen. She ultimately offered the authorities to take a virginity test in order to prove her innocence and was even accompanied to a medical facility by law-enforcement officials. The authorities eventually stopped pressuring her afterwards.[136] This case is extreme but shows the extent of state pressure exercised over women. Ultimately, this woman had to go through a humiliating physical examination to prove that she was not only morally but also politically virtuous.

Like in Soviet times, female clothing as well as women's attitudes embody the secular character and the Nation's progress. In the authorities' point of view, women bear both many domestic and public responsibilities. By dictating how to behave and to dress, women, as citizens and mothers, are expected to nurture patriotic and secular subjects. Paradoxically, conservative state narratives concur with some of the religious discourses, which emphasize traditional gender roles and reinforce patriarchal relations between men and women, and within families. Sadly, those responsibilities are exercised in less-than-ideal conditions as the country's socio-economic situation remains highly problematic, and particularly affect women. As I will detail at the end of the next chapter, state pressure, labour migration and poverty contribute to the creation of an oppressive environment for women. However, the tightening of state control over not only politics and religion, but over ways of being in the world on a day-to-day basis, increases the pressure on all citizens. The next chapter will reveal that even if some people agree with those neo socio-engineering attempts, the extent of state control inevitably provokes resentment among a significant portion of the population.

CHAPTER 5

OF BEING MUSLIM IN TAJIKISTAN

We hear that they are fighting for Islam, but why? 97 per cent of
our Republic is Muslim, so why fight over that?

MIRZOHUDJA AHMADOV

There are officially 97 per cent of Muslims in this country. But
what kind of Muslims are they? The kind who smoke, drink, and
wear mini-skirts?

KHUJAND BUSINESSMAN

In the epigraph above, Mirzohudja Ahmadov, a former commander who
fought with the United Tajik Opposition (UTO) during the civil war, is
commenting on the clashes between military forces and so-called
militants in the Rasht valley in the autumn of 2010.[1] His question
sounds simple, but it touches on the crucial issue of the place of religion
in society and the malaise it creates. Implicit in Ahmadov's observation
is the premise that problems should not arise if one nation shares
one faith, as is (nearly) the case in Tajikistan. Religious diversity in
Tajikistan is not defined by the cohabitation of different confessions, but
rather by diverse interpretations of what it means to be religious. As was
outlined in the previous chapter, public expressions of faith present a
problem for Tajik authorities, who try to temper such expressions with
laws, decrees, and threats. This control appears to take the form of a
disciplinary biopower *à la Foucault*, regulating the possibly bad practices
of strict believers, while promoting good secular ways of living.[2] These

include the appearance and clothing of people as well as their religious practice. Ostentatious religious signs such as the hijab and the beard are strongly discouraged, if not altogether prohibited in some instances. Citizens are expected to be pious but within the limits of piety established by state norms. Virtue and loyalty appear preferable to piety, which can potentially become subversive. Like the Soviets before them, Tajik authorities try to constrain religious practices within boundaries they consider beneficial and harmless for both the community at large and themselves. The problem that Ahmadov points out is that there is limited agreement on those boundaries. This chapter articulates this disagreement by presenting what can be broadly characterized as popular post-Soviet narratives about religion, which I collected during fieldwork within the broader population and IRPT circles. Although I will focus on those I label as 'strict believers,' whose behaviour appears to thwart the official narrative, I will also cite the opinions of those whom I refer to as 'secular-minded people,'[3] whose opinions align more closely with the authorities' in order to illuminate the complex texture of social tensions at the local level. As Asad rightfully indicated: 'Any discipline that seeks to understand "religion" must also try to understand its other.'[4]

Previous chapters highlighted the importance of the Soviet legacy for Tajik authorities' management of religious issues. I would now like to ask what the Soviet legacy has to do with the accelerating religious revival in Tajikistan. Although this question might seem paradoxical, this chapter will highlight the affinities between Soviet moral and social codes. Panchenko argues that New-Age religious movements in Russia inherited their 'peculiar moral culture' from Soviet collectivist practices with 'utopian expectations and totalistic forms of social control.'[5] I will argue that religious beliefs can partially counteract a totalizing social system, such as the Soviets,' which was characterized by its strong control of the economic, social, and, to some extent, personal lives of Soviet citizens. Yet, people do not simply perpetuate pre-existing circumstances, they accommodate and manoeuvre between available socio-political and personal repertoires. As Louw suggests, people 'interpret them [circumstances], contest, negotiate and nuance them, re-imagine them, protest against them and accommodate to them, as they strive to create a satisfying existence.'[6] The current chapter also shows how economic and political alienation can have a major impact on the redefinition of religious identities. These redefinitions in turn provoke tensions between groups who hold different conceptions of what they consider 'good behaviour.' The idea here is to account for the multiple and often conlicting moralities that coexist within Tajik society. I use interview material to articulate the two main theses of the book: the underlying continuity between the Soviet and post-Soviet orders, and between religious and secular realms.

Assessing Religion

Cefaï asserts that, prior to starting research, scholars should only entertain a vague idea of what they will investigate during fieldwork, because the research topic properly speaking can only emerge through a process of familiarization with the milieu and people.[7] If a complete absence of prejudices is perhaps desirable for a researcher, it is hardly achievable. Yanow explains that the ethnographer is 'understood to bring prior knowledge to his or her experiences, thereby giving shape to the myriad sensate stimuli [. . .] vying for attention.'[8] In Central Asia, assumptions about religious dynamics can lead researchers to overemphasize the prevalence of radical beliefs and conservative values. I myself was not wholly immune to that tendency. Prior to arriving in Tajikistan, I thought I would be confronted with two types of people – religious or secular – and that it would be easy to distinguish them. I expected that individuals and groups would express their faith in obvious ways. For instance, I was very much looking forward to attending a 'religious wedding,' which I expected to be a solemn religious experience. It turned out that there was not much religion involved in such a wedding except for the 'Nikoh,' during which the bride and the groom exchanged vows before God. The ceremony was not officiated by a religious authority, but rather by a respected elder relative. The Nikoh does not even require the presence of guests. Family and friends simply gather afterwards to celebrate the union in a reception hall or at someone's home. No alcohol is served, no music is played, and women and men sit in two separate rooms. The absence of alcohol and dancing is the primary difference between religious and secular marriages.

Another example is the observance of Ramadan, which I expected to be very solemn and contemplative. In July of 2010 I celebrated the first day of Ramadan sitting in an orchard with a bunch of men who, though they all identified as Muslims, did not scruple to make vodka toasts in celebration of the holy month. At the end of Ramadan, I accompanied a friend to visit her grandparents. Most people honour the end of Ramadan by visiting family elders and offering them presents. Someone said a short prayer, pronounced when we arrived (this was quite ordinary), and the conversation quickly turned to profane matters. Again, religious displays were not as prevalent as I expected them to be. I quickly realized that I needed to move past the religious-secular dichotomy in my thinking. Ethnographic immersion appeared to be the proper approach to investigate the region of overlap between religious and secular realms and to more subtly assess the meaning of behaviours that might seem obviously religious or secular. None of this is to say that categories are irrelevant, but rather to argue that they are primarily useful as starting points for understanding the complex dynamics of Tajik society. It will quickly become apparent in the case studies below why I needed to move beyond a rigid application of this duality.

As discussed in the Introduction, there is no doubt that religious observance is on the rise in Tajikistan. This section aims to go beyond statistical figures to depict this change from the perspective of the individuals who are living it. My focus is on 'born-again' believers who lived a secular life before 'discovering' faith and organizing their lives according to religious principles. I defend the position that people who have apparently distanced themselves most aggressively from Soviet ideals and embraced a life based on religious principles have done so in many instances because of the strong affinities between religious and Soviet moral codes. While born-agains as yet present only a minority of Tajiks, they constitute an important part of the growing segment whose opinions and behaviours are provoking social tensions. Set apart visually by their adherence to traditional Islamic dress codes – long, full robes, long beards, and small hats for men and full, conservative dresses and hijabs for women. They strictly observe the religious duties stipulated in the Qur'an – praying five times a day, fasting during Ramadan, frequenting only establishments that are halal (and avoiding restaurants that serve alcohol or where waitresses wear 'European clothes'), and whenever possible buying food and goods from 'good Muslims.' All of my interviewees, except the two women, had performed the Hajj, and in some cases more than once. One couple I met, Mera and Iskandar, were living in a polygynous marriage. Though they were very conservative and tended to surround themselves with people who shared their views, they were very courteous to me, and I never felt that my gender, religion, or ethnic origin presented an obstacle to our relationship. Their attitude contrasted with that of a few very conservative people whom I encountered briefly in Isfara, where some men would avoid not only talking to women, but even looking at them. I once asked Iskandar to comment on the difference between him and such conservative people, and he replied that he was a 'bad Muslim' and that he should be behaving more like those men so as to avoid temptation.

I was frequently asked if I was a believer or to which religion I belonged. These questions made me feel uneasy since I was afraid to disappoint my interlocutors. I refused to dodge these questions, so I would invariably answer: 'I'm Catholic,' which was honest enough, because I am baptized. At the same time, it did not necessarily mean that I was practising. In general, people would be satisfied with this answer. Most Muslims respect Christians, whom they regard as 'People of the Book.' In Islam, the Bible is a Holy Book, and Jesus a prophet, though suggesting that Jesus is God's son 'is a sin' (as I was told more than once). Some interviewees were not satisfied with this answer and asked me if I was practising, and I had to admit that I was not. They often saw this as an opportunity to proselytize. Iskandar was especially proactive in this regard. He told me countless times how my unbeliever's heart was black, that something bad would happen to me, that I would burn in hell if I did not accept Islam as the true religion. In the beginning, he seemed to be doing this pro forma. He could not understand why I was so interested in religion if I was not myself a believer. But the more we got to know each other, I believe he came to feel truly sorry for me. He truly did not want *me* to burn in hell. Iskandar once told me, 'I can see it in your eyes that you are a kind (*dobrii*) person because eyes are the mirror of the soul. But I also see that your soul is sick.' He even became convinced that I could not marry a Christian because my heart was not really Christian any more, but already half-Muslim.

On one occasion, thinking that I was going to a casual tea-drinking session with three women I met at the Islamic Party, I found myself having dinner with 11 members and militants from the IRPT. All of them were wearing their hijab even though there were no men in the house. The issue of my faith, or lack thereof, did not seem to pose a problem. On the contrary, they viewed me as a potential convert.

My non-judgemental attitude towards strict believers only fuelled their efforts to convert me. Over the course of the dinner, one of the women put it this way: 'It's much more interesting to sit with you than with our people (*rodnie*) because you come to our lessons, you want to learn about Islam, whereas our Tajik women are afraid to sit with us because they think we will force them to take Islam and wear hijabs.' Obviously, they too thought that my interest in their religion could be transformed into faith. Despite the overall sympathetic tone of conversation during dinner, a young girl in her early 20s was more insistent than the others. She was particularly emotional about her faith, even to the point of weeping when she described how much she loved Allah. Her tone became more aggressive when she said 'We respect you, but there is no other choice than to believe in Islam. It's the ultimate religion. Mohammed is the last prophet. Those who do follow Islam will stand higher than others when Judgement Day comes.' More or less the same dynamics were at play in Christian settings. Though I did not develop close relationships with my Christian interlocutors, I was also subjected to efforts to convert me. Overall, my own religious beliefs did not impede my research. Perhaps the fact that I was not very religious even helped me, because some religious people would invest time and energy conversing with me in the hope that they could convert me.

My basic knowledge of Tajik did not allow me to use it for interviews. I conducted all my interviews in Russian even though I was afraid it could be perceived as the 'colonial' language. However, Russian felt inappropriate on only one occasion. It was in an informal meeting with an imam-businessman from Mastchox, one of the conservative areas close to Khujand where Sufi lineages remained strong even during Soviet rule. After this meeting I realized that there is an aspect to the language issue that goes beyond the colonial associations with conversing in Russian – an aspect that reveals the divide between the 'traditional' Islam from the countryside and the 'new urban' Islam. The latter is mostly, but not completely, found in urban contexts. It is characterized by newly created religious networks that seek knowledge mostly from foreign literature and predicators. It contrasts with religious lineages that flourished or developed in the countryside as opposition movements against the Soviet regime in the 1960s and 1970s that are rather nationalistic.[9] On that matter, Iskandar's attitude was significant. He once told me that there was no need for me to learn Tajik since I already knew Russian and could easily get along with it in Tajikistan. According to him, I needed to learn Arabic because it was the Prophet's language. When I told him about people who sometimes refused to speak Russian, he said: 'This is not right. They are uneducated and don't understand. After all, it's God who created all languages on earth. But I understand why they do so. They have very bad memories from Soviet times.' Another of my interviewees, Hoji, received his education exclusively in Russian. He spoke Tajik very well, but had problems reading it. He did not read or listen to local poets and religious leaders, relying entirely on religious literature imported from Russia. He was also not attached to any mosque in particular and visited several different ones each week. As it will be discussed in subsequent sections, both the religious practices and the political views of these men were very different than the ones of a circle of friends in Gonchi, who regularly met in the village mosque to pray and read classic Tajik literature. Language usage can reflect not only political attitudes, but also the important divide between old-time believers and those I call born-again Muslims.

While some scholars refer to them as 'newly pious,'[10] I use the qualifier *born-again* to describe those persons whom I met who have left behind a mostly secular life to live according to Sharia or canonical laws, since I also include Christians in this category. Overall, the term *born-again* has mostly been used to refer to Christians in the United States, but its use remains controversial even in the American context.[11]

Interestingly, many men who described themselves as strict believers contrasted their current pious behaviour to their previous 'sinner's lifestyle,' typified by 'drinking, smoking and fooling around with women' (*ya pil, kuril i gulyal*). Born-again women, in contrast, tended to refer to their previous lives as ones in which they had not known God, so that they were neither praying nor wearing a hijab. Aged more or less between 30 and 50, my eight main interviewees had been educated and socialized in Soviet times. While some had taken part in religious rites before, their religious practice was limited and had more to do with customs than spiritual engagement. More importantly, they saw themselves as fundamentally changed since having begun living according to strict religious precepts. At the IRPT's headquarters in Sughd, many women I talked to recalled changing radically after they 'discovered' Islam. Interestingly, one woman who knew I was Canadian told me that while she used to be a hockey fan, she was no longer interested because 'thank God, after I converted, I changed 100 per cent and became different (*drugoi*).' In one case, the woman's decision to live religiously came as a shocking surprise for her family, which she described as 'communist nobility.'

I use the term 'conservative Muslims' or 'strict believers' interchangeably to describe individuals whose behaviours correspond to a lifestyle based on strict religious principles. I eschew the terms 'radical' and 'fundamentalist' because they convey a misleading sense of vague menace. Abashin suggests that 'the differentiation between 'traditional' and 'fundamentalist' Islam is just as dubious and politically charged as the opposition posited between 'official' and 'unofficial' Islam in the Soviet Union, which originated out of concerns over regional stability and conflict.'[12] Islam in Tajikistan is certainly trending more conservative, perhaps even to the point of becoming fundamentalist in some instances. It bears emphasizing that fundamentalism is not necessarily extremist or violent. In Tajikistan, at least, it entails a strong critique of the secular state coupled with a demand for the supremacy of Sharia in the Constitution and the right to oppose governmental decisions in the name of Sharia.[13]

Apparently dependant on their view of Islam, the Tajiks I interviewed would use either the neutral term 'believer' (*veruiushii*) or the pejorative term 'fanatic' (*fanat*) to indicate a person who lives strictly according to Sharia. The term (*veruiushii*), however, is ambiguous because many use it broadly to mean a person who has faith in God whether or not he lives according to strict religious principles. I therefore propose to use the terms *born-again* and *strict believer* to refer exclusively to those people who have (re)discovered faith and who live according to strict religious principles. These two terms seem more appropriate to define my interlocutors due to the conception of the Tajik, and in fact Central Asian, identity being seen as inseparable from an Islamic identity. Scholarly literature has clearly underlined the association between cultural identity and religion, and this matches my own field observations. For Abdulloh Rahnamo, a Tajik political scientist, using terms like 'Islamization' and 'Islamic factor' is nonsense in the Tajik context as one cannot talk about an Islamic factor in a society that is 99 per cent Muslim. Yet, I believe these terms are relevant to describe how more and more people turn to religion and how Islam comes to play a more important role in people's life.

In the course of my fieldwork, I often received strange looks and heard disapproving remarks when I used the Russian phrase *on/ona prinyal/ prinyala Islam* (literally, 'he/she took Islam') in reference to a person who had started living according to strict religious rules. Whether they were practising Muslims or not, most Tajiks considered the use of the word 'conversion' as tautological because Tajiks are born Muslims. Pelkmans suggests that the Soviet 'ethnicization of religion' reified this identity.[14] In 1973, the mullah of Tashkent's Shaykh Zaynuddin mosque proclaimed that 'only he who will publicly declare in front of all believers, in the mosque, that he no longer accepts Allah's commandments will cease to be considered a Muslim.'[15] However, this well predates the Soviet period. During the first USSR census, there was great confusion regarding what actually counted as an ethnic identity. Respondents in Central Asia often self-identified not as Tajiks or Kyrgyzs, but as Muslims.[16]

Consequently, the conversion of fellow Tajiks to other religions, such as Christianity, is strongly condemned. Pelkmans suggests that conversions to other religions provoke intensely passionate reactions because 'the ethnicization of religion meant that conversion acts had social consequences that reached far beyond specifically theological concerns.'[17] In 1994, Tajik Mufti Fathoullah Khan Sharifzade published an article in the journal *Religia i Nauka* stating that it was inadmissible for a Muslim to quit his religion and convert to another one. Nevertheless, he made it clear that he was ready to welcome Christians who wished to convert to Islam.[18] In Tajikistan, the discourse connecting Islam and national identity is pervading both individual and political narratives. This is an idea often asserted within political circles as the authorities have tried in the recent years to shape a national identity based on the values of Hanafism, which they have elevated to the status of a quasi-national religion.

The Believers

Mera and Iskandar

I consider Mera and Iskandar my main interviewees. They formed a joyful couple in their early 40s. I met them at the beginning of my fieldwork in 2010 in Khujand and spent a lot of time with them and some of their friends in 2010 and 2011. We bonded quickly, and not long after I met them, Iskandar was arrested and briefly detained by the police, in June 2010. Mera called me immediately to help her find him. He came back safe in the early evening that day. Our meetings were informal and amicable. We met at different places: the bazaar, Mera's workplace, teahouses (*chaikhonas*), and restaurants, as well as at my apartment. We also spoke on the phone regularly. They were devout Muslims who lived according to Sharia. Mera dressed in dark conservative robes and wore a hijab, while Iskandar sported a long beard and wore modest clothes. From the very beginning, they were very keen on converting me to Islam – 'the ultimate religion' – and trying to get me married to one of their friends.

Mera was Iskandar's second wife. She studied to work as a caregiver in kindergartens, but was not at the time working in her field because the wages were too low. She had been divorced for several years and had three children, but only the youngest one lived with her. It took me some time to realize that the boy was not Iskandar's son, because he treated him like his own. They were introduced to each other by a common friend, and they talked to each other only briefly before concluding the Nikoh in 2008. Iskandar explained that he was not very fond of her when they married, but said that he now loved her very much, that it is God who blesses us with love. Arranged marriages are the norm in Tajikistan, in religious and secular families alike. Sometimes, a conversation between the bride and groom is all that is required to seal the deal, but in some cases, couples have a chance to get to one another before accepting a marriage proposal. Iskandar and Mera's hasty marriage was unrelated to their religious beliefs. Iskandar first married when he was in his 20s and had four children from his first marriage. He had been trained as a carpenter and woodcarver, but he did not have a regular job and was subsisting on low-paid contracts. When I met them, they were selling religious literature and CDs at the main bazaar, but eventually they had to close down and find a different occupation. Their financial situation was very precarious. When we met again in the summer 2011, Mera had moved from the apartment where she used to live alone with her son to her husband's house, where they lived together with his first wife and their four children. Marred by jealousy and tensions, cohabitation was not easy, but they were managing 'with the help of God, because jealousy between wives is *haram*.' On a few occasions Iskandar even asked me to become his third wife.

In 2010 when I first asked Iskandar if he had been raised in a religious family, he said yes, but in the summer of 2011, he said that his family had not been very religious because it was impossible to be a believer in Soviet times. He explained that his father became religious only after they performed the Hajj together a few years ago. He himself discovered Islam late in his 20s after an uncle invited him to the mosque during Ramadan. He admitted that he used 'to drink, smoke and fool around' before he became a believer. Mera had not been religious at all before meeting Iskandar and had discovered her faith all of a sudden when she married him. She started praying and wearing a hijab only after they married. The unforeseen lifestyle change was a source of tension between Mera and her parents. Though I never met them, she described them as secular intellectuals who had a hard time accepting that their daughter would become a second wife and wear a hijab. Yet, she recalled that in her previous marriage, she used to be a reclusive housewife, whereas she was now working outside the house and socially active as she and Iskandar often went out. Recalling her first unhappy marriage, she admitted that her previous husband was disrespectful, unfaithful, and had bad habits (again, smoking, drinking and cheating). While cohabitation with the first wife was difficult, she found her marriage to Iskandar was both spiritually and personally liberating. She was, she said, living in faith, and yet she was more socially active than ever. Although Mera was socially active, her husband seemed to be the one making the decisions.

When I asked Iskandar if he missed the Soviet period, his answer was unequivocal: 'Not in the slightest bit! We did not have any freedom back then and did not have the liberty to make choices about our personal life. We were getting up, going to work and that was it. Now I'm free to do whatever I want.' At first, I did not find his answer particularly puzzling, and it was during a subsequent conversation that it came to me that despite his negative opinions about the Soviet system, his religion-centred worldview was perhaps modelled by the very system he despised. During one his many attempts to convert me to Islam, Iskandar said, 'there are three types of food pitanie in the world; material food for the body, intellectual for the mind, and spiritual for the soul. Without one of them, a person feels incomplete.' In order to find inspiration, Iskandar advised me to start fulfilling the duties of a Muslim, such as praying and wearing a hijab, saying it would not be difficult because I already dressed conservatively. He then added, 'but you will see,

Islam is a very limiting (*ogranichenaya*) religion. There are rules for everything in Islam; about how to eat, to dress and even how to appropriately go to the toilet, etc.' Indeed, Islam and its codes of conduct mark boundaries and set up rules that dictate personal and social behaviour. Like other Holy books, the Qur'an separates Good from Evil, provides daily, weekly, and yearly schedules, dictates food habits, offers guidelines for managing marital relations, for conducting business, and so on. If Sovietism was a totalizing ideology, Islamic codes of conduct are equally totalizing. Religion provides a sense of morality, 'an embodied disposition, one's everyday way of being in the world.'[19] I don't want to suggest that Iskandar felt 'complete' in Soviet times, since he does not seem to have been particularly interested in communism or politics. It can be seen as a quest for life direction, a strategy to cope with the disintegration of a social order. As Iskandar said, spiritual food, obviously lacking in the political discourse in post-Soviet Tajikistan, is provided by religion.

Jamshed and Tolib

Mera and Iskandar introduced me to many of their friends, and I had the chance to have lengthy discussions with two of them, Jamshed and Tolib. Though they wanted to introduce me to them to help me with my research, Mera and Iskandar also wanted me to marry one of them as they were both divorced. I met with Tolib on three occasions in 2010 (but not in 2011, since he had gone to Russia for work). Jamshed, a close friend of Iskandar, was a divorced businessman in his mid-30s. He and Iskandar were running a rather unsuccessful matchmaking agency located in Khujand's main bazaar. He also had other commercial ventures, and, unlike his friend Iskandar, he was in a secure financial situation. Also raised in a secular family, he had become religious a few years ago. Jamshed was straightforward when talking about his coming to faith. He recalled that while sitting on the street, a Russian man gave him a Bible. He started reading it, believed it all, and then went to the library to read more about Jesus. After noticing his reading, a woman asked him: 'Do you know what you are going to become if you read this? You are going to be a Christian' and gave him a Qur'an instead. He summarized his conversion experience as such: 'I used to live among Russians and I was thinking like them, but now I've changed. I think and act like a Muslim.' I met one on one with

Jamshed in 2011 a couple of times in his office, but I ultimately decided to stop seeing him after he made me a serious marriage proposal. Not knowing how to refuse his proposal politely, I argued that I could not marry him because I was not a believer and had habits that were contrary to Islam. He answered, 'It does not matter if you smoke and drink, this is the influence of Satan and it will go away eventually. When you will convert to Islam, faith will grow into you.'

Farangis

Farangis was a divorced mother in her mid-30s living in Khujand. I came into close contact with her because she was the sister of a good friend of mine. I spent much time in their house, and she also invited me to visit her workplace, wherein religious tolerance was put to the test. She dressed in colourful, yet modest, clothes and wore a hijab. Farangis was raised in a secular family with whom she moved back together with her daughter when she divorced. Though the rest of the family was not very pious, her faith did not cause any problem, and her family fully accepted her life choices. Farangis said she started questioning her secular lifestyle when she came in closer contact with her boss, Hoji, whom she greatly respected. Farangis said that she had already been praying five times a day before her conversion and that the main change for her consisted in swapping her European clothes for Islamic ones. As will be discussed later in the chapter, she faced many problems at work because of her hijab. It was also then that she started attending religious lessons with a *bibi-otun*, a female religious leader. *Bibi-otun* is an Uzbek word, but people in Sughd, heavily influenced by the Uzbek language, use it instead of the Tajik *bibi-khalifa*. These female religious leaders serve as something like unofficial mullahs, though they also act as healers and advisers. Though their teachings are not officially sanctioned, and are therefore technically illegal, female study circles are common in Tajikistan. Farangis's study circle was led by a *bibi-otun* who lived nearby and attracted neighbours seeking spiritual, but also matrimonial and personal, guidance. Interestingly, the *bibi-otun*, who was in her mid-50s, was seeking a new younger wife for her husband because she was no longer interested in having sexual relations with him. She had proposed Farangis, who was then actively looking for a husband. Farangis was hesitant to accept the *bibi-otun*'s offer since she found the man a little too old for her.

Hoji

Hoji, Farangis' boss, was a very pious man in his mid-40s. He lived in a large house with his wife and their three-year-old daughter in the city of Khujand. His parents were dead, and he was estranged from his brothers and sisters. His wife Samira was staying at home and taking care of their daughter. She was divorced and had a son from a previous marriage, but the boy was not living with them. Samira did not talk about him, and when their daughter accidentally brought up the topic I quickly understood that it was a sensitive one. Farangis later explained the matter to me. Unlike Iskandar, Hoji did not want to raise someone else's child, and the boy was living with his maternal grandmother. Hoji's daughter was only three, but she was already wearing a hijab, which is very unusual not only in Tajikistan, but also in other Muslim societies. Generally, girls are expected to start wearing the hijab when they reach puberty. When I asked why, the parents explained me that they wanted her to get used to it, otherwise, it would be hard to make her put on a veil at age 12.

Hoji 'discovered' Islam about ten years ago. He was reflective and self-aware concerning his religious shift. Remembering the days when he used to live a secular life (also depicted as drinking, smoking, and fooling around with women), he recalled feeling completely lost after his second divorce. He felt not only lost, but also lonely and useless, and he had problems wrestling with the meaning of life. He turned to religion for answers, and found them. Notwithstanding his personal experience, Hoji interpreted the growing popularity of Islam in Tajikistan as the fact that the Soviet system still provided people with an objective in their life, that people's lives were more or less determined by the system. After independence, people found themselves without systemic guiding. He said, 'a person needs to find a purpose in life. The Soviet system used to provide us with one, but now religion does.' At the Islamic Party headquarters in Khujand, many women in their early 40s whom I met in the course of my numerous visits also described feeling lost for most of their lives. They were, they said, 'looking for answers.' They said Islam provided them with the answers they needed. Hoji worked as an upper-middle manager in a governmental organization. He was also doing some business independently, and the family appeared to be well-off. Yet, piety made his life as an administrator in a governmental institution quite difficult because of his colleagues' mistrust. Farangis had told me that they could not understand why he had suddenly turned into a 'fanatic.' Hoji, for his part, thought that they were afraid of him because as a good Muslim. He was honest and refused to take bribes, which thereby made them appear corrupt.

Gulnora

Gulnora was a dynamic young educated woman in her late 20s with a rather complicated family history. Gulnora's husband used to be a prosperous businessman who was doing import-export between Russia and Tajikistan. In 2007, he was arrested and jailed in Russia. He received a ten-year sentence, and it was not clear to me what the charges against him were. Gulnora lived in a cozy apartment in Khujand with her four children and her sister-in-law, Munira. Gulnora's eldest son was in fact her nephew, the son of a brother who had died a couple of years ago. She adopted him when he lost his parents at age six. It was unclear to me how his parents died. Gulnora had told me that they died in a plane crash in Russia, but Munira later told me that the father had disappeared in Russia, while the mother later died in a hospital in Russia as well. Munira was also in her late 20s and did not have children. She had been briefly married to the brother of Gulnora's husband, but they had divorced after three months because they did not get along. She had never worked and was now living with Gulnora, helping out with the children and other household tasks. Another of Gulnora's brothers was a Shia Muslim. He had 'converted' while pursuing his studies in Iran in an Islamic institution. He came back from Iran in 2002 and was imprisoned upon his return to Tajikistan. Gulnora explained that it was right after the 2001 attacks and that the authorities were paranoid and accused him of being a terrorist. He spent two years in jail. I never had the chance to meet him, but I was told he was running a business in Dushanbe.

Gulnora was trained in journalism and spoke Russian, Uzbek, and Tajik, as well as English. She used to work as an English teacher in a secondary school, but despite being competent, she lost her job in 2011 because of her hijab. When I met her at the IRPT's headquarters in Khujand, she had recently been hired by the Party to give English lessons. Gulnora said she was raised in a family that was not particularly religious. She recalled studying with a *bibi-otun* during her studies, but she had not been much interested in religion at the time. She came back to it later when she started living with her husband. Since he did not allow her to work, she decided to keep herself busy with religion. She started reading books and studying the Qur'an and explained that faith 'grew in her.' She then decided to start wearing a hijab. Interestingly, her husband was not really in favour of it, even though Gulnora described him as a very religious man and a *Hoji*. Now that her husband was in jail and she had become her family's main breadwinner, she found it particularly ironic that her husband had refused to let her work back then.

Gulnora respected the secular character of the state, but she said she would like to live in an Islamic country in which her religious rights would not be infringed. In particular, she hoped her religious beliefs would not be a hindrance to her professional development. She complained that schools and even private media companies would not hire her because of her hijab. When I asked her about her relations with non-believers, she said she had no problem with atheists or non-believers. She claimed to have good friends who were not religious at all. Also, contrary to other interviewees who were also very religious, she did not mind the fact that Tajiks drank alcohol and did not worship. In the end, she said, 'It's not because you wear a hijab that you are better than others. It is the good things you do that make you a good person.'

Musin and the Gonchi imams

I was introduced to two imams, father and son, by an acquaintance in a village in the district of Gonchi (70km from Khujand) in 2010. The first time we met, I sat with them for a long interview in the newly renovated village mosque. The father understood Russian, but did not speak it very well, whereas the son was fluent in Russian. Later, I used to frequent this village, and I got to spend more time with the young imam and his family. I was on several occasions invited to their house as well as to their orchard. The family was originally from the Gonchi region, but the old man's grandfather had moved to Qurghonteppa (Kathlon viloyat) in Soviet times. When he was still a child in seventh or eighth grade, the old man started studying the Qur'an with a mentor. The lessons were organized in secrecy, and he recalled waking up in the middle of the night to go to his lesson by bike. His opinion of the Soviet government was fairly positive. He even said it was a very good government for everyone, since people lived well and had jobs, though, unfortunately, religion was forbidden. He had not foreseen the civil war, and he was shocked that Tajiks could kill each other. The family moved back to the north as refugees during the civil war. The young imam, who was in his early 30s, had studied the Qur'an with his father during his youth, after which he had entered the medresse in Khujand in 1995. He said his studies were quite easy since he was well prepared, but he still enjoyed learning about Islamic scriptures as well as other topics such as Persian literature. He finished in 1999. Father and son were businessmen. They had a small shop in the village as well as land on which they cultivated grapes and other fruits. Overall, people in the village were not very religious, but they reckoned that young people were becoming increasingly interested in religion.

My acquaintances in this village were not religious at all and had never been to the mosque and rarely spoke to the imam. When I was invited to dinner at their place, a friend of mine in her early 20s came with me and told me after that she was surprised by how warm the imam's family was. She was afraid that they would despise her because of her 'European looks.' There were definitely very tolerant of other peoples' beliefs. 'As representatives of Islam, we should not judge and speak badly of people who are not very religious. Our role is to propagate good messages, and people can make choices for themselves,' said the young imam. In fact, the young imam's wife was wearing not a hijab but a light scarf, though his sisters were wearing hijabs. When I asked them if girls had been forced to remove their hijab to go to school, they said such cases did not come up because no one was wearing it. However, they reported that a few years ago, some old people had been pressuring women to cover up, but complaints to the authorities had stopped the harassment.

The young imam wanted me to meet and talk to his good friend Musin, who according to the imam, 'was very educated and had a different, interesting perspective on religion.' Musin was a man in his late 30s who owned a big store in the centre of the village. He was married and had three children. He said he started being a practising Muslim while working in Russia few years ago. He had lived there together with other Tajik migrants who studied at the Khujand medresse, so they knew the Qur'an and taught others. Musin was considered overzealous by some in his neighbourhood, who told me that he had become 'strange' after his return from Russia. I first met him during the summer of 2010 when I visited his shop, but I did not have the chance to talk to him on that day. I was impressed and intimidated not only by the quantity of Islamic gear in the shop, but also by the huge, very loud flat-screen TV that was broadcasting a prayer from Mecca. The local imam introduced me to him few weeks later. Musin was a very pious man who recalled living a fairly secular life before. In his family, he remembered only his grandmother 'reading the prayers.' He said that Soviet rule had been very detrimental to religion. In Soviet times, he said, 'people wanted to know about Islam but they could not. Muslims were like people being starved. After we became free, people started building mosques and reading the Qur'an, but Islam had been destroyed.' According to him, the current situation was 100 per cent better because 'civilization was moving forward quickly; building mosques, studying religion.' Musin acknowledged that the USSR was good to some extent – for instance, 'for its universal social programs, schools, and healthcare system – but it was awful for religion. Some people remember that things were good in Soviet times, but we don't need *that* kind of good. People should think about eternal life.'

Khairullo

Another of my interviewees, Khairullo, was a man in his 50s. I had nearly daily contact with him, and we often discussed social and political affairs since he was a friendly and frank man. He was divorced, lived alone, and was employed in an international organization, which meant that he received a good salary relative to the local average. When I asked him to talk about Soviet times, his memories were very positive. He recalled his youth, the cafes and dancing parties where he and his friends would go. He remembered how easy life was, how you could find a good job and not worry about not having enough money to pay the bills. He described himself as religious, in the sense that he believed in God, but was not following strict religious precepts in his daily life. When I asked him about his prayers habits, he said, 'I'm religious, but I won't go to the mosque to pray five times a day. Who am I to do this? An idiot, or what?' He said he did not need for anyone to know about his religious beliefs, that they were between him and God. He was very worried about what he perceived as the radicalization of his society. He had trouble understanding young people who lived by strict religious rules. 'They cover themselves, they hide, and they sit at home, they have tea and never drink alcohol, they don't even listen to music! Why are they doing this to themselves? They should go out and enjoy life.' He was also extremely critical of those he called 'fundamentalists,' accusing fully half of them of being hypocrites who did not hold genuine religious beliefs and only showed off. Khairullo also used the spiritual food metaphor to describe evolving religious dynamics, but in a totally different way. In his opinion, people were turning to religion because of harsh living conditions: 'People freeze at work, they come home, they are still freezing, there is no gas, no electricity and in some cases, not much to eat. It makes people angry, they look for answers elsewhere, but people don't need spiritual nourishment. What they need is heat, electricity and something to eat.'

The Disorder of Things

The following sections refer to the issue of religiosity as a sense-making strategy and moral guideline in the *still*-deteriorating world people live in. Indeed, changing religious dynamics 'should be seen in light of the dislocations wrought by postsocialist change and the advance of free-market capitalism.'[20] The expression 'disorder of things' could be used as an alternative to the controversial concept of ideological vacuum discussed earlier. It seems more appropriate to describe the socio-economic turmoils and hardships that people found themselves going through after independence instead of emphasizing the discard of the Communist ideology *per se*. The USSR was defined by so much more than its Marxist ideology. Despite its brutal ways and injustices, for a lot of people, the USSR also meant stability, full employement, and accessible social care. McBrien summarizes this impression as 'a sense that some dreams could be reached.'[21]

It is in this sense that I argue that people turn to religion to fill the 'ideological vacuum' or rather to cope with the disorder of things. Both religious and non-religious interviewees expressed a great sense of injustice and instability, for economic as well as political reasons: harsh living conditions, corruption, and a perceived impunity of the political elite tend to make people feel powerless. Religiosity can be empowering and give a sense of purpose. As Iskandar remarked, Islam is a limiting *ogranichenaya* religion, yet one that provides guidelines to live a good life and gives hope for a better future. The issue of morality here is also of importance. Being perceived as a good Muslim can be seen as a strategy 'for regaining agency and a sense of social belonging and attempted to rebuild the shattered moral foundations of their lives.'[22]

Foreign observers often fail to grasp the symbolic violence, the full scope and scale of the suffering that followed the USSR's collapse.[23] Trying to make sense of the so-called 'ethnic violence' in Southern Kyrgyzstan in 2010, Noah Tucker asks, 'How we can measure or disentangle the traumas of the collapse of Soviet-built and sustained economy – and the collapse of the order of things that came with transition – from the ethnic antagonism that now exists and the sense of disorder and disorientation that I hear so often here?'[24] This was even more evident in war-torn Tajikistan, where poverty and hunger threatened large portions of the population. Many Tajiks relied on foreign food supplies to survive. For the Sughd region alone, the shipping of goods dropped by 95 per cent between 1991 and 2001.[25] The war resulted in a dramatic decline of living standards and increasing feelings of insecurity. Poverty is widespread and affects around 32 per cent of the population.[26] Access to quality healthcare and education is limited and affects the healthy development of communities. McMann's research shows that current state involvement and responsiveness in Central Asia is considered greatly deficient in comparison to the services the Soviet state provided.[27] In theory, the healthcare system in Tajikistan is free and universal, as it was in Soviet times. In practice, the quality and accessibility to healthcare has been greatly undermined since independence; hospitals and clinics lack professional equipment and competent personnel. Furthermore, private out-of-pocket payments count for a far larger portion of revenues than public sources, accounting for an estimated 76 per cent of total health care expenditure in 2007[28] and overall expenditures of primary health care patients appear to have doubled between 2005 and 2011.[29] Living conditions are difficult, especially in winter time when citizens in rural areas have access to only three to four hours of electricity a day. Indeed, because of power shortages in the autumn and winter, the national electricity company, Barqi Tojik, engages in electricity pruning in all regions of Tajikistan, with the exception of the capital. A Tajik NGO called 'Union of Consumers' even set up a website called barknest.tj (literally 'there's no power') that assesses power shortages by region on a daily basis.[30]

Among other factors, such as the heritage of the Soviet planned economy, the civil war, and the lack of natural resources, economic growth was inhibited by corruption. Tajikistan scored 152 out of 175 for the Corruption Perceptions Index established by Transparency International in 2014,[31] with both grand and petty corruption representing major socio-economic hindrances. Among many high-profile cases, the case of the toll road, briefly mentioned in Chapter 2, is particularly disconcerting. In June 23, 2009, the Tajik Parliament voted to amend the Law on Highways and Road Affairs to allow toll roads to operate in the country.[32] Later it was announced that the government of China would provide a loan of $280 million, which would be used to finance the construction of a road connecting the south to the north of the country, the Dushanbe-Khujand-Chanak highway. Deputies from the opposition parties raised the toll road issue in Parliament because there was no alternative route that drivers could use to avoid paying the tolls. It caused major discontent among the population living close to the toll road. In a very rare occurrence of popular mobilization, on April 22, 2010, residents gathered more than 10,000 signatures in support of an open letter sent to the President asking him to reduce tolls for locals. Eight days later, it was announced that the toll would be lowered by one-third for Varzob residents.[33]

The contract for administering of the road was awarded without tender to Innovative Road Solutions (IRS), a company which allegedly had extensive experience in road-management in 12 different countries. It proved impossible, however, to find information about its past commercial activities and its ownership was protected as a 'trade secret.' In his investigation of this whole affair, Tajik journalist Khairullo Mirsaidov[34] connected the ownership of the company to Jamoliddin Nuraliev, who was Deputy Minister of Finance at the time and the husband of Ozodi Rahmonova, the eldest daughter of Emomali Rahmon.[35] China provided not only the funding but also the labour. The government planned to raise $20 million annually to repay the loan. However, IRS is registered in the British Virgin Islands, which is a tax haven, so tax revenues on the tolls for the Tajik state will be very low, if not nonexistent. In this transaction alone, ordinary Tajik citizens lost on three fronts: the construction of the road did not create jobs; the expenses of drivers rose since they have no alternative road to use to travel between north and south; and the Chinese loan will be repaid collectively with tax-payers' money. State enterprises are also corrupt. One example is

Talco, a state-owned aluminium plant which uses nearly 40 per cent of the country's total electricity production. The company managed to transfer $1 billion to an offshore company in the British Virgin Islands between 2005 and 2008.[36] Corruption schemes are a heavy burden, but so is disillusionment.

Petty corruption affects all sectors of society: people pay bribes to find spots in kindergartens, schools, to get University diplomas, to avoid fines, to get construction permits, to get jobs, and so on. Many Tajiks complain that corruption makes business initiatives quite costly. Entrepreneurs, for instance, sometimes need to pay heavy bribes to get the proper authorizations and permits necessary to operate their business. Also, prosperous independent businesses can be taken over by better-connected people, on the false pretext of improper registration or tax issues. There are too many examples to report in full, but the following few cases illustrate the problem, giving a sense of the negative consequences for the country's economic development as money and personal connections replace competence and skills in the distribution of resources and responsibilities.

In general, people complain that the level of education has been going downward since independence. According to the popular narrative, textbooks are inadequate and professors are underpaid and corrupt as well as incompetent. A study conducted in 2012, which involved 2,000 graduates of institutions of higher education, revealed that 27 per cent of them could neither read nor write.[37] To give one specific example, a friend of mine was a recent graduate of the Faculty of Foreign Languages at Khujand State University in English in 2011. Yet, he could not hold a simple conversation in English even after having studied it for five years. He had simply bribed his way to the diploma, feeding professors and staff substantial sums of money in exchange for the trappings of academic success. Yet, while some professors' competence in English was questionable, I have met truly outstandingly language professors at the Khujand State University, so it was possible for students to become proficient in English if they wanted to. Corruption affects not only public institutions, but also private companies. An experienced trilingual, yet unemployed, flight attendant once told me he was asked to pay a $6,000 bribe when he applied for a job at one of the two local airline companies. Not only does this system favour society's wealthiest members, it also discourages risk-taking and personal investment, and provides no meaningful barriers to incompetence.

Though there are institutions and laws that putatively fight corruption, they provide few tangible results. Quite the contrary. To make things even murkier, in March 2015, the President appointed his 27-year-old son, Rustam Emomali, as the head of the Agency for State Financial Control and Combating Corruption.[38] As mentioned earlier, Tajikistan is also marked by nepotism, and many members of the President's extended family enjoy favourable economic and political positions. Nepotism extends beyond family ties to one's region or tribe as well. The civil war was as much a struggle for power between regional clans as an ideological confrontation, and the result of the conflict was a decisive shift in the balance of power shifted in favour of the Southern Kulobi factions.

Beyond negative economic consequences, it is the widespread feeling of injustice that these practices entail that poisons the whole society. The patterns of corruption that we see in Tajikistan today did not appear until well after independence, even though the political and economic turmoil, with its processes of decentralization and privatization, created many opportunities to take advantage of state resources. Corruption was diffuse in Soviet times, and it was not necessarily monetary. The Soviet economic system was marked by chronic shortages, which encouraged the development of alternative supply channels and the use of connections and acquaintances to obtain certain things and favours. As Ledeneva explains, 'The relative unimportance of money in the command economy brought into being this specific form of exchange, intermediary between commodity exchange and gift giving.'[39] Even though there was corruption in Soviet times, it appears to have been less detrimental than in the present, and it led to less inequality between citizens and public figures. Tajik journalist Nurali Davlat argues that there was greater control over the work of civil servants back then, not because they truly believed in Soviet ideals of equality, but because they knew that if a complaint filed against them reached Moscow, there might well be consequences, up to and including the loss of employment.[40] Davlat's assessment is representative of colloquial discourses as well. People feel that they had more resources at their disposition to advance a cause in Soviet times than they do today. Most people see today's formal bureaucratic mechanisms as ineffective so that informal rules prevail. This might be one of the reasons why former Soviet citizens sometimes feel nostalgic for Soviet times. In the summer of 2013, Gallup conducted a survey across the former Soviet Union about the consequences of the break-up.[41] Except for Russia, people in the poorer countries found that the breakup had done more harm than good. Results differed in oil-rich Kazakhstan, Azerbaijan, and Turkmenistan, where people saw greater benefits in independence even though a significant portion of the population saw more harm.

Nostalgia for the USSR constitutes a research topic in itself, and my point here is not to prove that Tajiks are nostalgic for the USSR, but simply to illustrate how people long for the security and stability that it provided. Soviet propaganda was definitely positive. Economic progress and material comfort were evidence of an ongoing movement. Without

Table 5.1 Gallup Survey 2013, Breakup of the Soviet Union more harmful than good

Breakup of Soviet Union More Harmful Than Good?

In general, did the breakup of the Soviet Union benefit or harm this country?

	Benefit (%)	Harm (%)	Neither (%)	Don't know/ Refused (%)
Total*	24	51	15	11
Armenia	12	66	10	12
Kyrgyzstan	16	61	8	14
Ukraine	23	56	10	10
Russia	19	55	18	8
Tajikistan	27	52	12	10
Moldova	26	42	10	22
Belarus	26	38	15	21
Georgia	37	33	9	21
Azerbaijan	44	31	8	18
Kazakhstan	45	25	12	19
Turkmenistan	62	8	9	22

Surveys conducted in 2013.

* This question was not asked in Uzbekistan, Lithuania, Estonia, or Latvia, which were also part of the Soviet Union.

GALLUP

aiming to go back in time and reinstate an oppressive system, people can certainly still feel abandoned and that they cannot rely on official structures to support and help them move forward. Even Tajik nationalists will admit that although corruption existed under Soviet rule, there was more fairness in everyday transactions. For instance, people recall that not only were there were official channels to express grievances in regards to jobs, apartments, and land, but that officials often ruled in favour of the claimant. Now, a sense of profound arbitrariness and unfairness infects conceptions of social and economic relations. When Hoji talked about the problems he was facing at work, mainly that his faith was bothering his colleagues, he said, 'Do you know why they don't like religious people? Because we are honest. I refuse to give or take bribes and that bothers them. What are *they* doing for their country? They only thing they want is to keep the money for themselves and drive Bentleys.'

Beyond financial insecurity, there is an unsettling feeling that the world they used to live in is gone. As Louw suggests, people feel 'alienated from social worlds they had formerly invested in, and which they felt had been active in shaping their very being.'[42] Alexei Yurchak's famous book title perfectly captures that feeling: 'Everything was forever, until it was no more.'[43] An Isfara pensioner expressed his disillusion of the system to me, favouring Islamic punishments (e.g., amputating hands and whipping, as is done in Saudi Arabia, because it sets an example). That is why, according to him, crime rates were very low in the Saudi kingdom. When his 35-year-old daughter expressed her fear of one day living in an Islamic Republic, the father instead viewed this possibility in a positive light, because he thought it would bring some order in the country. He was worried about social decay, condemning discotheques, for instance, and he thought the Western lifestyle was unworthy of imitation. On many occasions, he expressed anti-American feelings and his dislike for unfettered capitalism, but he praised the Soviet Union for its social and economic achievements. At the Baptist Church in Khujand, discourses were very similar. During a sermon, the pastor told worshippers, 'We live in a corrupt world, and we cannot escape it. It is our responsibility to protect children from society's bad influences: computers, forbidden sexual activity, and alcohol.' Likewise, as the citation about mini-skirts at the beginning of the chapter exemplifies, many religious people regard with disapproval the Tajik youth's lifestyle, especially clothing habits, and call for a return to conservative values. In this regard, Agadjanian highlights the fact that, like religious prescripts, the Soviet moral system was quite traditional and conservative and emphasized strong collective family-oriented values. There were few opportunities for individual expression and sexual freedom was restrained.[44] Anti-Western bias also resonates with Soviet propaganda, and perhaps even also with current public opinion and official discourses in Russia.

In the following section, my aim is to illustrate this disorientation and insecurity and to discuss how strong faith and the religious behaviour it entails are used as a strategy to cope with chaos. My argument concerns issues of order and opportunities, of repertoires and ideological frames. As Roberts suggests: 'Muslim communities in Central Asia find themselves stuck between the desire to revive religious practices, the legacy of Soviet atheism, and the forces of globalization and capitalism.'[45] For Louw, 'Muslimness' in the post-Soviet context is a morality in the making rather than a fixed concept and 'is able to give people meaningful answers as they struggle along, trying to cope with a changing social world.'[46] It will become clear that some of those strategies refer to 'moral authority alternative to those prescribed by socialism and nationalism,'[47] which inevitably makes some believers feel that they do not fit in because they do not correspond to the image of Islamic identity promoted by the authorities.

Contested Boundaries

Iskandar: Salam Hélène! Everything is good?
Hélène: Salam Iskandar! Yes everything is fine, thanks.
Iskandar: How come everything is always fine with you?
Hélène: Hum, I don't know. It's just like that.
Iskandar: Well, I know why. It's because you are not Muslim!

This remark came unexpectedly. At the time, I found it rather funny as Iskandar was quite the joking type. It was only later that I grasped a deeper meaning of Iskandar's suggestion that being a Muslim believer in today's Tajikistan might create feelings of uneasiness. As we saw in the previous chapter, the Tajik legal framework has become increasingly obtrusive for strict adherents and ordinary believers alike. The country may be 97 per cent Muslim, but the multiplicity of interpretations regarding the place of religion in the society fuel tensions between the authorities and strict believers who don't conform to the model prescribed by the former.

Iskandar, Tolib, and Jamshed were members of a circle of friends who met on a regular basis. The circle was informal, based on simple friendship and faith, but it acted much like a solidarity circle. They referred to one another as brothers, and they supported each other as they dealt with personal and financial issues. For example, when Mera and Iskandar were forced to close down their stall at the bazaar in 2011, Mera was hired by one of the 'brothers' to work at his small pierogi stall. At the same time, the wife and two children of one of the other 'brothers,' who was in prison in Russia at the time, temporarily occupied Mera's empty apartment. Iskandar and Jamshed had set up a small business together, so their friendship also included commercial ties. I once asked Iskandar if he was always proselytizing, as he did with me. He said he did not need to because everyone around him was a believer. He then asked, 'Do you hang out with drug addicts? No, you hang out with people like yourself, who are intellectual, interested in politics, etc. The same goes for me. I hang out with people like myself.'

Similarly, the young imam, Musin and friends of his in the Gonchi district formed a brotherhood centred on the village mosque. This group of men, all in their early 40s, met regularly for both business and religious activities. Since 2006 they had been rebuilding the old crumbling village mosque, which boasted sophisticated colourful wooden carvings and paintings. They received no support from the authorities, relying entirely on donations and volunteer work to complete the restoration. They specifically wanted to restore it 'in the Tajik tradition and not like the "European-style" mosque in Khujand.' They were making plans to add a kindergarten and a small kitchen attached to the mosque. They explained that this was part of *ashar*, volunteer work that good Muslim community members should perform. In daytime, the men were doing business, transporting goods bought in Khujand to their village where they would be sold in their respective shops. During their leisure time, of which they had little, they would meet to study the Qur'an, and write and read poetry. They were very fond of classical Persian poetry, though they also admired ancient poets from the area. They could recite favourite poems from memory. Musin had written poems that focused on spiritual topics, though his most recent ones were more political, addressing the new regulations and laws, to which he was opposed.

Similar dynamics structured the Christian communities I visited in the city of Khujand. The minority status of the congregation tended to heighten their sense of unity. Yet, their proselytizing activities also meant that they looked outward. They set up community events open to the public. For instance, the Evangelical Baptist Church of Khujand provided free meals to the community on certain days and offered special consultations for alcoholics and drug addicts. The Korean Sonmin Grace Church organized free language classes in its Khujand office, and once a year offered free medical consultations by visiting Korean doctors. These consultations were extremely popular among the local population as they were considered far superior to those received in local clinics. In the city of Buston, the Presbyterian Church offered computer and English languages classes. Still, material interests do not suffice to explain the popularity of these churches. Religious attachment provided a sense of community, a social network of mutual aid that to some extent replaced the social net that existed in Soviet times. For Peyrouse, the difficulty experienced by some individuals in coping with the disintegration of social structures leads them to compensate for this change by regrouping into 'situational networks.'[48] Religious affiliations are not uniquely intense in Tajik society, in which there are many robust support networks, not only family ties, but neighbours, acquaintances, and clans. Yet, religious circles represent special units in which faith helps forming a strong bond. People such as Iskandar and his friends would probably not have formed a supportive circle had they never met at the mosque. Scholars reckon that new non-traditional religious groups have emerged in the Ferghana Valley, involving wealthy businessmen who discuss religion and economic matters in local mosques. This represents a way of using religious capital to support one's business, 'of employing local traditions to advance modernization.'[49] This phenomenon has never been observed in Hizb ut-Tahrir circles, yet for Karagiannis, liberal economic policies clash with the Islamic values of solidarity and Sharia as a way to organize society, which explains to a certain extent why the radical ideas of the Hizb ut-Tahrir are appealing to some people.[50]

Strict believers often connect current socio-economic problems to the lack of piety among the population. Tolib, who accused the authorities of persecuting believers, said: 'The Qur'an stipulates that women should wear a veil and men a beard, but in this country, Muslims cannot even serve their God as they want. That is why things are going so wrong in Tajikistan.' Similarly, Iskandar mentioned that the Qur'an never insists on the necessity of having a fully Islamic government: 'If we were good Muslims, God would give us a good leader.' Also, he saw in the natural catastrophes and shootings happening in the United States 'punishment for the unjust wars they have been waging.' Likewise, an old imam from the Gonchi district hoped that maybe in 10,000 years everyone on Earth would be a Muslim. According to him, all the negative things that are happening in the world, like global warming, came about because people do not do behave properly. A global conversion to Islam would make things right and bring order to the world.

For many of my interviewees, Sharia contained all the necessary guidelines for the establishment of an ideal and just political society. Their opinion was motivated by the fact that they were bothered by the liberal lifestyle. Iskandar, for instance, was upset that women dressed in short skirts and that alcohol was available in every corner store. He even suggested that the Organisation for Security and Cooperation in Europe (OSCE), whose work in Tajikistan he thought was completely useless, should tackle this problem. Yet, others did not mind 'walking among' non-practising Muslims, though they regretted the fact that their faith seemed to hinder their personal, social, and professional lives. Iskandar also argued that the country needed tougher laws, along the same lines as those contained in the Sharia: 'When a thief is caught, he has his hand cut. You can be sure he will never do it again, and this serves as an example for others.' At times, however, Iskandar's opinions on crime and justice were much softer. When discussing the long sentences given to alleged members of Hizb ut-Tahrir in Tajikistan, he thought this was unfair. Instead, he thought they should be given short terms and provided with counselling sessions with a good imam, who could bring them back on the right track. A member of the IRPT in Khujand expressed her wish to live in an Islamic country not because she opposed the separation between state and religion, but because in an Islamic state, no one would bother

her because of her hijab: 'People in power, they don't understand us.' Indeed, many strict believers felt alienated from socio-political affairs. Tolib was really upset about the authorities' behaviour toward Muslims, and he accused the government of interfering with sincere religious practice with its strict regulations:

> Those who sit on the chairs, they don't care about Islam. What have I done to this government? Nothing and they bother me. They deprive me of my right to be a Muslim. They want us to be a certain type of Muslims, half-Muslim, but I don't want to be the kind of Muslim they want me to be.

Local human rights activists are equally concerned about human rights infringements in the country/region and the weakness of social justice movements. However, they look for ways to enforce the current laws and mechanisms to implement the rule of law. But many strict believers feel that such efforts are futile. Tolib, for example, insisted on the worthlessness of Tajik laws:

> You can talk about violation of rights as much as you want, stand here with an enormous sign saying: 'Here, Human Rights are violated' and even use a gigantic megaphone to scream it, but nobody will listen to you. Do you know what the Constitution is good for? To go to the toilet.

Tolib was particularly resentful about the lack of religious liberties and felt that the constant pressure of the authorities might eventually backfire:

> You know if a dog wants to die, it will walk by a Mosque, piss on it and leave. If people saw it and the dog comes back, they will kill it.

For him, the authorities's attitude was perceived as insulting to religion and ordinary Muslims. By using this metaphor, he implies that there might be consequences to the imposition of restrictions on ordinary believers. Tolib was not a member of any extremist organization nor inclined to violence but his resentment is symptomatic of the frustration and difficulties lived by many ordinary Muslims in Tajikistan.

All strict believers expressed strong dissatisfaction with politics and the lack of strong protections for religious freedom in Tajikistan. In fact, their religious views caused them no end of problems with the authorities. When I first met Mera and Iskandar, they were renting a tiny booth at Khujand's Panjshanbe bazaar where they were selling local religious literature, CDs, and DVDs, as well as religious accessories such as prayer mats, perfumes, prayer beads, and the like. In August 2010, the bazaar administration ordered them to start selling non-religious goods, otherwise they would be shut down. This is ultimately what happened in 2011 as they did not have enough money to buy new goods. This situation made them particularly bitter because nothing in the law specifically forbids the selling of Islamic CDs and books. In this case, political orientations appear to have trickled down from the top and to have affected the private sector. Perhaps this is not the result of clear directives coming from above, but rather simply self-censorship from the bazaar's administration in an effort to avoid problems with the authorities. In the end, the result is that religious rights are curtailed even though discrimination is not explicitly sanctioned. Even more disturbing, in the summer of 2010, the police detained Iskandar for a whole day for allegedly officiating a Muslim wedding during which a man took a second wife. He reported that he had not been physically hurt during his detention, but that police officers had 'beaten him with words.' Overall, strict believers felt discriminated against for not fitting the mould of Muslimness proposed by the authorities. Their constant difficulties fuelled their resentment. Their dissatisfaction with the current political situation in Tajikistan was combined with a feeling that there was very little opportunity to change the situation via electoral or legal means.

On the other hand, there were others who lived a fairly religious lifestyle who were not especially critical of the authorities. The imams of the Gonchi district for instance, expressed their faith in the system and in the country's leader, praising Rahmon, who had performed the Hajj and had the Qur'an translated into Tajik. During one conversation, the son insisted on the necessity of obeying authorities for maintaining order: 'If I am not going to obey my father, what is going to happen to our family? If one does not obey authority, he goes away from Islam.'

The father, a man who had studied Islam clandestinely in Soviet times, was among the most optimistic people I met concerning the current situation: 'Our current laws don't forbid anything regarding religion. I studied those laws, and there is not a word against religion in them. We should follow them.' He seemed fairly satisfied with the freedom he enjoyed as a Muslim, even praising the President for building new mosques and medresses and for translating the Qur'an into Tajik. For him, the path taken by Tajikistan was by far superior, in terms of freedom of religion, to the one of neighbouring countries, Uzbekistan especially. The pastor of the Baptist Church in Dushanbe expressed a similar respect for the law, claiming that the Law on Religious Organizations was necessary to protect the secular character of the state and was in fact the most permissive in the former Soviet Union.

Abashin's analysis of one religious conflict in the early 1990s in the Mastchox region illuminates the dynamics at play between parties who tried to impose their views of virtuous Islamic practices. He describes the rivalry between different regional lineages, which led them to accuse one another 'of greed and hypocrisy,' to insist 'upon their own versions of "correct" Islam and orthodoxy,' and to present themselves as "real" Muslims.'[51] In Tajikistan, piety functions as both a source of trust and distrust. On the one hand, strict believers see faith as ensuring just and harmonious social relations during a time when people feel increasingly threatened by arbitrariness and greed. Indeed, some people consider strict believers as being more likely to be honest because they fear God. At the bazaar for instance, 'good Muslims' bought from other 'good Muslims' because they believed their prices would be reasonable. Interestingly, that confidence was also shared by some non-practising or non-Muslims. For instance, a family of Russians living in Khujand I got to know well also had the habit of buying from a 'God-fearing' shopkeeper at the Panjshanbe bazaar, whom they trusted more than others for fair prices.

On the other hand, the differences between practising and non-practising Muslims led to tensions. Khairullo, whom I introduced earlier in this chapter, was particularly sensitive to this. He told me of tensions at the bazaar where he saw, for instance, merchants advising customers to buy their carrots from 'good Muslims' and to not buy 'sinful (*greshnie*) carrots' from secular merchants. Khairullo, who identified himself as a believer, but lived a fairly secular lifestyle, was very critical of highly observant people, many of whom he said were just faking it to look good in front of others in response to social pressure. He was very critical of piety, and insisted that appearances were often deceiving. He gave the example of all the fuss people were making about Hojis who made the pilgrimage to Mecca. He did not understand how someone's status could rise simply after performing the Hajj: 'A drunkard (*alkash*) goes to Mecca, comes back, and he is suddenly respectable? This is not serious!' Khairullo's distrust is representative of a trend. Indeed, pilgrims enjoy high regard, though ordinary believers who perform the Hajj are sometimes accused of doing it just for show, since they don't otherwise abide by strict religious rules. Also, the return of the Hojis is an occasion for the family to throw lavish returning parties, though such parties are forbidden according to the Law on Traditions, Celebrations, and Ceremonies. These celebrations can last many days, during which the pilgrim's extended family, friends, and the whole neighbourhood are invited to congratulate the Hojis, receive their blessings, eat, and socialize with other guests. I was invited to two such parties in 2011, one in Khujand and one in the Mastchox district. Large posters or carpets were made in effigy of the Hojis, and the whole process was recorded by a professional videographer. Such celebrations boost the prestige of Hojis, who use them to flaunt their piety as well as their wealth. Indeed, such celebrations are typically quite expensive, because every guest is fed and given a gift brought back from Mecca. Ironically, many of those religious goods, such as prayer beads and scarves, are made in China. In one case, perhaps 200 persons visited the returnee's house. Though pilgrimage is one of the five pillars of Islam, it is considered an obligation only for those who have the financial means to do it. However, at one party I attended, I learned that some people take out loans to cover the expensive fees for the holy journey ($3,500), a practice many consider a sin.

Believers and non-believers alike condemn what they consider to be 'fake' religious behaviour. In particular, secular people underline the paradox of rising religious practice and declining moral standards in social and economic spheres. Khairullo said, 'Our society has never been so religious, but immoral behaviour, such as cheating and stealing, has never been so prevalent. On the contrary, faith is supposed to improve morality, no?' For him, this apparent contradiction was the proof that many religious-looking people are not genuinely pious. For him, 'people should be judged according to the good they do, not because they go to the mosque.' Likewise, observant Muslims doubt some of their peers' devotion. Female IRPT members often told me they encountered lots of people who 'pretended to be religious,' but who were in fact behaving very badly. Like Khairullo, they condemned those who made the pilgrimage, yet did not improve their lifestyle upon returning. They accused them of making the pilgrimage merely to get social recognition, and not out of heartfelt piety. Similarly, even Hoji Ibodullo Kalonzoda, the imam-khatib of Nuri-Islam mosque, doubted the sincerity of some members of his mosque, who appeared 'too selfish to be worthy of good Muslims' – a view apparently based on their lack of courtesy towards others in and around the mosque.

The young imam from the Gonchi district also addressed the issue of righteousness in Islam. He recalled an agitated encounter with some men, whom he identified as Salafis, which had left him bitter. At the bazaar, he got into an argument with men sitting at a table nearby who criticized him for his use of a ringtone, which came from an Iranian movie that recounted the life of the prophet Yusuf (Joseph). The men were saying that the movie was *haram* because it had been financed with dirty Iranian (Shiite) money. The imam was upset not only at having his beliefs questioned based on something so trivial, but also at what he perceived as a very narrow interpretation of Islam. He speculated that these men were just blindly repeating what they had been taught without questioning the legitimacy and morality of their beliefs. He also argued that such intolerant people were giving Islam a bad reputation, which is why some non-believers were afraid of Islam. For him, true believers should try to help others to embrace faith, not judge them. He explained how Salafis misinterpret the idea of Jihad by forcing secular people to pray: 'If someone reads the Qur'an literally, he will think he has to fight everybody who is not praying, including his own parents. But the mother and the father are sacred in Islam. Islam's best chance of success is to live right and show others the example.'

These narratives show the great discrepancies about what it means to be Muslim and what role should religion play in society. Some try to build an aura of respectability through religious practice, while others doubt the sincerity of believers. Ultimately, the idea was not to gauge my interviewees' faith but to expose how they judge others based on their religiousness and sincerity. Those judgements provide them with ground rules and moral standards that help them interact with others and manage their everyday lives.

My intention has been to offer a perspective on the significance of religious revival in Tajikistan, and to examine some of its facets. I suggested that the totalizing character of the Soviet system has a parallel in the tendency of contemporary religious movements to lean toward offering a total or encompassing worldview for believers. Evidence from the narratives and life experiences laid out in this chapter reveal an interesting continuity between older Soviet values and developing religious beliefs, especially as concerns issues of social justice, mutual care, and economic order. Yet, as Luerhmann explains: 'Mutual influences may be so manifold that the causal question of what came first or which side is a reflection of the other is less important than insights into the shifting balance of power between secular and religious institutions and the contribution of each side to helping people live through wider historical changes.'[52] My intention in this book has been to investigate the political and economic context that structures the debate over the place of religion in society. As I have discussed in the previous chapter, the debate over religious identities also entails a redefinition of gender roles. In that regard, the issue of polygyny brings up a challenging secular-religious puzzle: is it because Islamic practices permit polygyny that it has become a growing phenomenon acceptable to many? Or is it that economic conditions and demographic imbalances that now favour polygyny have made it so widespread that it needs to be reframed as a religious tradition?

Polygyny and Traditional Gender Roles

A father was on his death bed and yet his daughter refrained from visiting him because her husband was away and he had told her not to leave the house in his absence. The woman sought advice from the Prophet who suggested her to listen to her husband, which she did. The father eventually died without seeing his daughter one last time. The husband came back and when he learned what has happened, he went to the Prophet to ask him why he did not tell

his wife to visit her dying father. Then the Prophet said: 'The
father will go to heaven for he has raised such a docile woman.'
    LESSON FROM THE QUR'AN as told by an IRPT MILITANT

Polygyny is on the rise in Tajikistan and the phenomenon is inextricably
connected to labour migration.[53] According to the Russian Federal
Migration Service, as of January 2015 there were 999,169 migrants from
Tajikistan residing in Russia, including 182,262 women.[54] In 2014,
41 per cent of the Tajik GDP came from the revenues of migrant workers,
making Tajikistan one of the most remittance-dependent countries in the
world.[55] In the absence of men, women are compelled to play more
important roles as they become the families' and sometimes communities'
main pillars. Theoretically, this situation could lead to the empowerment
of women but the lack of economic opportunities hinders such
development. What is especially alarming is the rapid increase of suicide
rates, especially among young women. The national suicide rate in
Tajikistan among the youth (15–19 years old) increased 63 per cent from
2.8 to 4.5 per 100,000 between 2008 and 2010. Female suicide rates
increased 176 per cent, from 1.9 to 5.2 per 100,000, while males
experienced only a 6 per cent increase, from 3.6 to 3.9 per 100,000.
In 2011, more than 200 women committed suicide in the northern
province of Sughd alone, which has a population of around 2.2 million.
The reasons cited are poverty, lack of life prospects, and domestic
violence.[56] A survey conducted in 2012 reported that 25 per cent of
women in Sughd had suffered from violence perpetrated by their spouse
while only 12 per cent reported such cases in the central region called
District under Republican Subordination.[57] It is impossible to know if the
regional variations are due to discrepancies in the actual number of cases or
to a higher level of awareness in the Sughd region. In any case, exact
numbers might be higher since domestic violence is often perpetrated by
in-laws, and not necessarily by spouses, a question neglected by the survey.
The government passed a Law on the Prevention of Domestic Violence in
2013 that might encourage more women to denounce abuses and change
the widespread perception that domestic violence is acceptable. Finally,
another sign of distress is the exposure of a number of horrendous cases of
infanticide since 2008, to a point where journalists are wondering if this is
turning into a sombre pattern.[58] These gloomy numbers reflect the social
and economic distress that is prevalent in today's Tajikistan, which

especially affects women. Additionally, labour migration to Russia exacerbates the precariousness of family stability.

As mentioned earlier, marriages are often arranged in Tajikistan and it is unusual to find couples who married 'out of love,' especially in rural areas where socializing opportunities are limited. Parents usually select potential candidates and present their son or daughter with a choice. If most marriages are arranged, they are rarely forced. In most instances, children may oppose their parents' choice and even propose someone they like. Despite a law adopted in 2011 that raised the legal age of marriage from 17 to 18, underage marriage persists in Tajikistan. The government has also adopted a law that outlaws consanguineous marriages since it has become a public health issue. Indeed, it was reported that there are 26,430 disabled children in Tajikistan and 35 per cent of these were born in consanguineous marriages.[59] Families either rely on Nikoh or bribe officials if they want an official registration (*Zapis Aktov Grazhdanskogo Sostoyaniya*, simply known as ZAGS).[60] Nikoh is almost always performed, even by non-religious people. It is seen as a symbolic gesture that complements the formal state wedding registration and that respects tradition. Sometimes, when divorcees remarry or when a man takes a second or third wife, the Nikoh is the only ceremony performed. It is done to legitimize the union, from not only a religious but also a social point of view. An unofficially married couple who would not have performed the Nikoh would be considered illegitimate.

Even though society is quite conservative, divorce is common in Tajikistan, even among the most religious people. In 2012, 7,608 divorces were officially registered in Tajikistan, which is 11 per cent more than in 2011. In 2013, the number of divorces increased again by 7 per cent in comparison to the previous year. In 2013, the number of marriages registered was slightly lower than the number of divorces.[61] In today's rapidly evolving world, the fragility of loveless arranged marriages at a young age might explain the increasing number of divorces. And labour migration also has an important impact on divorce rates. Oinikhol Bobonazarova, former would-be presidential candidate in 2013 and social activist, explained how living far from home changed people's expectations and their view of the constraints of tradition.[62] While in Russia, many Tajik men seize the opportunity to have romantic affairs with Russian women who are more socially active and sexually liberated than their Tajik wives. This becomes a problem when men return home and start seeing their wife as 'boring.' Harris explored the tensions lived by migrant couples when men return home. Though feeling unsatisfied by their marriage, men would not want to replicate the lifestyle they had with their Russian girlfriends, especially the sexual pleasure, because they feared that it would encourage their wives to be more independent and, even worse, sexually active.[63] Such strained relationships put couples to the test and many men end up divorcing while in migration. In Sunni Islam, men can divorce their wives by saying *Talaq* three times and many migrants end up divorcing over the phone while in Russia. Faced with this phenomenon, in April 2011, the Council of Ulemas of Tajikistan announced its intention to issue a fatwa that would ban SMS-divorces.[64] In 2013 alone, more than 1,700 women sought help from the Committee on Women and Family Affairs and the Council of Ulemas to resolve such litigations. Yet, in January 2014, the Council announced that it could not stop the phenomenon and concluded that it was not contrary to Sharia.[65]

Alone with children, without money, and with few employment opportunities, divorcees struggle to make a living. Such precarious economic conditions certainly contribute to the rise of polygyny in Tajikistan. I use the term 'polygyny' instead of the commonly used 'polygamy' since it is more specific. In Tajikistan, as in most countries where it is practised, polygamy refers to the marriage of one man and at least two women and the opposite is extremely rare. It is also a better translation of the Russian term *mnogozhenstvo* (many wives).

Though legally forbidden, polygyny is common. Because it is outlawed, it is difficult to have an accurate portrait of polygyny in Tajikistan. In 2000, a pilot survey conducted by the World Health Organization (WHO) in Tajikistan reported that 21 per cent of married women in a sample of 840 had polygamous husbands. However, a different survey conducted in 2003 reported that less than one per cent of households were in polygamous marriages.[66] More recently in 2010, a survey conducted by a Tajik research institute revealed that about 10 per cent of Tajik men were engaged in polygynous relationships[67] but the number could be higher. The evolving structure of the Tajik family model forced discussions in the country. In order to protect the rights of second or third wives, some civic organizations even favour the legalization of polygyny.[68] This is perhaps one of the reasons why the government designated 2015 the Year of the Family and planned on adopting a series of measures to support families. The President also announced that a new topic, 'culture of family life,' was in preparation and would be introduced in schools to prepare youth for adult life.[69]

Polygyny has become so widespread that Tajiks discuss it without any restraint. Many believers genuinely thought that polygyny was justified since women greatly outnumbered men in the world, as written in the Qur'an. Yet, when I mentioned that official statistics confirmed that the number of men and women was nearly even, I was looked at with incredulity and the conversation fell flat. Others were under the impression that the great numbers of war widows resulted in an imbalance between the number of men and women in Tajikistan. In fact, the number of casualties during the civil war resulted in a demographic gender imbalance in Tajikistan but its effects today are insignificant. Surprisingly, according to the most recent census, the number of women in Tajikistan is in fact lower than the number of men by 2 per cent.[70] Yet, given the number of labour migrants, the actual number of men present on the territory is likely inferior than that of women. Stepping away from statistics, one observer in rural Tajikistan will quickly notice how some villages seem to have been deserted by men.

Interestingly, Uehling argues that: 'marital infidelity was reframed as a Muslim tradition called polygyny, lending it an aura of respectability.'[71] My personal experience points in this direction. Despite social conservatism, infidelity is widespread and even if prostitution remains taboo, it is common in major cities. I was myself more than once confronted with 'romantic' invitations: I received a number of marriage proposals from married men to become a second or third wife, from divorced men to become the first wife and repeatedly asked on dates by married men. In a particularly embarrassing moment of my fieldwork, Iskandar asked me to teach him how to use the internet. I accepted and agreed to meet him at an internet café. Once there, I found out that his true intention was to register to a Muslim dating site and needed my help for it. He explained that he was planning to travel to Chechnya, Russia for work and wanted to find a local wife while working there. His intention was to perform the Nikoh, the religious marriage, so that the union would be in accordance with Islamic Law. Iskandar, who already had two wives, confessed that: 'he could not live without a woman.' Were it not for the plan to bless the marriage by performing the

Nikoh, Iskandar's behaviour would certainly be interpreted as adultery. Ultimately, I refused to do it and never told Mera about it even though she was aware that Iskandar might eventually take another wife. In fact, he had once proposed me to become his third wife right in front of her.

Later, when I asked Iskandar about the proper way for Muslim men to 'acquire' more wives, he pledged that a man could marry a second or third time without the consent or approval of his other wife or wives. When I asked Hoji the same question, he said consent was not always mandatory. He explained, for example, that if a man is 'hot' and his wife is 'frigid,' he can secretly marry. In other cases, he said the couple should take the decision together. As I will tell in the next chapter, some women even take the matter in their own hands and actively look for second wives.

During a dinner with IRPT female militants that I recalled earlier, the issue of polygyny eventually came up. When I asked them whether or not a husband should consult his wife before deciding to marry again, opinions were divergent. The youngest of the group, whom I found rather conservative and intransigent, answered that the husband should get permission from his wife but the older women interrupted her and said that it is the husband's decision alone. She quickly retracted and went on explaining that women have to listen to their husband and not even go out of the house without his permission. She concluded that a woman should not be jealous, she should welcome a new wife as her own sister and be happy because these are the laws of God: 'If you love god, you will accept it.' This was an uneasy topic since most women seemed to be uncomfortable with the idea of having to share their husband. One of them even murmured: 'Easier said than done.'

Discourses on traditional gender roles have become pervasive in Tajikistan. They particularly affect women since men have more social and political leverage. It is a multi-faceted phenomenon triggered by a combination of political, religious, social, economic, and demographic factors. It is difficult to tell which of those aspects prevails but there are two sides of the phenomenon to distinguish. On the one hand, increasing piety contributes to retraditionalization since the rediscovery of Islamic scriptures and practices entail the reaffirmation of certain traditional values and gender roles. While I have not met women who admitted to being forced to wear a hijab, it is likely that in some conservative milieus, women experience social and peer pressure to cover themselves. Yet, conservatives do not necessarily advocate the reclusion of women; in fact, some very religious men boast about favouring the emancipation of women, who they think should play an active role in society. I have indeed met a number of very conservative women who were socially active, either working or engaged in social work. Also, the education of women is often praised and encouraged. Most conservatives will acknowledge that Islam favours the education of women, but this is mostly associated with the idea that educated women make better mothers. In this regard, the position of conservatives is not so different from the state's. Akin to the IRPT's stance on the hijab, Mera and Iskandar mentioned the impact that the hijab ban could have on the education of women, which, they said, was valued in Islam. Even though he framed the hijab ban as a hindrance to the right to education for women, in reality, Iskandar did not seem to attach much importance to women's education. When I asked Mera about how she learned the Islamic scriptures, she said that she never really studied and relied on her husband to teach her the prayers instead. Despite that, most people will follow traditional gender roles of obedience and maintain that women should obey their husband. Iskandar once told me that the best quality a woman could have was to be 'obedient' (*poslushnaya*), while a man should be 'kind' (*dobrii*). Moreover, Iskandar and his friend Tolib once argued with me that women only possessed 50 per cent of the intellectual capacities of men. When I expressed doubts, they explained that it was written as such in the Qur'an and assured me that scientists had proven it already. Also, according to them, the fact that parliaments all over the world were in majority dominated by men was yet another proof that women were intellectually inferior.

Interestingly, some of the above conservative attitudes echo state narratives. Talking about Egypt, Hatem notices the convergence of secularist and Islamist discourses, especially with regards to the 'domesticity as part of their definitions of femininity.'[72] While official discourses insist on secular values and praise the secular character of the state and society, they are also extremely conservative and intersect with religious ones by insisting on obedience and traditional gender roles. Despite a certain willingness to protect women from obscurantism, official discourses actually prevent women from pursuing more decisive roles outside the house by emphasizing their nurturing role as mothers. And like Islamic scriptures, state discourses also impose dress and conduct codes. Veiled women have become the target of secular authorities who label them as outsiders and even, on some occasions, as dangerous individuals. The authorities do not hesitate to use legal as well as physical coercion to enforce their ideological orientations. Finally, economic and political conditions do not encourage anyone, and even less so women, to become socially and politically empowered. Eventually, such patronizing practices can only foster resentment toward a privileged and commanding political elite.

Peyrouse argues that religiousness should be seen as a resurgence of religious institutions rather than as a revival of personal faith among individuals, that there is little change in the intensity of personal religious feelings, but rather a change in the political expression of those feelings.[73] As the discourses outlined above show, one important aspect of people's renewed faith is the presumed congruity of religious liberties, Islam, and social harmony. My interviewees saw faith as emancipating, despite numerous limitations, including the increased likelihood of getting into trouble because of one's religious practices. I have tried to show that Islam and Islamic values are sometimes seen as a way to find a sense of justice in the absence of a legitimate channel for expressing discontent. In other cases, Tajiks view their faith simply as part of a personal spiritual life, without any strong connection to political aspirations or ideals. Still other narratives have shown the limitations of the categories of religious and secular in understanding what is today happening in Tajikistan. While some people feel discriminated against for their religious beliefs, others believe that the current leadership is providing a healthy environment for Islam to flourish and religious beliefs to be manifested.

On the one hand, religion is limiting as it imposes strict codes of conduct concerning social and personal behaviour in daily life, which matches a desire for social order in a difficult economic environment plagued by widespread corruption. The economic collapse in Tajikistan is clearly not the main cause of increasing religiosity, but it certainly adds to the sentiment of disorientation, which has been a common feature of Tajik life since independence. On the other hand, faith can also be liberating. By this, I mean that relying on God's will relieves an individual from having to take complete responsibility not only for his or her personal destiny, but also for the community's well-being. In this sense, religious guidance acts as a forceful governing authority in much the way that the Soviet totalitarian system did in much the way that the Soviet totalitarian system did. Religious affiliation also provides a sense of community and mutual assistance that compensates for the sense of disorientation and dispossession that has dogged Tajik society since independence.

CONCLUSION

The twentieth century was the century of atheism; the twenty-first century will be the century of Islam.

REPRESENTATIVE OF THE IRPT's WOMEN'S COMMITTEE

From the beginning, my main intention has been to explore the tensions and connections between the Soviet legacy and the religious revival in Tajikistan. I have favoured a theoretical approach, which I have called 'neo-institutionalist ethnography,' which acknowledges the agency of political actors without neglecting the ideational frames that structure their actions. I have argued that in Tajikistan, Soviet culture, in the largest sense, but particularly its atheist policies, its emphasis on collectivism, and its holistic collectivist ideology, continues to influence policy-making, people's understanding of the proper place of religion in society, and the articulation of religious identities. I traced the Soviet legacy and its impact in the making of moral choices and redefinitions of the self. Most significantly, I clarified some of the most important meanings assigned to religious practice in Tajikistan.

This project required a detailed account of the Soviet secularization process in order to analyse how it informed the understanding of religion in society in Tajikistan. Both scholarly and Western public opinion tend to picture the Soviet socio-political project as something spectacular and unique, set apart from the historical development of secularization in the Western world. Such a view emphasizes the brutality and totalitarian ambition of the Soviet project while neglecting the agency of the socio-political actors actually engaged in the process.[1]

Still, under the Soviet regime, state involvement in socialization and education was overwhelming and coercive. For several decades, Soviet authorities successfully imposed many behaviours and inhibited many others. I dismissed interpreting the modernization process in terms of an external imposition and passive assimilation of social norms; it is rather the internal, active transformation and appropriation of such norms that shapes today's social, political, and religious dynamics in the former Soviet states. At bottom, I have argued that the concept of *accommodation*, rather than *resignation* or *resistance*, best reflects the attitude of the peoples of the former Soviet states toward modernization and the legacy of Soviet values.

It seemed important to undertake a more focused analysis and investigate the popular aspects of religious revival. To paraphrase Khalid, how can we speak of political Islam in Tajikistan if we do not understand what Islam means for the people in Tajikistan? I stressed the relevance and appropriateness of an ethnographic approach for the study of religious politics, because it offers a way to accommodate human agency of both the researcher and the people from whom we seek knowledge.[2] Research on personal religious practices touches on very intimate aspects of one's life. I therefore expected that my interviewees would be reluctant to address those issues. I was surprised to see how open and enthusiastic people were when asked about their religious experiences and feelings. The possibility of producing thick descriptions is an important methodological advantage of ethnographic fieldwork. The use of investigative approaches that require prolonged observation, acceptance, and trust-building positions scholars to make sense of complex socio-political dynamics. As I have argued throughout the book, academic research should not rely on fixed categories, but should deliberately leave room open for imagination and a diversity of perspectives.

When I compared Tajikistan's current religious policies with previous Soviet ones, I emphasized formal rules and political discourses that pervade the politico-religious field. I argued the resilience of both Soviet values and the presumption of state control over religious life. However, while Soviet-style authoritarian institutions have been maintained, the authorities seem incapable of delivering a unifying and inspiring secular message. They instead fall back on authoritarian practices and propagate a paternalistic and nationalist discourse that draws on diluted Islamic references. These official narratives are lost on a certain portion of the population, which sees Islam as a source of inspiration for the making and remaking of identities.

My intention was to demonstrate that the state is not necessarily monolithic and that state actors can also have equivocal positions on religious issues. In particular, I used discrepancies in the application of the law and in justifications for police interventions to demonstrate that local contexts and dynamics matter. Moreover, not everyone sees the state as hostile to Islam. Although this was not the main focus of my investigation, I showed that a portion of the population, including some clerics, actually supports state policies. Also, a significant portion of the population, traumatized by the horrors of the war, bears with authoritarian practices so long as they perceive that they stabilize the country.[3] Still, the war ended 17 years ago, and the current generation does not remember or relate to wartime. This disconnect might be a game changer in the near future.

A nuanced understanding of *ideological vacuum* was useful to describe the instability created by the sudden dissolution of an ideological and socio-economic project that had held the nation together for decades. The same concept was helpful when I described the arbitrariness and social disorganization of social interactions in Tajikistan, as compared with the memory of past practices, even though the Soviet political and economic system had also been characterized by informal rules and transactions. I asserted that the holistic and collectivist values of the Soviet regime continue to operate – if perhaps unconsciously – as normative references, even for religious people who despised Soviet atheism. I have argued that the redefinition of religious identities may be triggered by a multiplicity of factors, but I have nevertheless insisted on the overarching effects of the ideological vacuum in Tajikistan and the sense of dismay that followed the collapse of the USSR. The shockwave was intense, but its effect was aggravated in Tajikistan as the country descended into civil war. My fieldwork focused on Tajikistan's most Sovietized and industrialized region, which was not directly affected by the war. Nevertheless, the region has been experiencing rapid Islamization. I argued that a strict adherence to religion could be interpreted as a 'sense-making' strategy, as it provides authoritative guidelines for personal comportment and social relations in an environment marked by poverty, corruption, and limited political liberties. Strict believers often feel politically, socially, and economically alienated. If some expressed support for the establishment of an Islamic state, this may have more to do with resentment against the current authorities' anti-religious bias than a fundamental animus against the secular state as such.[4] Yet, such a strategy undermines the authority of the state.

My findings indicate that the current dearth of broadly current socio-political landmarks and the challenging economic situation contribute to an increase in religiosity. I also demonstrated that, as in Soviet times, there exists no bright and reliable demarcation between the religious and the secular, as these two spheres overlap constantly, depending on circumstantial definitions of appropriate behaviour. Depending on the situation, I found it necessary in some instances to conceptualize people's attitudes and behaviours in terms of *crossing* the boundary between the secular and the religious, and in other instances as *redefining* that boundary.[5] Both types of moves or plays appear to be motivated by a desire to redefine moral standards. I also demonstrated that the weight of social pressure must be considered, as some people feel pressured to adopt certain religious behaviours in order to wrap themselves in the respectability of Islamic values. Some people's stories also revealed that different degrees of religiosity can contribute to social tensions, mainly between those who identify as secular or as moderate believers on the one hand, and those who live by strict religious principles on the other. Such tensions are not due to the growth of religion per se, but by the fear that such growth inspires in the secular segments of society. For most moderate believers, strictly observant Muslims are seen as dupes or victims of fanaticism. And while some strict believers have no trouble envisaging an Islamic democracy, moderate believers see little (if any) compatibility between Islam and democracy and a greatly restricted space for individual freedom within a Sharia-based society. Most religious moderates understandably view the reaffirmation of religious values as a return to obscurantist ways.

The focus of my research was hyper-local but many of the conclusions are not. Cefaï mentions that a good ethnographic account should engender concepts that apply to a particular case, but which aspire to be tested on other cases – not by applying such concepts unthinkingly as preformed templates, but as sources of inspiration, as starting points for shaping observation and reflection.[6] The issue of conflicting moralities not only reveals much about domestic Tajik politics, but also exemplifies the difficulties of nation-building in post-Soviet countries. Yet, such struggles are not limited to the former USSR. The issue of the place of religion in the society and the respect of religious freedoms is common to many societies. Recent debates over religious freedoms in the increasingly multicultural societies of Europe and North America illustrate the difficulties of establishing the boundaries regarding the expression of faith. Even in these overwhelmingly non-Muslim communities, the hijab and other religious garments are the object of controversies. At variance with, North African countries appear as potentially interesting comparative cases. Despite having very different political systems, parallels can be drawn in regards to the regulation of religion. The presence in many North African states of an official clergy, a closed political environment, and an Islamic opposition[7] reinforce the comparative advantage. Such comparisons naturally leads us away from the specifics of the Soviet legacy and closer to the general idea that authoritarianism might be a significant factor when accounting for the emergence of religious conflicts. I believe that such comparisons are likely to reveal that Central Asian states have coped with religious dynamics by using strategies that go beyond the simple reproduction of Soviet norms, and which respond to the specific domestic challenges they face. Moreover, the example of China, a non-Islamic authoritarian state in which the government interferes strongly in people's religious affairs, shows that the dynamic I am discussing extends beyond the Muslim world. The Chinese Communist Party has since 1949 controlled religious elements that might pose a threat to its interests through the strategies of cooptation, cooperation, and repression. In so many contexts, we find that the place of religion in public and political spheres epitomizes the fundamental struggle for political inclusion and social justice.

Islam in Tajikistan: National and International Influences

Olivier Roy has qualified the IRPT as a movement led by modern intellectuals who saw Islam as a political ideology capable of holding the state together.[8] Roy's characterization of IRPT leaders as 'modern intellectuals' touches on a crucial aspect of the politico-religious discord in Tajikistan. As the following quote suggests, strict believers hold that the atheist and secular policies that shaped Soviet – and continue to shape post-Soviet – political orientations belong to another era. For instance, many IRPT members have complained that the current political leadership in Tajikistan are still driven by an atheist outlook, which means that they are disconnected from current Tajik society. Ilhom Yakubov, former Chairman of the IRPT in Sughd, has summarized this opinion very well:

> They have a twentieth century mentality. They don't understand us, but we understand how and why they think the way they do. They have been educated in the Soviet system. They call themselves believers, but they are not. They think religion is something of the past and that traditions should be forgotten, but they are themselves of the past! Let me give you an example. When I sent my application to the regional Hukumat for the elections last year (2010), they told me to send a fax! Fax. Isn't that a twentieth century technology? Who uses fax these days when you have the internet? People at the Hukumat don't have computers and don't even know how to use them. How can they possibly understand society? Ninety-eight per cent of our society is Muslim but they don't want to acknowledge it.

Strict believers claim to offer a distinctive perspective on modernity that redefines notions of equality and social justice from a different, non-Western angle. Indeed, far from being anti-modern, they aspire to a pious and moral modernity, with all the material benefits that come with it. In light of the ban of the IRPT in 2015, there seems little chance for an Islamic strain of modern political thought to flourish in Tajikistan. Strengthening authoritarian practices increases the cost of opposition for formal political actors as well as for ordinary citizens. With poor economic indicators and few prospects for improvement, resentment could grow even stronger. My research has led me to view claims about the radicalization of Islam in Central Asia as alarmist. While I do not deny the existence of radicalism, the threat of an armed insurgency is unlikely. Yet, religiosity in general seems unlikely to decrease. As oppositional spaces are shrinking in Tajikistan, it seems relevant to look at the development of political or religious movements of Tajiks abroad. Labour migration induces new socio-political dynamics that redefine religious identities. The story of Musin, a village trader from the Gonchi district who became religious while living with devout Tajiks in Moscow, suggests a potential connection between acculturation and/or labour exploitation and religious attitudes. Musin's experience is representative of an accelerating tendency as more and more migrants cope with their unsettling working experience by turning to religion.[9] Islam, with its unifying message, provides migrants guidance and moral landmarks. Roy's study of fundamentalism in Europe describes the difficulties faced by Muslims in trying to assert their identity in a non-Muslim context.[10] Roy suggests that uprooted Muslims, in search of new identities, are vulnerable to being seduced by fundamentalist aspirations to establish an imaginary Ummah. However, their engagement is not necessarily political and often takes place outside the purview of the state. Despite its references to 'the fundamentals' and calls to return to purer (ancient) forms of Islamic polity, Roy argues that fundamentalism is not anti-modern. On the contrary, it is precisely modernity or post-modernity that created the conditions for European fundamentalism to emerge. Social isolation and the use of the internet create room for the emergence of a global Islamic identity not necessarily grounded in local communities and the everyday life of the believers.[11] As discussed briefly earlier, many ISIS frighters from Central Asia were recruited via the internet in Russia while working as labour migrants.[12] Alienated from the host society and sometimes disconnected from their own community back in Central Asia, migrants can present easy targets for recruiters. The forces of globalization powerfully affect Central Asian societies in many ways. Because they are exposed to alternative lifestyles, with varied attitudes toward individual freedom and religion, labour migrants challenge the patriarchal secular order that prevails in Tajik society. Some lean towards more liberal lifestyles, others towards more conservative or illiberal ones.

Both scholars[13] and journalists[14] have also repeatedly warned about the threat posed by the Taliban on the southern border, especially after the withdrawal of foreign troops in 2014. Yet, history shows that the connections between the Taliban, at the exception of the IMU that has now relocated even further from Central Asia, and other groups are tenuous. The Taliban ruled over Afghanistan for over five years between

1996 and 2001 with limited impact on Central Asian states. Even though they are now gaining more territory in northern Afghanistan, it is difficult to imagine a fundamentalist spillover into Tajikistan. Ultimately, the drug trade might be a more disruptive factor for Central Asia. Given their basically secular character, Tajik and Central Asian societies remain largely immune to full-fledged radicalization as there is limited support for radical ideologies and even less so for armed militancy. The portrait I have painted of contemporary Tajikistan does not, in short, depict the emergence of Islamic extremism, but rather a fragile and intricate intermingling of ways of being in the world in unsettling times.

NOTES

Introduction   Religious Revival in Tajikistan

1. Saodat Olimova and Muzaffar Olimov, 'The Withdrawal of NATO Forces from Afghanistan: Consequences for Tajikistan,' Afghanistan Regional Forum, March 6, 2013, http://centralasiaprogram.org/blog/2013/03/06/the-withdrawal-of-nato-forces-from-afghanistan-consequences-for-tajikistan-2/, 2.
2. Formerly Kurgan-Tyube.
3. Statistical Agency under the President of the Republic of Tajikistan, 'Informatsia O Chislenosti Musul'man v Respublike Tadzhikistana (Information on the Number of Muslims in the Republic of Tajikistan),' 2013, http://stat.tj/ru/news/186/.
4. Froese cites a dubious survey published in the *World Christian Encyclopaedia* in 2001. He himself acknowledges that the use of surveys in authoritarian environments cannot realistically provide trustworthy data. According to the survey, the number of believers (including all religions) in Tajikistan has increased from 66 per cent to 85 per cent between 1970 and 1995 and is now one of the highest rates in the former Soviet states. Paul Froese, *The Plot to Kill God: Findings from the Soviet Experiment in Secularization* (Berkeley: University of California Press, 2008). Different statistics show that in 1987, 45 per cent of Tajiks identified as believers. Dilip Hiro, *Between Marx and Muhammad: The Changing Face of Central Asia* (London: HarperCollins, 1994), 197.
5. EurasiaNet, 'Tajikistan: Prayer Rooms Targeted for Demolition,' *EurasiaNet*, February 25, 2016, http://www.eurasianet.org/node/77536.
6. Steven Wagner, 'Public Opinion in Tajikistan: 1996 Findings' (Washington: International Foundation for Electoral Systems (IFES), 1997), 111.
7. Participants were asked about the number of times they prayed a day; 41 per cent of the respondents prayed 1 to 5 times a day, but only 1 per cent prayed 5 times a day.

8. Michael Taarnby, 'Islamist Radicalization in Tajikistan: An Assessment of Current Trends' (Dushanbe: Korshinos, 2012), 36.

9. Islam News, 'V Tadzhikistane v mesyats' Ramazan 88% naseleniya sobliudaiut post (In Tajikistan, 88% of the Population Fast During Ramadan),' *Islam News*, August 13, 2012, http://islamnews.tj/tajikistan/471-v-tadzhikistane-v-mesyac-ramazan-88-naseleniya-soblyudayut-post.html.

10. SADUM stands for the Russian acronym *Sredne Aziatskoe Dukhovnoe Upravlenie Musulman*. Established in Tashkent in 1943, the SADUM was responsible for elaborating and implementing the broad religious orientations for the Central Asian Republics.

11. International Crisis Group, 'Central Asia: Islam and the State,' Asia Report (International Crisis Group, 2003), http://www.crisisgroup.org/en/regions/asia/central-asia/059-central-asia-islam-and-the-state.aspx.

12. Maria Elisabeth Louw, *Everyday Islam in Post-Soviet Central Asia* (New York: Routledge, 2007).

13. Shirin Akiner, 'The Politicisation of Islam in Postsoviet Central Asia,' *Religion, State and Society* 31, no. 2 (2003): 97–122; Alexei Malashenko, 'Islam And Politics In Central Asian States,' in *Political Islam and Conflicts in Eurasia*, ed. Lena Jonson and Murad Esenov (Stockholm: CA&CC Press, 1999); Petra Steinberger, '"Fundamentalism" in Central Asia: Reasons, Reality and Prospects,' in *Central Asia: Aspects of Transition*, ed. Tom Everett-Heath (New York: Routledge, 2003), 219–43; Laurent Vinatier, *L'islamisme en Asie centrale* (Paris: Armand Colin, 2002); Malashenko, 'Islam And Politics In Central Asian States.'

14. John Heathershaw and Nick Megoran, 'Contesting Danger: A New Agenda for Policy and Scholarship on Central Asia,' *International Affairs* 87, no. 3 (2011): 589–612.

15. Freedom House, 'Nations in Transit: Tajikistan' (Washington: Freedom House, September 29, 2015), https://freedomhouse.org/report/nations-transit/2015/tajikistan.

16. Edward Schatz, 'Ethnographic Immersion and the Study of Politics,' in *Political Ethnography: What Immersion Contributes to the Study of Power*, ed. Edward Schatz (Chicago: The University of Chicago Press, 2009), 1–22.

17. Paul Froese, *The Plot to Kill God: Findings from the Soviet Experiment in Secularization* (Berkeley: University of California Press, 2008), 147–8.

18. Shahram Akbarzadeh, 'Islamic Clerical Establishment in Central Asia,' *South Asia: Journal of South Asian Studies* 20, no. 2 (1997): 73–102.

19. Taarnby, 'Islamist Radicalization in Tajikistan: An Assessment of Current Trends,' p. 34.

20. S. A. Tokarev, 'Religion and Religions from the Historical-Ethnographic Viewpoint,' in *Secularization in Multi-Religious Societies Indo-Soviet Perspectives*, ed. S. C. Dube and V. N. Basilov (New Delhi: Concept Publishing Company, 1983), 125–39.

21. Pew Research Center, 'U.S. Religious Knowledge Survey' (Washington: Pew Research Center, 2010), http://www.pewforum.org/2010/09/28/u-s-religious-knowledge-survey-about-the-project/.
22. Louw, *Everyday Islam in Post-Soviet Central Asia* (London: Routledge, 2007).
23. Stephane A. Dudoignon and Christian Noack, eds, *Allah's Kolkhozes: Migration, De-Stalinisation, Privatisation and the Emergence of New Muslim Religious Communities in the USSR, and After (1950s–2000s)*, Klaus Schwarz Verlag (Berlin: Klaus Schwarz, 2014).

Chapter 1 A Neo-Institutionalist Ethnography of Religious Revival

1. While some scholars include Mongolia and Afghanistan in their definition of Central Asia, the reference I use encompasses the five ex-Soviet republics of Kazakhstan, Kyrgyzstan, Tajikistan, Turkmenistan and Uzbekistan. Use of this denomination became widespread in the 1990s, whereas in Soviet times the region was referred to as 'Middle Asia' (Srednaya Aziya) and it excluded Kazakhstan.
2. Hélène Carrère d'Encausse, *L'Empire Éclaté: La Révolte Des Nations En URSS* (Paris: Flammarion, 1978).
3. Alexandre Bennigsen and Chantal Lemercier-Quelquejay, *L'Islam en Union soviétique* (Paris: Payot, 1968); Alexandre Bennigsen and Chantal Lemercier-Quelquejay, *Le Soufi et le commissaire: Les confréries musulmanes en URSS* (Éd. du Seuil, 1986).
4. James Critchlow, 'Islam and Nationalism in Soviet Central Asia,' in *Religion and Nationalism in Soviet Union and East European Politics* (Duke: Duke Press Policy Studies, 1984), 104–20.
5. Vitaly V. Naumkin, *Radical Islam in Central Asia: Between Pen and Rifle* (Lanham, MD: Rowman & Littlefield Publishers, 2005); Richard Weitz, 'Storm Clouds over Central Asia: Revival of the Islamic Movement of Uzbekistan (IMU)?,' *Studies in Conflict & Terrorism* 27, no. 6 (2004): 505–30, doi:10.1080/10576100490513558; Igor Rotar, 'Will the Fergana Valley Become a Hotbed of Destabilization in Central Asia?' *Jamestown* 9, no. 180 (October 3, 2012), https://jamestown.org/program/will-the-fergana-valley-become-a-hotbed-of-destabilization-in-central-asia/. Akiner, 'The Politicisation of Islam in Postsoviet Central Asia;' Malashenko, 'Islam And Politics In Central Asian States;' Steinberger, '"Fundamentalism" in Central Asia: Reasons, Reality and Prospects;' Vinatier, *L'islamisme en Asie centrale*; Malashenko, 'Islam And Politics In Central Asian States.'
6. Ahmed Rashid, *Taliban: Islam, Oil and the New Great Game in Central Asia* (London: I.B.Tauris, 2008); Alexander Cooley, *Great Games, Local Rules: The New Power Contest in Central Asia* (New York: Oxford University Press, 2012).
7. Jesse Driscoll, *Warlords & Coalition Politics in Post-Soviet States* (New York: Cambridge University Press, 2015).

8. Lawrence P. Markowitz, 'Tajikistan: Authoritarian Reaction in a Postwar State,' *Democratization* 19, no. 1 (2012): 98–119, doi:10.1080/13510347.2012.641299.

9. Kirill Nourzhanov, 'Saviours of the Nation or Robber Barons? Warlord Politics in Tajikistan,' *Central Asian Survey* 24, no. 2 (2005): 109–30.

10. John Heathershaw, 'The Paradox of Peacebuilding: Peril, Promise, and Small Arms in Tajikistan,' *Central Asian Survey* 24, no. 1 (2005): 21–38, doi:10.1080/13648470500049958.

11. Markowitz, 'Tajikistan.'

12. John Heathershaw, 'Seeing like the International Community: How Peacebuilding Failed (and Survived) in Tajikistan,' *Journal of Intervention and Statebuilding* 2, no. 3 (2008): 329–51, doi:10.1080/17502970802436346.

13. Dudoignon and Noack, *Allah's Kolkhozes: Migration, De-Stalinisation, Privatisation and the Emergence of New Muslim Religious Communities in the USSR, and After (1950s–2000s)*; Parviz Mullojanov, 'The Islamic Clergy in Tajikistan since the End of the Soviet Period,' in *Islam in Politics in Russia and Central Asia (Early Eighteenth to Late Twentieth Centuries)*, ed. Stephane A. Dudoignon and Hisao Komatsu (New York: Kegan Paul, 2001), 221–50; Tim Epkenhans, 'Defining Normative Islam: Some Remarks on Contemporary Islamic Thought in Tajikistan – Hoji Akbar Turajonzoda's Sharia and Society,' *Central Asian Survey* 30, no. 1 (2011): 81–96; Muzaffar Olimov and Sulmon Khamadov, 'Neformalnoe Liderstvo v Stranax Tsentralnoi Azii: Kakimi Budut Novie Vojdi? (Informal Leaders in Central Asian Countries: Who Will the New Leaders Be?),' in *Musul'manskie Lideri: Sotsialnaya Rol i Avtoritet (Muslim Leaders: Social Role and Legitimacy)*, ed. Muzaffar Olimov and Saodat Olimova (Dushanbe: Sharq Research Center, 2003), 47–53; Parviz Mullojanov, 'The Islamic Clergy in Tajikistan since the End of the Soviet Period,' in *Islam in Politics in Russia and Central Asia (Early Eighteenth to Late Twentieth Centuries)*, ed. Stephane A. Dudoignon and Hisao Komatsu (New York: Kegan Paul, 2001), 221–50.

14. Louw, *Everyday Islam in Post-Soviet Central Asia*, 2007; Jarrett Zigon, *Multiple Moralities and Religions in Post-Soviet Russia* (New York: Berghahn Books, 2011); Johan Rasanayagam, *Islam in Post-Soviet Uzbekistan: The Morality of Experience* (Cambridge: Cambridge University Press, 2010); Mathijs Pelkmans, *Conversion After Socialism: Disruptions, Modernisms and Technologies of Faith in the Former Soviet Union* (Berghahn Books, 2009); Julie McBrien, 'Extreme Conversations: Secularism, Religious Pluralism, and the Rhetoric of Islamic Extremism in Southern Kyrgyzstan,' in *The Postsocialist Religious Question: Faith and Power in Central Asia and East-Central Europe*, ed. Hann (Berlin: LIT Verlag Münster, 2006), 47–74; Julie McBrien, 'Mukadas's Struggle: Veils and Modernity in Kyrgyzstan,' *Journal of the Royal Anthropological Institute* 15 (2009): S127–44, doi:10.1111/j.1467-9655.2009.01546.x.

15. Devin Deweese, 'Islam and the Legacy of Sovietology: A Review Essay on Yaacov Ro'i's Islam in the Soviet Union,' *Journal of Islamic Studies* 13, no. 3 (2002): 298–330.

16. Mark Beissinger and M. Crawford Young, *Beyond State Crisis?: Post-Colonial Africa and Post-Soviet Eurasia in Comparative Perspective* (Washington, DC: Woodrow Wilson Center Press, 2002); Valerie Bunce, 'Should Transitologists Be Grounded?' *Slavic Review* 55 (1995): 111–27; Shirin Akiner, 'Nation-Building and the Islamic Revival in Post-Soviet Central Asia,' in *The OSCE and the Multiple Challenges of Transition: The Caucasus and Central Asia*, ed. Farian Sabahi and Daniel Warner (Aldershot, UK: Ashgate, 2004), 71–89; Martha Brill Olcott, 'Roots of Radical Islam in Central Asia,' *Carnegie Endowment for International Peace*, no. 77 (2007), http://carnegieendowment.org/2007/01/17/roots-of-radical-islam-in-central-asia; Mehrdad Haghayeghi, *Islam and Politics in Central Asia* (New York: St. Martin's Press, 1995); Eren Tatari and Renat Shaykhutdinov, 'State Response to Religious Revivalism in Post-Soviet Central Asia,' *European Journal of Economic and Political Studies* 3, no. 2 (2010): 85–110.

17. Peter A. Hall and Rosemary C. R. Taylor, 'Political Science and the Three New Institutionalisms,' *Political Studies* 44, no. 5 (1996): 938.

18. David Bates Pauline Jones Luong, 'Sources of Institutional Continuity: The Soviet Legacy in Central Asia' (Annual Meeting of the American Political Science Association, Washington, DC, 2000), 2.

19. Haghayeghi, *Islam and Politics in Central Asia*, 157.

20. Anthony Gill is considered to be the reference for this approach: Anthony Gill, 'Religion and Comparative Politics,' *Annual Review of Political Science* 4, no. 1 (2001): 117–38; Froese, *The Plot to Kill God*; Christopher Marsh, *Religion and the State in Russia and China: Suppression, Survival, and Revival* (London: Continuum, 2011).

21. Louw, *Everyday Islam in Post-Soviet Central Asia*, 2007; Sonja Luehrmann, *Secularism Soviet Style: Teaching Atheism and Religion in a Volga Republic* (Bloomington, IN: Indiana University Press, 2011); Alexander A. Panchenko, 'Morality, Utopia, Discipline. New Religious Movements and Soviet Culture,' in *Multiple Moralities and Religions in Post-Soviet Russia*, ed. Jarrett Zigon (London: Berghahn Books, 2011), 119–45; Mathijs Pelkmans, 'Introduction: Post-Soviet Space and the Unexpected Turns of Religious Life,' in *Conversion After Socialism: Disruptions, Modernisms and Technologies of Faith in the Former Soviet Union*, ed. Mathijs Pelkmans (London: Berghahn Books, 2009), 1–16; Rasanayagam, *Islam in Post-Soviet Uzbekistan*; Catherine Wanner, 'Multiple Moralities, Multiple Secularisms,' in *Multiple Moralities and Religions in Post-Soviet Russia*, ed. Jarrett Zigon (London: Berghahn Books, 2011), 214–25.

22. Froese, *The Plot to Kill God*, 20.

23. Lisa Weeden, 'Ethnography as Interpretive Enterprise,' in *Political Ethnography: What Immersion Contributes to the Study of Power*, ed. Edward Schatz (Chicago: The University of Chicago Press, 2009), 85.

24. Cedric Jourde, 'The Ethnographic Sensibility: Overlooked Authoritarian Dynamics and Islamic Ambivalences in West Africa,' in *Political Ethnography: What Immersion Contributes to the Study of Power*, ed. Edward Schatz (Chicago: The University of Chicago Press, 2009), 206.

25. Daniele Caramani, 'Introduction to Comparative Politics,' in *Comparative Politics*, ed. Daniele Caramani (New York: Oxford University Press, 2008), 3.

26. Lorraine Bayard de Volo, 'Participant Observation, Politics, and Power Relations: Nicaraguan Mothers and US Casino Waitresses,' in *Political Ethnography: What Immersion Contributes to the Study of Power*, ed. Edward Schatz (Chicago: The University of Chicago Press, 2009), 217–36.

27. Pelkmans, 'Introduction: Post-Soviet Space and the Unexpected Turns of Religious Life,' 5.

28. Andreas Glaeser, 'Theory by Way of Ethnography,' Perspectives: Newsletter of the ASA Theory Section 27, no. 1 (2004), 7.

29. Maria Louw, 'Pursuing "Muslimness": Shrines as Sites for Moralities in the Making in Post-Soviet Bukhara,' *Central Asian Survey* 25, no. 3 (2006): 321.

30. Grace Davie, 'Discerning and Explaining Pattern' (Research Meeting of The Religion and Diversity Project, Université de Montréal, 14 March 2013).

31. Jourde, 'The Ethnographic Sensibility: Overlooked Authoritarian Dynamics and Islamic Ambivalences in West Africa,' 206.

32. Louw, *Everyday Islam in Post-Soviet Central Asia*, 2007, 130.

33. Emmanuel Karagiannis, *Political Islam in Central Asia: The Challenge of Hizb Ut-Tahrir* (Routledge, 2010), 93.

34. Jarrett Zigon, 'Multiple Moralities: Discourses, Practices, and Breakdowns in Post-Soviet Russia,' in *Multiple Moralities and Religions in Post-Soviet Russia*, ed. Jarrett Zigon (London: Berghahn Books, 2011), 1–15.

35. Luehrmann, *Secularism Soviet Style*, 2011, 199.

36. Peter R. Grahame, 'Ethnography, Institutions, and the Problematic of the Everyday World,' *Human Studies* 21, no. 4 (1998), 350.

37. B. Z. Muhammadieva, 'Natsionalnii Sostav, Vladene Yazikami I Grazhdantsvo Naselenie Respubliki Tajikistan (Ethnic Composition and Language Skills, Citizenship of the Republic of Tajikistan)' (Dushanbe (Tajikistan): Statistical Agency under the President of the Republic of Tajikistan (Agentstvo po statistike pri Prezidente Respubliki Tadzhikistan), 2010), http://www.stat.tj/en/img/526b8592e834fcaaccec26a22965ea2b_1355502192.pdf, 7.

38. Martha Brill Olcott, *Vtoroi shans Tsentralnoi Azii (Central Asia's Second Chance)* (Washington, DC: Carnegie Endowment for International Peace, 2005), http://carnegie.ru/publications/?fa=35896, p. 25.

39. Igor Rotar, 'Tajikistan: Central Asian Powerkeg,' Prism, March 8, 1996, http://www.jamestown.org/single/?tx_ttnews%5Btt_news%5D=19457&tx_ttnews%5BbackPid%5D=218&no_cache=1.

40. Ahmed Rashid, *The Resurgence of Central Asia: Islam or Nationalism?* (Oxford: Oxford University Press, 2003), 162.

41. Vincent Fourniau, *Histoire de l'Asie Centrale* (Paris: PUF, 1994).

42. Abdukakhor Saidov, Abdulkhamid Anarbaev, and Valentina Goriyacheva, 'The Pre-Colonial Legacy,' in *Ferghana Valley: The Heart of Central Asia*, ed. Stephen Frederick Starr (Armonk: M.E. Sharpe, 2011), 3–28.

194 NOTES TO PAGES 17–23

43. Bobodzhan Gafurovich Gafurov, *Central Asia: Pre-Historic to Pre-Modern Times* (New Delhi: Shipra Publications, 2005).

44. Jean-Paul Roux, *L'Asie Centrale: Histoire et Civilisations* (Paris: Fayard, 1997), 385.

45. Fourniau, *Histoire de l'Asie Centrale*, 56.

46. Geoffrey Wheeler, *The Modern History of Soviet Central Asia* (London: Weidenfeld & Nicolson, 1964).

47. Adeeb Khalid, *The Politics of Muslim Cultural Reform: Jadidism in Central Asia* (University of California Press, 1998).

48. Firouzeh Nahavandi, 'L'idée de Nation En Asie Centrale: L'exemple Du Kazakhstan et de l'Ouzbékistan,' *Transitions* 37, no. 2 (1996), p. 153.

49. Fourniau, *Histoire de l'Asie Centrale*, 107.

50. Ibid., p. 108.

51. Marco Buttino, 'Ethnicité et Politique Dans La Guerre Civile: À Propos Du Basmacestvo Au Fergana,' *Cahiers Du Monde Russe* 38, no. 1–2 (1997): 195–222.

52. Ibid., 201.

53. Zukhra Madamidzhanova and Ildar Mukhtarov, 'Cultural Life in the Ferghana Valley Under Krushchev and Brezhnev,' in *Ferghana Valley: The Heart of Central Asia*, ed. Stephen Frederick Starr (Armonk: M.E. Sharpe, 2011), 164–77.

54. Bahrom Fayzulloyev, 'Chkalovsk Renamed Shohkant,' *Asia Plus*, 26 June 2015, http://news.tj/en/news/chkalovsk-renamed-shohkant.

55. Ravshan Nazarov and Pulat Shozimov, 'The Khrushchev and Brezhnev Eras,' in *Ferghana Valley: The Heart of Central Asia*, ed. Stephen Frederick Starr (Armonk: M. E. Sharpe, 2011), 140–63.

56. Keith Martin, 'Welcome to the Republic of Leninabad,' *Central Asia & Central Caucasus* 10, no. 4 (1997), http://www.ca-c.org/dataeng/st_06_martin.shtml.

57. Rotar, 'Tajikistan.'

58. B. Z. Muhammadieva, 'Regiony Respubliki Tadzhikistan (Regions of the Republic of Tajikistan)' (Dushanbe (Tajikistan): Agentstvo po statistike pri Prezidente Respubliki Tadzhikistan, 2011), http://stat.tj/en/img/fafa4ed7 64f8e9b9cad5fd57b6c819fa_1322470826.pdf.

59. Tajikistan, 'Natsionalnii Sostav, Vladene Yazikami I Grazhdantsvo Naselenie Respublik Tajikistan (Ethnic Composition and Language Skills, Citizenship of the Republic of Tajikistan)' (Agentstvo po statistike pri Prezidente Respubliki Tadzhikistan, 2012), http://www.stat.tj/en/img/526b8592e834fcaaccec26a22965ea2b_1355502192.pdf, 110.

60. Ibid., 7.

61. Ibid., 50.

62. Daniel Cefaï, 'Postface,' in *L'engagement Ethnographique* (Paris: École des hautes études en sciences sociales, 2010), 548.

63. Lorraine Bayard de Volo and Edward Schatz, 'From the Inside Out: Ethnographic Methods in Political Research,' *PS: Political Science & Politics* null, no. 02 (2004), 268.

64. This is a quote repeatedly spoken by Sukhov, a kind-hearted Red Army officer, in Soviet cult-movie *Beloe solntse pustyni* – The White Sun of the Desert.

Released in 1970, the movie recalls the Basmachi rebellion in Central Asia during the Civil war.

65. Hale C. Bolak, 'Studying One's Own in the Middle East: Negotiating Gender and Self-Other Dynamics in the Field,' *Qualitative Sociology* 19, no. 1 (1996): 109, doi:10.1007/BF02393250.

66. Ibid.

67. Marjorie DeVault, 'Theory by Way of Ethnography,' *Perspectives: Newsletter of the ASA Theory Section* 27, no. 1 (2004).

68. Gary King, Robert O. Keohane, and Sidney Verba, *Designing Social Inquiry: Scientific Inference in Qualitative Research* (Princeton University Press, 1994); Mark Irving Lichbach and Alan S. Zuckerman, 'Paradigms and Pragmatism: Comparative Politics during the Past Decade,' in *Comparative Politics: Rationality, Culture, and Structure*, ed. Mark Irving Lichbach and Alan S. Zuckerman (New York: Cambridge University Press, 2009), 1–17; Sir Karl Raimund Popper, *Objective Knowledge: An Evolutionary Approach* (Oxford: Clarendon Press, 1972).

69. Bayard de Volo, 'Participant Observation, Politics, and Power Relations: Nicaraguan Mothers and US Casino Waitresses.'

70. Laura L. Adams, 'The Mascot Researcher: Identity, Power, and Knowledge in Fieldwork,' *Journal of Contemporary Ethnography* 28, no. 4 (1999): 332.

71. Theresa Baker, *Doing Social Research* (New York: McGraw Hill, 1988), 74.

72. Susan Palmer, 'Caught Up in the Cult Wars: Confessions of a Canadian Researcher,' in *Religion and Canadian Society. Traditions, Transitions, and Innovations* (Toronto: Canadian Scholars' Press, 2006), 174.

73. Adams, 'The Mascot Researcher: Identity, Power, and Knowledge in Fieldwork,' 1999.

74. Jessica Allina-Pisano, 'How to Tell an Axe-Murderer: An Essay on Ethnography, Truth, and Lies,' in *Political Ethnography: What Immersion Contributes to the Study of Power*, ed. Edward Schatz (Chicago: The University of Chicago Press, 2009), 69.

75. Carol A. B. Warren and Paul K. Rasmussen, 'Sex and Gender in Field Research,' *Urban Life* 6, no. 3 (1977): 352.

76. In Tajikistan, very few houses have beds in the Western understanding of the term. People sleep on 'kurpachas,' thick colourful cotton mattresses that are unfolded at night for sleeping and put away in the morning. Therefore, there are no 'bedrooms' per se, and many family members can sleep together in one room.

77. Jillian Schwedler, 'The Third Gender: Western Female Researchers in the Middle East,' *PS: Political Science & Politics* 39, no. 03 (2006): 425–8.

78. Warren and Rasmussen, 'Sex and Gender in Field Research,' 350.

79. Readers might find it amusing that during my time in Tajikistan, I have heard an unprecedented plethora of negative comments towards short people, such as: 'short persons should marry between each other.' On another occasion, Iskandar was telling me that his friend Jamshed, to whom he wanted me to marry, had found a new wife. He claimed that she was nice but

not as tall as me unfortunately. Beyond aesthetic considerations, a short woman is often perceived as fragile and therefore unfit to fulfill household duties.

80. John Gledhill, *Power & Its Disguises: Anthropological Perspectives on Politics* (Pluto Press, 1994), 124.

Chapter 2   The Soviet Secularization Project

1. Marsh, *Religion and the State in Russia and China*, 13.
2. Ibid., 2.
3. A Okulov, 'Constitution of the USSR and Problems of Freedom of Conscience,' in *Secularization in Multi-Religious Societies Indo-Soviet Perspectives*, ed. S. C. Dube and V. N. Basilov (New Delhi: Concept Publishing Company, 1983), 176.
4. Dimitry Pospielovsky, *A History of Marxist-Leninist Atheism and Soviet Antireligious Policies* (Boulder, CO: St. Martin's Press, 1987), 6.
5. Ibid., 22.
6. John Burdon Sanderson Haldane and Frederick Engels, 'Preface,' in *Dialectics of Nature*, ed. Clemens Dutt (New York: International Publishing, 1949), http://trove.nla.gov.au/work/12853174.
7. P. K. Kurochkin, 'The Creative Role of the Scientific and Materialist Atheistic Weltanschauung in Moulding a New Type of Man,' in *Secularization in Multi-Religious Societies Indo-Soviet Perspectives*, ed. S. C. Dube and V. N. Basilov (New Delhi: Concept Publishing Company, 1983), 142.
8. Ladislao Kania, *Bolshevism and Religion* (New York: Polish Library, 1946), 18.
9. Kurochkin, 'The Creative Role of the Scientific and Materialist Atheistic Weltanschauung in Moulding a New Type of Man,' 142.
10. Serguei Danilovich Skazkin, *Nastolnaya kniga ateista (The Atheist's Handbook)* (Moscow: Izdatelstvo Politicheskoii Literatury, 1981), 44.
11. Okulov, 'Constitution of the USSR and Problems of Freedom of Conscience,' 177.
12. First published in 1968 and re-edited 1981, the book was a very influential one and considered to be the 'Bible' of Party-members, professors, atheist propagandists, and the like.
13. Skazkin, *Nastolnaya kniga ateista (The Atheist's Handbook)*, 1981, 49.
14. Yuri Alexandrovich Rosenbaum, *Sovetskoe gosudarstvo i tserkov (The Soviet state and the Church)* (Moscow: Nauka, 1985), 32.
15. V. G. Sadur, 'Musulmane v SSSR: istorya i sovremennost (Muslims in the Soviet Union: History and Modernity),' in *Perestroika: Glastnost, Demokratiya, Socialism. Na puti k svobode sovesti (Perestroika: Glastnost, Democracy, Socialism. On the Road to Freedom of Conscience)*, ed. Dimitri Efimovich Furman (Moscow: Progress, 1989), 415.
16. Serguei Danilovich Skazkin, *Nastolnaya kniga ateista (The Atheist's Handbook)* (Moscow: Izdatelstvo Politicheskoii Literatury, 1968), 49.

17. This is not the wording used in the Qur'an but the idea refers to the 6th Surate, which states that everything in the world is a reflection of God's will. Ibid., 249.
18. Skazkin, *Nastolnaya kniga ateista (The Atheist's Handbook)*, 1981, 225.
19. Ibid., 431.
20. The absence of other parties was justified by the fact that such parties can exist only in societies which contain antagonistic classes whereas in the USSR, there were only two united classes: peasants and workers. Kania, *Bolshevism and Religion*, 5.
21. Dimitri Efimovich Furman, 'Religiya, Ateizm i Perestroika,' in *Perestroika: Glastnost, Democratiya, Socialism. Na puti k svobode sovesti (Perestroika: Glastnost, Democracy, Socialism. On the road to freedom of conscience)*, ed. Dimitri Efimovich Furman (Moscow: Progress, 1989), 7.
22. Marsh, *Religion and the State in Russia and China*, 18.
23. Alexander Agadjanian, 'Exploring Religiosity as a Source of Morality Today,' in *Multiple Moralities and Religions in Post-Soviet Russia*, ed. Jarrett Zigon (New York: Berghahn Books, 2011), 16–26; Marsh, *Religion and the State in Russia and China*.
24. Giovanni Codevilla, *The Attitude of the Soviet State Towards Religion* (Milan: Russia Cristiana, 1971), 26.
25. Vlamidir Illich Lenin, 'The Three Sources and Three Component Parts of Marxism,' *Marxists Internet Archive*, 1913, https://www.marxists.org/archive/lenin/works/1913/mar/x01.htm.
26. Codevilla, *The Attitude of the Soviet State Towards Religion*, 30.
27. Pospielovsky, *A History of Marxist-Leninist Atheism and Soviet Antireligious Policies*, 93.
28. Ibid., 21.
29. Agadjanian, 'Exploring Religiosity as a Source of Morality Today,' 2011, 16.
30. Froese, *The Plot to Kill God*, 16.
31. Sometimes referred to as the League of Militant Godless, it was an atheistic and antireligious organization of workers.
32. *Komsomol* is a contraction of three Russian words, *Kommunistitcheskii soyuz molodezhi*, The Young Communist League.
33. Froese, *The Plot to Kill God*, 20–40.
34. Ibid., 34.
35. Ibid., 70.
36. Ernest Gellner, 'Islam and Marxism: Some Comparisons,' *International Affairs (Royal Institute of International Affairs 1944–)* 67, no. 1 (1991): 1.
37. Pospielovsky, *A History of Marxist-Leninist Atheism and Soviet Antireligious Policies*, 21.
38. Luehrmann, *Secularism Soviet Style*, 2011, 7.
39. José Casanova, 'Rethinking Secularization: A Global Comparative Perspective,' *Hedgehog Review* 8, no. 1–2 (2006): 7–22.
40. Bruce J. Berman, Rajeev Bhargava, and Andre Laliberte, 'Introduction,' in *Secular States and Religious Diversity* (Vancouver: UBC Press, 2013), 8.

41. David Ernest Apter, *The Politics of Modernization* (Chicago: The University of Chicago Press, 1965); Peter L. Berger, *The Sacred Canopy: Elements of a Sociological Theory of Religion* (Garden City, NY: Doubleday, 1967).
42. Marsh, *Religion and the State in Russia and China*, 1.
43. Edward Schatz, 'Leninism's Long Shadow in Central Asia,' in *Multination States in Asia: Accommodation or Resistance*, ed. Jacques Bertrand and Andre Laliberte (New York: Cambridge University Press, 2010), 249.
44. William Husband, *'Godless Communists': Atheism and Society in Soviet Russia, 1917–1932* (De Kalb, IL: Northern Illinois University Press, 2000), 35.
45. Shoshana Keller, *To Moscow, Not Mecca: The Soviet Campaign Against Islam in Central Asia, 1917–1941* (Westport, CT: Greenwood Publishing Group, 2001), 53.
46. John Riddell, *To See the Dawn: Baku, 1920: First Congress of the Peoples of the East* (New York: Pathfinder, 1993), 251.
47. Ibid., 263.
48. John Dunstan, 'Soviet Schools, Atheism and Religion,' in *Religious Policy in the Soviet Union*, ed. Sabrina Petra Ramet (Cambridge: Cambridge University Press, 1993), 158.
49. Sadur, 'Musulmane v SSSR: istorya i sovremennost (Muslims in the Soviet Union: History and Modernity),' 427.
50. Authors disagree on the extent of their influence. Fourniau for example, argues that the Jadid movement was not politically significant in Central Asia and found echoes among a few secret societies in the Emirate of Bukhara Fourniau, *Histoire de l'Asie Centrale*, 100. Others, however, give it much significance in the political and intellectual history of the region. Stephane A. Dudoignon, 'Djadidisme, Mirasisme, Islamisme,' *Cahiers Du Monde Russe* 37, no. 1 (1996): 13–40; Keller, *To Moscow, Not Mecca*.
51. Dudoignon, 'Djadidisme, Mirasisme, Islamisme.'
52. Northern Tajikistan (Sughd) belonged to the Kokand Khanate.
53. Sadur, 'Musulmane v SSSR: istorya i sovremennost (Muslims in the Soviet Union: History and Modernity),' 430–2.
54. These regions partly encompass today's Sughd Viloyat.
55. The uprising occurred after the declaration of an Imperial Decree stating that non-Russians too were to be called to serve for labour duties in the Russian Army engaged in World War I. The decree unleashed a wave of violent protests severely repressed by the Russians.
56. Fourniau, *Histoire de l'Asie Centrale*, 107.
57. In 1918, the chaotic environment and the harsh economic conditions set up the stage for the development of widespread thievery in the new Republic. For this reason the Basmachi movement (in local Turkic languages, a *basmak* or *basmach* is a thief) was rapidly associated with the marauders in order to discredit its action. Buttino admits that many combatants were also involved in some kind of larceny. Buttino, 'Ethnicité et Politique Dans La Guerre Civile: À Propos Du Basmacestvo Au Fergana,'

195. Fighters referred to themselves as Qurbashi (nightwatchmen), a term also found in official Communist documents. Keller, *To Moscow, Not Mecca*, 47.

58. Pan-Turkism, an ideology calling for the unification of all Turkic people, was steered in Central Asia by former Turkish Minister of War, Enver Pasha. As Roy argues, while the movement was ethnicized in Turkey, 'among Russian Muslims, pan-Turkism was merely a variant of pan-Islamism.' Olivier Roy, *L'Asie Centrale Contemporaine* (Paris: PUF, 2001), 38.

59. Wheeler, *The Modern History of Soviet Central Asia*, 111.

60. Sergei Petrovich Poliakov, *Everyday Islam: Religion and Tradition in Rural Central Asia* (Armonk: M.E. Sharpe, 1992), 19.

61. Properties given as endowments to mosques, schools, hospitals, and so on.

62. Skazkin, *Nastolnaya kniga ateista (The Atheist's Handbook)*, 1981, 418.

63. Pospielovsky, *A History of Marxist-Leninist Atheism and Soviet Antireligious Policies*, 27.

64. Skazkin, *Nastolnaya kniga ateista (The Atheist's Handbook)*, 1981, 419–20.

65. Keller, *To Moscow, Not Mecca*, 41–50.

66. Niccolò Pianciola and Paolo Sartori, 'Waqf in Turkestan: The Colonial Legacy and the Fate of an Islamic Institution in Early Soviet Central Asia, 1917–1924,' *Central Asian Survey* 26, no. 4 (2007), 493.

67. Local, pre or extra Islamic customary Law.

68. Keller, *To Moscow, Not Mecca*, 38.

69. Ibid., 84.

70. Ibid., 40.

71. Sergei Abashin et al., 'Soviet Rule and the Delineation of Borders,' in *Ferghana Valley: The Heart of Central Asia*, ed. Stephen Frederick Starr (Armonk: M.E. Sharpe, 2011), 103.

72. Keller, *To Moscow, Not Mecca*, 204.

73. Douglas Taylor Northrop, *Veiled Empire: Gender & Power in Stalinist Central Asia* (Ithaca, NY: Cornell University Press, 2004), 12.

74. Mark Savage, 'The Law of Abortion in the Union of Soviet Socialist Republics and the People's Republic of China: Women's Rights in Two Socialist Countries,' *Stanford Law Review* 40, no. 4 (1988): 1030.

75. Massell (1974) was the first to use this term. Gregory J. Massell, *The Surrogate Proletariat: Moslem Women and Revolutionary Strategies in Soviet Central Asia, 1919–1929* (Princeton: Princeton University Press, 1974).

76. Sometimes spelled *Hudjum*. That word can be translated as 'assault,' in the sense of an attack against the traditional organization of the family and the society.

77. *Zhenotdel*, later called *Zhensektor* is a contraction of 'zhenskii,' which is the adjective 'female' and 'otdel,' which means 'department.' It was closed in 1934 but in Central Asia, due, among other things to the veil issue, it remained until 1937. Northrop, *Veiled Empire*, 9.

78. Walter Kolarz, *Islam in the Soviet Union, 1917–1960* (Karachi: East Press, 1960), 25.

79. Yaacov Ro'i, *Islam in the Soviet Union: From the Second World War to Gorbachev* (New York: Columbia University Press, 2000), 544.

80. Ibid., 254.

81. Marsh, *Religion and the State in Russia and China*, 53.

82. Galiev was arrested in 1923, released in 1924, then again arrested in 1937 and executed in 1940 because his calls to unite Muslims of Russia and Central Asia were interpreted as a threat to national unity by Stalin. He has been the first party member arrested for 'national-deviationism.' Nicolas Werth, *Histoire de l'Union soviétique: de l'Empire russe à la Communauté des Etats indépendants, 1900–1991* (Paris: Presses universitaires de France, 1992), 170.

83. Sadur, 'Musulmane v SSSR: istorya i sovremennost (Muslims in the Soviet Union: History and Modernity),' 433.

84. Keller, *To Moscow, Not Mecca*, 122–34.

85. Ibid., 53.

86. Ibid., 139.

87. Sadur, 'Musulmane v SSSR: istorya i sovremennost (Muslims in the Soviet Union: History and Modernity),' 431.

88. Keller, *To Moscow, Not Mecca*, 145.

89. Ibid., 241.

90. Hiro, *Between Marx and Muhammad*, 32.

91. Keller, *To Moscow, Not Mecca*, 241.

92. Ro'i, *Islam in the Soviet Union*, 371.

93. Established in 1944 and renamed the Council for Religious Affairs (CRA) in 1965, it was a governmental body with extended powers attached to the Moscow-based Council of Ministers of the Soviet Union. Akbarzadeh, 'Islamic Clerical Establishment in Central Asia,' 74.

94. Ro'i, *Islam in the Soviet Union*, 460.

95. Wheeler, *The Modern History of Soviet Central Asia*, 139.

96. Sadur, 'Musulmane v SSSR: istorya i sovremennost (Muslims in the Soviet Union: History and Modernity),' 431.

97. She was reportedly born in 1800 in Istaravshan (present-day Tajikistan) and died in Kokand (present-day Uzbekistan) in 1905.

98. Viktor Dubovitskii and Khaydarbek Bababekov, 'The Rise and Fall of the Kokand Khanate,' in *Ferghana Valley: The Heart of Central Asia*, ed. Stephen Frederick Starr (Armonk: M.E. Sharpe, 2011), 61.

99. Bashorat Saifitdinovna Asimova and Magomet Izmailovich Isaev, *Iazykovoe stroitelstvo v Tadzhikistane, 1920–1940 (Language Building in Tajikistan)* (Dushanbe: Izdotelstvo Donish, 1982), 14.

100. Okulov, 'Constitution of the USSR and Problems of Freedom of Conscience,' 174.

101. Adeeb Khalid, 'Backwardness and the Quest for Civilization: Early Soviet Central Asia in Comparative Perspective,' *Slavic Review* 65, no. 2 (2006): 250.

102. Ernest Gellner, *Nations and Nationalism* (Ithaca, NY: Cornell University Press, 2008).

103. Keller, *To Moscow, Not Mecca*, 209.

104. Hiro, *Between Marx and Muhammad*, 30.

105. Mark S. Johnson, 'The Legacy of Russian and Soviet Education and the Shaping of Ethnic, Religious and National Identities in Central Asia,' in *The Challenges of Education in Central Asia*, ed. Stephen P. Heyneman and Alan J. DeYoung (Greenwich, CT: Information Age Publishing, 2004), 30.

106. David E. Powell, 'Religion and Secularization in the Soviet Union: The Role of Antireligious Cartoons,' in *Religion and Modernization in the Soviet Union*, ed. Dennis J. Dunn (Boulder, CO: Westview Press, 1977), 136.

107. Kirill Nourzhanov and Christian Bleuer, *Tajikistan: A Political and Social History* (Canberra: ANU Press, 2013), 70.

108. Peter Kenez, *The Birth of the Propaganda State: Soviet Methods of Mass Mobilization, 1917–1929* (Cambridge: Cambridge University Press, 1985), 8.

109. Kurochkin, 'The Creative Role of the Scientific and Materialist Atheistic Weltanschauung in Moulding a New Type of Man,' 144.

110. Rosenbaum, *Sovetskoe gosudarstvo i tserkov (The Soviet state and the Church)*, 29.

111. Sadur, 'Musulmane v SSSR: istorya i sovremennost (Muslims in the Soviet Union: History and Modernity),' 434.

112. Keller, *To Moscow, Not Mecca*, 208.

113. Eid el-Adha in Arabic, the 'Festival of sacrifice.'

114. Keller, *To Moscow, Not Mecca*, 207.

115. Luehrmann, *Secularism Soviet Style*, 2011, 8.

116. Pospielovsky, *A History of Marxist-Leninist Atheism and Soviet Antireligious Policies*, 100.

117. Skazkin, *Nastolnaya kniga ateista (The Atheist's Handbook)*, 1968, 479.

118. Larry E Holmes, 'Schools and Religion in Soviet Russia, 1917–1941,' in *Religious Policy in the Soviet Union*, ed. Sabrina Petra Ramet (Cambridge: Cambridge University Press, 1993), 130.

119. Narrodnyi komissariat Prosveshcheniya.

120. Pospielovsky, *A History of Marxist-Leninist Atheism and Soviet Antireligious Policies*, 112.

121. Ibid., 68.

122. The Russian word is 'обыденный,' which can be understood as homely, banal or trivial.

123. T. G. Gaidurova, '"Zavisimost" obydennovo religioznovo soznaniya veruiushhix ot uslovii ix zhizni (Believers' Ordinary Religious Consciousness Depends on Their Living Conditions),' in *Konkretno-sotsiologicheskoe uizuchenie sostoyaniya religioznosti i opyta ateisticheskoe vospitaniya (Empirical Sociological Study of the State of Religion and the Experience of Atheistic Education)*, ed. Ilya Dominovich Pantsxava (Moscow: Moscow University, 1969), 12.

124. Okulov, 'Constitution of the USSR and Problems of Freedom of Conscience,' 175.

125. Akbarzadeh, 'Islamic Clerical Establishment in Central Asia,' 79.
126. Mary Buckley, *Soviet Social Scientists Talking: An Official Debate about Women* (London: The Macmillan Press, 1986).
127. Skazkin, *Nastolnaya kniga ateista (The Atheist's Handbook)*, 1968, 483.
128. Gaidurova, '"Zavisimost" obydennovo religioznovo soznaniya veruiushhix ot uslovii ix zhizni (Believers' Ordinary Religious Consciousness Depends on Their Living Conditions),' 18.
129. Ro'i, *Islam in the Soviet Union*, 42.
130. Abdulla Abdulgani, 'Musul'mane v uslovyax glasnosti, perestroika i novovo mishelnya (Muslims in the conditions of glasnost, perestroika and new thoughts),' in *Perestroika: Glastnost, Democratiya, Socialism. Na puti k svobode sovesti (Perestroika: Glastnost, Democracy, Socialism. On the road to freedom of conscience)*, ed. Dimitri Efimovich Furman (Moscow: Progress, 1989), 404.
131. Ro'i, *Islam in the Soviet Union*, 30–2.
132. USSR, 'Konstitutsiya Soyuza Sovetskikh Sotsialisticheskikh Respublik (Constitution of the Union of Soviet Socialist Republics),' 1936, http://www.hist.msu.ru/ER/Etext/cnst1936.htm.
133. USSR, 'Konstitutsiya Soyuza Sovetskikh Sotsialisticheskikh Respublik (Constitution of the Union of Soviet Socialist Republics),' 1977, http://www.hist.msu.ru/ER/Etext/cnst1977.htm.
134. Russian Soviet Federative Socialist Republic (RSFSR), 'Postanovlene ob osvobozhdenii ot voinskoy povinnosti po religioznym ubezhdeniyam, o trudovoy povinnosti sluzhiteley kul'ta, ob izdanii religioznoy literatury i o religioznykh gruppakh, ob'edineniyakh i s'ezdakh (Decree on the Exemption from Conscription due to Religious Convictions, Labour service of Priests and on the Publication of Religious Literature by Religious Groups Associations, and Congresses),' 1921, http://www.libussr.ru/doc_ussr/ussr_1053.htm.
135. An Islamic tax to help support the poor.
136. Powell, 'Religion and Secularization in the Soviet Union: The Role of Antireligious Cartoons,' 139.
137. Pospielovsky, *A History of Marxist-Leninist Atheism and Soviet Antireligious Policies*, 81.
138. This law can be seen as the ancestor of the 2011 Tajik Law on Parental responsibility in the upbringing and education of children, which I will discuss further.
139. Karl Marx, 'K Kritike gegelevskoi filosofiya prava: Vvdenie (Critique of Hegel's Philosophy of Right: Introduction),' in *O religii i tserkvi: Sbornik viskazanii klassikov marksima-leninisma, dokumentov KPSS i sovetskovo gosudarstva (Collection of Quotes of Marxist-Leninist Classics, Documents of the CPSU and the Soviet state)*, ed. Anatoliy Vasil'yevich Belov (Moscow: Politizdat, 1977), 126.
140. Ghoncheh Tazmini, 'The Islamic Revival in Central Asia: A Potent Force or a Misconception?,' *Central Asian Survey* 20, no. 1 (2001): 65.
141. Ro'i, *Islam in the Soviet Union*, 100.

142. Ibid., 23.

143. Haghayeghi, *Islam and Politics in Central Asia*, 25–6.

144. Bakhtiar Babajanov, 'Sredneazitaskoe Duxovnoe Upravlene Musulman (Spiritual Muslim Board of Central Asia: Origin and Consequences of the Collapse),' in *Mnogomerne Granitsy Tsentralnoii Azii (The Multidimensional Frontiers of Central Asia)*, ed. Martha Brill Olcott and Alexei Malashenko (Moscow: Gendalf, 2000), 81.

145. Abdumannob Polat, 'The Islamic Revival in Uzbekistan: A Threath to Stability,' in *Islam and Central Asia: An Enduring Legacy or an Evolving Threat?*, ed. Susan Eisenhower and Roald Sagdeev (Washington: Center for Political and Strategic Studies, 2000), 40.

146. Ro'i, *Islam in the Soviet Union*, 104.

147. Stephane A. Dudoignon, 'From Revival to Mutation: The Religious Personnel of Islam in Tajikistan, from de-Stalinization to Independence (1955–91),' *Central Asian Survey* 30, no. 1 (2011): 55.

148. Keller, *To Moscow, Not Mecca*, 251.

149. Fourniau, *Histoire de l'Asie Centrale*, 118.

150. Dominique Arel, 'Introduction: Theorizing the Politics of Cultural Identities in Russia and Ukraine,' in *Rebounding Identities: The Politics of Identity in Russia and Ukraine*, ed. Dominique Arel and Blair A. Ruble (Washington, DC: Woodrow Wilson Center Press, n.d.), 18.

151. Pelkmans, 'Introduction: Post-Soviet Space and the Unexpected Turns of Religious Life,' 6.

152. Schatz, 'Leninism's Long Shadow in Central Asia,' 253.

153. Eren Murat Tasar, 'Soviet and Muslim: The Institutionalization of Islam in Central Asia, 1943–1991' (Harvard University, 2010).

154. In total, there had been four Muftis: Ishan Babakhan (1943–57), Ziyauddin Babakhan (1957–82), Shamsuddin Babakhan (1982–9), and Muhammad-Sodiq Muhammad Yusuf (1989–93). Brill Olcott, *Vtoroi shans Tsentralnoii Azii (Central Asia's Second Chance)*, 357–8.

155. 'Musulmane Sovetskovo Vostoka' was founded in 1968. By 1977, its circulation increased by five times and reached 35,000 copies published in 33 countries.

156. Akbarzadeh, 'Islamic Clerical Establishment in Central Asia,' 82.

157. Shirin Akiner, *Tajikistan: Disintegration Or Reconciliation?* (London: Royal Institute of International Affairs, 2001), 29.

158. Akbarzadeh, 'Islamic Clerical Establishment in Central Asia,' 82.

159. Ro'i, *Islam in the Soviet Union*, 30.

160. Otto Luchterhandt, 'The Council for Religious Affairs,' in *Religious Policy in the Soviet Union*, ed. Sabrina Petra Ramet (Cambridge: Cambridge University Press, 1993), 72.

161. Babajanov, 'Sredneazitaskoe Duxovnoe Upravlene Musulman (Spiritual Muslim Board of Central Asia: Origin and Consequences of the Collapse).'

162. A person responsible for observing and maintaining religious morality.

163. Sadur, 'Musulmane v SSSR: istorya i sovremennost (Muslims in the Soviet Union: History and Modernity),' 437.

164. Tim Epkenhans, 'Muslims Without Learning, Clergy Without Faith: Institutions of Islamic Learning in the Republic of Tajikistan,' in *Islamic Education in the Soviet Union and Its Successor States*, ed. Michael Kemper, Raoul Motika, and Stefan Reichmuth (New York: Routledge, 2010), 317.

165. Akbarzadeh, 'Islamic Clerical Establishment in Central Asia,' 76.

166. Ro'i, *Islam in the Soviet Union*, 161.

167. Sadur, 'Musulmane v SSSR: istorya i sovremennost (Muslims in the Soviet Union: History and Modernity),' 433.

168. Babajanov, 'Sredneazitaskoe Duxovnoe Upravlene Musulman (Spiritual Muslim Board of Central Asia: Origin and Consequences of the Collapse),' 152.

169. Yaacov Ro'i, 'The Task of Creating the New Soviet Man: "Atheistic Propaganda" in the Soviet Muslim Areas,' *Soviet Studies* 36, no. 1 (1984): 28.

170. Ibid., 35.

171. A Abdusamedov and A Masaliev, 'Obzor zhurnala 'Musul'mane Sovetskovo Vostoka' (1979–1982) (Survey of the Journal "Muslims of the Soviet East" (1979–1982)),' in *Obzor religioznix zhurnalov, izdavemix v SSSR (Survey of religious journals published in the USSR)* (Moscow: Seksia ateisticheskovo vospitania pri Pravlenii Ordena Lenina Vsesoyuznovo obshestvo 'Znane,' 1984), 80–1.

172. Dudoignon, 'From Revival to Mutation,' 71–2.

173. Ro'i, *Islam in the Soviet Union*, 696.

174. Akbarzadeh, 'Islamic Clerical Establishment in Central Asia,' 80.

175. Dudoignon, 'From Revival to Mutation,' 61.

176. Tasar, 'Soviet and Muslim: The Institutionalization of Islam in Central Asia, 1943–1991,' 528.

177. Babajanov, 'Sredneazitaskoe Duxovnoe Upravlene Musulman (Spiritual Muslim Board of Central Asia: Origin and Consequences of the Collapse),' 83–7.

178. Dudoignon, 'From Revival to Mutation.'

179. Ro'i, *Islam in the Soviet Union*, 354.

180. Ibid., 285.

181. Tasar, 'Soviet and Muslim: The Institutionalization of Islam in Central Asia, 1943–1991,' 524.

182. Ibid.

183. Dudoignon, 'From Revival to Mutation,' 59.

184. Ro'i, *Islam in the Soviet Union*, 382.

185. Mullojanov, 'The Islamic Clergy in Tajikistan since the End of the Soviet Period,' 2001, 235.

186. Luchterhandt, 'The Council for Religious Affairs,' 55–7.

187. Ro'i, *Islam in the Soviet Union*, 12.

188. Ibid., 23–8.

189. Luchterhandt, 'The Council for Religious Affairs,' 57.
190. Ro'i, *Islam in the Soviet Union*, 553.
191. Pospielovsky, *A History of Marxist-Leninist Atheism and Soviet Antireligious Policies*, 118–19.
192. Ernest Gellner, 'Islam and Marxism: Some Comparisons,' *International Affairs (Royal Institute of International Affairs 1944–)* 67, no. 1 (1991): 1.
193. William Fierman, *Soviet Central Asia: The Failed Transformation* (Boulder, CO: Westview Press, 1991).
194. Michael Rywkin, *Moscow's Muslim Challenge: Soviet Central Asia* (Armonk: M. E. Sharpe, 1982).
195. Roy, *L'Asie Centrale Contemporaine*.
196. Naumkin, *Radical Islam in Central Asia*.
197. Will Myer, *Islam and Colonialism: Western Perspectives on Soviet Asia* (New York: Routledge, 2002), 169.
198. Deweese, 'Islam and the Legacy of Sovietology,' 302.
199. Laura L. Adams, 'Tha Mascot Researcher: Identity, Power, and Knowledge in Fieldwork,' *Journal of Contemporary Ethnography* 28, no. 4 (1999), 336.
200. Froese, *The Plot to Kill God*.
201. Poliakov, *Everyday Islam*.
202. Alexandre Bennigsen and Chantal Lemercier-Quelquejay, *L'Islam en Union soviétique* (Payot, 1968).
203. Myer, *Islam and Colonialism*, 181.
204. Ro'i, *Islam in the Soviet Union*, 288.
205. Abdulgani, 'Musul'mane v uslovyax glastnosti, perestroika i novovo mishelnya (Muslims in the conditions of glasnost, perestroika and new thoughts),' 405.
206. Poliakov, *Everyday Islam*. Sergei Petrovich Poliakov is a Russian ethnographer who published an influential book in the USSR in 1989 about everyday Islam in Central Asia although his research focuses mainly on Northern Tajikistan. His main findings point to the failure of Soviet policies and the continuing influence of the clergy and traditional ideas among the population. For Deweese, Poliakov's work, described as 'a disturbingly ethnocentric example of prescriptive ethnography,' is the quintessence of a Soviet view of religious life. Deweese, *Islam and the Legacy of Sovietology*, 315.
207. Ro'i, *Islam in the Soviet Union*, 358.
208. Ibid., 694.
209. Rasanayagam, *Islam in Post-Soviet Uzbekistan*, 81.
210. Dudoignon, 'From Revival to Mutation.'
211. Tasar, 'Soviet and Muslim: The Institutionalization of Islam in Central Asia, 1943–1991.'
212. J. Glenn, *The Soviet Legacy in Central Asia* (New York: St. Martin's Press, 1999), 91.
213. Saodat Olimova, 'Islam and the Tajik Conflict,' in *Islam and Central Asia: An Enduring Legacy or an Evolving Threat?*, ed. Susan Eisenhower and

Roald Sagdeev (Washington, DC: Center for Political and Strategic Studies, 2000), 59.

214. Northrop, *Veiled Empire*, 356.

215. James C. Scott, *Weapons of the Weak: Everyday Forms of Peasant Resistance* (New Haven, CT: Yale University Press, 1985), 29.

216. Husband, *Godless Communists*, 150.

217. Ibid., 162.

218. Northrop, *Veiled Empire*, 351.

219. Ibid., 115.

220. Alexei Yurchak, 'Soviet Hegemony of Form: Everything Was Forever, Until It Was No More,' *Comparative Studies in Society and History* 45, no. 03 (2003), 499.

221. Ronald Grigor Suny, 'The Contradictions of Identity: Being Soviet and National in the USSR and After,' in *Soviet and Post-Soviet Identities*, ed. Mark Bassin and Catriona Kelly (New York: Cambridge University Press, 2012), 23.

222. Christel Lane, 'Legitimacy and Power in the Soviet Union through Socialist Ritual,' *British Journal of Political Science* 14, no. 2 (1984), 215.

223. Suny, 'The Contradictions of Identity: Being Soviet and National in the USSR and After,' 17.

224. Wanner, 'Multiple Moralities, Multiple Secularisms,' 219.

225. Sergei Abashin, 'Les Descendants de Saints En Asie Centrale : Élite Religieuse Ou Nationale?,' *Cahiers d'Asie Centrale*, no. 13/14 (2004): 215.

Chapter 3   Tajikistan's Political Landscape in the Aftermath of the Civil War

1. Heathershaw, 'Seeing like the International Community,' 234.

2. Roy, *L'Asie Centrale Contemporaine*, 153.

3. Olivier Roy, *L'Islam Mondialisé* (Paris: Éditions du Seuil, 2002), 41.

4. Nourzhanov and Bleuer, *Tajikistan*, 275.

5. Jesse Driscoll, 'Commitment Problems or Bidding Wars? Rebel Fragmentation as Peace Building,' *The Journal of Conflict Resolution* 56, no. 1 (2012): 157.

6. In Tajik, it is called Viloyati Mukhtori Kuhistoni Badakhshan (Mountainous Badakhshan Autonomous Province) but it is mostly referred to in Russian as Gorno-Badakhshan avtonomnaya oblast' (GBAO). This is an isolated region bordering Afghanistan where Pamiris live, an ethno-linguistic and religious minority. Most Pamiris speak an Iranian language different than Tajik and are Ismaili Shia Muslims.

7. Driscoll, 'Commitment Problems or Bidding Wars?,' 123.

8. Aziz Niyazi, 'The Year of the Tumult: Tajikistan After February 1990,' in *State, Religion and Society in Central Asia. A Post-Soviet Critique*, ed. Vitaly Naumkin (Reading, UK: Ithaca Press, 1993), 267.

9. Shahram Akbarzadeh, 'Why Did Nationalism Fail in Tajikistan?,' *Europe-Asia Studies* 48, no. 7 (1996): 1108.

10. Haidar Shodiev and Khumairoi Bakhtior, 'Neokonchennaya missiya "Rastokheza" (The Unfinished Mission of "Rastokhez"),' *Asia Plus*, 16 September 2014, http://www.news.tj/ru/news/neokonchennaya-missiya-rastokheza.

11. A. I. Kuzmin, 'The Causes and Lessons of the Civil War,' in *Central Asia. Political and Economic Challenges in the Post-Soviet Era*, ed. Alexei Vassiliev (London: Saqi Books, 2001), 182.

12. Naumkin, *Radical Islam in Central Asia*, 208–209.

13. Akiner, *Tajikistan*.

14. V. I. Bushkov and D. V. Mikul'skii, *Anatomiya grazhdanskoii voiny v Tadzhikistane (Anatomy of the Civil War in Tajikistan)* (Moscow: Institute for Ethnology and Anthropology (Institut Etnologii i Antropologii RAN), 1996), http://www.ca-c.org/datarus/st_08_bush.shtml.

15. Akbarzadeh, 'Why Did Nationalism Fail in Tajikistan?' 1111.

16. Felix Corley, 'Obituary: The Chief Mufti of Tajikistan,' *Independent*, January 23, 1996, http://www.independent.co.uk/news/people/obituary-the-chief-mufti-of-tajikistan-1325372.html.

17. Ahmed Rashid, *Jihad: The Rise of Militant Islam in Central Asia* (New York: Penguin Books, 2003).

18. Hiro, *Between Marx and Muhammad*.

19. Kamoludin Abdullaev and Shahram Akbarzadeh, *Historical Dictionary of Tajikistan* (Lanham, MD: Scarecrow Press, 2002), 278.

20. Stephane A. Dudoignon, 'Une segmentation peut en cacher une autre : régionalismes et clivages politico-économiques au Tadjikistan,' *Cahiers d'Etudes sur la Méditerranée Orientale et le monde Turco-Iranien*, no. 18 (1994): 73–129.

21. Akbarzadeh, 'Why Did Nationalism Fail in Tajikistan?' 1112.

22. Naumkin, *Radical Islam in Central Asia*, 214.

23. Stephane A. Dudoignon and Sayyid Ahmad Qalandar, '"They Were All from the Country." The Revival and Politicisation of Islam in the Lower Wakhsh River Valley of the Tajik SSE (1947–1997),' in *Allah's Kolkhozes: Migration, De-Stalinisation, Privatisation and the Emergence of New Muslim Religious Communities in the USSR, and After (1950s–2000s)* (Berlin: Klaus Schwarz Verlag, 2014), 47–122.

24. Roy, *L'Asie Centrale Contemporaine*, 131.

25. Akbarzadeh, 'Why Did Nationalism Fail in Tajikistan?,' 1111.

26. Akbarzadeh, 'Islamic Clerical Establishment in Central Asia,' 77.

27. Hiro, *Between Marx and Muhammad*, 209.

28. Dudoignon, 'Une segmentation peut en cacher une autre.'

29. Bess Brown, 'The Civil War in Tajikistan, 1992–1993,' in *Tajikistan: The Trials of Independence*, ed. Mohammad-Reza Djalili, Frédéric Grare, and Shirin Akiner (New York: St. Martin's Press, 1997), 86–96.

30. Naumkin, *Radical Islam in Central Asia*, 217.
31. Stephane A. Dudoignon, *Communal Solidarity and Social Conflicts in Late 20th Century Central Asia : The Case of the Tajik Civil War* (Tokyo: Islamic Area Studies Project, 1998), 14.
32. Nourzhanov, 'Saviours of the Nation or Robber Barons?,' 112.
33. Akbarzadeh, 'Why Did Nationalism Fail in Tajikistan?,' 1113.
34. Kuzmin, 'The Causes and Lessons of the Civil War,' 195–203.
35. Ibid., 179.
36. Nourzhanov, 'Saviours of the Nation or Robber Barons?' 124.
37. Kuzmin, 'The Causes and Lessons of the Civil War,' 207.
38. Vinatier, *L'islamisme en Asie centrale.*
39. Olimov and Khamadov, 'Neformalnoe Liderstvo v Stranax Tsentralnoi Azii: Kakimi Budut Novie Vojdi? (Informal Leaders in Central Asian Countries: Who Will the New Leaders Be?),' 52.
40. Nourzhanov, 'Saviours of the Nation or Robber Barons?,' 124.
41. Naumkin, *Radical Islam in Central Asia*, 242.
42. Heathershaw, 'Seeing like the International Community,' 334.
43. John Heathershaw and Sophie Roche, 'Islam and Political Violence in Tajikistan: An Ethnographic Perspective on the Causes and Consequences of the 2010 Armed Conflict in the Kamarob Gorge,' *Ethnopolitics Papers*, no. 8 (2011): 4, https://www.psa.ac.uk/psa-communities/specialist-groups/ethnopolitics/news/ethnopolitics-paper-8-islam-and-political.
44. Nourzhanov, 'Saviours of the Nation or Robber Barons?,' 123–4.
45. Bruce Pannier, 'Tajikistan: Government Launches Military Operation Against Hostage-Takers,' *Radio Free Europe/Radio Liberty*, June 22, 2001, http://www.rferl.org/content/article/1096760.html.
46. Bruce Pannier, 'The Demise Of Tajikistan's Islamic Party,' September 4, 2015, Qishloq Ovozi, http://www.rferl.org/content/qishloq-ovozi-demise-of-tajik-islamic-party/27227509.html.
47. Driscoll, 'Commitment Problems or Bidding Wars?' 164.
48. Asia Plus, 'Gunmen Kill Six Prison Wardens, Free 25 Prisoners,' *Asia Plus*, August 23, 2010, http://news.tj/en/news/gunmen-kill-six-prison-wardens-free-25-prisoners.
49. Asia Plus, 'Otvetstvennost za vzryv v Khujande vzyala na sebya ranee neizvestnaya islamskaya gruppirvoka (Responsibility for the Khujand Bombing Claimed by a Previously Unknown Islamic Group),' *Asia Plus*, September 8, 2010, http://www2.asiaplus.tj/news/47/69110.html.
50. Radio Free Europe/Radio Liberty, 'Tajikistan Claims Militant Leader Killed,' *Radio Free Europe/Radio Liberty*, April 15, 2011, http://www.rferl.org/content/tajikistan_says_militant_leader_killed/3558497.html.
51. Heathershaw and Roche, 'Islam and Political Violence in Tajikistan: An Ethnographic Perspective on the Causes and Consequences of the 2010 Armed Conflict in the Kamarob Gorge,' 13.

52. Pravda, 'Poiman poslednii iz 25 sbezhavshix iz SIZO Tadzhikistana (The last of the 25 escapees from Tajik prison was caught),' *Pravda*, November 13, 2011, http://www.pravda.ru/news/accidents/13-11-2011/1098468-prison-0/.

53. Asia Plus, 'Otvetstvennost za vzryv v Khujande vzyala na sebya ranee neizvestnaya islamskaya gruppirvoka (Responsibility for the Khujand Bombing Claimed by a Previously Unknown Islamic Group).'

54. Asia Plus, 'Prokuror Sogda: Informatsiya o sushchestvovanii ekstremistskoii gruppirovki "Dzhamaat Ansarullakh" ne sootvetstvuyet deystvitel'nosti (Sughd Attorney: Information on the Existence of an Extremist Group "Jamaat Ansarullah" Does Not Correspond to Reality),' *Asia Plus*, October 22, 2010, http://news.tj/ru/news/prokuror-sogda-informatsiya-o-sushchestvovanii-ekstremistskoi-gruppirovki-dzhamaat-ansarullakh-.

55. Radio Free Europe/Radio Liberty, '14 Suspected Terrorists Detained In Northern Tajikistan,' *Radio Free Europe/Radio Liberty*, October 14, 2010, http://www.rferl.org/content/Fourteen_Suspected_Terrorists_Detained_In_Northern_Tajikistan/2190807.html.

56. Nargis Hamrabaeva, 'MVD podozrevaet vo vzryve v Khujande IDY (Interior Ministry Suspects IMU in Khujand Bombing),' *Asia Plus*, September 3, 2010, [http://news.tj/ru/news/mvd-podozrevaet-vo-vzryve-v-khudzhande-idu.

57. RFE/RL's Tajik Service, 'Tajik Opposition Security Official Assassinated In Knife Attack,' July 22, 2012, sec. Tajikistan, http://www.rferl.org/content/tajik-opposition-security-official-killed-in-knife-attack/24652924.html.

58. Radio Free Europe/Radio Liberty, 'Disarming Continues In East Tajikistan,' *Radio Free Europe/Radio Liberty*, August 3, 2012, http://www.rferl.org/content/article/24665487.html.

59. Salimjon Aioubov, 'Surrendered Tajik Opposition Commander: "We Don't Want To Fight. We Want Peace.",' *Radio Free Europe/Radio Liberty*, August 13, 2012, http://www.rferl.org/content/interview-surrendered-tajik-opposition-commander-says-wanted-issues-to-be-solved-lawfully/24675373.html.

60. 'Tajik Opposition Security Official Assassinated In Knife Attack.'

61. Ramsia Mirzobekova, 'V Khoroge Nespokoiino. V Region Styagivayutsya Voiiska (Agitation in Khorog. Troops Tightened in the Region),' *Asia Plus*, July 13, 2012, http://www.news.tj/ru/news/v-khoroge-nespokoino-v-region-styagivayutsya-voiska.

62. Pairav Chorshanbiev, 'B. Zukhurov: Odna pulya popala v provoda, poetomu s Khorogom net svyaz (B. Zuhurov: One bullet hit the wires, that is why there is no contact with Khorog),' *Asia Plus*, July 26, 2012, http://www.news.tj/ru/news/b-zukhurov-odna-pulya-popala-v-provoda-poetomu-s-khorogom-net-svyazi.

63. Regnum, 'Vlasti Tadzhikistana otvergli predlozheniye amnistirovat' uchastnikov besporyadkov v Khoroge (Tajik Authorities Have Rejected a Proposal to Grant Amnesty to Protestors in Khorog),' *Information Agency Regnum*, 26 May 2014, http://regnum.ru/news/1806348.html.

64. Farangis Najibullah, 'Explainer: What's Going On In Tajikistan's Gorno-Badakhshan?,' *Radio Free Europe/Radio Liberty*, May 29, 2014, http://www.rferl. org/content/tajikistan-explainer-gorno-badakhshan/25403342.html.

65. Filippo De Danieli, 'Counter-Narcotics Policies in Tajikistan and Their Impact on State Building,' *Central Asian Survey* 30, no. 1 (1 March 2011): 131–40, doi:10.1080/02634937.2011.554067.

66. Ahmed Rashid, 'Why Afghanistan's Neighbours Fear Drugs Influx,' *BBC News*, July 2, 2015, http://www.bbc.com/news/world-asia-33139652.

67. Radio Ozodi, 'Po faktu izbiyeniya Umara Babadzhanova vozbuzhdeno ugolovnoye delo (A Criminal Case Was Opened in Connection to the Beating of Umar Babadjanov),' *Radio Ozodi*, August 31, 2015, http://rus.ozodi.org/ content/article/27218543.html; Radio Ozodi, 'Umar Bobodzhonov skonchalsya posle nedel'nogo nakhozhdeniya v kome (Umar Bobojonov Died After Being in a Coma For a Week),' *Radio Ozodi*, September 5, 2015, http://rus. ozodi.org/content/article/27228170.html.

68. Radio Ozodi, 'V Vakhdate soversheno napadeniye na otdel militsii (Attack on a Police Station in Vahdat),' *Radio Ozodi*, September 4, 2015, http://rus.ozodi. org/content/article/27225781.html.

69. Radio Free Europe/Radio Liberty, 'Tajik Police Say 17 Killed In "Terrorist" Attacks,' *Radio Free Europe/Radio Liberty*, September 4, 2015, http://www.rferl. org/content/tajikistan-attacks-airport-deaths/27226045.html.

70. 'V Tadzhikistane likvidirovan myatezhnyy general Nazarzoda' (Mutiny General Nazarzoda eliminated in Tajikistan), *Asia Plus*, September 16, 2015, http://news.tj/ru/news/v-tadzhikistane-likvidirovan-myatezhnyi-general-nazarzoda.

71. Temur Varki, 'Zayavleniye Generala Abdukhalima Nazarzoda Rasstavlyayet Tochki Nad "i"? (Does the Statement of General Abduhalimov Nazarzoda Dot the "i's"?),' *Internet Portal Tajikskoi Oppozitsii*, September 7, 2015, http://www. tajinfo.org/post/2015/09/07/635772091024432224.

72. 'Pravitel'stvennoye SMI obvinyayet lidera PIVT v popytke gosperevorota (Government media accused IRPT's leader in the coup attempt),' *Asia Plus*, September 10, 2015, http://news.tj/ru/node/214494.

73. Asia Plus, 'Vlasti: PIVT namerevalas' atakovat' nekotoryye gosuchrezhdeniya (Authorities: The IRPT Planned to Attack Few State Institutions),' *Asia Plus*, September 22, 2015, http://asiaplus.tj/ru/node/215124.

74. Charles King, 'The Micropolitics of Social Violence,' *World Politics* 56, no. 03 (2004): 449.

75. Varki, 'Zayavleniye Generala Abdukhalima Nazarzoda Rasstavlyayet Tochki Nad "i"? (Does the Statement of General Abduhalimov Nazarzoda Dot the "i's"?).'

76. Radio Free Europe/Radio Liberty, 'Tajikistan's Ruling Party Wins Election Decried As "Farce",' *Radio Free Europe/Radio Liberty*, March 2, 2015, http://www.rferl.org/content/tajik-elections-rahmon-party-victory/ 26877105.html.

77. Office for Democratic Institutions and Human Rights (ODHIR), 'Tajikistan, Parliamentary Elections, 1 March 2015: Final Report' (Warsaw: Office for Democratic Institutions and Human Rights (ODHIR), May 15, 2015), http://www.osce.org/odihr/elections/tajikistan/158081.

78. Zafar Abdullaev, 'Tajikistan: Referendum Result Controversy,' *Institute for War and Peace Reporting*, February 21, 2005, https://iwpr.net/global-voices/tajikistan-referendum-result-controversy.

79. Asia Plus, 'Lider Natsii : U Rulya Do Kontsa (Leader of the Nation : At the Wheel Until the End),' *Asia Plus*, December 15, 2015, http://news.tj/ru/news/lider-natsii-u-rulya-do-kontsa.

80. EurasiaNet, 'Tajikistan: Weary Population Resigned to a President-for-Life,' *EurasiaNet*, May 23, 2016, http://www.eurasianet.org/node/78871.

81. Saodat Olimova, 'Regionalism and Its Perception by Major Political and Social Powers of Tajikistan,' in *Tajikistan at a Crossroad: The Politics of Decentralization*, ed. Luigi De Martino, Cimera, 2004, 86–119.

82. Radio Free Europe/Radio Liberty, 'Tajik President Appoints Daughter Chief Of Staff, Seen As Move To Consolidate Power,' *Radio Free Europe/Radio Liberty*, January 27, 2016, http://www.rferl.org/content/tajikistan-rahmon-daughter-chief-of-staff-consolidate-power/27514819.html.

83. David Trilling, 'Tajikistan's Strongman Appoints Son to Lead Corruption Fight,' *EurasiaNet*, March 16, 2015, http://www.eurasianet.org/node/72546.

84. 'Tajik President Makes Son Capital's Mayor,' *Radio Free Europe/Radio Liberty*, January 12, 2017, http://www.rferl.org/a/tajikistan-rahmon-appoints-son-dushanbe-mayor/28228061.html.

85. Abdulfattoh Shafiev, '"I Am Shuhrat": Tajiks Come to Jailed Lawyer's Defence on Facebook",' *Global Voices*, January 17, 2015, https://globalvoices.org/2015/01/17/i-am-shuhrat-tajiks-come-to-jailed-lawyers-defence-on-facebook/.

86. BBC News, 'Tajik Opposition Leader Kuvatov Shot Dead in Turkey,' *BBC News*, March 6, 2015, http://www.bbc.com/news/world-middle-east-31760810.

87. Radio Ozodi, 'Sulaymon Kayumov obvinil v ubiystve Kuvvatova evo telokhranitelya (Sulaymon Kayumov Accused in the Murder of Kuvvatov Was His Bodyguard),' *Radio Ozodi*, March 21, 2015, http://rus.ozodi.org/content/article/26913204.html.

88. Tohir Pallaev, 'YouTube Blocked in Tajikistan After Video of President Dancing Goes Viral,' *Global Voices*, September 25, 2015, https://globalvoices.org/2013/05/27/tajikistan-famous-wedding-singer-splits-opinion/.

89. Asia Plus, 'Press-konferentsiya PIVT v otele "Sheraton" segodnya byla sorvana (IRPT's Press-Conference in Sheraton Hotel Prevented today),' *Asia Plus*, August 27, 2015, http://news.tj/ru/news/press-konferentsiya-pivt-v-otele-sheraton-segodnya-byla-sorvana.

90. Fergana News, 'Amnesty International prizyvayet tadzhikskiye vlasti razreshit' deyatel'nost' NPO "Amparo" (Amnesty International Calls on the Tajik authorities to Allow the Activities of the NGO 'Amparo'),'

Fergana News, January 21, 2013, http://www.fergananews.com/news.php? id=20095.

91. Radio Free Europe/Radio Liberty, 'Tajik Court Upholds Closure Of Human Rights NGO,' *Radio Free Europe/Radio Liberty*, April 30, 2013, http://www.rferl.org/content/tajikistan-ngo-human-rights/24972595.html.

92. International Center for Non-Profit Law, 'NGO Law Monitor: Tajikistan,' *ICNL The International Center for Non-Profit Law*, September 28, 2015, http://www.icnl.org/research/monitor/tajikistan.html.

93. Jennifer Gandhi and Adam Przeworski, 'Cooperation, Cooptation, and Rebellion Under Dictatorships,' *Economics & Politics* 18, no. 1 (2006): 1–26, doi:10.1111/j.1468-0343.2006.00160.x.

94. Olivier Roy, *The Failure of Political Islam* (Harvard University Press, 1994), 36.

95. Dudoignon and Qalandar, '"They Were All from the Country." The Revival and Politicisation of Islam in the Lower Wakhsh River Valley of the Tajik SSE (1947–1997).'

96. Dudoignon, 'Une segmentation peut en cacher une autre,' 110.

97. Vinatier, *L'islamisme en Asie centrale*, 221.

98. Abdullo Rahnamo, *Hizbi Dini va Davlati Dunyavi (The Religious Party and the Secular State)* (Dushanbe: Irfon, 2008).

99. Naumkin, *Radical Islam in Central Asia*, 239.

100. Farangis Najibullah, 'Islamic Party Leader In Tajikistan Says He Supports Secular System,' *Radio Free Europe/Radio Liberty*, September 15, 2009, http://www.rferl.org/content/Islamic_Party_Leader_In_Tajikistan_Says_He_Supports_Secular_System_/1823086.html.

101. Roy, *L'Islam Mondialisé*.

102. 'Opros TSI: svyshe 50% oproshennykh dushanbintsev nazvali PIVT terroristicheskoy (CSS Survey: More than 50% Respondents Called the IRPT 'Terrorist'),' *Asia Plus*, October 2, 2015, http://www.news.tj/ru/news/opros-tssi-svyshe-50-oproshennykh-dushanbintsev-nazvali-pivt-terroristicheskoi.

103. Mehrangez Tursunzoda, 'Vlasti zakryli izdatel'stvo PIVT za "ne obespecheniye sotrudnikov lechebno-meditsinskim pitaniyem" (Authorities Closed the IRPT's Publishing House for 'Not Providing Employees With Sufficient Healthy Food'),' *Asia Plus*, August 13, 2015, http://asiaplus.tj/ru/node/213041.

104. Radio Ozodi, 'VS ob'yavil PIVT terroristicheskoy organizatsiyey (Supreme Court Declares the IRPT a Terrorist Organization),' *Radio Ozodi*, September 29, 2015, http://rus.ozodi.org/content/article/27277328.html.

105. Schatz, 'Leninism's Long Shadow in Central Asia,' 260.

106. Unicef, 'Study of Prevalence and Dynamics of Suicide Among Children and Young People (12–24 Years of Age) in Sughd Region, Tajikistan' (Dushanbe (Tajikistan), 2013), vii.

107. Khairullo Mirsaidov, 'Platnye dorogi v Tadzhikistane sdelali gosudarstvennoy tainoii (Toll Roads in Tajikistan Made a State Secret),' *Deutsche Welle*, July 6, 2010, платные-дороги-в-таджикис тане-сделали-государственной-тайной/a-5762913.

108. Najibullah, 'Islamic Party Leader In Tajikistan Says He Supports Secular System.'

109. Tilav Rasulzade, 'Tadzhikistan: Shkol'nitsy Prigrozili Samoubiystvom Za Zapret Nosit' Musul'manskiy Platok (Tajikistan: Schoolgirls Threatened to Kill Themselves Over the Hijab Interdiction),' *Fergana News*, October 7, 2010, http://www.fergananews.com/news.php?id=15695&mode=snews.

110. Musafirbek Ozod, 'Muhiddin Kabiri: V novom zakone o religii slishkom mnogo ogranicheni (Muhiddin Kabiri: Too Many Limitations in the Law on Religion),' *Fergana News*, March 16, 2009, http://www.fergananews.com/article.php?id=6097.

111. Stephane A. Dudoignon, 'From Ambivalence to Ambiguity? Some Paradigms of Policy Making in Tajikistan,' in *Tajikistan at a Crossroad: The Politics of Decentralization*, ed. Luigi De Martino, Cimera, 2004, 126.

112. Radio Free Europe/Radio Liberty, 'Tajik President Creates Opposition-Free Government,' *Radio Free Europe/Radio Liberty*, December 6, 2006, http://www.rferl.org/content/article/1073258.html.

113. Radio Free Europe/Radio Liberty, 'Main Tajik Opposition Party Won't Make Presidential Bid,' *Radio Free Europe/Radio Liberty*, September 25, 2006, http://www.rferl.org/content/article/1071612.html.

114. Dudoignon and Qalandar, '"They Were All from the Country." The Revival and Politicisation of Islam in the Lower Wakhsh River Valley of the Tajik SSE (1947–1997).'

115. Asia Plus, 'Bobonazarova schitayet, chto antireklama protiv PIVT ne pozvolila sobrat' nuzhnoye kolichestvo podpisey (Bobonazarova Believes that the Negative Publicity Against the IRPT Prevented to Collect the Required Number of Signatures),' *Asia Plus*, October 19, 2013, http://news.tj/ru/node/174087.

116. Farangis Najibullah and Khiromon Baqozoda, 'Tajik Islamic Party Labels Sex Video An "Attack" Ahead Of Elections,' *Radio Free Europe/Radio Liberty*, July 23, 2014, http://www.rferl.org/content/tajikistan-sex-video-politics-elections/26715229.html.

117. Radio Free Europe/Radio Liberty, 'A Pyrrhic Victory In Tajik Parliamentary Elections,' *Radio Free Europe/Radio Liberty*, March 5, 2015, http://www.rferl.org/content/tajikistan-islam-elections-parliament-history/26883637.html.

118. Bakhtior Khumairo, 'Imam-khatiby na pyatnichnoy molitve prizovut zakryt' PIVT? (Will Imam-Khatibs Call to Close Down the IRPT at the Friday Prayer?),' *Asia Plus*, March 27, 2015, http://news.tj/ru/news/imam-khatiby-na-pyatnichnoi-molitve-prizovut-zakryt-pivt.

119. Radio Free Europe/Radio Liberty, 'Calls Made For Tajik Islamic Party To Be Declared Terror Group,' *Radio Free Europe/Radio Liberty*, April 2, 2015, http://www.rferl.org/content/calls-made-for-tajik-islamic-party-to-be-declared-terror-group/26935070.html.

120. Asia Plus, 'Polnii tekst obrashcheniya Politsoveta PIVT k Prezidentu Respubliki Tadzhikistan (Full text of the IRPT's Political Council's Appeal to the President of the Republic),' *Asia Plus*, June 16, 2015, http://news.tj/ru/node/210078.

121. Asia Plus, 'PIVT obratilas' k stranam-garantam mezhtadzhikskogo soglasheniya (The IRPT Addressed the Guarantor-countries of the Inter-Tajik Agreement),' *Asia Plus*, July 1, 2015, http://news.tj/ru/node/210889.

122. Avaz Yuldashev, 'Kompartiya: Tam, gde OBSE, ES i OON, net ni mira, ni soglasiya (Communist Party: Where the OSCE, the EU and the UN Are There Is No Peace, No Agreement),' *Asia Plus*, July 6, 2015, http://news.tj/ru/news/kompartiya-tam-gde-obse-es-i-oon-net-ni-mira-ni-soglasiya.

123. Politrus, 'Muhiddin Kabiri: V Tadzhikistane nachalsa "37-ii god" (Muhiddin Kabiri: the Year 1937 Started in Tajikistan),' *Politrus*, June 24, 2015, http://www.politrus.com/2015/06/24/mukhiddin-kabiri/.

124. Radio Free Europe/Radio Liberty, 'The Painful Last Days Of Umed Tojiev,' *Radio Free Europe/Radio Liberty*, January 22, 2014, http://www.rferl.org/content/last-days-of-umed-tojiev/25238683.html.

125. Fergana News, 'PIVT: "Zakrytye dveri ili snesennye zdaniya ne oslablyayet nash dukh" (IRPT: 'The Closure of Doors or Destruction of Buildings Does Not Weaken Our Spirit),' *Fergana News*, June 23, 2014, http://www.fergananews.com/articles/8176.

126. Mehrangez Tursunzoda, 'V Tadzhikistane opechatan ofis pravyashchey v strane NDPT (The Office of Ruling Party NDPT Was Shutdown in Tajikistan),' *Asia Plus*, August 20, 2015, http://news.tj/ru/news/v-tadzhikistane-opechatan-ofis-pravyashchei-v-strane-ndpt.

127. Farangis Najibullah, 'Islamic Party Members Resign En Masse In Tajikistan,' *Radio Free Europe/Radio Liberty*, June 24, 2015, http://www.rferl.org/content/tajikistan-islamic-renaissance-party-resignations-en-masse/27091440.html.

128. Asia Plus, 'Genprokuratura: PIVT teryayet status politicheskoy partii (Prosecutor General: the IRPT Loses Its Status as a Political Party),' *Asia Plus*, July 8, 2015, http://news.tj/ru/node/211301.

129. Avaz Yuldashev, 'PIVT gotovit otvet Miniusti i prodolzhaet podgotovku k svoemu sezdu (The IRPT Prepares Its Answer to the Minsitry of Justice and Goes on with the Organization of Its Congress),' *Asia Plus*, September 1, 2015, http://asiaplus.tj/ru/node/213981.

130. Radio Ozodi, 'VS ob'yavil PIVT terroristicheskoy organizatsiyey (Supreme Court Declares the IRPT a Terrorist Organization).'

131. Internet Portal of the Tajik Opposition, 'Zaderzhan Nuriddin Makhkamov? (Is Nuriddin Mahkamov being detained?),' *Internet Portal Tajikskoi oppozitsii*, October 20, 2015, http://tajinfo.org/post/2015/10/22/635811340464225957.

132. Radio Ozodi, 'Buzurgmekhr Yorov podozrevayetsya v moshennichestve i poddelke dokumentov (Buzurgmehr Yorov Suspected of Fraud and Forgery),' *Radio Ozodi*, September 29, 2015, http://rus.ozodi.org/content/article/27276622.html.

133. Asia Plus, 'Zaderzhan Vtoroy Advokat Aktivistov PIVT (A Second Lawyer and Activist of the IRPT Was Detained),' *Asia Plus*, October 26, 2015, http://news.tj/ru/news/zaderzhan-vtoroi-advokat-aktivistov-pivt.

134. Catherine Putz, 'Tajikistan's Attack on Lawyers,' *The Diplomat*, May 5, 2016, http://thediplomat.com/2016/05/tajikistans-attack-on-lawyers/.

135. Bruce Pannier, 'Why Does Tajikistan Need A Referendum?,' *Radio Free Europe/Radio Liberty*, May 20, 2016, http://www.rferl.org/content/qishloq-ovozi-tajikistan-referendum-rahmon/27747496.html.

136. Emmanuel Karagiannis, 'The Challenge of Radical Islam in Tajikistan: Hizb Ut-Tahrir Al-Islami,' *Nationalities Papers* 34, no. 1 (2006): 16.

137. Olimova, 'Islam and the Tajik Conflict,' 70.

138. Daler Gufronov, 'A. Rahmamo: "Nevozmozhno Razdelit Islamskii Faktor i Naselenie" (A. Rahmamo: "It Is Impossible to Separate the Islamic Factor and Society")," *Asia Plus*, June 13, 2011, https://www.news.tj/ru/node/104952.

139. Bakhtiar Babajanov, 'Islam in Uzbekistan: From the Struggle for Religious Purity to Political Activism,' in *Central Asia: A Gathering Storm?*, ed. Boris Z. Rumer (New York: M.E. Sharpe, 2002), 299.

140. John Heathershaw and David W. Montgomery, 'The Myth of Post-Soviet Muslim Radicalization in the Central Asian Republics' (Chatam House, 2015), https://www.chathamhouse.org//node/16207.

141. There are different ways of transliterating the name of this organization: Tabligh-i Jamaat, Jamoati Tabligh, and Таблиги Джамоат in Russian. I recopied the name as used in the articles I quote.

142. Bayram Balci, 'The Rise of the Jama'at Al Tabligh in Kyrgyzstan: The Revival of Islamic Ties Between the Indian Subcontinent and Central Asia?,' *Central Asian Survey* 31, no. 1 (2012): 61–76.

143. Naumkin, *Radical Islam in Central Asia*.

144. Adeeb Khalid, 'L'Islam et l'État post-soviétique en Asie centrale,' *Revue internationale et stratégique*, no. 64 (2006): 101–10; Taarnby, 'Islamist Radicalization in Tajikistan: An Assessment of Current Trends.'

145. They actually jumped on the stage where Islam Karimov was giving a speech, grabbed the microphone from the President's hands, and called for the establishment of an Islamic state. A video footage of the incident is available on Youtube: https://www.youtube.com/watch?v=xwVS8CQg2s4.

146. Rashid, *Jihad*, 51.

147. Ibid., 51–2.

148. Fergana News, 'Takhir Yuldash: "Krakh SSHA Blizok, Zhdite Nas v Vashingtone" (Tahir Yuldash: 'The Collapse of the US Is near, Wait for Us in Washington'),' *Fergana News*, October 15, 2007, http://www.fergananews.com/articles/5403.

149. Olcott, 'Roots of Radical Islam in Central Asia,' 28.

150. Bruce Pannier, 'What Next For The Islamic Movement Of Uzbekistan?,' *Radio Free Europe/Radio Liberty*, August 23, 2015, http://www.rferl.org/content/qishloq-ovozi-imu-ghazi-uzbekistan-pakistan/27204379.html.

151. Heathershaw and Montgomery, 'The Myth of Post-Soviet Muslim Radicalization in the Central Asian Republics.'
152. Rashid, *Jihad*, 115.
153. Mariam Abou Zahab and Olivier Roy, *Islamist Networks: The Afghan-Pakistan Connection* (New York: Columbia University Press, 2004).
154. Rashid, *Jihad*, 121–31.
155. Karagiannis, 'The Challenge of Radical Islam in Tajikistan: Hizb Ut-Tahrir Al-Islami,' 4.
156. Al-Jazeera, *Breeding Discontent*, 2010, http://www.aljazeera.com/programmes/peopleandpower/2010/01/201012062540517354.html.
157. International Crisis Group, 'Central Asia.'
158. 'New Arrests of Hizb Ut Tahrir Members in Tajikistan!' *Khilafah.Com*, April 27, 2015, http://www.khilafah.com/new-arrests-of-hizb-ut-tahrir-members-in-tajikistan/.
159. Deweese, 'Islam and the Legacy of Sovietology,' 317.
160. Alexander Knysh, 'A Clear and Present Danger: "Wahhabism" as a Rhetorical Foil,' *Die Welt Des Islams* 44, no. 1 (2004): 3–26.
161. US Bureau of Counterterrorism, 'Country Reports on Terrorism: South and Central Asia,' Report (US Department Of State. The Office of Website Management, Bureau of Public Affairs, June 18, 2015) http://www.state.gov/j/ct/rls/crt/2014/239408.htm.
162. Human Rights Watch, 'Illusion of Justice: Human Rights Abuses in US Terrorism Prosecutions' (Human Rights Watch, 2014), 2, https://www.hrw.org/report/2014/07/21/illusion-justice-human-rights-abuses-us-terrorism-prosecutions.
163. George Camm, 'Tajikistan Ramps Up Terror Convictions, Life Sentences,' *EurasiaNet*, January 11, 2012, http://www.eurasianet.org/node/64818.
164. Rashid, *Jihad*, 108.
165. Najibullah, 'Islamic Party Leader In Tajikistan Says He Supports Secular System.'
166. BBC Monitoring Service, 'Renowned Tajik Cleric Urges Party to Back Outlawed Islamic Organization,' *Tojikiston*, December 24, 2009.
167. BBC News, 'Tajikistan Special Forces Chief Gulmurod Khalimov "Joins IS",' *BBC News*, May 28, 2015, http://www.bbc.com/news/world-asia-32917311.
168. Noah Tucker, 'Islamic State Messaging to Central Asians Migrant Workers in Russia,' Central Asia Program CERIA Brief, March 2015, http://centralasiaprogram.org/?p=6982.
169. Noah Tucker, 'Central Asian Involvement in the Conflict in Syria and Iraq: Drivers and Responses' (USAID, 2015), https://www.usaid.gov/sites/default/files/documents/1866/CVE_CentralAsiansSyriaIraq.pdf, 9.
170. Noah Tucker, 'Islamic State Messaging to Central Asians Migrant Workers in Russia,' Central Asia Program CERIA Brief, March 2015, 1, http://centralasiaprogram.org/?p=6982.

171. Radio Free Europe/Radio Liberty, 'Authorities Say Up To 1,000 Tajiks Joined IS In Syria, Iraq,' *Radio Free Europe/Radio Liberty*, January 25, 2016, http://www.rferl.org/content/tajikistan-double-estimate-of-islamic-state-members/27509293.html.

172. Edward J. Lemon, 'Daesh and Tajikistan: The Regime's (In)Security Policy,' *The RUSI Journal* 160, no. 5 (2015): 68–76.

173. Joshua Kucera, '95,000 Russian Troops Practice "Containing" Central Asian Conflict,' *EurasiaNet*, September 21, 2015, http://www.eurasianet.org/node/75191.

174. Markowitz, 'Tajikistan.'

175. Robert Alan Dahl, *Regimes and Oppositions* (New Haven: Yale University Press, 1973), 13.

Chapter 4   State Policies and Discourses in Independent Tajikistan

1. John Schoeberlein, 'The Ubiquitous State: Scholarship of Central Eurasia and the Sovietological Legacy' (European Society for Central Asian Studies, Ankara, 2007).

2. 'Tajikistan: On the Road to Failure,' Asia Report (Brussels: International Crisis Group, 2009), 15.

3. Haghayeghi, *Islam and Politics in Central Asia*, 157.

4. Berman, Bhargava, and Laliberte, 'Introduction.'

5. Lemon, 'Daesh and Tajikistan,' 73.

6. Abdullaev, 'Tajikistan.'

7. I reproduced in their integrity, excerpts from the English version of the Tajik Constitution available on the Parliament's website. Therefore, typos are not mine. Tajikistan, 'The Constitution of the Republic of Tajikistan,' accessed May 4, 2017, http://en.parlament.tj/konstitutsiyai-jt/.

8. Olimova, 'Islam and the Tajik Conflict.'

9. Tajikistan, 'The Constitution of the Republic of Tajikistan.'

10. Jonathan Fox, 'Separation of Religion and State and Secularism in Theory and in Practice,' *Religion, State and Society* 39, no. 4 (2011): 384–401.

11. Interestingly, in the South Caucasus, only Azerbaijan's Constitution specifies the secular character of the State while Georgian and Armenian texts mention the exclusive historical mission of their respective Churches.

12. See for instance Felix Corley, 'President Signs Repressive Religion Law,' *Forum 18*, March 29, 2009, http://www.forum18.org/archive.php?article_id=1274; Office for Democratic Institutions and Human Rights (ODHIR), 'Comments on The Draft Law of the Republic of Tajikistan "The Law of the Republic of Tajikistan on Freedom of Conscience and Religious Associations",' 2006, http://legislationline.org/download/action/download/id/782/file/2e2ebcda04dce962d620711d6be9.pdf, Office for Democratic Institutions and Human Rights (ODHIR), 'Comments on The Draft Law of the Republic

of Tajikistan "The Law of the Republic of Tajikistan on Freedom of Conscience and Religious Associations",' 2008, http://www.legislationline.org/topics/country/49/topic/78; Ozod, 'Muhiddin Kabiri: V novom zakone o religii slishkom mnogo ogranicheni (Muhiddin Kabiri: Too Many Limitations in the Law on Religion).'

13. Tajikistan, 'Zakon Respubliki Tadzhikistan o svobode sovesti i religioznix obedenieniyax (Law of the Republic of Tajikistan on Freedom of Conscience and Religious Organizations),' 2009, http://www.mmk.tj/ru/legislation/legislation-base/2009/.

14. Avaz Yuldashev, 'Hanafi School Recognized as Official Religion of Tajikistan,' *Asia Plus*, March 5, 2009, http://www.news.tj/en/news/hanafi-school-recognized-official-religion-tajikistan.

15. Olcott, 'Roots of Radical Islam in Central Asia.'

16. Radio Ozodi, 'Polkovnik MVD: vsyakiy, kto deystvuyet ne po Khanafitskomu mazkhabu, budet doproshen (Colonel of Interior Ministry: Those Who Do Not Act According to the Hanafi school Will Be Questioned),' *Radio Ozodi*, August 7, 2015, http://rus.ozodi.org/content/article/27176052.html.

17. Office for Democratic Institutions and Human Rights (ODHIR), 'Comments on The Draft Law of the Republic of Tajikistan "The Law of the Republic of Tajikistan on Freedom of Conscience and Religious Associations"' (2006).

18. Epkenhans, 'Muslims Without Learning, Clergy Without Faith: Institutions of Islamic Learning in the Republic of Tajikistan.'

19. Valerii Arkadevich Bryanov, *Ateisticheskoe vospitane studentov (The Atheistic Education of Students)* (Moscow: Izdatelstvo Vyshaya Shkola, 1986).

20. Igor Rotar, 'Baptist Missionary Killed While Praying,' *Forum 18*, January 14, 2004, http://www.forum18.org/archive.php?article_id=229.

21. Taarnby, 'Islamist Radicalization in Tajikistan: An Assessment of Current Trends.'

22. Farangis Najibullah, 'Tajik Cleric Says Textbooks Misinterpret Islam,' *EurasiaNet*, December 19, 2008, http://www.eurasianet.org/departments/insight/articles/pp122008.shtml.

23. Radio Free Europe/Radio Liberty, 'Tajikistan Introduces New Islamic Curriculum To Schools,' *Radio Free Europe/Radio Liberty*, March 6, 2009, http://www.rferl.org/content/article/1506565.html.

24. Radio Ozodi, 'Islamskoe prosveshhenie zamenili "Istorii tadzhikskovo naroda" (Islamic Instruction Replaced by 'History of the Tajik People'),' *Radio Ozodi*, February 4, 2011, http://rus.ozodi.org/content/no_islamic_education_in_tajik_schools_/9586323.html.

25. Farangis Najibullah, 'Tajiks Stopped From Traveling To Iran, Pakistan For Religious Courses,' *Radio Free Europe/Radio Liberty*, September 8, 2010, http://www.rferl.org/content/Tajiks_Stopped_From_Traveling_to_Iran_Pakistan_For_Religious_Courses/2152337.html.

26. Karim Orzuy, 'Ixroji keudakon az Masojid baxsi makomot bo reuxonion (Banning Children From Mosques: Authorities' Dialogue With Clerics),'

BBC Tajik, July 10, 2010, http://www.bbc.co.uk/tajik/news/2010/07/100710_ea_ak_children_mosque.shtml.

27. BBC Monitoring Service, 'Tajik Leader Voices Concern About "Secret" Islamic Schools' (Dushanbe: First Channel, April 30, 2007).

28. International Crisis Group, 'Central Asia.'

29. Dolina Mira, 'Analiz konfliktogennyx faktorov v religioznoii sfere Ferganskoii Doliny (Analysis of Factors of contention in Fergana Valley's Religious Sphere)' (Dolina Mira, 2010), http://www.dolinamira.org/issledovaniya.html.

30. Mavlouda Rafiyeva, '"Madrasah" Operation Ends up in Northern Tajikistan,' *Asia Plus*, June 17, 2011, http://news.tj/en/news/madrasah-operation-ends-northern-tajikistan.

31. Saiirahmon Nazryev, 'Na yuge Tadzhikistana vyavleno 47 nezakonno deiistvuyushhix religioznyx shkol (47 Illegally Operating Religious Schools Uncovered in the South of Tajikistan),' *Asia Plus*, July 1, 2011, http://news.tj/ru/news/na-yuge-tadzhikistana-vyyavleno-47-nezakonno-deistvuyushchikh-religioznykh-shkol.

32. Radio Free Europe/Radio Liberty, 'Five Of Six Legally-Run Tajik Madrasahs Suspended,' *Radio Free Europe/Radio Liberty*, July 12, 2013, http://www.rferl.org/content/tajikistan-madrasahs-closed/25044410.html.

33. Islam News, 'Zdaniye Islamskoy gimnazii peredano pod obshchezhitiye Peduniversiteta (The Building of the Islamic Gymnasium Given for Pedagogical University's Residences),' *Islam News*, June 18, 2015, http://islamnews.tj/tajikistan/1161-zdanie-islamskoy-gimnazii-peredano-pod-obschezhitie-peduniversiteta.html.

34. The equivalent of secondary 3 in the US and Canada.

35. Michele E. Commercio, 'Retraditionalization in Post-Soviet Kyrgyzstan and Tajikistan: Rejected by Elites, Embraced by Young Women' (Association for the Studies of Nationalities, New York, 2013), 18–22.

36. Emomali Rahmon, 'Obrashcheniye Prezidenta Respubliki Tadzhikistan Emomali Rakhmona Na Obshchestvennoye Sobraniye Po Regulirovaniyu Natsional'nykh Obychayev I Religioznykh Ritualakh (Address of the President of the Republic of Tajikistan Emomali Rahmon at the Public Gathering on Regulating National Customs and Religious Rituals)' (Dushanbe, May 24, 2007), http://www.prezident.tj/rus/vistupleniy240507.htm (Broken link).

37. Asia Plus, 'V RT sozdan islamskii institut s izucheniem gumanitarnyx nauk (An Islamic Institute With The Study of Humanities Was Created in the Tajik Republic),' *Asia Plus*, November 16, 2007, http://www.news.tj/ru/news/v-rt-sozdan-islamskii-institut-s-izucheniem-gumanitarnykh-nauk.

38. Avaz Yuldashev, 'President Signs Decree Announcing 2009 as Year of Imam Azam in Tajikistan,' *Asia Plus*, September 15, 2008, http://www.news.tj/en/news/president-signs-decree-announcing-2009-year-imam-azam-tajikistan.

39. Mehrangez Tursunzoda, 'U. Nazarov: 'Ne kazhdii nash student idet rabotat' v Mechet' (Not All Of Our Student Go Work at a Mosque),' *Asia Plus*, January 19, 2012, http://www.news.tj/ru/newspaper/interview/u-nazarov-ne-kazhdyi-nash-student-idet-rabotat-v-mechet.

40. Islam News, 'Studenty islamskogo vuza nachali obuchatsyapo novomu posobiyupo russkomu yazyku (Students of Islamic University Began to Study Russian with New Manuals),' *Islam News*, January 22, 2013, http://www.islamnews.tj/tajikistan/583-studenty-islamskogo-vuza-nachali-obuchatsya-po-novomu-posobiyu-po-russkomu-yazyku.html.

41. International Crisis Group, '"Central Asia"; Ahmadali Todzhiddinov, 'Kuda delis studenty vernuvshiesya iz Islamkix stran? (Where Are the Students Who Returned From Islamic countries?),' *Asia Plus*, September 27, 2011, http://www.news.tj/ru/news/kuda-delis-studenty-vernuvshiesya-iz-islamskikh-stran.

42. Fardin Isazade, 'Shafig Pshikhachev: "Nasha tsel" – konsolidatsiya musul'man na postsovetskom prostranstve (Shafig Pshihachev: 'Our Goal – The Consolidation of Muslims in the Post-Soviet Space'),' *Islam.az*, April 29, 2013, http://islam.az/news/a-13529.html.

43. Religioscope, 'Islam in Tajikistan - Interview with Abdullo Hakim Rahnamo,' *Religioscope*, April 25, 2004, http://religion.info/english/interviews/article_34.shtml#.VtXpGkC8qSo.

44. Najibullah, 'Tajiks Stopped From Traveling To Iran, Pakistan For Religious Courses.'

45. Khairullo Mirsaidov, Tilav Rasulzade, and Turko Dikaev, 'Vozrashenie studentov – Vorpos politicheskii? (Students' Return – A Political Issue?),' *Centrasia*, December 1, 2010, http://www.centrasia.ru/newsA.php?st=1291175400.

46. Radio Free Europe/Radio Liberty, 'Tajiks Who Studied Abroad Face Criminal Charges,' *Radio Free Europe/Radio Liberty*, August 19, 2011, http://www.rferl.org/content/tajiks_who_studied_abroad_face_criminal_charges/24301913.html.

47. Najibullah, 'Tajiks Stopped From Traveling To Iran, Pakistan For Religious Courses.'

48. Todzhiddinov, 'Kuda delis studenty vernuvshiesya iz Islamkix stran? (Where Are the Students Who Returned From Islamic countries?).'

49. Tajikistan, 'Zakon Respubliki Tadzhikistan Ob Obtvetstvennosti Roditelei Za Vospitane i Obuchene Detei (Law of the Republic of Tajikistan on Parental Responsibility in the Upbringing and Education of Children),' 2011, http://www.mmk.tj/ru/legislation/legislation-base/2011/.

50. Avaz Yuldashev, 'V Tadzhikistane v silu vstupil zakon ob otvetstvennosti roditeleii (Law on Parental Responsibility Came Into Force in Tajikistan),' *Asia Plus*, August 6, 2011, http://news.tj/ru/news/v-tadzhikistane-v-silu-vstupil-zakon-ob-otvetstvennosti-roditelei.

51. Avaz Yuldashev, 'Vosstanovlena mechet' pri PIVT, povrezhdennaya pri pozhare (IRPT's Mosque Damaged by Fire Was Restored),' *Asia Plus*,

September 22, 2011, http://news.tj/ru/news/vosstanovlena-mechet-pri-pivt-povrezhdennaya-pri-pozhare.

52. 'Statement by the Head of Delegation of Tajikistan Ambassador Nuriddin Shamsov' (870th the OSCE Permanent Council Meeting, Vienna, June 23, 2011), http://www.osce.org/library/.

53. Bayram Mushfig, 'Legal Restrictions on Parents' and Children's Religious Freedom,' *Forum 18*, March 15, 2011, http://www.forum18.org/archive.php?article_id=1552.

54. Parvina Hamidova, 'Marxabo Dzhabborov: 'Tol'ko zakon mozhet vsex razbudit' (Marxabo Dzhabborova: 'Only the Law Can Wake Us All Up'),' *Asia Plus*, June 30, 2011, http://news.tj/ru/newspaper/article/markhabo-dzhabborova-tolko-zakon-mozhet-vsekh-razbudit.

55. Yuldashev, 'V Tadzhikistane v silu vstupil zakon ob otvetstvennosti roditeleii (Law on Parental Responsibility Came Into Force in Tajikistan).'

56. 'Statement by the Head of Delegation of Tajikistan Ambassador Nuriddin Shamsov.'

57. Islam News, 'Na severe Tadzhikistana vyyavili deteii, kotorye vo vremya ucheby poseshali mecheti (Children at Mosque During School Time Discovered in Northern Tajikistan),' *Islam News*, March 27, 2012, http://islamnews.tj/tajikistan/352-na-severe-tadzhikistana-vyyavili-detey-kotorye-vovremya-ucheby-poseschali-mecheti.html.

58. Hiro, *Between Marx and Muhammad*, 209.

59. Farangis Najibullah, 'Tajikistan Moves To Ban Arabic Names, Marriages Between First Cousins,' *Radio Free Europe/Radio Liberty*, January 13, 2016, http://www.rferl.org/content/tajikistan-ban-arabic-names-marriage-between-cousins/27486012.html.

60. The Moscow Times, 'Tajikistan's President Changes His Name,' *The Moscow Times*, March 29, 2007, http://www.themoscowtimes.com/news/article/tajikis tans-president-changes-his-name/198084.html.

61. In Tajik, 'Shuroi Ulamo,' in Russian 'Soviet Ulemov.'

62. Similar institutions are found in all Central Asian republics as well as in Russia.

63. Epkenhans, 'Muslims Without Learning, Clergy Without Faith: Institutions of Islamic Learning in the Republic of Tajikistan,' 327.

64. Akbarzadeh, 'Islamic Clerical Establishment in Central Asia,' 98.

65. Akiner, 'The Politicisation of Islam in Postsoviet Central Asia,' 119.

66. Mavdzhuda Hasanova, 'Izbran novyii predsedatel' Soveta ulemov Islamskovo Tsentra (A new Chairman for the Council of Ulemas of the Islamic Center of Tajikistan Was Chosen),' *Centrasia*, October 13, 2010, http://www.centrasia.ru/newsA.php?st=1286948700.

67. For the organization chart, see http://islamnews.tj/ulema-council.html.

68. Antoine Blua, 'Tajikistan: Government To Vet Islamic Clerics,' *Radio Free Europe/Radio Liberty*, August 7, 2002, http://www.rferl.org/content/article/1100477.html.

69. Farangis Najibullah, 'Tajikistan: Authorities Impose Religious Tests On Imams,' *Radio Free Europe/Radio Liberty*, August 8, 2007, http://www.rferl.org/content/article/1078040.html.

70. Islam News, 'V Tadzhikistane zaregistrirovan tsentr po podgotovke imam-khatibov (Training Center for Imam-khatibs Registered in Tajikistan),' *Islam News*, August 29, 2012, http://islamnews.tj/tajikistan/484-v-tadzhikistane-zaregistrirovan-centr-po-podgotovke-imam-hatibov.html.

71. Epkenhans, 'Muslims Without Learning, Clergy Without Faith: Institutions of Islamic Learning in the Republic of Tajikistan,' 328.

72. Islam News, 'V Tadzhikistane v mechetyakh menyaiut imam-khatibov po prichine ne prokhozheniya attestatsii (Imam-Khatibs Replaced After Failing Certification in Tajikistan),' *Islam News*, December 27, 2011, http://islam news.tj/tajikistan/267-v-tadzhikistane-v-mechetyah-menyayut-imam-hatibov-po-prichine-ne-prohozhdeniya-attestacii.html.

73. Negmatullo Mirsaidov, 'Sughd Wraps up 1st Stage of Imam Certification,' *Central Asia Online*, June 2, 2011, http://centralasiaonline.com/en_GB/articles/caii/features/politics/2011/06/02/feature-02.

74. Emomali Rahmon, 'Televizionnoe pozdravlenie po sluchayu nastupleniya svyashhennovo mesyatsa Ramazan (Television congratulation of the President of the Republic of Tajikistan Emomali Rahmon at the Occasion of the Holy Month of Ramadan),' August 7, 2007, http://www.prezident.tj/ru/node/1418.

75. Emomali Rahmon, 'Vystuplenie Na Vstreche s Predstavitelyami Obshhestvennosti Strany (Speech at a Meeting With Representatives of the Country's Community),' July 4, 2013, http://www.prezident.tj/ru/node/4669.

76. Islam News, 'Zarplata Imam-Khatibam: Nezakonno i Neobosnovanno? (Salary for Imam-Khatibs: Illegal and Unreasonable?),' *Islam News*, July 23, 2013, http://islamnews.tj/analitic/769-zarplata-imam-hatibam-nezakonno-i-neobosnovanno.html.

77. Roja Assadi, 'Tajik Government Pays Salaries to Imams for First Time,' *BBC News*, March 17, 2014, http://www.bbc.com/news/world-asia-26579613.

78. Russia Today, 'Closer to God: Tajik President's Speech to Be Explained in Mosques,' *Russia Today*, May 10, 2013, https://www.rt.com/news/rahmon-address-imams-mosques-106/.

79. Farangis Najibullah, 'Tajik Imams Get A Makeover,' *Radio Free Europe/Radio Liberty*, January 18, 2014, sec. Tajikistan, http://www.rferl.org/content/tajikistan-imams-makeover/25234064.html.

80. Islam News, 'V Mecheti "Muhammadya" Novyii imam-khatib (New Imam-Khatib in the Muhammadya Mosque),' *Islam News*, December 14, 2011, http://islamnews.tj/tajikistan/251-v-mecheti-muhammadiya-novyy-imam-hatib.html.

81. Avaz Yuldashev, 'Vlasti priostanovili deyatel'nost' mecheti sem'i Turadzhonzoda (Authorities Have Suspended the Activities of Turajonzoda's Family Mosque),' *Asia Plus*, December 12, 2011, http://news.tj/ru/news/vlasti-priostanovili-deyatelnost-mecheti-semi-turadzhonzoda.

82. Islam News, 'Mechet' Turadzhonzoda ofitsial'no lishena statusa pyatnichnoy mecheti (Turajonzoda's Mosque Officially Stripped of Its Friday Mosque Status),' *Islam News*, May 3, 2012, http://islamnews.tj/tajikistan/394-mechet-turadzhonzoda-oficialno-lishena-statusa-pyatnichnoy-mecheti.html.

83. Islam News, 'Hoji Akbar Turajonzoda: Tsel'iu byl ne ya, a moii starshii brat Huriddin (Hoji Akbar Turajonzoda: The Objective Was Not Me, But My Older Brother Nuriddin),' *Islam News*, December 19, 2011, http://islamnews. tj/tajikistan/257-hodzhi-akbar-turadzhonzoda-celyu-byl-ne-ya-a-moy-starshiy-brat-nuriddin.html.

84. Asia Plus, 'V otnoshenii odnogo iz izvestnykh duhovnykh liderov Tadzhikistana mozhet byt' vozbuzhdeno ugolovnoe delo (A criminal Case Might Be Opened In Connection to A Well-known Religious Leader in Tajikistan),' *Asia Plus*, November 28, 2008, http://www.news.tj/ru/news/v-otnoshenii-odnogo-iz-izvestnykh-dukhovnykh-liderov-tadzhikistana-mozhet-byt-vozbuzhdeno-ugolo.

85. Adeeb Khalid, *Islam After Communism: Religion and Politics in Central Asia* (Berkeley: University of California Press, 2007), 186–7.

86. International Crisis Group, 'Central Asia.'

87. Igor Rotar, 'Tajikistan: Council of Ulems – An Instrument Of State Control,' *Forum 18*, June 8, 2006, http://www.forum18.org/archive.php?article_id=796.

88. Rahmon, 'Obrashcheniye Prezidenta Respubliki Tadzhikistan Emomali Rakhmona Na Obshchestvennoye Sobraniye Po Regulirovaniyu Natsional'-nykh Obychayev i Religioznykh Ritualakh (Address of the President of the Republic of Tajikistan Emomali Rahmon at the Public Gathering on Regulating National Customs and Religious Rituals).'

89. Taarnby, 'Islamist Radicalization in Tajikistan: An Assessment of Current Trends,' 38.

90. Epkenhans, 'Defining Normative Islam,' 84.

91. Isazade, 'Shafig Pshikhachev: "Nasha tsel" – konsolidatsiya musul'man na postsovetskom prostranstve (Shafig Pshihachev: 'Our Goal – The Consolidation of Muslims in the Post-Soviet Space').'

92. The Committee has its own website: [http://www.din.tj/]/

93. International Crisis Group, 'Central Asia'; Epkenhans, 'Muslims Without Learning, Clergy Without Faith: Institutions of Islamic Learning in the Republic of Tajikistan,' 326.

94. Epkenhans, 'Muslims Without Learning, Clergy Without Faith: Institutions of Islamic Learning in the Republic of Tajikistan,' 325.

95. Tajikistan, 'Zakon Respubliki Tadzhikistan Ob uporyadochenii traditsiy, torzhestv i obryadov v RT (Law of the Republic of Tajikistan on On regulation of Traditions, Celebrations and ceremonies in Tajikistan),' 2007, http://www.mmk.tj/ru/legislation/legislation-base/2007/.

96. Rahmon, 'Obrashcheniye Prezidenta Respubliki Tadzhikistan Emomali Rakhmona Na Obshchestvennoye Sobraniye Po Regulirovaniyu Natsional'-

nykh Obychayev i Religioznykh Ritualakh (Address of the President of the Republic of Tajikistan Emomali Rahmon at the Public Gathering on Regulating National Customs and Religious Rituals).'

97. Radio Free Europe/Radio Liberty, 'Tajik Authorities Demand Payment In Dollars For Hajj,' *Radio Free Europe/Radio Liberty*, August 22, 2011, http://www.rferl.org/content/tajik_authorities_demand_payment_in_dollars_for_hajj/24304426.html.

98. Mehrangez Tursunzoda, 'Dlya tadzhikskix palomnikov ustanovlen edinii standart odezhdy (A Unique Standard Dress for Tajik Pilgrims,' *Asia Plus*, October 1, 2011, http://news.tj/ru/news/dlya-tadzhikskikh-palomnikov-ustanovlen-edinyi-standart-odezhdy.

99. Radio Free Europe/Radio Liberty, 'Tajikistan Bans Hajj Pilgrimage For Citizens Younger Than 35,' *Radio Free Europe/Radio Liberty*, April 14, 2015, sec. Tajikistan, http://www.rferl.org/content/tajikisyanm-bans-hajj-pilgirm age-for-citizens-younger-than-35/26955080.html.

100. Ahmet T. Kuru, 'Passive and Assertive Secularism: Historical Conditions, Ideological Struggles, and State Policies toward Religion,' *World Politics* 59, no. 4 (2007): 571.

101. Islam News, 'M. Kabiri: V Tadzhikistane neobxodimo nachat' novuiyu fazu peregovorov (M. Kabiri: We Need to Start a New Phase of Negotiations in Tajikistan),' *Islam News*, February 21, 2012, http://islamnews.tj/tajikistan/323-m-kabiri-v-tadzhikistane-neobhodimo-nachat-novuyu-fazu-peregovorov.html.

102. Panchenko, 'Morality, Utopia, Discipline. New Religious Movements and Soviet Culture.'

103. She used to wear a 'traditional' scarf. As recalled in Chapter 2, she started wearing a hijab in 2013, after which problems started for her. Her small human rights promotion NGO was shutdown on the pretext of administrative irregularities few months later.

104. McBrien, 'Mukadas's Struggle,' 136.

105. Igor Rotar, 'Tajikistan: Mosque Visits and Hijabs Banned for Children,' *Forum 18*, October 31, 2005, http://www.forum18.org/archive.php?article_id=679.

106. Sally Peck, 'Tajikistan Bans Miniskirts and Head Scarves,' *The Telegraph*, April 18, 2007, http://www.telegraph.co.uk/news/worldnews/1549005/Tajikistan-bans-miniskirts-and-head-scarves.html.

107. Farangis Najibullah, 'Tajikistan: New Curbs Target Islamic Students,' *Radio Free Europe/Radio Liberty*, January 17, 2008, sec. Tajikistan, http://www.rferl.org/content/article/1079366.html.

108. 'Rakhmonov: "Pust" vashikh detey uchat mully' (Rakhmonov: 'Go Ahead and Let Your Children Study With Mullahs'),' *Asia Plus*, September 17, 2010, http://news.tj/en/node/1321.

109. Radio Ozodi, 'V pedagogicheskom universitete vveden zapret na vysokiye kabluki (High Heels Now Forbidden at the Pedagogical University),'

Radio Ozodi, March 27, 2013, http://rus.ozodi.org/content/article/24940302. html.

110. Edward J. Lemon and Hélène Thibault, 'Counter-Extremism, Power and Authoritarian Governance in Tajikistan,' (30 June 2017) *Central Asian Survey*, 10.1080/02634937.2017.1336155.

111. Tilav Rasulzade, 'Tadzhikistan: Shkol'nitsy prigrozili samoubiystvom za zapret nosit' musul'manskiy platok' (Tajikistan: Schoolgirls threatened to kill themselves over the hijab interdiction),' *Fergana News*, October 7, 2010, http://www.fergananews.com/news.php?id=15695&mode=snews.

112. 'Women Appeal Against "Impending Hijab Ban" At Tajik City Market,' *Radio Free Europe/Radio Liberty*, August 24, 2010, http://www.rferl.org/content/ Women_Appeal_Against_Impending_Hijab_Ban_At_Tajik_City_Market/ 2136688.html.

113. 'Tajik Pressure Said To Be Growing Over Islamic Dress,' *Radio Free Europe/Radio Liberty*, September 17, 2010, http://www.rferl.org/content/Tajik_Pressure_ Said_To_Be_Growing_Over_Islamic_Dress/2160501.html.

114. Farangis Najibullah, 'Tajikistan: Authorities Exclude Miniskirt, Hejab On Campuses,' *Radio Free Europe/Radio Liberty*, April 12, 2007, http://www.rferl. org/content/article/1075841.html.

115. Fergana News, 'Tadzhikistan: Sovet ulemov prizyvayet zhenshchin nosit' tol'ko natsional'nuyu odezhdu (Tajikistan: The Council of Ulemas Calls on Women to Only Wear National Clothes),' *Fergana News*, September 30, 2010, http://www.fergananews.com/news.php?id=15647.

116. Najibullah, 'Islamic Party Leader In Tajikistan Says He Supports Secular System.'

117. Farangis Najibullah and Ganj Ganjinai, 'Tajik Prostitutes Seek Protection In The Hijab,' *Radio Free Europe/Radio Liberty*, March 14, 2015, http://www.rferl. org/content/tajikistan-prostitutes-hijab/26900935.html.

118. Bakhrom Fayzullayev, 'Na Severe Tadzhikistana Nosheniye Khidzhaba Vzyali Pod Kontrol (Hijab Under Control in Northern Tajikistan),' *Asia Plus*, March 27, 2015, http://news.tj/ru/news/na-severe-tadzhikistana-noshenie-khidzhaba-vzyali-pod-kontrol.

119. Avaz Yuldashev, 'Mer Dushanbe "ob'yavil voynu" chuzhdoy tadzhikam odezhde (Dushanbe Mayor "Declared War" Against Foreign Clothes),' *Asia Plus*, August 20, 2015, http://news.tj/ru/news/mer-dushanbe-obyavil-voinu-chuzhdoi-tadzhi kam-odezhde.

120. *Radio Ozodi*, August 7, 2015.

121. Mehrangez Tursunzoda, 'Komitet po delam religii ob'yasnil, chto takoye "odezhda, chuzhdaya dlya Tadzhikistana" (Committee for Religious Affairs Explained That Such 'Clothes are Foreign to Tajikistan'),' *Asia Plus*, January 12, 2016, http://news.tj/ru/news/komitet-po-delam-religii-obyasnil-chto-takoe-odezhda-chuzhdaya-dlya-tadzhikistana.

122. Asia Plus, 'V OVD stolitsy breyut borody ... I fotografiruyut za den'gi (The Capital's Department of International Affairs Shave Beards ... And Take

Photos For Money),' *Asia Plus*, January 12, 2011, http://news.tj/ru/newspaper/article/v-ovd-stolitsy-breyut-borody-i-fotografiruyut-za-dengi.

123. NewsRU, 'Sovet ulemov Tadzhikistana opredelil, kakoy dolzhna byt' boroda u mestnykh musul'man' (Tajik Council of Ulemas Determines How the Beards of Local Muslims Should Be),' *NewsRU*, November 21, 2012, http://www.newsru.com/religy/21nov2012/barba.html.

124. Asia Plus, 'V OVD stolitsy breyut borody ... I fotografiruyut za den'gi (The Capital's Department of International Affairs Shave Beards ... And Take Photos For Money).'

125. Radio Free Europe/Radio Liberty, 'What Would You Choose?' *Radio Free Europe/Radio Liberty*, April 19, 2011, http://www.rferl.org/content/tajik_football_player_barred_because_of_his_beard/9498409.html.

126. Mavdjuda Hasanova, 'Komitet po delam religii: V Tadzhikistane nikto ne zapreshchayet nosit' khidzhab i borodu (Committee for Religious Affairs: No one in Tajikistan forbids to wear a hijab or a beard),' *Asia Plus*, October 11, 2010, http://news.tj/ru/news/komitet-po-delam-religii-v-tadzhikistane-nikto-ne-zapreshchaet-nosit-khidzhab-i-borodu.

127. Al-Jazeera, 'Tajikistan Shaves 13,000 Beards in "Radicalism" Battle,' *Al-Jazeera*, January 21, 2016, http://www.aljazeera.com/news/2016/01/tajikistan-shaves-13000-men-beards-radicalism-160120133352747.html.

128. Morgan Liu, 'Post-Soviet Paternalism and Personhood: Why Culture Matters to Democratization in Central Asia,' in *Prospects for Democracy in Central Asia*, ed. Birgit N. Schlyter (Istanbul: Swedish Research Institute in Istanbul, 2005), 225–37.

129. Jessica Allina-Pisano, 'How to Tell an Axe-Murderer: An Essay on Ethnography, Truth, and Lies,' in *Political Ethnography: What Immersion Contributes to the Study of Power*, ed. Edward Schatz (Chicago: The University of Chicago Press, 2009), 69.

130. Emomali Rahmon, 'Televizionnoye Poslaniye v Chest' Dnya Materi (Television Discourse in Honor of Mother's Day)' (Dushanbe, March 6, 2016), http://prezident.tj/ru/node/10859.

131. Emomali Rahmon, 'Vystupleniye Po Sluchayu Dnya Materi (Discourse at the Occasion of Mother's Day)' (Dushanbe, March 6, 2015), http://www.president.tj/ru/node/8400.

132. Elizabeth Ann Constantine, 'Public Discourse and Private Lives: Uzbek Women under Soviet Rule, 1917–1991' (Bloomington: University of Indiana, 2001), 281.

133. Iskandar Aliev and Daisy Sindelar, 'Tajikistan: Top Islamic Body Bans Women From Attending Mosque Services,' *Radio Free Europe/Radio Liberty*, October 20, 2004, http://www.rferl.org/content/article/1055440.html.

134. Bruce Pannier, 'Tajikistan: President's Remarks On Women And Mosques Draw Sharp Reactions,' *Radio Free Europe/Radio Liberty*, November 11, 2004, http://www.rferl.org/content/article/1055829.html.

135. Bryanov, *Ateisticheskoe vospitane studentov (The Atheistic Education of Students)*.

136. Mirzo Salimov and Frud Bezhan, 'The Islamic Party, The Reporter, And The Virginity Test,' *Radio Free Europe/Radio Liberty*, January 7, 2016, http://www.rferl.org/content/tajikistan-islamic-renaissance-party-love-virginity-test-reporter-kabiri/27473804.html.

Chapter 5   Of Being Muslim in Tajikistan

1. Olga Tutubalina, 'M. Akhmadov: "My dostanem ix v pravitelstve" (M. Ahmadov: We Will Hand Them Over to the Authorities),' *Asia Plus*, January 12, 2011, http://news.tj/ru/newspaper/article/m-akhmadov-my-dostanem-ikh-i-v-pravitelstve.

2. Lemon and Thibault, 'Counter-Extremism, Power and Authoritarian Governance in Tajikistan.'

3. Though they refer to them as 'secularists,' I use Pelkmans and McBrien's definition of people who 'though they did not apply the term "secular" to themselves, they increasingly identified themselves in contrast to those they labelled as "religious" and denied the keeping of any religious observance' except for their belief in God and participation in life-cycle rituals. Mathijs Pelkmans and Julie McBrien, 'Turning Marx on his Head Missionaries, "Extremists" and Archaic Secularists in Post-Soviet Kyrgyzstan,' *Critique of Anthropology* 28/1 (2008), p. 89.

4. Talal Asad, *Formations of the Secular: Christianity, Islam, Modernity* (Stanford: Stanford University Press, 2003), 16.

5. Alexander A Panchenko, 'Morality, Utopia, Discipline. New religious movements and Soviet culture,' in Jarrett Zigon (ed). *Multiple moralities and Religions in Post-Soviet Russia* (New York: Bergham Books, 2011), 120.

6. Louw, *Everyday Islam in Post-Soviet Central Asia*, 2007, 10.

7. Daniel Cefaï, 'Qu'est-ce que l'ethnographie? Débats contemporains.' Originally published as '¿Qué es la etnografía? Debates contemporáneos. Primera parte. Arraigamientos, operaciones y experiencias del trabajo de campo,' *Persona y sociedad* 27/3 (2013), 101–19.

8. Dvora Yanow, 'Thinking Interpretively: Philosophical Presuppositions and the Human Science,' in Peregrine Schwartz-Shea and Dvora Yanow (eds) *Interpretation And Method: Empirical Research Methods And the Interpretive Turn* (New York: M.E. Sharpe, 2006), 9.

9. Dudoignon and Noack, *Allah's Kolkhozes: Migration, De-Stalinisation, Privatisation and the Emergence of New Muslim Religious Communities in the USSR, and After (1950s–2000s)*.

10. McBrien, 'Mukadas's Struggle.'

11. Slightly different versions of a same question led to quite different results in two surveys conducted the same year in the United States. Thirty-five per cent of respondents of a Gallup survey answered yes to the question: 'Would you say that you have been "born again" or have had a "born-again" experience – that is, a turning point in your life when you committed yourself to Jesus Christ?'

whereas 56 per cent of respondents did when asked the shorter question: 'Would you say that you are a "born-again" Christian?' Dixon Richard D, Diane E. Levy and Roger C. Lowery, 'Asking The "Born-Again" Question,' *Review of Religious Research* 30 (1988), 34–5.

12. Sergei Abashin, 'The Logic of Islamic Practice: a Religious Conflict in Central Asia,' *Central Asian Survey* 25/3 (2006), 268.
13. Olivier Roy, *L'Islam mondialisé*, Seuil (Paris, 2009); 50–1.
14. Mathijs Pelkmans, 'Introduction: Post-Soviet Space and the Unexpected Turns of Religious Life,' in Mathijs Pelkmans (ed.), *Conversion after socialism: disruptions, modernisms and technologies of faith in the former Soviet Union* (Oxford: Bergahn Books, 2009), p. 6.
15. Sarah Kendzior, 'Redefining Religion: Uzbek Atheist Propaganda in Gorbachev-Era Uzbekistan,' *Nationalities Papers* 34/5 (2006), p. 536.
16. Juliette Cadiot, *Le laboratoire impérial: Russie-URSS 1860–1940* (Paris: CNRS, 2007).
17. Pelkmans, 'Introduction,' p. 6.
18. Sébastien Peyrouse, *Des Chrétiens Entre Athéisme et Islam: Regards Sur La Question Religieuse En Asie Centrale Soviétique et Post-Soviétique* (Paris: Maisonneuve et Larose, 2003), 236.
19. Zigon, 'Multiple Moralities: Discourses, Practices, and Breakdowns in Post-Soviet Russia,' 10.
20. Pelkmans, 'Introduction: Post-Soviet Space and the Unexpected Turns of Religious Life,' 2.
21. McBrien, 'Mukadas's Struggle,' 133.
22. Louw, *Everyday Islam in Post-Soviet Central Asia*, 2007, 40.
23. John Heathershaw and Nick Megoran, 'Contesting danger: a new agenda for policy and scholarship on Central Asia,' *International Affairs* 87/3 (2011), 589–612.
24. Noah Tucker, '"Ordinary People" and the Violence of Collapse (Osh, Part III),' *Registan.Net*, June 26, 2011, http://registan.net/2011/06/26/ordinary-people-and-the-violence-of-collapse-osh-part-iii/.
25. Alijon Boymatov, 'Economic Relations between Centre and Regions: The Case of Sughd Province,' in *Tajikistan at a Crossroad: The Politics of Decentralization*, ed. Luigi De Martino, Cimera, Situation Report 4 (Geneva, 2004), p. 54.
26. World Bank, 'Tajikistan Data,' *World Bank*, 2014, http://data.worldbank.org/country/tajikistan.
27. Kelly McMann, 'The Shrinking of the Welfare State: Central Asians' Assessments of Soviet and Post-Soviet Governance,' in *Everyday Life in Central Asia Past and Present* (Bloomington: Indiana University Press, 2007), 233–47.
28. Ghafur Khodjamurodov and Rechel Bernd, 'Tajikistan: Health System Review,' *Health Systems in Transition* 12, no. 2 (2010), xvi.
29. Joëlle Schwarz et al., 'Out-of-Pocket Expenditures for Primary Health Care in Tajikistan: A Time-Trend Analysis,' *BMC Health Services Research* 13 (2013), 6.

30. The government has undertaken the construction of the Rogun hydroelectric power plant, a project started by the Soviets in the 1970s but later abandoned. Every Tajik family was officially asked to buy shares for a minimum of 3,000 somoni ($450), but fieldwork revealed that many were actually forced to. The project, which would greatly improve Tajikistan's energetic independence, has stalled due to a fierce dispute with neighbouring Uzbekistan which fears a negative impact on its own downstream irrigation system. The government resumed construction in late 2015.

31. Transparency International, 'Tajikistan,' *Transparency International*, n.d., http:// www.transparency.org/country#TJK 2.

32. 'Prezident Tadzhikistana Povelel: Kazhdaya Sem'ya Dolzhna Kupit' Aktsii Rogunskoy GES (The President of Tajikistan Ordered: Each Family Must Buy Shares of the Rogun Hydroelectric Power Station),' *Fergana News*, December 2, 2009, http://www.fergananews.com/news.php?id=13563&mode=snews.

33. Pairav Chorshanbiev, 'Road Tolls Lowered for Residents of Varzob District,' *Asia Plus*, April 30, 2010, http://www.asiaplus.tj/en/news/road-tolls-lowered-residents-varzob-district.

34. Mirsaidov has worked for the German Deutsche Welle and Tajik Asia Plus before. He has been involved in Khujand-based KVN (Club of the Funny and Inventive People) in the last few years, trying to push forward the Tajik team on the international stage. They were facing financial problems and he publicly denounced the lack of support and corruption of the local authorities in November. Following that, he has been arrested and charged with 'national enmity and false denunciation'. *Asia-Plus*, 2017, 'Head of Khujand-based KVN team faces charges of inciting national enmity and false denunciation', Asia Plus, December 8, https://news.tj/en/node/248428.

35. Mirsaidov, 'Platnye dorogi v Tadzhikistane sdelali gosudarstvennoy tainoii (Toll Roads in Tajikistan Made a State Secret).'

36. Transparency International, 'Tajikistan.' To add insult to the injury, in 2011, a portion of the company's declining profits were used to finance the construction of the world's tallest flagpole, reputed to have cost around $5 million, to commemorate the twentieth anniversary of Tajik independence.

37. 'V Tadzhikistane 27% diplomirovannix molodix liudiei ne mogut chitat' (In Tajikistan, 27% of Degree Holders Cannot Read nor Write),' *Radio Ozodi*, September 1, 2015, http://rus.ozodi.org/content/article/27219776. html.

38. Trilling, 'Tajikistan's Strongman Appoints Son to Lead Corruption Fight.'

39. Alena V. Ledeneva, 'Practices of Exchange and Networking in Russia,' *Soziale Welt* 48/2 (1997), 153.

40. Nurali Davlat, 'Korruptsiya Reshaet vse (Corruption Determines Everything),' *Asia Plus*, August 6, 2015, http://asiaplus.tj/ru/news/korruptsiya-reshaet-vse.

41. Neli Esipova and Julie Ray, 'Former Soviet Countries See More Harm From Breakup' (Gallup, December 19, 2013), http://www.gallup.com/poll/166538/ former-soviet-countries-harm-breakup.aspx.

42. Maria Elisabeth Louw, *Everyday Islam in Post-Soviet Central Asia* (New York: Routledge, 2007), 15.
43. Alexei Yurchak, 'Soviet Hegemony of Form: Everything Was Forever, Until It Was No More,' *Comparative Studies in Society and History* 45, no. 3 (2003): 480–510.
44. Alexander Agadjanian, 'Exploring Religiosity as a Source of Morality Today,' in *Multiple Moralities and Religions in Post-Soviet Russia*, ed. Jarrett Zigon (New York: Berghahn Books, 2011), 17.
45. Sean E. Roberts, 'Everyday Negotiations of Islam in Central Asia,' in *Everyday Life in Central Asia Past and Present* (Bloomington: Indiana University Press, 2007), 352.
46. Maria Louw, 'Pursuing "Muslimness": Shrines as Sites for Moralities in the Making in Post-Soviet Bukhara,' *Central Asian Survey* 25/3 (2006), 336.
47. David M. Abramson and Elyor E. Karimov, 'Sacred Sites, Profane Ideologies: Religious Pilgrimage and He Uzbek State,' in *Everyday Life in Central Asia: Past and Present* ed. Russell G. Zanca and Jeff Sahadeo (Bloomington: Indiana University Press, 2007), p. 319.
48. Peyrouse, *Des Chrétiens Entre Athéisme et Islam*, 306.
49. Pulat Shozimov, Joomart Sulaimanov, and Shamshad Abdullaev, 'Culture in the Ferghana Valley Since 1991: The Issue of Identity,' in *Ferghana Valley: The Heart of Central Asia*, ed. Stephen Frederick Starr (New York: M.E. Sharpe, 2011), p. 283.
50. Emmanuel Karagiannis, *Political Islam in Central Asia: The Challenge of Hizb Ut-Tahrir* (New York: Routledge, 2010), 94.
51. Sergei Abashin, 'The Logic of Islamic Practice: A Religious Conflict in Central Asia,' *Central Asian Survey* 25, no. 3 (2006): 269.
52. Sonja Luehrmann, *Secularism Soviet Style: Teaching Atheism and Religion in a Volga Republic* (Bloomington: Indiana University Press, 2011), p. 17.
53. I have explored the topic in greater depth in Thibault, Hélène. 2017. 'Labour Migration, Sex, and Polygyny: Negotiating Patriarchy in Tajikistan', Ethnic and Racial Studies. Online first: http://www.tandfonline.com/doi/full/10.1080/0141 9870.2017.1400086.
54. Fergana News, 'Ofitsial'nye dannye FMS oprovergli slukhi o massovom vyezde trudovykh migrantov (Official Data From the Federal Migration Agency Deny Rumors About the Mass Departure of Labour Migrants),' *Fergana News*, January 23, 2015, http://www.fergananews.com/news/23008.
55. World Bank, 'Personal Remittances, Received (% of GDP),' *World Bank*, http://data.worldbank.org/indicator/BX.TRF.PWKR.DT.GD.ZS.
56. Unicef, 'Study of Prevalence and Dynamics of Suicide Among Children and Young People (12–24 Years of Age) in Sughd Region, Tajikistan.'
57. 'The DHS Program – Tajikistan: 2012,' Demographic and Health Surveys (USAID, 2013), http://dhsprogram.com/publications/publication-FR279-DHS-Final-Reports.cfm.

58. 'U ubiystva – zhenskoye litso. V Tadzhikistane snova mat' ubila svoyego rebenka (Murder with a Female Face. Another Mother Killed Her Baby in Tajikistan),' *Asia Plus*, November 12, 2015, http://www.news.tj/ru/news/u-ubiistva-zhenskoe-litso-v-tadzhikistane-snova-mat-ubila-svoego-rebenka.

59. Nulifar Karimova, 'Teenage Marriage Persists in Tajikistan,' *Institute for War and Peace Reporting*, May 14, 2014, https://iwpr.net/global-voices/teenage-marriage-persists-tajikistan.

60. Radio Ozodi, 'V Tadzhikistane podgotovlen zakonoproyekt, zapreshchayush-chiy rodstvennyye braki (A Bill Banning Consanguineous Marriages Drafted in Tajikistan),' *Radio Ozodi*, June 18, 2015, http://rus.ozodi.org/content/article/27079037.html.

61. Tilav Rasulzade, 'Tadzhikistan: Domovodstvo v shkolakh kak sredstvo ot razvodov (Tajikistan: Housekeeping at Schools Against Divorces),' *Fergana News*, June 25, 2014, http://www.fergananews.com/articles/8180.

62. Rahmonali Dodarkhujaev, 'Tajik Labour Migration Boosts Divorce Rates,' *Institute for War and Peace Reporting*, January 27, 2015, https://iwpr.net/global-voices/tajik-labour-migration-boosts-divorce-rates.

63. Colette Harris, 'Desire versus Horniness: Sexual Relations in the Collectivist Society of Tajikistan,' *Social Analysis: The International Journal of Social and Cultural Practice* 49, no. 2 (2005), 90–1.

64. Farangis Najibullah, 'Tajik Fatwa Bans SMS-Divorce,' *Radio Free Europe/Radio Liberty*, April 11, 2011, http://www.rferl.org/content/tajik_fatwa_bans_sms_divorces/3553754.html.

65. Radio Ozodi, 'Sovet ulemov: Shariat dopuskayet SMS-razvody (Council of Ulemas: Sharia Permits SMS-Divorces),' *Radio Ozodi*, January 22, 2014, http://rus.ozodi.org/content/sms-divorces-are-allowed/25238766.html.

66. Olga Shemyakina, 'The Marriage Market and Tajik Armed Conflict,' HiCN Working Paper (Households in Conflict Network, October 2009), 10, http://econpapers.repec.org/paper/hicwpaper/66.htm.

67. Zarina Khushvakt, 'Qarordodi izdivoç: Rohi muqoвala во candzanī? (Marriage Contracts: The Way to Deal With Polygyny?),' *BBC Tajik*, August 19, 2010, http://www.bbc.co.uk/tajik/news/2010/08/100819_zkh_marriage_contract.shtml.

68. Juliette Cleuziou, '"A Second Wife Is Not Really a Wife": Polygyny, Gender Relations and Economic Realities in Tajikistan,' *Central Asian Survey* 35, no. 1 (2016): 76–90.

69. Rahmon, 'Vystupleniye Po Sluchayu Dnya Materi (Discourse at the Occasion of Mother's Day).'

70. A Kulov, 'Gendernie Aspekty Demografii (Gender Aspects of Demography)' (Agentstvo po statistike pri Prezidente Respubliki Tadzhikistan, 2014), 2, http://stat.tj/img/ru/genderruss.pdf.

71. Greta Uehling, 'Dinner With Akhmet,' in *Everyday Life in Central Asia: Past and Present*, ed. Jeff Sahadeo and Russell Zanca (Bloomington: Indiana University Press, 2007), 128.

72. Mervat F. Hatem, 'Egyptian Discourses on Gender and Political Liberalization: Do Secularist and Islamist Views Really Differ?' *Middle East Journal* 48, no. 4 (1994), 676.

73. Peyrouse, *Des Chrétiens Entre Athéisme et Islam*, 301–3.

Conclusion

1. Yurchak, 'Soviet Hegemony of Form,' 2003.

2. Schatz, 'Ethnographic Immersion and the Study of Politics.'

3. Christophe Zürcher, 'Building Democracy While Building Peace,' *Journal of Democracy* 22, no. 1 (2011), 86.

4. Berman, Bhargava, and Laliberte, 'Introduction.' In *Secular States and Religious Diversity*, 1–25. (Vancouver: UBC Press, 2013).

5. Pelkmans, 'Introduction: Post-Soviet Space and the Unexpected Turns of Religious Life.'

6. Daniel Cefaï, '¿Qué es la etnografía? Segunda parte. Inscripciones, extensiones y recepciones del trabajo de campo,' *Persona y Sociedad* 27, no. 3 (2013): 11–32.

7. Mohamed Tozy, 'L'évolution du champ religieux marocain au défi de la mondialisation,' *Revue internationale de politique comparée* 16, no. 1 (2009): 63–81.

8. Roy, *L'Asie Centrale Contemporaine*.

9. Sophie Roche, 'The Role of Islam in the Lives of Central Asian Migrants in Moscow,' Central Asia Program CERIA Brief, October 2014, http://centralasiaprogram.org/blog/2014/10/05/the-role-of-islam-in-the-lives-of-central-asian-migrants-in-moscow-2/.

10. Roy, *L'Islam Mondialisé*.

11. Ibid.

12. Tucker, 'Islamic State Messaging to Central Asians Migrant Workers in Russia,' March 2015.

13. Rashid, *Taliban: Islam, Oil and the New Great Game in Central Asia*.

14. Uran Botobekov, 'Taliban: New Challenges for Central Asia,' *The Diplomat*, April 11, 2017, http://thediplomat.com/2017/04/taliban-new-challenges-for-central-asia/; Farangis Najibullah, 'Taliban Threat – Real Or Useful Fear Mongering?' *Radio Free Europe/Radio Liberty*, June 12, 2009, http://www.rferl.org/a/Threat_Of_Taliban_Incursion_Raised_In_Central_Asia__Again/1752944.html.

BIBLIOGRAPHY

Abashin, Sergei. 2004. 'Les Descendants de Saints En Asie Centrale: Élite Religieuse Ou Nationale?' *Cahiers d'Asie Centrale* no. 13/14: 215–29.

———. 2006. 'The Logic of Islamic Practice: A Religious Conflict in Central Asia.' *Central Asian Survey* 25 (3): 267–86.

Abashin, Sergei, Kamoludin Abdullaev, Ravshan Abdullaev, and Arslan Koichiev. 2011. 'Soviet Rule and the Delineation of Borders.' In *Ferghana Valley: The Heart of Central Asia*, edited by Stephen Frederick Starr, 94–118. Armonk: M.E. Sharpe.

Abdulgani, Abdulla. 1989. 'Musul'mane v uslovyax glastnosti, perestroika i novovo mishelnya (Muslims in the conditions of glasnost, perestroika and new thoughts).' In *Perestroika: Glastnost, Democratiya, Socialism. Na puti k svobode sovesti (Perestroika: Glastnost, Democracy, Socialism. On the road to freedom of conscience)*, edited by Dimitri Efimovich Furman, 402–47. Moscow: Progress.

Abdullaev, Kamoludin and Shahram Akbarzadeh. 2002. *Historical Dictionary of Tajikistan*. Lanham, MD: Scarecrow Press.

Abdullaev, Zafar. 2005. 'Tajikistan: Referendum Result Controversy.' *Institute for War and Peace Reporting*, February 21. https://iwpr.net/global-voices/tajikistan-referendum-result-controversy.

Abdusamedov, A. and A. Masaliev. 1984. 'Obzor zhurnala 'Musul'mane Sovetskovo Vostoka' (1979–1982)' (Survey of the Journal 'Muslims of the Soviet East' (1979–1982)). In *Obzor religioznix zhurnalov, izdavemix v SSSR (Survey of religious journals published in the USSR)*, 70–96. Moscow: Seksia ateisticheskovo vospitania pri Pravlenii Ordena Lenina Vsesoyuznovo obshestvo 'Znane.'

Abramson, David M. and Elyor E. Karimov. 2007. 'Sacred Sites, Profane Ideologies: Religious Pilgrimage and He Uzbek State.' In *Everyday Life in Central Asia: Past and Present*, edited by Russell G. Zanca and Jeff Sahadeo, 319–38. Bloomington, IN: Indiana University Press.

Adams, Laura L. 1999. 'The Mascot Researcher: Identity, Power, and Knowledge in Fieldwork.' *Journal of Contemporary Ethnography* 28 (4): 331–63.

———. 2008. 'Can We Apply Postcolonial Theory to Central Eurasia?' *Central Eurasian Studies Review* 7 (1): 2–7.

———. 2010. *The Spectacular State: Culture and National Identity in Uzbekistan*. Durham, NC: Duke University Press.

Agadjanian, Alexander. 2011. 'Exploring Religiosity as a Source of Morality Today.' In *Multiple Moralities and Religions in Post-Soviet Russia*, edited by Jarrett Zigon, 16–26. New York: Berghahn Books.

Aioubov, Salimjon. 2012. 'Surrendered Tajik Opposition Commander: "We Don't Want To Fight. We Want Peace".' *Radio Free Europe/Radio Liberty*, August 13. http://www.rferl.org/content/interview-surrendered-tajik-opposition-commander-says-wanted-issues-to-be-solved-lawfully/24675373.html.

Akbarzadeh, Shahram. 1996. 'Why Did Nationalism Fail in Tajikistan?' *Europe-Asia Studies* 48 (7): 1105–29.

———. 1997. 'Islamic Clerical Establishment in Central Asia.' *South Asia: Journal of South Asian Studies* 20 (2): 73–102.

Akiner, Shirin. 1995. 'Tadjikistan: Catalyseur Ou Anticorps Pour Les États Voisins d'Asie Centrale?' In *Le Tadjikistan à l'épreuve de l'indépendance*, edited by Mohammad-Reza Djalili, Frédéric Grare, and Shirin Akiner, 135–48. Paris: Institut universitaire des hautes études internationales.

———. 2001. *Tajikistan: Disintegration Or Reconciliation?* London: Royal Institute of International Affairs.

———. 2003. 'The Politicisation of Islam in Postsoviet Central Asia.' *Religion, State and Society* 31 (2): 97–122.

———. 2004. 'Nation-Building and the Islamic Revival in Post-Soviet Central Asia.' In *The OSCE and the Multiple Challenges of Transition: The Caucasus and Central Asia*, edited by Farian Sabahi and Daniel Warner, 71–89. Aldershot, UK: Ashgate.

Al Jazeera. 2010. *Breeding Discontent*. http://www.aljazeera.com/programmes/peopleandpower/2010/01/201012062540517354.html.

———. 2016. 'Tajikistan Shaves 13,000 Beards in "Radicalism" Battle.' *Al-Jazeera*, January 21. http://www.aljazeera.com/news/2016/01/tajikistan-shaves-13000-men-beards-radicalism-160120133352747.html.

Al Jazeera English. 2010. *People and Power – Breeding Discontent*. https://www.youtube.com/watch?v=zckWipmOxG8.

Aliev, Iskandar and Daisy Sindelar. 2004. 'Tajikistan: Top Islamic Body Bans Women From Attending Mosque Services.' *Radio Free Europe/Radio Liberty*, October 20. http://www.rferl.org/content/article/1055440.html.

Allina-Pisano, Jessica. 2009. 'How to Tell an Axe-Murderer: An Essay on Ethnography, Truth, and Lies.' In *Political Ethnography: What Immersion Contributes to the Study of Power*, edited by Edward Schatz, 53–73. Chicago: The University of Chicago Press.

Apter, David Ernest. 1965. *The Politics of Modernization*. Chicago: The University of Chicago Press.

Arel, Dominique. n.d. 'Introduction: Theorizing the Politics of Cultural Identities in Russia and Ukraine.' In *Rebounding Identities: The Politics of Identity in Russia and Ukraine*, edited by Dominique Arel and Blair A. Ruble, 1–30. Washington, DC: Woodrow Wilson Center Press.

Asad, Talal. 2003. *Formations of the Secular: Christianity, Islam, Modernity*. Stanford: Stanford University Press.

Asia Plus. 2007. 'V RT sozdan islamskii institut s izucheniem gumanitarnyx nauk (An Islamic Institute With The Study of Humanities Was Created in the Tajik Republic).' *Asia Plus*, November 16. http://www.news.tj/ru/news/v-rt-sozdan-islamskii-institut-s-izucheniem-gumanitarnykh-nauk.

————. 2008. 'V otnoshenii odnogo iz izvestnykh duhovnykh liderov Tadzhikistana mozhet byt' vozbuzhdeno ugolovnoe delo (A Criminal Case Might Be Opened In Connection to A Well-known Religious Leader in Tajikistan).' *Asia Plus*, November 28. http://www.news.tj/ru/news/v-otnoshenii-odnogo-iz-izvestnykh-dukhovnykh-liderov-tadzhikistana-mozhet-byt-vozbuzhdeno-ugolo.

————. 2010a. 'Gunmen Kill Six Prison Wardens, Free 25 Prisoners.' *Asia Plus*, August 23. http://news.tj/en/news/gunmen-kill-six-prison-wardens-free-25-prisoners.

————. 2010b. 'Otvetstvennost za vzryv v Khujande vzyala na sebya ranee neizvestnaya islamskaya gruppirvoka (Responsibility for the Khujand Bombing Claimed by a Previously Unknown Islamic Group).' *Asia Plus*, September 8. http://www2.asiaplus.tj/news/47/69110.html.

————. 2010c. 'Rakhmonov: Pust' Vashikh Detey Uchat Mully' (Rakhmonov: Go Ahead and Let Your Children Study With Mullahs').' *Asia Plus*, September 17. http://news.tj/en/node/1321.

————. 2010d. 'Prokuror Sogda: Informatsiya o sushchestvovanii ekstremistskoii gruppirovki "Dzhamaat Ansarullakh" ne sootvetstvuyet deystvitel'nosti (Sughd Attorney: Information on the Existence of an Extremist Group "Jamaat Ansarullah" Does Not Correspond to Reality).' *Asia Plus*, October 22. http://news.tj/ru/news/prokuror-sogda-informatsiya-o-sushchestvovanii-ekstremistskoi-gruppirovki-dzhamaat-ansarullakh-.

————. 2011. 'V OVD stolitsy breyut borody ... I fotografiruyut za den'gi (The Capital's Department of International Affairs Shave Beards ... And Take Photos For Money).' *Asia Plus*, January 12. http://news.tj/ru/newspaper/article/v-ovd-stolitsy-breyut-borody-i-fotografiruyut-za-dengi.

————. 2013. 'Bobonazarova schitayet, chto antireklama protiv PIVT ne pozvolila sobrat' nuzhnoye kolichestvo podpisey (Bobonazarova Believes that the Negative Publicity Against the IRPT Prevented to Collect the Required Number of Signatures).' *Asia Plus*, October 19. http://news.tj/ru/node/174087.

————. 2015a. 'Polnii tekst obrashcheniya Politsoveta PIVT k Prezidentu Respubliki Tadzhikistan (Full text of the IRPT's Political Council's Appeal to the President of the Republic).' *Asia Plus*, June 16. http://news.tj/ru/node/210078.

————. 2015b. 'Kabiri uveren, chto na rodine yemu ugrozhayet ugolovnoye presledovaniye (Kabiri Believes He Will Face Prosecution at Home).' *Asia Plus*, June 18. http://news.tj/ru/node/210186.

————. 2015c. 'PIVT obratilas' k stranam-garantam mezhtadzhikskogo soglasheniya (The IRPT Addressed the Guarantor-countries of the Inter-Tajik Agreement).' *Asia Plus*, July 1. http://news.tj/ru/node/210889.

————. 2015d. 'Genprokuratura: PIVT teryayet status politicheskoy partii (Prosecutor General: the IRPT Loses Its Status as a Political Party).' *Asia Plus*, July 8. http://news.tj/ru/node/211301.

————. 2015e. 'Trudovaya migratsia iz Tadzhikistana v Tsifrax (Labour Migration From Tajikistan in Figures).' *Asia Plus*, July 10. http://asiaplus.tj/ru/news/trudovaya-migratsiya-iz-tadzhikistana-v-tsifrakh.

————. 2015f. 'Press-konferentsiya PIVT v otele "Sheraton" segodnya byla sorvana (IRPT's Press-Conference in Sheraton Hotel Prevented today).' *Asia Plus*, August 27. http://news.tj/ru/news/press-konferentsiya-pivt-v-otele-sheraton-segodnya-byla-sorvana.

———. 2015g. 'Pravitel'stvennoye SMI obvinyayet lidera PIVT v popytke gosperevorota (Government Media Accused IRPT's Leader in Coup Attempt).' *Asia Plus*, September 10. http://news.tj/ru/node/214494.

———. 2015h. 'V Tadzhikistane likvidirovan myatezhnyy general Nazarzoda (Mutiny General Nazarzoda Eliminated in Tajikistan).' *Asia Plus*, September 16. http://news.tj/ru/news/v-tadzhikistane-likvidirovan-myatezhnyi-general-nazarzoda.

———. 2015i. 'V Tdzhikistane zaderzhivaiut aktivnix chlenov PIVT (Active IRPT Members Detained in Tajikistan).' *Radio Ozodi*, September 17. http://rus.ozodi.org/content/article/27252994.html.

———. 2015j. 'Vlasti: PIVT namerevalas' atakovat' nekotoryye gosuchrezhdeniya (Authorities: The IRPT Planned to Attack Few State Institutions).' *Asia Plus*, September 22. http://asiaplus.tj/ru/node/215124.

———. 2015k. 'Opros TSI: svyshe 50% oproshennykh dushanbintsev nazvali PIVT terroristicheskoy (CSS Survey: More than 50% Respondents Called the IRPT "Terrorist").' *Asia Plus*, October 2. http://www.news.tj/ru/news/opros-tssi-svyshe-50-oproshennykh-dushanbintsev-nazvali-pivt-terroristicheskoi.

———. 2015l. 'Tadzhikskim chinovnikam zapretili poseshchat' pyatnichnyye molitvy (Tajik Officials Banned from Attending Friday Prayers).' *Asia Plus*, October 12. http://www.news.tj/ru/node/216190.

———. 2015m. 'Syn Mukhiddina Kabiri obvinyayetsya v posobnichestve myatezhnikam (Son of Muhiddin Kabiri Accused of Aiding Rebels).' *Asia Plus*, October 26. http://news.tj/ru/news/syn-mukhiddina-kabiri-obvinyaetsya-v-posobnichestve-myatezhnikam.

———. 2015n. 'Zaderzhan Vtoroy Advokat Aktivistov PIVT (A Second Lawyer and Activist of the IRPT Was Detained).' *Asia Plus*, October 26. http://news.tj/ru/news/zaderzhan-vtoroi-advokat-aktivistov-pivt.

———. 2015o. 'U ubiystva – zhenskoye litso. V Tadzhikistane snova mat' ubila svoyego rebenka (Murder with a Female Face. Another Mother Killed Her Baby in Tajikistan).' *Asia Plus*, November 12. http://www.news.tj/ru/news/u-ubiistva-zhenskoe-litso-v-tadzhikistane-snova-mat-ubila-svoego-rebenka.

———. 2015p. 'Lider Natsii: U Rulya Do Kontsa (Leader of the Nation: At the Wheel Until the End).' *Asia Plus*, December 15. http://news.tj/ru/news/lider-natsii-u-rulya-do-kontsa.

———. 2017, "Head of Khujand-based KVN team faces charges of inciting national enmity and false denunciation", *Asia Plus*, December 8, https://news.tj/en/node/248428.

Asimova, Bashorat Saifitdinovna and Magomet Izmailovich Isaev. 1982. *Iazykovoe stroitelstvo v Tadzhikistane, 1920–1940 (Language Building in Tajikistan)*. Dushanbe: Izdotelstvo Donish.

Assadi, Roja. 2014. 'Tajik Government Pays Salaries to Imams for First Time.' *BBC News*, March 17. http://www.bbc.com/news/world-asia-26579613.

Babajanov, Bakhtiar. 2000a. 'Islam Officiel Contre Islam Politique En Ouzbékistan Aujourd'hui: La Direction Des Musulmans et Les Groupes Non-Hanafî.' *Revue d'études Comparatives Est-Ouest* 31 (3): 151–64.

———. 2000b. 'Sredneazitaskoe Duxovnoe Upravlene Musulman (Spiritual Muslim Board of Central Asia: Origin and Consequences of the Collapse).' In *Mnogomerne Granitsy Tsentralnoii Azii (The Multidimensional Frontiers of Central Asia)*, edited by Martha Brill Olcott and Alexei Malashenko, 80–90. Moscow: Gendalf.

————. 2002. 'Islam in Uzbekistan: From the Struggle for Religious Purity to Political Activism.' In *Central Asia: A Gathering Storm?*, edited by Boris Z. Rumer, 299–330. New York: M.E. Sharpe.

Baker, Theresa. 1988. *Doing Social Research*. New York: McGraw Hill.

Balci, Bayram. 2012. 'The Rise of the Jama'at Al Tabligh in Kyrgyzstan: The Revival of Islamic Ties Between the Indian Subcontinent and Central Asia.' *Central Asian Survey* 31 (1): 61–76.

Bayard de Volo, Lorraine. 2009. 'Participant Observation, Politics, and Power Relations: Nicaraguan Mothers and US Casino Waitresses.' In *Political Ethnography: What Immersion Contributes to the Study of Power*, edited by Edward Schatz, 217–36. Chicago: The University of Chicago Press.

Bayard de Volo, Lorraine and Edward Schatz. 2004. 'From the Inside Out: Ethnographic Methods in Political Research.' *PS: Political Science & Politics* (02): 267–71.

BBC Monitoring Service. 2007a. *Tajik Leader Voices Concern About 'Secret' Islamic Schools*. First Channel.

————. 2007b. 'Tajik Leader Voices Concern about "Secret" Islamic Schools Source: Tajik Television First Channel, Dushanbe.' *BBC Monitoring Service*, April 30.

————. 2009a. 'Tajik MPs Approve Freedom of Faith Bill.' *Asia Plus*, March 5.

————. 2009b. 'Renowned Tajik Cleric Urges Party to Back Outlawed Islamic Organization.' *Tojikiston*, December 24.

BBC News. 2015a. 'Tajik Opposition Leader Kuvatov Shot Dead in Turkey.' *BBC News*, March 6. http://www.bbc.com/news/world-middle-east-31760810.

————. 2015b. 'Tajikistan Special Forces Chief Gulmurod Khalimov "Joins IS".' *BBC News*, May 28. http://www.bbc.com/news/world-asia-32917311.

Beissinger, Mark R. 2006. 'Soviet Empire as "Family Resemblance".' *Slavic Review* 65 (2): 294–303.

Beissinger, Mark and M. Crawford Young. 2002. *Beyond State Crisis?: Post-Colonial Africa and Post-Soviet Eurasia in Comparative Perspective*. Washington, DC: Woodrow Wilson Center Press.

Bennigsen, Alexandre and Chantal Lemercier-Quelquejay. 1968. *L'Islam en Union soviétique*. Paris: Payot.

Berger, Peter L. 1967. *The Sacred Canopy: Elements of a Sociological Theory of Religion*. Garden City, NY: Doubleday.

————. 1999. *The Desecularization of the World: Resurgent Religion and World Politics*. Grand Rapids, MI: Eerdmans Publishing.

Berman, Bruce J., Rajeev Bhargava, and Andre Laliberte. 2013. 'Introduction.' In *Secular States and Religious Diversity*, 1–25. Vancouver: University of British Columbia Press.

Blua, Antoine. 2002. 'Tajikistan: Government To Vet Islamic Clerics.' *Radio Free Europe/Radio Liberty*, August 7. http://www.rferl.org/content/article/1100477.html.

Bolak, Hale C. 1996. 'Studying One's Own in the Middle East: Negotiating Gender and Self-Other Dynamics in the Field.' *Qualitative Sociology* 19 (1): 107–30. doi:10.1007/BF02393250.

Botobekov, Uran. 2017. 'Taliban: New Challenges for Central Asia.' *The Diplomat*, April 11. http://thediplomat.com/2017/04/taliban-new-challenges-for-central-asia/.

Boymatov, Alijon. 2004. 'Economic Relations between Centre and Regions: The Case of Sughd Province.' In *Tajikistan at a Crossroad: The Politics of Decentralization*, edited by Luigi De Martino, Cimera, 47–85.

238 TRANSFORMING TAJIKISTAN

Brill Olcott, Martha. 2005. *Vtoroi shans Tsentralnoii Azii (Central Asia's Second Chance)*. Moscow: Carnegie Endowment for International Peace. http://carnegie.ru/publications/?fa=35896.

Bromwich, Carl and Maeve Shearlaw. 2015. 'My Summer in a Soviet Pioneer Camp.' *Guardian*. April 2. http://www.theguardian.com/world/2014/jul/03/soviet-pioneer-camp-communism-scouts-belarus.

Brown, Bess. 1997. 'The Civil War in Tajikistan, 1992–1993.' In *Tajikistan: The Trials of Independence*, edited by Mohammad-Reza Djalili, Frédéric Grare, and Shirin Akiner, 86–96. New York: St. Martin's Press.

Bryanov, Valerii Arkadevich. 1986. *Ateisticheskoe vospitane studentov (The Atheistic Education of Students)*. Moscow: Izdatelstvo Vyshaya Shkola.

Buckley, Mary. 1986. *Soviet Social Scientists Talking: An Official Debate about Women*. London: The Macmillan Press.

Bunce, Valerie. 1995. 'Should Transitologists Be Grounded?' *Slavic Review* 55: 111–27.

Bushkov, V. I. and D. V. Mikul'skii. 1996. *Anatomiya grazhdanskoii voiny v Tadzhikistane (Anatomy of the Civil War in Tajikistan)*. Moscow: Institute for Ethnology and Anthropology (Institut Etnologii i Antropologii RAN). http://www.ca-c.org/datarus/st_08_bush.shtml.

Buttino, Marco. 1997. 'Ethnicité et Politique Dans La Guerre Civile: À Propos Du Basmacestvo Au Fergana.' *Cahiers Du Monde Russe* 38 (1–2): 195–222.

Cadiot, Juliette. 2007. *Le laboratoire impérial: Russie-URSS 1860–1940*. Paris: CNRS.

Camm, George. 2012. 'Tajikistan Ramps Up Terror Convictions, Life Sentences.' *EurasiaNet*, January 11. http://www.eurasianet.org/node/64818.

Caramani, Daniele. 2008. 'Introduction to Comparative Politics.' In *Comparative Politics*, edited by Daniele Caramani, 1–19. New York: Oxford University Press.

Casanova, José. 1994. *Public Religions in the Modern World*. Chicago: University of Chicago Press.

———. 2006. 'Rethinking Secularization: A Global Comparative Perspective.' *Hedgehog Review* 8 (1–2): 7–22.

Cefaï, Daniel. 2010. 'Postface.' In *L'engagement Ethnographique*, 547–98. Paris: École des hautes études en sciences sociales.

———. 2013. '¿Qué es la etnografía? Segunda parte. Inscripciones, extensiones y recepciones del trabajo de campo.' *Persona y Sociedad* 27 (3): 11–32.

Center for History and New Media. n.d. 'Guide Rapide Pour Débuter.' http://zotero.org/support/quick_start_guide.

Chorshanbiev, Pairav. 2010. 'Road Tolls Lowered for Residents of Varzob District.' *Asia Plus*, April 30. http://news.tj/en/news/road-tolls-lowered-residents-varzob-district.

———. 2012. 'B. Zukhurov: Odna pulya popala v provoda, poetomu s Khorogom net svyaz (B. Zuhurov: One bullet hit the wires, that is why there is no contact with Khorog).' *Asia Plus*, July 26. http://www.news.tj/ru/news/b-zukhurov-odna-pulya-popala-v-provoda-poetomu-s-khorogom-net-svyazi.

CIA. Central Intelligence Agency. n.d. 'CIA. The World Factbook.' https://www.cia.gov/library/publications/the-world-factbook/.

Cleuziou, Juliette. 2016. '"A Second Wife Is Not Really a Wife": Polygyny, Gender Relations and Economic Realities in Tajikistan.' *Central Asian Survey* 35 (1): 76–90. doi:10.1080/02634937.2015.1088228.

Cleuziou, Juliette and Lucia Direnberger. 2016. 'Gender and Nation in Post-Soviet Central Asia: From National Narratives to Women's Practices.' *Nationalities Papers* 44 (2): 195–206. doi:10.1080/00905992.2015.1082997.

Codevilla, Giovanni. 1971. *The Attitude of the Soviet State Towards Religion*. Milan: Russia Cristiana.

Collins, Kathleen. 2006. *Clan Politics and Regime Transition in Central Asia*. New York: Cambridge University Press.

Commercio, Michele E. 2013. 'Retraditionalization in Post-Soviet Kyrgyzstan and Tajikistan: Rejected by Elites, Embraced by Young Women.' In. New York.

———. 2015. 'The Politics and Economics of "Retraditionalization" in Kyrgyzstan and Tajikistan.' *Post-Soviet Affairs* 31 (6): 529–56. doi:10.1080/1060586X. 2014.986870.

Constantine, Elizabeth Ann. 2001. 'Public Discourse and Private Lives: Uzbek Women under Soviet Rule, 1917–1991.' University of Indiana.

Cooley, Alexander. 2012. *Great Games, Local Rules: The New Power Contest in Central Asia*. Oxford University Press.

Corley, Felix. 1996. 'Obituary: The Chief Mufti of Tajikistan.' *Independent*, January 23. http://www.independent.co.uk/news/people/obituary-the-chief-mufti-of-tajikistan-1325372.html.

———. 2009. 'President Signs Repressive Religion Law.' *Forum 18*. March 29. http://www.forum18.org/archive.php?article_id=1274.

Dahl, Robert Alan. 1973. *Regimes and Oppositions*. New Haven, CT: Yale University Press.

Danieli, Filippo De. 2011. 'Counter-Narcotics Policies in Tajikistan and Their Impact on State Building.' *Central Asian Survey* 30 (1): 129–45. doi:10.1080/ 02634937.2011.554067.

Davie, Grace. 2013. 'Discerning and Explaining Pattern.' Presented at the Research Meeting of The Religion and Diversity Project, Université de Montréal, March 14.

Davlat, Nurali. 2015. 'Korruptsiya reshaet vse (Corruption determines everything).' *Asia Plus*, August 6. http://news.tj/ru/news/korruptsiya-reshaet-vse.

De Martino, Luigi. 2004. 'Contradictory Forces at the Heart of the Tajik Political System.' In *Tajikistan at a Crossroad: The Politics of Decentralization*, edited by Luigi De Martino, Cimera, 152–9.

DeVault, Marjorie. 2004. 'Theory by Way of Ethnography.' *Perspectives: Newsletter of the ASA Theory Section* 27 (1).

Deweese, Devin. 2002. 'Islam and the Legacy of Sovietology: A Review Essay on Yaacov Ro'i's Islam in the Soviet Union.' *Journal of Islamic Studies* 13 (3): 298–330.

Dixon, Richard D., Diane E. Levy, and Roger C. Lowery. 1988. 'Asking the "Born-Again" Question.' *Review of Religious Research* 30 (1): 33–9.

Dodarkhujaev, Rahmonali. 2015. 'Tajik Labour Migration Boosts Divorce Rates.' *Institute for War and Peace Reporting*, January 27. https://iwpr.net/global-voices/tajik-labour-migration-boosts-divorce-rates.

Dolina Mira. 2010. 'Analiz konfliktogennyx faktorov v religioznoii sfere Ferganskoii Doliny (Analysis of Factors of contention in Fergana Valley's Religious Sphere).' Dolina Mira. http://www.dolinamira.org/issledovaniya.html.

Driscoll, Jesse. 2012. 'Commitment Problems or Bidding Wars? Rebel Fragmentation as Peace Building.' *The Journal of Conflict Resolution* 56 (1): 118–49.

Dubovitskii, Viktor and Khaydarbek Bababekov. 2011. 'The Rise and Fall of the Kokand Khanate.' In *Ferghana Valley: The Heart of Central Asia*, edited by Stephen Frederick Starr, 29–68. Armonk: M.E. Sharpe.

Dudoignon, Stephane A. 1994. 'Une segmentation peut en cacher une autre : régionalismes et clivages politico-économiques au Tadjikistan.' *Cahiers d'Etudes sur la Méditerranée Orientale et le monde Turco-Iranien*, no. 18: 73–129.

———. 1996. 'Djadidisme, Mirasisme, Islamisme.' *Cahiers Du Monde Russe* 37 (1): 13–40.

———. 1998. *Communal Solidarity and Social Conflicts in Late 20th Century Central Asia: The Case of the Tajik Civil War.* Tokyo: Islamic Area Studies Project.

———. 2004. 'From Ambivalence to Ambiguity? Some Paradigms of Policy Making in Tajikistan.' In *Tajikistan at a Crossroad: The Politics of Decentralization*, edited by Luigi De Martino, Cimera, 120–51.

———. 2011. 'From Revival to Mutation: The Religious Personnel of Islam in Tajikistan, from de-Stalinization to Independence (1955–91).' *Central Asian Survey* 30 (1): 53–80.

Dudoignon, Stephane A. and Christian Noack, eds. 2014. *Allah's Kolkhozes: Migration, De-Stalinisation, Privatisation and the Emergence of New Muslim Religious Communities in the USSR, and After (1950s–2000s).* Klaus Schwarz Verlag. Berlin.

Dudoignon, Stephane A. and Sayyid Ahmad Qalandar. 2014. '"They Were All from the Country." The Revival and Politicisation of Islam in the Lower Wakhsh River Valley of the Tajik SSE (1947–1997).' In *Allah's Kolkhozes: Migration, De-Stalinisation, Privatisation and the Emergence of New Muslim Religious Communities in the USSR, and After (1950s–2000s)*, 47–122. Berlin: Klaus Schwarz Verlag.

Dunstan, John. 1993. 'Soviet Schools, Atheism and Religion.' In *Religious Policy in the Soviet Union*, edited by Sabrina Petra Ramet, 158–86. Cambridge: Cambridge University Press.

Dushanbeeva, Manija and Khurshed Khalilbekov. 2015. 'Zhizn' bez muzhchin. Zhony emigrantov o Rossii, migratsii i zhizni bez muzhey (Life Without Men. Wives of Emigrants About Russia, Migration and Life Without a Husband).' *Rossiya dlya vsex*, November 11. http://tjk.rus4all.ru/exclusive/20151111/726296417.html.

Dushanbieva, Sayyokhat. 2014. 'The Impacts of Migration: The Tajik Women's. Experiences of Their Husband's Migration.' Budapest: Central European University.

Epkenhans, Tim. 2010. 'Muslims Without Learning, Clergy Without Faith: Institutions of Islamic Learning in the Republic of Tajikistan.' In *Islamic Education in the Soviet Union and Its Successor States*, edited by Michael Kemper, Raoul Motika, and Stefan Reichmuth, 313–48. New York: Routledge.

———. 2011. 'Defining Normative Islam: Some Remarks on Contemporary Islamic Thought in Tajikistan – Hoji Akbar Turajonzoda's Sharia and Society.' *Central Asian Survey* 30 (1): 81–96.

———. 2015. 'The Islamic Revival Party of Tajikistan: Episodes of Islamic Activism, Postconflict Accommodation, and Political Marginalization.' *Central Asian Affairs* 2 (4): 321–46.

Esipova, Neli and Julie Ray. 2013. 'Former Soviet Countries See More Harm From Breakup.' Gallup. http://www.gallup.com/poll/166538/former-soviet-countries-harm-breakup.aspx.

'Eurasian Development Bank: Eurasian Integration Yearbook 2013.' 2015. September 11. http://www.eabr.org/e/research/publications/IntegrationYearbook/IntegrationYearbook2013/index.php?id_4=387.

EurasiaNet. 2016a. 'Tajikistan: Prayer Rooms Targeted for Demolition.' *EurasiaNet*, February 25. http://www.eurasianet.org/node/77536.

———. 2016b. 'Tajikistan: Weary Population Resigned to a President-for-Life.' *EurasiaNet*, May 23. http://www.eurasianet.org/node/78871.

Fasxhutdinov, Galim. 2015. 'Posledstviya migratsii: broshennyye zheny i razrushennyye sem'i (Consequences of Migration: Abandoned Wives and Broken Families).' *Deutsche Welle*, March 6.

Fayzullayev, Bahrom. 2015. 'Na Severe Tadzhikistana Nosheniye Khidzhaba Vzyali Pod Kontrol (Hijab Under Control in Northern Tajikistan).' *Asia Plus*, March 27. http://news.tj/ru/news/na-severe-tadzhikistana-noshenie-khidzhaba-vzyali-pod-kontrol.

———. 2015. 'Chkalovsk Renamed Shohkant.' *Asia Plus*, June 26. http://news.tj/en/news/chkalovsk-renamed-shohkant.

Fergana News. 2007. 'Takhir Yuldash: "Krakh SSHA Blizok, Zhdite Nas v Vashingtone" (Tahir Yuldash: "The Collapse of the US Is near, Wait for Us in Washington").' *Fergana News*, October 15. http://www.fergananews.com/articles/5403.

———. 2009. 'Prezident Tadzhikistana povelel: Kazhdaya sem'ya dolzhna kupit' aktsii Rogunskoy GES (The President of Tajikistan ordered: Each Family Must Buy Shares of the Rogun Hydroelectric Power Station).' *Fergana News*, December 2. http://www.fergananews.com/news.php?id=13563&mode=snews.

———. 2010. 'Tadzhikistan: Sovet ulemov prizyvayet zhenshchin nosit' tol'ko natsional'nuyu odezhdu (Tajikistan: The Council of Ulemas Calls on Women to Only Wear National Clothes).' *Fergana News*, September 30. http://www.fergananews.com/news.php?id=15647.

———. 2013. 'Amnesty International prizyvayet tadzhikskiye vlasti razreshit' deyatel'nost' NPO "Amparo" (Amnesty International Calls on the Tajik authorities to Allow the Activities of the NGO "Amparo").' *Fergana News*, January 21. http://www.fergananews.com/news.php?id=20095.

———. 2014. 'PIVT: "Zakrytve dveri ili snesennye zdaniya ne oslablyayet nash dukh" (IRPT: "The Closure of Doors or Destruction of Buildings Does Not Weaken Our Spirit").' *Fergana News*, June 23. http://www.fergananews.com/articles/8176.

———. 2015. 'Ofitsial'nye dannye FMS oprovergli slukhi o massovom vyezde trudovykh migrantov (Official Data From the Federal Migration Agency Deny Rumors About the Mass Departure of Labour Migrants).' *Fergana News*, January 23. http://www.fergananews.com/news/23008.

FIDH/Memorial. 2014. 'From Tajikistan to Russia: Vulnerability and Abuse of Migrant Workers and Their Families.' Federation Internationale des Ligues des Droits de l'Homme/Memorial. https://www.fidh.org/en/region/europe-central-asia/tajikistan/16619-whether-or-not-you-want-to-you-have-to-go.

Fierman, William. 1991. *Soviet Central Asia: The Failed Transformation*. Boulder, CO: Westview Press.

Forum 18. 2014. 'Kazakhstan: Religious Freedom Survey.' *Forum 18*. March 20. http://www.forum18.org/archive.php?article_id=1939.

Fourniau, Vincent. 1994. *Histoire de l'Asie Centrale*. Paris: PUF.

Fox, Jonathan. 2006. 'World Separation of Religion and State Into the 21st Century.' *Comparative Political Studies* 39 (5): 537–69.

―――. 2011. 'Separation of Religion and State and Secularism in Theory and in Practice.' *Religion, State and Society* 39 (4): 384–401.

Freedom House. 2015. 'Nations in Transit: Tajikistan.' Washington, DC: Freedom House. https://freedomhouse.org/report/nations-transit/2015/tajikistan.

Froese, Paul. 2004. 'After Atheism: An Analysis of Religious Monopolies in the Post-Communist World.' *Sociology of Religion* 65 (1): 57–75.

―――. 2008. *The Plot to Kill God: Findings from the Soviet Experiment in Secularization.* Berkeley: University of California Press.

Furman, Dimitri Efimovich. 1989. 'Religiya, Ateizm i Perestroika.' In *Perestroika: Glastnost, Democratiya, Socialism. Na puti k svobode sovesti (Perestroika: Glastnost, Democracy, Socialism. On the road to freedom of conscience)*, edited by Dimitri Efimovich Furman, 7–18. Moscow: Progress.

Gafurov, Bobodzhan Gafurovich. 2005. *Central Asia: Pre-Historic to Pre-Modern Times.* New Delhi: Shipra Publications.

Gaidurova, T.G. 1969. 'Zavisimost' obydennovo religioznovo soznaniya veruiushhix ot uslovii ix zhizni (Believers' Ordinary Religious Consciousness Depends on Their Living Conditions).' In *Konkretno-sotsiologicheskoe uizuchenie sostoyaniya religioznosti i opyta ateisticheskoe vospitaniya (Empirical Sociological Study of the State of Religion and the Experience of Atheistic Education)*, edited by Ilya Dominovich Pantsxava, 12–31. Moscow: Moscow University.

Gandhi, Jennifer and Adam Przeworski. 2006. 'Cooperation, Cooptation, and Rebellion Under Dictatorships.' *Economics & Politics* 18 (1): 1–26. doi:10.1111/j.1468-0343.2006.00160.x.

Gellner, Ernest. 1991. 'Islam and Marxism: Some Comparisons.' *International Affairs (Royal Institute of International Affairs 1944–)* 67 (1): 1–6.

―――. 2008. *Nations and Nationalism.* Ithaca, NY: Cornell University Press.

Gill, Anthony. 2001. 'Religion and Comparative Politics.' *Annual Review of Political Science* 4 (1): 117–38.

Glaeser, Andreas. 2004. 'Theory by Way of Ethnography.' *Perspectives: Newsletter of the ASA Theory Section* 27 (1).

Gledhill, John. 1994. *Power & Its Disguises: Anthropological Perspectives on Politics.* London: Pluto Press.

Glenn, J. 1999. *The Soviet Legacy in Central Asia.* New York: St. Martin's Press.

Grahame, Peter R. 1998. 'Ethnography, Institutions, and the Problematic of the Everyday World.' *Human Studies* 21 (4): 347–60.

Gufronov, Daler. 2011. 'A. Rahnamo: "Nevozmozhno Razdelit Islamskii Faktor i Naselenie" (A. Rahnamo: "It Is Impossible to Separate the Islamic Factor and Society").' *Asia Plus*, June 13. https://www.news.tj/ru/node/104952.

Haghayeghi, Mehrdad. 1995. *Islam and Politics in Central Asia.* New York: St. Martin's Press.

Haldane, John Burdon Sanderson, and Frederick Engels. 1949. 'Preface.' In *Dialectics of Nature*, edited by Clemens Dutt. New York: International Publishing. http://trove.nla.gov.au/work/12853174.

Hall, Peter A. and Rosemary C. R. Taylor. 1996. 'Political Science and the Three New Institutionalisms*.' *Political Studies* 44 (5): 936–57.

Hamidova, Parvina. 2011. 'Marxabo Dzhabborov: "Tol'ko zakon mozhet vsex razbudit" (Marxabo Dzhabborova: "Only the Law Can Wake Us All Up").' *Asia Plus*, June 30. http://news.tj/ru/newspaper/article/markhabo-dzhabborova-tolko-zakon-mozhet-vsekh-razbudit.

Hamrabaeva, Nargis. 2010. 'MVD podozrevaet vo vzryve v Khujande IDY (Interior Ministry Suspects IMU in Khujand Bombing).' *Asia Plus*, September 3. http://news.tj/ru/news/mvd-podozrevaet-vo-vzryve-v-khudzhande-idu.

Harris, Colette. 2005. 'Desire Versus Horniness: Sexual Relations in the Collectivist Society of Tajikistan.' *Social Analysis: The International Journal of Social and Cultural Practice* 49 (2): 78–95.

———. 2011. 'State Business: Gender, Sex and Marriage in Tajikistan.' *Central Asian Survey* 30 (1): 97–111. doi:10.1080/02634937.2011.554057.

Hasanova, Mavdzhuda. 2010. 'Izbran novyii predsedatel' Soveta ulemov Islamskovo Tsentra (A new Chairman for the Council of Ulemas of the Islamic Center of Tajikistan Was Chosen).' *Centrasia*, October 13. http://www.centrasia.ru/newsA.php?st=1286948700.

Hatem, Mervat F. 1994. 'Egyptian Discourses on Gender and Political Liberalization: Do Secularist and Islamist Views Really Differ?' *Middle East Journal* 48 (4): 661–76.

Heathershaw, John. 2008. 'Seeing like the International Community: How Peacebuilding Failed (and Survived) in Tajikistan.' *Journal of Intervention and Statebuilding* 2 (3): 329–51. doi:10.1080/17502970802436346.

Heathershaw, John and Nick Megoran. 2011. 'Contesting Danger: A New Agenda for Policy and Scholarship on Central Asia.' *International Affairs* 87 (3): 589–612.

Heathershaw, John and David W. Montgomery. 2015. 'The Myth of Post-Soviet Muslim Radicalization in the Central Asian Republics.' Chatham House. https://www.chathamhouse.org//node/16207.

Heathershaw, John and Sophie Roche. 2011. 'Islam and Political Violence in Tajikistan: An Ethnographic Perspective on the Causes and Consequences of the 2010 Armed Conflict in the Kamarob Gorge.' *Ethnopolitics Papers* no. 8. https://www.psa.ac.uk/psa-communities/specialist-groups/ethnopolitics/news/ethno politics-paper-8-islam-and-political.

Hiro, Dilip. 1994. *Between Marx and Muhammad: The Changing Face of Central Asia*. London: HarperCollins.

Holmes, Larry E. 1993. 'Schools and Religion in Soviet Russia, 1917–1941.' In *Religious Policy in the Soviet Union*, edited by Sabrina Petra Ramet, 125–57. Cambridge: Cambridge University Press.

Human Rights Watch. 2014. 'Illusion of Justice: Human Rights Abuses in US Terrorism Prosecutions.' Human Rights Watch. https://www.hrw.org/report/2014/07/21/illusion-justice/human-rights-abuses-us-terrorism-prosecutions.

Husband, William. 2000. *'Godless Communists': Atheism and Society in Soviet Russia, 1917–1932*. De Kalb, IL: Northern Illinois University Press.

International Center for Non-Profit Law. 2015. 'NGO Law Monitor: Tajikistan.' *ICNL The International Center for Non-Profit Law*. September 28. http://www.icnl.org/research/monitor/tajikistan.html.

International Crisis Group. 2003. 'Central Asia: Islam and the State.' 59. Asia Report. International Crisis Group. http://www.crisisgroup.org/en/regions/asia/central-asia/059-central-asia-islam-and-the-state.aspx.

———. 2009. 'Tajikistan: On the Road to Failure.' 162. Asia Report. Brussels: International Crisis Group. http://www.crisisgroup.org/en/regions/asia/central-asia/tajikistan/162-tajikistan-on-the-road-to-failure.aspx.

International Foundation for Electoral Systems (IFES). 2010. 'Public Opinion in Tajikistan 2010: Findings from an IFES Survey.' Washington, DC: International Foundation for Electoral Systems (IFES). http://www.ifes.org/surveys/public-opinion-tajikistan-2010-findings-ifes-survey.

Isazade, Fardin. 2013. 'Shafig Pshikhachev: "Nasha tsel" – konsolidatsiya musul'man na postsovetskom prostranstve (Shafig Pshihachev: "Our Goal – The Consolidation of Muslims in the Post-Soviet Space").' *Islam.az*, April 29. http://islam.az/news/a-13529.html.

Islam News. 2011a. 'V Mecheti "Muhammadya" Novyii imam-khatib (New Imam-Khatib in the Muhammadya Mosque).' *Islam News*, December 14. http://islam news.tj/tajikistan/251-v-mecheti-muhammadiya-novyy-imam-hatib.html.

———. 2011b. 'Hoji Akbar Turajonzoda: Tsel'iu byl ne ya, a moii starshii brat Huriddin (Hoji Akbar Turajonzoda: The Objective Was Not Me, But My Older Brother Nuriddin).' *Islam News*, December 19. http://islamnews.tj/tajikistan/257-hodzhi-akbar-turadzhonzoda-celyu-byl-ne-ya-a-moy-starshiy-brat-nuriddin.html.

———. 2011c. 'V Tadzhikistane v mechetyakh menyaiut imam-khatibov po prichine ne prokhozheniya attestatsii (Imam-Khatibs Replaced After Failing Certification in Tajikistan).' *Islam News*, December 27. http://islamnews.tj/tajikistan/267-v-tadzhikistane-v-mechetyah-menyayut-imam-hatibov-po-prichine-ne-prohozhdeniya-attestacii.html.

———. 2012a. 'M. Kabiri: V Tadzhikistane neobxodimo nachat' novuiyu fazu peregovorov (M. Kabiri: We Need to Start a New Phase of Negotiations in Tajikistan).' *Islam News*, February 21. http://islamnews.tj/tajikistan/323-m-kabiri-v-tadzhikistane-neobhodimo-nachat-novuyu-fazu-peregovorov.html.

———. 2012b. 'Na severe Tadzhikistana vyyavili deteii, kotorye vo vremya ucheby poseshali mecheti (Children at Mosque During School Time Discovered in Northern Tajikistan).' *Islam News*, March 27. http://islamnews.tj/tajikistan/352-na-severe-tadzhikistana-vyyavili-detey-kotorye-vovremya-ucheby-poseschali-mecheti.html.

———. 2012c. 'Mechet' Turadzhonzoda ofitsial'no lishena statusa pyatnichnoy mecheti (Turajonzoda's Mosque Officially Stripped of Its Friday Mosque Status).' *Islam News*, May 3. http://islamnews.tj/tajikistan/394-mechet-turadzhonzoda-oficialno-lishena-statusa-pyatnichnoy-mecheti.html.

———. 2012d. 'V Tadzhikistane v mesyats' Ramazan 88% naseleniya sobliudaiut post (In Tajikistan, 88% of the Population Fast During Ramadan).' *Islam News*, August 13. http://islamnews.tj/tajikistan/471-v-tadzhikistane-v-mesyac-ram azan-88-naseleniya-soblyudayut-post.html.

———. 2012e. 'V Tadzhikistane zaregistrirovan tsentr po podgotovke imam-khatibov (Training Center for Imam-khatibs Registered in Tajikistan).' *Islam News*, August 29. http://islamnews.tj/tajikistan/484-v-tadzhikistane-zaregistri rovan-centr-po-podgotovke-imam-hatibov.html.

———. 2013a. 'Studenty islamskogo vuza nachali obuchatsyapo novomu posobiyupo russkomu yazyku (Students of Islamic University Began to Study Russian with New Manuals).' *Islam News*, January 22. http://www.islamnews.tj/tajikistan/583-studenty-islamskogo-vuza-nachali-obuchatsya-po-novomu-posobiyu-po-russkomu-yazyku.html.

———. 2013b. 'Zarplata Imam-Khatibam: Nezakonno i Neobosnovanno? (Salary for Imam-Khatibs: Illegal and Unreasonable?).' *Islam News*, July 23.

http://islamnews.tj/analitic/769-zarplata-imam-hatibam-nezakonno-i-neobos novanno.html.

———. 2015. 'Zdaniye Islamskoy gimnazii peredano pod obshchezhitiye Peduniversiteta (The Building of the Islamic Gymnasium Given for Pedagogical University's Residences).' *Islam News*, June 18. http://islamnews.tj/tajikistan/1161-zdanie-islamskoy-gimnazii-peredano-pod-obschezhitie-peduniversiteta.html.

'Islamic State and Central Asia.' 2015. *Central Asia Program*. April 14. http://centralasiaprogram.org/blog/2015/02/23/islamic-state-messaging-to-central-asians-migrant-workers-in-russia/.

Johnson, Mark S. 2004. 'The Legacy of Russian and Soviet Education and the Shaping of Ethnic, Religious and National Identities in Central Asia.' In *The Challenges of Education in Central Asia*, edited by Stephen P. Heyneman and Alan J. DeYoung, 21–35. Greenwich, CT: Information Age Publishing.

Jourde, Cedric. 2009. 'The Ethnographic Sensibility: Overlooked Authoritarian Dynamics and Islamic Ambivalences in West Africa.' In *Political Ethnography: What Immersion Contributes to the Study of Power*, edited by Edward Schatz, 201–16. Chicago: The University of Chicago Press.

Kabiri, Muhiddin. 2002. 'The Islamic Renaissance Party in Tajikistan as a Partner to Ruling Authorities: Achievements and Problems.' Cimera Conference Procceeding 1: Islam and Society in Central Asia. Dushanbe (Tajikistan): Cimera.

Kandiyoti, Deniz. 1988. 'Bargaining with Patriarchy.' *Gender & Society* 2 (3): 274–90. doi:10.1177/089124388002003004.

Kania, Ladislao. 1946. *Bolshevism and Religion*. New York: Polish Library.

Karagiannis, Emmanuel. 2006. 'The Challenge of Radical Islam in Tajikistan: Hizb Ut-Tahrir Al-Islami.' *Nationalities Papers* 34 (1): 1–20.

———. 2007. 'The Rise of Political Islam in Kazakhstan: Hizb Ut-Tahrir Al Islami.' *Nationalism and Ethnic Politics* 13 (2): 297–322. doi:10.1080/13537110 701293567.

———. 2010. *Political Islam in Central Asia: The Challenge of Hizb Ut-Tahrir*. New York: Routledge.

Karimova, Nulifar. 2014. 'Teenage Marriage Persists in Tajikistan.' *Institute for War and Peace Reporting*. May 14. https://iwpr.net/global-voices/teenage-marriage-persists-tajikistan.

Kasymova, Sofia. 2006. 'Tadzhikskoye obshchestvo: traditsiya i praktika mnogozhenstva (Tajik Society: Tradition and Practice of Polygyny).' *Vestnik Evrazii*, no. 4: 97–115.

Keevil, Genesee. 2013. 'Tajikistan: Migrant Laborers Dying to Work in Russia.' *EurasiaNet*, February 26. http://www.eurasianet.org/node/66602.

Keller, Shoshana. 2001. *To Moscow, Not Mecca: The Soviet Campaign Against Islam in Central Asia, 1917–1941*. Westport, CT: Greenwood Publishing Group.

Kendzior, Sarah. 2006. 'Redefining Religion: Uzbek Atheist Propaganda in Gorbachev-Era Uzbekistan.' *Nationalities Papers* 34 (5): 533–48.

Kenez, Peter. 1985. *The Birth of the Propaganda State: Soviet Methods of Mass Mobilization, 1917–1929*. Cambridge: Cambridge University Press.

Khalid, Adeeb. 1998. *The Politics of Muslim Cultural Reform: Jadidism in Central Asia*. University of California Press.

———. 2006a. 'Backwardness and the Quest for Civilization: Early Soviet Central Asia in Comparative Perspective.' *Slavic Review* 65 (2): 231–51.

———. 2006b. 'L'Islam et l'État post-soviétique en Asie centrale.' *Revue internationale et stratégique*, no. 64: 101–10.

———. 2007. *Islam After Communism: Religion and Politics in Central Asia*. Berkeley, CA: University of California Press.

Khodjamurodov, Ghafur and Rechel Bernd. 2010. 'Tajikistan: Health System Review.' *Health Systems in Transition* 12 (2): 1–154.

Khumairo, Bakhtior. 2015. 'Imam-khatiby na pyatnichnoy molitve prizovut zakryt' PIVT? (Will Imam-Khatibs Call to Close Down the IRPT at the Friday Prayer?).' *Asia Plus*, March 27. http://news.tj/ru/news/imam-khatiby-na-pyatnichnoi-molitve-prizovut-zakryt-pivt.

Khushvakt, Zarina. 2010. 'Qarordodi izdivoç: Rohi muqoBala Bo candzanī? (Marriage Contracts: The Way to Deal With Polygyny?).' *BBC Tajik*, August 19. http://www.bbc.co.uk/tajik/news/2010/08/100819_zkh_marriage_contract.shtml.

King, Charles. 2004. 'The Micropolitics of Social Violence.' *World Politics* 56 (03): 431–55.

King, Gary, Robert O. Keohane, and Sidney Verba. 1994. *Designing Social Inquiry: Scientific Inference in Qualitative Research*. Princeton, NJ: Princeton University Press.

Kolarz, Walter. 1960. *Islam in the Soviet Union, 1917–1960*. Karachi: East Press.

Kucera, Joshua. 2015. '95,000 Russian Troops Practice "Containing" Central Asian Conflict.' *EurasiaNet*, September 21. http://www.eurasianet.org/node/75191.

Kulov, A. 2014. 'Gendernie Aspekty Demografii (Gender Aspects of Demography).' Agentstvo po statistike pri Prezidente Respubliki Tadzhikistan. http://stat.tj/img/ru/genderruss.pdf.

Kurochkin, P. K. 1983. 'The Creative Role of the Scientific and Materialist Atheistic Weltanschauung in Moulding a New Type of Man.' In *Secularization in Multi-Religious Societies Indo-Soviet Perspectives*, edited by S. C. Dube and V. N. Basilov, 141–9. New Delhi: Concept Publishing Company.

Kuru, Ahmet T. 2007. 'Passive and Assertive Secularism: Historical Conditions, Ideological Struggles, and State Policies toward Religion.' *World Politics* 59 (4): 568–94.

Kuzmin, A. I. 2001. 'The Causes and Lessons of the Civil War.' In *Central Asia. Political and Economic Challenges in the Post-Soviet Era*, edited by Alexei Vassiliev, 175–219. London: Saqi Books.

Lane, Christel. 1984. 'Legitimacy and Power in the Soviet Union through Socialist Ritual.' *British Journal of Political Science* 14 (2): 207–17.

Ledeneva, Alena V. 1997. 'Practices of Exchange and Networking in Russia.' *Soziale Welt* 48 (2): 151–70.

Lemon, Edward J. 2015a. 'Daesh and Tajikistan: The Regime's (In)Security Policy.' *The RUSI Journal* 160 (5): 68–76.

———. 2015b. 'Daesh and Tajikistan: The Regime's (In)Security Policy.' *The RUSI Journal* 160 (5): 68–76. doi:10.1080/03071847.2015.1102550.

Lemon, Edward J. and Hélène Thibault. 2017. 'Counter-Extremism, Power and Authoritarian Governance in Tajikistan.' *Central Asian Survey* 30 June, 10.1080/02634937.2017.1336155.

Lenin, Vlamidir Illich. 1913. 'The Three Sources and Three Component Parts of Marxism.' *Marxists Internet Archive*. https://www.marxists.org/archive/lenin/works/1913/mar/x01.htm.

Lichbach, Mark Irving and Alan S. Zuckerman. 2009. 'Paradigms and Pragmatism: Comparative Politics during the Past Decade.' In *Comparative Politics:*

Rationality, Culture, and Structure, edited by Mark Irving Lichbach and Alan S. Zuckerman, 1–17. Cambridge: Cambridge University Press.

Liu, Morgan. 2005. 'Post-Soviet Paternalism and Personhood: Why Culture Matters to Democratization in Central Asia.' In *Prospects for Democracy in Central Asia*, edited by Birgit N. Schlyter, 225–37. Istanbul: Swedish Research Institute in Istanbul.

Louw, Maria. 2006. 'Pursuing "Muslimness": Shrines as Sites for Moralities in the Making in Post-Soviet Bukhara.' *Central Asian Survey* 25 (3): 319–39.

Louw, Maria Elisabeth. 2007. *Everyday Islam in Post-Soviet Central Asia*. New York: Routledge.

Luchterhandt, Otto. 1993. 'The Council for Religious Affairs.' In *Religious Policy in the Soviet Union*, edited by Sabrina Petra Ramet, 55–83. Cambridge: Cambridge University Press.

Luehrmann, Sonja. 2011. *Secularism Soviet Style: Teaching Atheism and Religion in a Volga Republic*. Bloomington, IN: Indiana University Press.

Madamidzhanova, Zukhra and Ildar Mukhtarov. 2011. 'Cultural Life in the Ferghana Valley Under Krushchev and Brezhnev.' In *Ferghana Valley: The Heart of Central Asia*, edited by Stephen Frederick Starr, 164–77. Armonk: M.E. Sharpe.

Malashenko, Alexei. 1994. 'Islam and Politics in the Southern Zone of the Former USSR.' In *Central Asia and Transcaucasia: Ethnicity and Conflict*, edited by Vitaly V. Naumkin, 109–25. Wesport, CT: Greenwood Press.

———. 1999. 'Islam And Politics In Central Asian States.' In *Political Islam and Conflicts in Eurasia*, edited by Lena Jonson and Murad Esenov. Stockholm: CA&CC Press.

Mann, Poonam. 2001. 'Taliban at the Doorstep of Central Asia.' *Strategic Analysis* 25 (1): 139–42. doi:10.1080/09700160108458945.

Marsh, Christopher. 2010. *Religion and the State in Russia and China: Suppression, Survival, and Revival*. London: Continuum.

Martin, David. 1978. *A General Theory of Secularization*. New York: Harper & Row.

Martin, Keith. 1997. 'Welcome to the Republic of Leninabad.' *Central Asia & Central Caucasus* 10 (4). http://www.ca-c.org/dataeng/st_06_martin.shtml.

Marx, Karl. 1977. 'K Kritike gegelevskoi filosofiya prava: Vvdenie (Critique of Hegel's Philosophy of Right: Introduction).' In *O religii i tserkvi: Sbornik viskazanii klassikov marksima-leninisma, dokumentov KPSS i sovetskovo gosudarstva (Collection of Quotes of Marxist-Leninist Classics, Documents of the CPSU and the Soviet state)*, edited by Anatoliy Vasil'yevich Belov. Moscow: Politizdat.

Massell, Gregory J. 1974. *The Surrogate Proletariat: Moslem Women and Revolutionary Strategies in Soviet Central Asia, 1919–1929*. Princeton, NJ: Princeton University Press.

McBrien, Julie. 2006. 'Extreme Conversations: Secularism, Religious Pluralism, and the Rhetoric of Islamic Extremism in Southern Kyrgyzstan.' In *The Postsocialist Religious Question: Faith and Power in Central Asia and East-Central Europe*, edited by Hann, 47–74. LIT Verlag Münster.

———. 2009. 'Mukadas's Struggle: Veils and Modernity in Kyrgyzstan.' *Journal of the Royal Anthropological Institute* 15: S127–44. doi:10.1111/j.1467-9655.2009.01546.x.

McBrien, Julie and Mathijs Pelkmans. 2008. 'Turning Marx on His Head: Missionaries, "Extremists" and Archaic Secularists in Post-Soviet Kyrgyzstan.' *Critique of Anthropology* 28 (1): 87–103.

McMann, Kelly. 2007. 'The Shrinking of the Welfare State: Central Asians' Assessments of Soviet and Post-Soviet Governance.' In *Everyday Life in Central Asia Past and Present*, 233–47. Bloomington, IN: Indiana University Press.

Mirsaidov, Khairullo. 2010. 'Platnye dorogi v Tadzhikistane sdelali gosudarstvennoy tainoii (Toll Roads in Tajikistan Made a State Secret).' *Deutsche Welle*, July 6. http://www.dw.com/ru/платные-дороги-в-таджикистане-сделали-государственной-тайной/a-5762913.

Mirsaidov, Khairullo, Tilav Rasulzade, and Turko Dikaev. 2010. 'Vozrashenie studentov – Vorpos politicheskii? (Students' Return – A Political Issue?).' *Centrasia*, December 1. http://www.centrasia.ru/newsA.php?st=1291175400.

Mirsaidov, Negmatullo. 2011. 'Sughd Wraps up 1st Stage of Imam Certification.' *Central Asia Online*, June 2. http://centralasiaonline.com/en_GB/articles/caii/features/politics/2011/06/02/feature-02.

Mirzobekova, Ramsia. 2012. 'V Khoroge Nespokoiino. V Region Styagivayutsya Voiiska (Agitation in Khorog. Troops Tightened in the Region).' *Asia Plus*, July 23. http://www.news.tj/ru/news/v-khoroge-nespokoino-v-region-styagivayuts ya-voiska.

Morrison, Claudio, Richard Croucher, and Olga Cretu. 2012. 'Legacies, Conflict and "Path Dependence" in the Former Soviet Union.' *British Journal of Industrial Relations* 50 (2): 329–51. doi:10.1111/j.1467-8543.2010.00840.x.

Muhammadieva, B. Z. 2010. 'Natsionalnii Sostav, Vladene Yazikami i Grazhdantsvo Naselenie Respubliki Tajikistan (Ethnic Composition and Language Skills, Citizenship of the Republic of Tajikistan).' 3. Dushanbe (Tajikistan): Agentstvo po statistike pri Prezidente Respubliki Tadzhikistan. http://www.stat.tj/en/img/526b8592e834fcaaccec26a22965ea2b_1355502192.pdf.

———. 2011. 'Regiony Respubliki Tadzhikistan (Regions of the Republic of Tajikistan).' Dushanbe (Tajikistan): Agentstvo po statistike pri Prezidente Respubliki Tadzhikistan. http://stat.tj/en/img/fafa4ed764f8e9b9cad5fd57b6c 819fa_1322470826.pdf.

Mullojanov, Parviz. 2001. 'The Islamic Clergy in Tajikistan since the End of the Soviet Period.' In *Islam in Politics in Russia and Central Asia (Early Eighteenth to Late Twentieth Centuries)*, edited by Stephane A. Dudoignon and Hisao Komatsu, 221–50. New York: Kegan Paul.

Mushfig, Bayram. 2011. 'Legal Restrictions on Parents' and Children's Religious Freedom.' *Forum 18*. March 15. http://www.forum18.org/archive.php?article_ id=1552.

Myer, Will. 2002. *Islam and Colonialism: Western Perspectives on Soviet Asia*. New York: Routledge.

Nahavandi, Firouzeh. 1996. 'L'idée de Nation En Asie Centrale: L'exemple Du Kazakhstan et de l'Ouzbékistan.' *Transitions* 37 (2): 143–73.

Najibullah, Farangis. 2007a. 'Tajikistan: Authorities Exclude Miniskirt, Hejab On Campuses.' *Radio Free Europe/Radio Liberty*, April 12. http://www.rferl.org/content/article/1075841.html.

———. 2007b. 'Tajikistan: Authorities Impose Religious Tests On Imams.' *Radio Free Europe/Radio Liberty*, August 8. http://www.rferl.org/content/article/1078040.html.

————. 2008a. 'Tajikistan: New Curbs Target Islamic Students.' *Radio Free Europe/ Radio Liberty*, January 17. http://www.rferl.org/content/article/1079366.html.
————. 2008b. 'Tajik Cleric Says Textbooks Misinterpret Islam.' *EurasiaNet*, December 19. http://www.eurasianet.org/departments/insight/articles/pp122008.shtml.
————. 2009a. 'Taliban Threat – Real Or Useful Fear Mongering?' *Radio Free Europe/Radio Liberty*, June 12. http://www.rferl.org/a/Threat_Of_Taliban_Incursion_Raised_In_Central_Asia__Again/1752944.html.
————. 2009b. 'Islamic Party Leader In Tajikistan Says He Supports Secular System.' *Radio Free Europe/Radio Liberty*, September 15. http://www.rferl.org/content/Islamic_Party_Leader_In_Tajikistan_Says_He_Supports_Secular_System_/1823086.html.
————. 2010. 'Tajiks Stopped From Traveling To Iran, Pakistan For Religious Courses.' *Radio Free Europe/Radio Liberty*, September 8. http://www.rferl.org/content/Tajiks_Stopped_From_Traveling_to_Iran_Pakistan_For_Religious_Courses/2152337.html.
————. 2011. 'Tajik Fatwa Bans SMS-Divorce.' *Radio Free Europe/Radio Liberty*, April 11. http://www.rferl.org/content/tajik_fatwa_bans_sms_divorces/3553754.html.
————. 2014a. 'Tajik Imams Get A Makeover.' *Radio Free Europe/Radio Liberty*, January 18, sec. Tajikistan. http://www.rferl.org/content/tajikistan-imams-makeover/25234064.html.
————. 2014b. 'Explainer: What's Going On In Tajikistan's Gorno-Badakhshan?' *Radio Free Europe/Radio Liberty*, May 29. http://www.rferl.org/content/tajikistan-explainer-gorno-badakhshan/25403342.html.
————. 2015. 'Islamic Party Members Resign En Masse In Tajikistan.' *Radio Free Europe/Radio Liberty*, June 24. http://www.rferl.org/content/tajikistan-islamic-renaissance-party-resignations-en-masse/27091440.html.
————. 2016. 'Tajikistan Moves To Ban Arabic Names, Marriages Between First Cousins.' *Radio Free Europe/Radio Liberty*, January 13. http://www.rferl.org/content/tajikistan-ban-arabic-names-marriage-between-cousins/27486012.html.
Najibullah, Farangis and Khiromon Baqozoda. 2014. 'Tajik Islamic Party Labels Sex Video An "Attack" Ahead Of Elections.' *Radio Free Europe/Radio Liberty*, July 23. http://www.rferl.org/content/tajikistan-sex-video-politics-elections/26715229.html.
Najibullah, Farangis and Ganj Ganjinai. 2015. 'Tajik Prostitutes Seek Protection In The Hijab.' *Radio Free Europe/Radio Liberty*, March 14. http://www.rferl.org/content/tajikistan-prostitutes-hijab/26900935.html.
Naumkin, Vitaly V. 1993. *State, Religion and Society in Central Asia*. See Comments.
————. 2005. *Radical Islam in Central Asia: Between Pen and Rifle*. Lanham, MD: Rowman & Littlefield Publishers.
Nazarov, Ravshan, and Pulat Shozimov. 2011. 'The Khrushchev and Brezhnev Eras.' In *Ferghana Valley: The Heart of Central Asia*, edited by Stephen Frederick Starr, 140–63. Armonk: M.E. Sharpe.
Nazarzoda, Abduxalima. 2015. 'Statement of General Abdukhalim Nazarzoda (Zayavleniye Generala Abdukhalima Nazarzoda).' *Internet Portal Tajikskoi oppozitsii*. September 6. http://www.tajinfo.org/post/2015/09/06/6357716674 52118699.
Nazryev, Saiirahmon. 2011. 'Na yuge Tadzhikistana vyavleno 47 nezakonno deiistvuyushhix religioznyx shkol (47 Illegally Operating Religious Schools

Uncovered in the South of Tajikistan).' *Asia Plus*, July 1. http://news.tj/ru/news/na-yuge-tadzhikistana-vyyavleno-47-nezakonno-deistvuyushchikh-religioznykh-shkol.

Ness, Immanuel. 2013. 'Labor Migration: An Overview.' In *The Encyclopedia of Global Human Migration*. Blackwell Publishing Ltd. http://onlinelibrary.wiley.com/doi/10.1002/9781444351071.wbeghm331/abstract.

NewsRU. 2012. 'Sovet ulemov Tadzhikistana opredelil, kakoy dolzhna byt' boroda u mestnykh musul'man' (Tajik Council of Ulemas Determines How the Beards of Local Muslims Should Be).' *NewsRU*, November 21. http://www.newsru.com/religy/21nov2012/barba.html.

Niyazi, Aziz. 1993. 'The Year of the Tumult: Tajikistan After February 1990.' In *State, Religion and Society in Central Asia. A Post-Soviet Critique*, edited by Vitaly Naumkin, 262–89. Reading, UK: Ithaca Press.

Northrop, Douglas Taylor. 2004. *Veiled Empire: Gender & Power in Stalinist Central Asia*. Ithaca, NY: Cornell University Press.

Nourzhanov, Kirill. 2005. 'Saviours of the Nation or Robber Barons? Warlord Politics in Tajikistan.' *Central Asian Survey* 24 (2): 109–30.

Nourzhanov, Kirill and Christian Bleuer. 2013. *Tajikistan: A Political and Social History*. Canberra: ANU Press.

NTV. 2015. 'V Dushanbe mat' ubila trekh svoikh detey i pytalas' utopit'sya (In Dushanbe a mother killed her three children and tried to drown).' *NTV*, November 18. http://www.ntv.ru/novosti/1437496.

Office for Democratic Institutions and Human Rights (ODHIR). 2006. 'Comments on The Draft Law of the Republic of Tajikistan "The Law of the Republic of Tajikistan on Freedom of Conscience and Religious Associations".' http://legislationline.org/download/action/download/id/782/file/2e2ebcda04dce962d620711d6be9.pdf.

———. 2008. 'Comments on The Draft Law of the Republic of Tajikistan "The Law of the Republic of Tajikistan on Freedom of Conscience and Religious Associations".' http://www.legislationline.org/topics/country/49/topic/78.

———. 2015. 'Tajikistan, Parliamentary Elections, 1 March 2015: Final Report.' Warsaw: Office for Democratic Institutions and Human Rights (ODHIR). http://www.osce.org/odihr/elections/tajikistan/158081.

Okulov, A. 1983. 'Constitution of the USSR and Problems of Freedom of Conscience.' In *Secularization in Multi-Religious Societies Indo-Soviet Perspectives*, edited by S. C. Dube and V. N. Basilov, 171–9. New Delhi: Concept Publishing Company.

Olcott, Martha Brill. 2007. 'Roots of Radical Islam in Central Asia.' *Carnegie Endowment for International Peace*, no. 77. http://carnegieendowment.org/2007/01/17/roots-of-radical-islam-in-central-asia.

Olimov, Muzaffar and Sulmon Khamadov. 2003. 'Neformalnoe Liderstvo v Stranax Tsentralnoi Azii: Kakimi Budut Novie Vojdi? (Informal Leaders in Central Asian Countries: Who Will the New Leaders Be?).' In *Musul'manskie Lideri: Sotsialnaya Rol i Avtoritet (Muslim Leaders: Social Role and Legitimacy)*, edited by Muzaffar Olimov and Saodat Olimova, 47–53. Dushanbe: Sharq Research Center.

Olimova, Saodat. 2000. 'Islam and the Tajik Conflict.' In *Islam and Central Asia: An Enduring Legacy or an Evolving Threat?*, edited by Susan Eisenhower and

Roald Sagdeev, 59–71. Washington, DC: Center for Political and Strategic Studies.

———. 2004. 'Regionalism and Its Perception by Major Political and Social Powers of Tajikistan.' In *Tajikistan at a Crossroad: The Politics of Decentralization*, edited by Luigi De Martino, Cimera, 86–119.

Olimova, Saodat and Muzaffar Olimov. 2013. 'The Withdrawal of NATO Forces from Afghanistan: Consequences for Tajikistan.' 6. Afghanistan Regional Forum. http://centralasiaprogram.org/blog/2013/03/06/the-withdrawal-of-nato-forces-from-afghanistan-consequences-for-tajikistan-2/.

Omelicheva, Mariya Y. 2011. 'Islam in Kazakhstan: A Survey of Contemporary Trends and Sources of Securitization.' *Central Asian Survey* 30 (2): 243–56. doi:10.1080/02634937.2011.567069.

———. 2016. 'Islam and Power Legitimation: Instrumentalisation of Religion in Central Asian States.' *Contemporary Politics* 22 (2): 144–63. doi:10.1080/13569775.2016.1153287.

Orzuy, Karim. 2010. 'Ixroji keudakon az Masojid baxsi makomot bo reuxonion (Banning Children From Mosques: Authorities' Dialogue With Clerics).' *BBC Tajik*, July 10. http://www.bbc.co.uk/tajik/news/2010/07/100710_ea_ak_children_mosque.shtml.

Osakwe, Chris. 1976. 'Contemporary Soviet Criminal Law: An Analysis Of The General Principles And Major Institutions Of Post-1958 Soviet Criminal Law.' *Georgia Journal of International and Comparative Law* 6: 437–91.

Ozod, Musafirbek. 2009. 'Muhiddin Kabiri: V novom zakone o religii slishkom mnogo ogranicheni (Muhiddin Kabiri: Too Many Limitations in the Law on Religion).' *Fergana News*, March 16. http://www.fergananews.com/article.php?id=6097.

Pallaev, Tohir. 2015. 'YouTube Blocked in Tajikistan After Video of President Dancing Goes Viral.' *Global Voices*. September 25. https://globalvoices.org/2013/05/27/tajikistan-famous-wedding-singer-splits-opinion/.

Palmer, Susan. 2006. 'Caught Up in the Cult Wars: Confessions of a Canadian Researcher.' In *Religion and Canadian Society. Traditions, Transitions, and Innovations*, 161–78. Toronto: Canadian Scholars' Press.

Panchenko, Alexander A. 2011. 'Morality, Utopia, Discipline. New Religious Movements and Soviet Culture.' In *Multiple Moralities and Religions in Post-Soviet Russia*, edited by Jarrett Zigon, 119–45. London: Berghahn Books.

Pannier, Bruce. 2001. 'Tajikistan: Government Launches Military Operation Against Hostage-Takers.' *Radio Free Europe/Radio Liberty*, June 22. http://www.rferl.org/content/article/1096760.html.

———. 2004. 'Tajikistan: President's Remarks On Women And Mosques Draw Sharp Reactions.' *Radio Free Europe/Radio Liberty*, November 11. http://www.rferl.org/content/article/1055829.html.

———. 2015a. 'What Next For The Islamic Movement Of Uzbekistan?' *Radio Free Europe/Radio Liberty*, August 23. http://www.rferl.org/content/qishloq-ovozi-imu-ghazi-uzbekistan-pakistan/27204379.html.

———. 2015b. 'The Demise Of Tajikistan's Islamic Party.' *Radio Free Europe/Radio Liberty*, September 4. http://www.rferl.org/content/qishloq-ovozi-demise-of-tajik-islamic-party/27227509.html.

———. 2016. 'Why Does Tajikistan Need A Referendum?' *Radio Free Europe/Radio Liberty*, May 20. http://www.rferl.org/content/qishloq-ovozi-tajikistan-referendum-rahmon/27747496.html.

Pauline Jones Luong, David Bates. 2000. 'Sources of Institutional Continuity: The Soviet Legacy in Central Asia.' presented at the Annual Meeting of the American Political Science Association, Washington, DC.

Peck, Sally. 2007. 'Tajikistan Bans Miniskirts and Head Scarves.' *The Telegraph*, April 18. http://www.telegraph.co.uk/news/worldnews/1549005/Tajikistan-bans-miniskirts-and-head-scarves.html.

Pelkmans, Mathijs. 2009a. *Conversion After Socialism: Disruptions, Modernisms and Technologies of Faith in the Former Soviet Union*. London: Berghahn Books.

———. 2009b. 'Introduction: Post-Soviet Space and the Unexpected Turns of Religious Life.' In *Conversion After Socialism: Disruptions, Modernisms and Technologies of Faith in the Former Soviet Union*, edited by Mathijs Pelkmans, 1–16. London: Berghahn Books.

Pew Research Center. 2010. 'U.S. Religious Knowledge Survey.' Washington, DC: Pew Research Center. http://www.pewforum.org/2010/09/28/u-s-religious-knowledge-survey-about-the-project/.

Peyrouse, Sébastien. 2003. *Des Chrétiens Entre Athéisme et Islam: Regards Sur La Question Religieuse En Asie Centrale Soviétique et Post-Soviétique*. Paris: Maisonneuve et Larose.

Pianciola, Niccolò and Paolo Sartori. 2007. 'Waqf in Turkestan: The Colonial Legacy and the Fate of an Islamic Institution in Early Soviet Central Asia, 1917–1924.' *Central Asian Survey* 26 (4): 475–98.

Polat, Abdumannob. 2000. 'The Islamic Revival in Uzbekistan: A Threath to Stability.' In *Islam and Central Asia: An Enduring Legacy or an Evolving Threat?*, edited by Susan Eisenhower and Roald Sagdeev, 39–58. Washington, DC: Center for Political and Strategic Studies.

Poliakov, Sergei Petrovich. 1992. *Everyday Islam: Religion and Tradition in Rural Central Asia*. Armonk: M.E. Sharpe.

Politrus. 2015. 'Muhiddin Kabiri: V Tadzhikistane nachalsa "37-ii god" (Muhiddin Kabiri: the Year 1937 Started in Tajikistan).' *Politrus*, June 24. http://www.politrus.com/2015/06/24/mukhiddin-kabiri/.

Popper, Sir Karl Raimund. 1972. *Objective Knowledge: An Evolutionary Approach*. Oxford: Clarendon Press.

Pospielovsky, Dimitry. 1987. *A History of Marxist-Leninist Atheism and Soviet Antireligious Policies*. Boulder, CO: St. Martin's Press.

Powell, David E. 1977. 'Religion and Secularization in the Soviet Union: The Role of Antireligious Cartoons.' In *Religion and Modernization in the Soviet Union*, edited by Dennis J. Dunn, 136–201. Boulder, CO: Westview Press.

Pravda. 2011. 'Poiman poslednii iz 25 sbezhavshix iz SIZO Tadzhikistana (The last of the 25 escapees from Tajik prison was caught).' *Pravda*, November 13. http://www.pravda.ru/news/accidents/13-11-2011/1098468-prison-0/.

Putz, Catherine. 2016. 'Tajikistan's Attack on Lawyers.' *The Diplomat*, May 5. http://thediplomat.com/2016/05/tajikistans-attack-on-lawyers/.

Qureshi, Kaveri, Katharine Charsley, and Alison Shaw. 2014. 'Marital Instability among British Pakistanis: Transnationality, Conjugalities and Islam.' *Ethnic and Racial Studies* 37 (2): 261–79. doi:10.1080/01419870.2012.720691.

Radio Free Europe/Radio Liberty. 2006a. 'Main Tajik Opposition Party Won't Make Presidential Bid.' *Radio Free Europe/Radio Liberty*, September 25. http://www.rferl.org/content/article/1071612.html.

————. 2006b. 'Tajik President Creates Opposition-Free Government.' *Radio Free Europe/Radio Liberty*, December 6. http://www.rferl.org/content/article/ 1073258.html.

————. 2009. 'Tajikistan Introduces New Islamic Curriculum To Schools.' *Radio Free Europe/Radio Liberty*, March 6. http://www.rferl.org/content/article/ 1506565.html.

————. 2010a. 'Tajik Pressure Said To Be Growing Over Islamic Dress.' *Radio Free Europe/Radio Liberty*, September 17. http://www.rferl.org/content/Tajik_Pressure_ Said_To_Be_Growing_Over_Islamic_Dress/2160501.html.

————. 2010b. '14 Suspected Terrorists Detained In Northern Tajikistan.' *Radio Free Europe/Radio Liberty*, October 14. http://www.rferl.org/content/ Fourteen_Suspected_Terrorists_Detained_In_Northern_Tajikistan/2190807. html.

————. 2011a. 'Tajikistan Claims Militant Leader Killed.' *Radio Free Europe/Radio Liberty*, April 15. http://www.rferl.org/content/tajikistan_says_militant_ eader_killed/3558497.html.

————. 2011b. 'What Would You Choose?' *Radio Free Europe/Radio Liberty*, April 19. http://www.rferl.org/content/tajik_football_player_barred_because_of_his_ beard/9498409.html.

————. 2011c. 'Tajiks Who Studied Abroad Face Criminal Charges.' *Radio Free Europe/Radio Liberty*, August 19. http://www.rferl.org/content/tajiks_who_ studied_abroad_face_criminal_charges/24301913.html.

————. 2011d. 'Tajik Authorities Demand Payment In Dollars For Hajj.' *Radio Free Europe/Radio Liberty*, August 22. http://www.rferl.org/content/tajik_ authorities_demand_payment_in_dollars_for_hajj/24304426.html.

————. 2012a. 'Tajik Opposition Security Official Assassinated In Knife Attack.' *Radio Free Europe/Radio Liberty*, July 22. http://www.rferl.org/content/tajik- opposition-security-official-killed-in-knife-attack/24652924.html.

————. 2012b. 'Disarming Continues In East Tajikistan.' *Radio Free Europe/Radio Liberty*, August 3. http://www.rferl.org/content/article/24665487.html.

————. 2013a. 'Tajik Court Upholds Closure Of Human Rights NGO.' *Radio Free Europe/Radio Liberty*, April 30. http://www.rferl.org/content/tajikistan-ngo- human-rights/24972595.html.

————. 2013b. 'Five Of Six Legally-Run Tajik Madrasahs Suspended.' *Radio Free Europe/Radio Liberty*, July 12. http://www.rferl.org/content/tajikistan-madrasahs -closed/25044410.html.

————. 2014. 'The Painful Last Days Of Umed Tojiev.' *Radio Free Europe/Radio Liberty*, January 22. http://www.rferl.org/content/last-days-of-umed-tojiev/ 25238683.html.

————. 2015a. 'Tajikistan's Ruling Party Wins Election Decried As "Farce".' *Radio Free Europe/Radio Liberty*, March 2. http://www.rferl.org/content/tajik-elections- rahmon-party-victory/26877105.html.

————. 2015b. 'Calls Made For Tajik Islamic Party To Be Declared Terror Group.' *Radio Free Europe/Radio Liberty*, April 2. http://www.rferl.org/content/calls- made-for-tajik-islamic-party-to-be-declared-terror-group/26935070.html.

————. 2015c. 'Tajikistan Bans Hajj Pilgrimage For Citizens Younger Than 35.' *Radio Free Europe/Radio Liberty*, April 14, sec. Tajikistan. http://www.rferl.org/ content/tajikisyanm-bans-hajj-pilgirmage-for-citizens-younger-than-35/ 26955080.html.

————. 2015d. 'Tajik Police Say 17 Killed In "Terrorist" Attacks.' *Radio Free Europe/Radio Liberty*, September 4. http://www.rferl.org/content/tajikistan-attacks-airport-deaths/27226045.html.

————. 2016a. 'Authorities Say Up To 1,000 Tajiks Joined IS In Syria, Iraq.' *Radio Free Europe/Radio Liberty*, January 25. http://www.rferl.org/content/tajikistan-double-estimate-of-islamic-state-members/27509293.html.

————. 2016b. 'Tajik President Appoints Daughter Chief Of Staff, Seen As Move To Consolidate Power.' *Radio Free Europe/Radio Liberty*, January 27. http://www.rferl.org/content/tajikistan-rahmon-daughter-chief-of-staff-consolidate-power/27514819.html.

————. 2017. 'Tajik President Makes Son Capital's Mayor.' January 12. http://www.rferl.org/a/tajikistan-rahmon-appoints-son-dushanbe-mayor/28228061.html.

Radio Ozodi. 2011. 'Islamskoe prosveshhenie zamenili "Istoriei tadzhikskovo naroda" (Islamic Instruction Replaced by 'History of the Tajik People').' *Radio Ozodi*, February 4. http://rus.ozodi.org/content/no_islamic_education_in_tajik_schools_/9586323.html.

————. 2013a. 'V pedagogicheskom universitete vveden zapret na vysokiye kabluki (High Heels Now Forbidden at the Pedagogical University).' *Radio Ozodi*, March 27. http://rus.ozodi.org/content/article/24940302.html.

————. 2014. 'Sovet ulemov: Shariat dopuskayet SMS-razvody (Council of Ulemas: Sharia Permits SMS-Divorces).' *Radio Ozodi*, January 22. http://rus.ozodi.org/content/sms-divorces-are-allowed/25238766.html.

————. 2015a. 'Sulaymon Kayumov obvinil v ubiystve Kuvvatova evo telokhranitelya (Sulaymon Kayumov Accused in the Murder of Kuvvatov Was His Bodyguard).' *Radio Ozodi*, March 21. http://rus.ozodi.org/content/article/26913204.html.

————. 2015b. 'V Tadzhikistane podgotovlen zakonoproyekt, zapreshchayushchiy rodstvennyye braki (A Bill Banning Consanguineous Marriages Drafted in Tajikistan).' *Radio Ozodi*, June 18. http://rus.ozodi.org/content/article/27079037.html.

————. 2015c. 'Polkovnik MVD: vsyakiy, kto deystvuyet ne po Khanafitskomu mazkhabu, budet doproshen (Colonel of Interior Ministry: Those Who Do Not Act According to the Hanafi school Will Be Questioned).' *Radio Ozodi*, August 7. http://rus.ozodi.org/content/article/27176052.html.

————. 2015d. 'Po faktu izbiyeniya Umara Babadzhanova vozbuzhdeno ugolovnoye delo (A Criminal Case Was Opened in Connection to the Beating of Umar Babadjanov).' *Radio Ozodi*, August 31. http://rus.ozodi.org/content/article/27218543.html.

————. 2015e. 'V Tadzhikistane 27% diplomirovannix molodix liudiei ne mogut chitat' (In Tajikistan, 27% of Degree Holders Cannot Read nor Write).' *Radio Ozodi*, September 1. http://rus.ozodi.org/content/article/27219776.html.

————. 2015f. 'V Vakhdate soversheno napadeniye na otdel militsii (Attack on a Police Station in Vahdat).' *Radio Ozodi*, September 4. http://rus.ozodi.org/content/article/27225781.html.

————. 2015g. 'Umar Bobodzhonov skonchalsya posle nedel'nogo nakhozhdeniya v kome (Umar Bobojonov Died After Being in a Coma For a Week).' *Radio Ozodi*, September 5. http://rus.ozodi.org/content/article/27228170.html.

————. 2015h. 'Buzurgmekhr Yorov podozrevayetsya v moshennichestve i poddelke dokumentov (Buzurgmehr Yorov Suspected of Fraud and Forgery).' *Radio Ozodi*, September 29. http://rus.ozodi.org/content/article/27276622. html.

————. 2015i. 'VS ob'yavil PIVT terroristicheskoy organizatsiyey (Supreme Court Declares the IRPT a Terrorist Organization).' *Radio Ozodi*, September 29. http://rus.ozodi.org/content/article/27277328.html.

Rafiyeva, Mavlouda. 2011. '"Madrasah" Operation Ends up in Northern Tajikistan.' *Asia Plus*, June 17. http://news.tj/en/news/madrasah-operation-ends-northern-tajikistan.

Rahmon, Emomali. 2007a. 'Obrashcheniye Prezidenta Respubliki Tadzhikistan Emomali Rakhmona Na Obshchestvennoye Sobraniye Po Regulirovaniyu Natsional'nykh Obychayev i Religioznykh Ritualakh (Address of the President of the Republic of Tajikistan Emomali Rahmon at the Public Gathering on Regulating National Customs and Religious Rituals).' Dushanbe, May 24. http://www.prezident.tj/rus/vistupleniy240507.htm.

————. 2007b. 'Televizionnoe pozdravlenie po sluchayu nastupleniya svyashhennovo mesyatsa Ramazan (Television congratulation of the President of the Republic of Tajikistan Emomali Rahmon at the Occasion of the Holy Month of Ramadan.' August 7. http://www.prezident.tj/ru/node/1418.

————. 2013. 'Vystuplenie Na Vstreche s Predstavitelyami Obshhestvennosti Strany (Speech at a Meeting With Representatives of the Country's Community).' July 4. http://www.prezident.tj/ru/node/4669.

————. 2015. 'Vystupleniye Po Sluchayu Dnya Materi (Discourse at the Occasion of Mother's Day).' Dushanbe, March 6. http://www.president.tj/ru/node/8400.

————. 2016. 'Televizionnoye Poslaniye v Chest' Dnya Materi (Television Discourse in Honor of Mother's Day).' Dushanbe, March 6. http://prezident.tj/ru/node/10859.

Rahnamo, Abdullo. 2008. *Hizbi Dini va Davlati Dunyavi (The Religious Party and the Secular State)*. Dushanbe: Irfon.

Rasanayagam, Johan. 2010. *Islam in Post-Soviet Uzbekistan: The Morality of Experience*. Cambridge: Cambridge University Press.

Rashid, Ahmed. 2001. *Taliban: Militant Islam, Oil, and Fundamentalism in Central Asia*. Yale University Press.

————. 2003a. *Jihad: The Rise of Militant Islam in Central Asia*. New York: Penguin Books.

————. 2003b. *The Resurgence of Central Asia: Islam or Nationalism?* Oxford: Oxford University Press.

————. 2008. *Taliban: Islam, Oil and the New Great Game in Central Asia*. London: I.B.Tauris.

————. 2015. 'Why Afghanistan's Neighbours Fear Drugs Influx.' *BBC News*, July 2. http://www.bbc.com/news/world-asia-33139652.

Rasulzade, Tilav. 2010. 'Tadzhikistan: Shkol'nitsy Prigrozili Samoubiystvom Za Zapret Nosit' Musul'manskiy Platok (Tajikistan: Schoolgirls Threatened to Kill Themselves Over the Hijab Interdiction).' *Fergana News*, October 7. http://www.fergananews.com/news.php?id=15695&mode=snews.

Reeves, Madeleine. 2011. 'Staying Put? Towards a Relational Politics of Mobility at a Time of Migration.' *Central Asian Survey* 30 (3–4): 555–76. doi:10.1080/02634937.2011.614402.

256 TRANSFORMING TAJIKISTAN

Regnum. 2014. 'Vlasti Tadzhikistana otvergli predlozheniye amnistirovat' uchastnikov besporyadkov v Khoroge (Tajik Authorities Have Rejected a Proposal to Grant Amnesty to Protestors in Khorog).' *Information Agency Regnum*, May 26. http://regnum.ru/news/1806348.html.

Religioscope. 2004. 'Islam in Tajikistan – Interview with Abdullo Hakim Rahnamo.' *Religioscope*, April 25. http://religion.info/english/interviews/article_34.shtml#.VtXpGkC8qSo.

Ria Novosti. 2014. 'FMS naschitala v Rossii 3,7 mln nelegal'nykh migrantov (FMS Counted 3,7 Million Illegal Migrants in Russia).' April 29. http://ria.ru/society/20140429/1005882745.html.

Riddell, John. 1993. *To See the Dawn: Baku, 1920-First Congress of the Peoples of the East*. New York: Pathfinder.

Roberts, Sean E. 2007. 'Everyday Negotiations of Islam in Central Asia.' In *Everyday Life in Central Asia Past and Present*, 337–54. Bloomington, IN: Indiana University Press.

Roche, Sophie. 2014. 'The Role of Islam in the Lives of Central Asian Migrants in Moscow.' 2. Central Asia Program CERIA Brief. http://centralasiaprogram.org/blog/2014/10/05/the-role-of-islam-in-the-lives-of-central-asian-migrants-in-moscow-2/.

———. 2016. 'A Sound Family for a Healthy Nation: Motherhood in Tajik National Politics and Society.' *Nationalities Papers* 44 (2): 207–24. doi:10.1080/00905992.2015.1087486.

Ro'i, Yaacov. 1984. 'The Task of Creating the New Soviet Man: "Atheistic Propaganda" in the Soviet Muslim Areas.' *Soviet Studies* 36 (1): 26–44.

———. 2000. *Islam in the Soviet Union: From the Second World War to Gorbachev*. New York: Columbia University Press.

Rosenbaum, Yuri Alexandrovich. 1985. *Sovetskoe gosudarstvo i tserkov (The Soviet state and the Church)*. Moscow: Nauka.

Rotar, Igor. 2004. 'Baptist Missionary Killed While Praying.' *Forum 18*. January 14. http://www.forum18.org/archive.php?article_id=229.

———. 2005. 'Tajikistan: Mosque Visits and Hijabs Banned for Children.' *Forum 18*. October 31. http://www.forum18.org/archive.php?article_id=679.

———. 2006. 'Tajikistan: Council of Ulems – An Instrument Of State Control.' *Forum 18*. June 8. http://www.forum18.org/archive.php?article_id=796.

———. 2012. 'Will the Fergana Valley Become a Hotbed of Destabilization in Central Asia?' *Jamestown* 9 (180). https://jamestown.org/program/will-the-fergana-valley-become-a-hotbed-of-destabilization-in-central-asia/.

Roux, Jean-Paul. 1997. *L'Asie Centrale: Histoire et Civilisations*. Paris: Fayard.

Roy, Olivier. 1994. *The Failure of Political Islam*. Harvard University Press.

———. 2001. *L'Asie Centrale Contemporaine*. Paris: PUF.

———. 2002. *L'Islam Mondialisé*. Paris: Éditions du Seuil.

Russia Today. 2013. 'Closer to God: Tajik President's Speech to Be Explained in Mosques.' *Russia Today*, May 10. https://www.rt.com/news/rahmon-address-imams-mosques-106/.

Rywkin, Michael. 1982. *Moscow's Muslim Challenge: Soviet Central Asia*. Armonk: M.E. Sharpe.

Sadur, V.G. 1989. 'Musulmane v SSSR: istorya i sovremennost (Muslims in the Soviet Union: History and Modernity).' In *Perestroika: Glastnost, Democratiya, Socialism. Na puti k svobode sovesti (Perestroika: Glastnost, Democracy, Socialism.*

On the Road to Freedom of Conscience), edited by Dimitri Efimovich Furman, 402–47. Moscow: Progress.

Sahadeo, Jeff, and Russell G. Zanca, eds. 2007. *Everyday Life in Central Asia: Past and Present*. Bloomington, IN: Indiana University Press.

Salimov, Mirzo, and Frud Bezhan. 2016. 'The Islamic Party, The Reporter, And The Virginity Test.' *Radio Free Europe/Radio Liberty*, January 7. http://www.rferl.org/content/tajikistan-islamic-renaissance-party-love-virginity-test-reporter-kabiri/27473804.html.

Savage, Mark. 1988. 'The Law of Abortion in the Union of Soviet Socialist Republics and the People's Republic of China: Women's Rights in Two Socialist Countries.' *Stanford Law Review* 40 (4): 1027–117.

Schatz, Edward. 2009. 'Ethnographic Immersion and the Study of Politics.' In *Political Ethnography: What Immersion Contributes to the Study of Power*, edited by Edward Schatz, 1–22. Chicago, IL: The University of Chicago Press.

———. 2010. 'Leninism's Long Shadow in Central Asia.' In *Multination States in Asia: Accommodation or Resistance*, edited by Jacques Bertrand and Andre Laliberte, 244–62. New York: Cambridge University Press.

Schoeberlein, John. 2007. 'The Ubiquitous State: Scholarship of Central Eurasia and the Sovietological Legacy.' European Society for Central Asian Studies, Ankara.

Schwarz, Joëlle, Kaspar Wyss, Zulfiya M. Gulyamova, and Soleh Sharipov. 2013. 'Out-of-Pocket Expenditures for Primary Health Care in Tajikistan: A Time-Trend Analysis.' *BMC Health Services Research* 13: 103.

Schwedler, Jillian. 2006. 'The Third Gender: Western Female Researchers in the Middle East.' *PS: Political Science & Politics* 39 (03): 425–8.

Scott, James C. 1985. *Weapons of the Weak: Everyday Forms of Peasant Resistance*. New Haven, CT: Yale University Press.

Service, RFE/RL's Tajik. 2012. 'Tajik Opposition Security Official Assassinated In Knife Attack.' July 22, sec. Tajikistan. http://www.rferl.org/content/tajik-opposition-security-official-killed-in-knife-attack/24652924.html.

Shafiev, Abdulfattoh. 2015. '"I Am Shuhrat": Tajiks Come to Jailed Lawyer's Defence on Facebook".' *Global Voices*. January 17. https://globalvoices.org/2015/01/17/i-am-shuhrat-tajiks-come-to-jailed-lawyers-defence-on-facebook/.

Shahrani, Nazif. 1995. 'Shaharani, M. Nazif. 1995. Islam and the Political Culture of "Scientific Atheism".' In *The Politics of Religion in Russia and the New States of Eurasia*, edited by Michael Bourdeaux, 273–92. Armonk: M.E. Sharpe.

Shemyakina, Olga. 2009. 'The Marriage Market and Tajik Armed Conflict.' HICN Working Paper 66. Households in Conflict Network. http://econpapers.repec.org/paper/hicwpaper/66.htm.

Shodiev, Haidar and Khumairoi Bakhtior. 2014. 'Neokonchennaya missiya "Rastokheza" (The Unfinished Mission of "Rastokhez").' *Asia Plus*, September 16. http://www.news.tj/ru/news/neokonchennaya-missiya-rastokheza.

Shozimov, Pulat, Joomart Sulaimanov, and Shamshad Abdullaev. 2011. 'Culture in the Ferghana Valley Since 1991: The Issue of Identity.' In *Ferghana Valley: The Heart of Central Asia*, edited by Stephen Frederick Starr, 278–95. Armonk: M.E. Sharpe.

Silvestri, Sara. 2011. 'Faith Intersections and Muslim Women in the European Microcosm: Notes towards the Study of Non-Organized Islam.' *Ethnic and Racial Studies* 34 (7): 1230–47. doi:10.1080/01419870.2011.565779.

Skazkin, Serguei Danilovich. 1968. *Nastolnaya kniga ateista (The Atheist's Handbook)*. Moscow: Izdatelstvo Politicheskoii Literatury.

———. 1981. *Nastolnaya kniga ateista (The Atheist's Handbook)*. Moscow: Izdatelstvo Politicheskoii Literatury.

'Statement by the Head of Delegation of Tajikistan Ambassador Nuriddin Shamsov.' 2011. presented at the 870th the OSCE Permanent Council Meeting, Vienna, June 23. http://www.osce.org/library/.

Statistical Agency under the President of the Republic of Tajikistan. 2013. 'Informatsia o chislenosti musul'man v respublike Tadzhikistana (Information on the Number of Muslims in the Republic of Tajikistan).' http://stat.tj/ru/news/186/.

Steinberger, Petra. 2003. 'Fundamentalism in Central Asia: Reasons, Reality and Prospects.' In *Central Asia: Aspects of Transition*, edited by Tom Everett-Heath, 219–43. New York: Routledge.

Suny, Ronald Grigor. 2012. 'The Contradictions of Identity: Being Soviet and National in the USSR and After.' In *Soviet and Post-Soviet Identities*, edited by Mark Bassin and Catriona Kelly, 17–36. New York: Cambridge University Press.

'Syria Calling: Radicalisation in Central Asia – International Crisis Group.' 2015. April 14. http://www.crisisgroup.org/en/regions/asia/central-asia/b072-syria-calling-radicalisation-in-central-asia.aspx.

Taarnby, Michael. 2012. 'Islamist Radicalization in Tajikistan: An Assessment of Current Trends.' Dushanbe: Korshinos.

Tajikistan. 2007. 'Zakon Respubliki Tadzhikistan Ob uporyadochenii traditsiy, torzhestv i obryadov v RT (Law of the Republic of Tajikistan on On regulation of Traditions, Celebrations and ceremonies in Tajikistan).' http://www.mmk.tj/ru/legislation/legislation-base/2007/.

———. 2009. 'Zakon Respubliki Tadzhikistan o svobode sovesti i religioznix obedenieniyax (Law of the Republic of Tajikistan on Freedom of Conscience and Religious Organizations).' http://www.mmk.tj/ru/legislation/legislation-base/2009/.

———. 2011. 'Zakon Respubliki Tadzhikistan Ob Obtvetstvennosti Roditelei Za Vospitane i Obuchene Detei (Law of the Republic of Tajikistan on Parental Responsibility in the Upbringing and Education of Children).' http://www.mmk.tj/ru/legislation/legislation-base/2011/.

———. 2012. 'Natsionalnii Sostav, Vladene Yazikami i Grazhdantsvo Naselenie Respubliki Tajikistan (Ethnic Composition and Language Skills, Citizenship of the Republic of Tajikistan).' 3. Agentstvo po statistike pri Prezidente Respubliki Tadzhikistan. http://www.stat.tj/en/img/526b8592e834fcaacc ec26a22965ea2b_1355502192.pdf.

'Tajikistan: Country Gender Assessment.' 2006. Asian Development Bank. http://www.adb.org/documents/tajikistan-country-gender-assessment.

'Tajikistan's Strongman Appoints Son to Lead Corruption Fight.' 2015. *EurasiaNet. Org*. March 16. http://www.eurasianet.org/node/72546.

Tatari, Eren and Renat Shaykhutdinov. 2010. 'State Response to Religious Revivalism in Post-Soviet Central Asia.' *European Journal of Economic and Political Studies* 3 (2): 85–110.

Tazmini, Ghoncheh. 2001. 'The Islamic Revival in Central Asia: A Potent Force or a Misconception?' *Central Asian Survey* 20 (1): 63–83.

'The DHS Program – Tajikistan: 2012.' 2013. Demographic and Health Surveys. USAID. http://dhsprogram.com/publications/publication-FR279-DHS-Final-Reports.cfm.

The Moscow Times. 2007. 'Tajikistan's President Changes His Name.' *The Moscow Times*, March 29. http://www.themoscowtimes.com/news/article/tajikistans-president-changes-his-name/198084.html.

Thibault, Hélène. 2013. 'The Secular and the Religious in Tajikistan Contested Political Spaces.' *Studies in Religion/Sciences Religieuses* 42 (2): 173–89. doi:10.1177/0008429813479297.

———. 2016. 'Female Virtue, Religion and State Ideology in Tajikistan.' 10. The Central Eurasia – Religion in International Affairs (CERIA). Central Asia Program. http://centralasiaprogram.org/blog/2016/01/04/female-virtue-religion-and-state-ideology-in-tajikistan/.

———. 2017. 'Labour Migration, Sex, and Polygyny: Negotiating Patriarchy in Tajikistan', *Ethnic and Racial Studies*. Online first: http://www.tandfonline.com/doi/full/10.1080/01419870.2017.1400086.

Todzhiddinov, Ahmadali. 2011. 'Kuda delis studenty vernuvshiesya iz Islamkix stran? (Where Are the Students Who Returned From Islamic countries?).' *Asia Plus*, September 27. http://www.news.tj/ru/news/kuda-delis-studenty-vernuvshiesya-iz-islamskikh-stran.

Tokarev, S. A. 1983. 'Religion and Religions from the Historical-Ethnographic Viewpoint.' In *Secularization in Multi-Religious Societies Indo-Soviet Perspectives*, edited by S. C. Dube and V. N. Basilov, 125–39. New Delhi: Concept Publishing Company.

Tozy, Mohamed. 2009. 'L'évolution du champ religieux marocain au défi de la mondialisation.' *Revue internationale de politique comparée* 16 (1): 63–81.

Transparency International. n.d. 'Tajikistan.' *Transparency International*. http://www.transparency.org/country#TJK 2.

Trilling, David. 2015. 'Tajikistan's Strongman Appoints Son to Lead Corruption Fight.' *EurasiaNet*, March 16. http://www.eurasianet.org/node/72546.

Tucker, Noah. 2011. '"Ordinary People" and the Violence of Collapse (Osh, Part III).' *Registan.Net*. June 26. http://registan.net/2011/06/26/ordinary-people-and-the-violence-of-collapse-osh-part-iii/.

———. 2015a. 'Central Asian Involvement in the Conflict in Syria and Iraq: Drivers and Responses.' USAID. https://www.usaid.gov/sites/default/files/documents/1866/CVE_CentralAsiansSyriaIraq.pdf.

———. 2015b. 'Islamic State Messaging to Central Asians Migrant Workers in Russia.' 6. Central Asia Program CERIA Brief. http://centralasiaprogram.org/?p=6982.

———. 2016. 'Public and State Responses to ISIS Messaging: Kazakhstan.' Central Asia Program CERIA Brief.

Tursunzoda, Mehrangez. 2011. 'Dlya tadzhikskix palomnikov ustanovlen edinii standart odezhdy (A Unique Standard Dress for Tajik Pilgrims.' *Asia Plus*, October 1. http://news.tj/ru/news/dlya-tadzhikskikh-palomnikov-ustanovlen-edinyi-standart-odezhdy.

———. 2012. 'U. Nazarov: 'Ne kazhdii nash student idet rabotat' v Mechet' (Not All Of Our Student Go Work at a Mosque).' *Asia Plus*, January 19. http://www.news.tj/ru/newspaper/interview/u-nazarov-ne-kazhdyi-nash-student-idet-rabotat-v-mechet.

————. 2015a. 'Vlasti zakryli izdatel'stvo PIVT za "ne obespecheniye sotrudnikov lechebno-meditsinskim pitaniyem" (Authorities Closed the IRPT's Publishing House for "Not Providing Employees With Sufficient Healthy Food").' *Asia Plus*, August 13. http://asiaplus.tj/ru/node/213041.

————. 2015b. 'V Tadzhikistane opechatan ofis pravyashchey v strane NDPT (The Office of Ruling Party NDPT Was Shutdown in Tajikistan).' *Asia Plus*, August 20. http://news.tj/ru/news/v-tadzhikistane-opechatan-ofis-pravyashchei -v-strane-ndpt.

————. 2016. 'Komitet po delam religii ob'yasnil, chto takoye "odezhda, chuzhdaya dlya Tadzhikistana" (Committee for Religious Affairs Explained That Such "Clothes are Foreign to Tajikistan").' *Asia Plus*, January 12. http:// news.tj/ru/news/komitet-po-delam-religii-obyasnil-chto-takoe-odezhda-chuzhdaya-dlya-tadzhikistana.

Tutubalina, Olga. 2011. 'M. Akhmadov: "My dostanem ix v pravitelstve" (M. Ahmadov: We Will Hand Them Over to the Authorities).' *Asia Plus*, January 12. http://news. tj/ru/newspaper/article/m-akhmadov-my-dostanem-ikh-i-v-pravitelstve.

Uehling, Greta. 2007. 'Dinner With Akhmet.' In *Everyday Life in Central Asia: Past and Present*, edited by Jeff Sahadeo and Russell Zanca, 127–40. Bloomington, IN: Indiana University Press.

Unicef. 2013. 'Study of Prevalence and Dynamics of Suicide Among Children and Young People (12–24 Years of Age) in Sughd Region, Tajikistan.' Dushanbe (Tajikistan). http://ki.se/sites/default/files/suicide_study_report_for_web_eng1. pdf.

United Nations. n.d. 'Tajikistan.' *United Nations*. https://data.un.org/CountryPro-file.aspx?crName=TAJIKISTAN.

US Bureau of Counterterrorism. 2015. 'Country Reports on Terrorism: South and Central Asia.' Report. US Department Of State. The Office of Website Management, Bureau of Public Affairs. http://www.state.gov/j/ct/rls/crt/2014/239408.htm.

USSR. 1936. 'Konstitutsiya Soyuza Sovetskikh Sotsialisticheskikh Respublik (Constitution of the Union of Soviet Socialist Republics).' http://www.hist.msu. ru/ER/Etext/cnst1936.htm.

————. 1977. 'Konstitutsiya Soyuza Sovetskikh Sotsialisticheskikh Respublik (Constitution of the Union of Soviet Socialist Republics).' http://www.hist.msu. ru/ER/Etext/cnst1977.htm.

Verkhovsky, Alexander. 2016. 'The Ultra-Right Movement under Pressure: Xenophobia and Radical Nationalism in Russia, and Efforts to Counteract Them in 2015.' Moscow: Sova. http://www.sova-center.ru/en/xenophobia/ reports-analyses/2016/04/d34247.

Vinatier, Laurent. 2002. *L'islamisme en Asie centrale*. Paris: Armand Colin.

Wagner, Steven. 1997. 'Public Opinion in Tajikistan: 1996 Findings.' Washington, DC: International Foundation for Electoral Systems (IFES).

Wanner, Catherine. 2011. 'Multiple Moralities, Multiple Secularisms.' In *Multiple Moralities and Religions in Post-Soviet Russia*, edited by Jarrett Zigon, 214–25. London: Berghahn Books.

Warren, Carol A. B. and Paul K. Rasmussen. 1977. 'Sex and Gender in Field Research.' *Urban Life* 6 (3): 349–70.

Weeden, Lisa. 2009. 'Ethnography as Interpretative Enterprise.' In *Political Ethnography: What Immersion Contributes to the Study of Power*, edited by Edward Schatz, 75–95. Chicago, IL: The University of Chicago Press.

Weitz, Richard. 2004. 'Storm Clouds over Central Asia: Revival of the Islamic Movement of Uzbekistan (IMU)?' *Studies in Conflict & Terrorism* 27 (6): 505–30. doi:10.1080/10576100490513558.

Werth, Nicolas. 1992. *Histoire de l'Union soviétique: de l'Empire russe à la Communauté des Etats indépendants, 1900–1991*. Paris: Presses universitaires de France.

Wheeler, Geoffrey. 1964. *The Modern History of Soviet Central Asia*. London: Weidenfeld & Nicolson.

World Bank. 2014. 'Tajikistan Data.' *World Bank*. http://data.worldbank.org/country/tajikistan.

———. 2016. 'Female Labor Force – Tajikistan.' *World Bank*. http://data.worldbank.org/indicator/SL.TLF.TOTL.FE.ZS.

———. 2016. 'Personal Remittances, Received (% of GDP).' *World Bank*. Accessed February 15. http://data.worldbank.org/indicator/BX.TRF.PWKR.DT.GD.ZS.

Yanow, Dvora. 2006. 'Thinking Interpretively: Philosophical Presuppositions and the Human Science.' In *Interpretation And Method: Empirical Research Methods And the Interpretive Turn*, edited by Dvora Yanow and Peregrine Schwartz-Shea, 5–26. Armonk: M.E. Sharpe.

Yanow, Dvora and Peregrine Schwartz-Shea. 2006. *Interpretation and Method: Empirical Research Methods and the Interpretive Turn*. Armonk: M.E. Sharpe.

Yemelianova, Galina and Zumrat Salmorbekova, eds. 2010. 'Islam and Islamism in the Ferghana Valley.' In *Radical Islam in the Former Soviet Union*, 211–43. New York: Routledge.

Yuldashev, Avaz. 2008. 'President Signs Decree Announcing 2009 as Year of Imam Azam in Tajikistan.' *Asia Plus*, September 15. http://www.news.tj/en/news/presi dent-signs-decree-announcing-2009-year-imam-azam-tajikistan.

———. 2009. 'Hanafi School Recognized as Official Religion of Tajikistan.' *Asia Plus*, March 5. http://www.news.tj/en/news/hanafi-school-recognized-official-religion-tajikistan.

———. 2011a. 'V Tadzhikistane v silu vstupil zakon ob otvetstvennosti roditeleii (Law on Parental Responsibility Came Into Force in Tajikistan).' *Asia Plus*, August 6. http://news.tj/ru/news/v-tadzhikistane-v-silu-vstupil-zakon-ob-otvetstvennosti-roditelei.

———. 2011b. 'Vosstanovlena mechet' pri PIVT, povrezhdennaya pri pozhare (IRPT's Mosque Damaged by Fire Was Restored).' *Asia Plus*, September 22. http://news.tj/ru/news/vosstanovlena-mechet-pri-pivt-povrezhdennaya-pri-pozhare.

———. 2011c. 'Vlasti priostanovili deyatel'nost' mecheti sem'i Turadzhonzoda (Authorities Have Suspended the Activities of Turajonzoda's Family Mosque).' *Asia Plus*, December 12. http://news.tj/ru/news/vlasti-priostanovili-deyatelnos t-mecheti-semi-turadzhonzoda.

———. 2015a. 'Politsovet PIVT obratilsya k prezidentu Tadzhikistana (IRPT's Political Council Appealed to Tajikistan President).' *Asia Plus*, June 16. http://news.tj/ru/node/210031.

———. 2015b. 'Kompartiya: Tam, gde OBSE, ES i OON, net ni mira, ni soglasiya (Communist Party: Where the OSCE, the EU and the UN Are There Is No Peace, No Agreement).' *Asia Plus*, July 6. http://news.tj/ru/news/kompartiya-tam-gde-obse-es-i-oon-net-ni-mira-ni-soglasiya.

———. 2015c. 'Mer Dushanbe "ob'yavil voynu" chuzhdoy tadzhikam odezhde (Dushanbe Mayor "Declared War" Against Foreign Clothes).' *Asia Plus*,

August 20. http://news.tj/ru/news/mer-dushanbe-obyavil-voinu-chuzhdoi-tadzhikam-odezhde.

————. 2015d. 'PIVT gotovit otvet Miniusti i prodolzhaet podgotovku k svoemu sezdu (The IRPT Prepares Its Answer to the Minsitry of Justice and Goes on with the Organization of Its Congress).' *Asia Plus*, September 1. http://asiaplus.tj/ru/node/213981.

————. 2016. 'Grazhdane Tadzhikistana vpred' do 40 let ne smogut sovershat' khadzh (Tajik Citizens Under 40 Years Old Cannot Perform the Hajj).' *Asia Plus*, January 15. http://news.tj/ru/news/grazhdane-tadzhikistana-vpred-do-40-let-ne-smogut-sovershat-khadzh.

Yurchak, Alexei. 2003. 'Soviet Hegemony of Form: Everything Was Forever, Until It Was No More.' *Comparative Studies in Society and History* 45 (03): 480–510.

Zahab, Mariam Abou and Olivier Roy. 2004. *Islamist Networks: The Afghan-Pakistan Connection*. New York: Columbia University Press.

Zevaco, Ariane. n.d. 'From Old to New Macha: Mass Resettlement and the Redefinition of Islamic Practice between Tajikistan's Upper Valleys and Cotton Lowlands.' In *Allah's Kolkhozes: Migration, De-Stalinisation, Privatisation and the Emergence of New Muslim Religious Communities in the USSR, and After (1950s–2000s)*, edited by Stephane A. Dudoignon and Christian Noack, Klaus Schwarz Verlag, 148–201. Berlin.

Zigon, Jarrett. 2011a. 'Multiple Moralities: Discourses, Practices, and Breakdowns in Post-Soviet Russia.' In *Multiple Moralities and Religions in Post-Soviet Russia*, edited by Jarrett Zigon, 1–15. London: Berghahn Books.

————. 2011b. *Multiple Moralities and Religions in Post-Soviet Russia*. London: Berghahn Books.

Zürcher, Christophe. 2011. 'Building Democracy While Building Peace.' *Journal of Democracy* 22 (1): 81–95.

Zviagelskaya, Irina. 2000. 'Tadzhikistan kak zerkalo "islamskoi revolutsii" (Tajikistan as a Mirror of the 'Islamic Revolution').' *Pro et Contra* 5 (3): 48–623.

INDEX

Lightning Source UK Ltd.
Milton Keynes UK
UKHW022332190223
417299UK00009B/281